Collection Evaluation in
Academic Libraries

COLLECTION EVALUATION IN ACADEMIC LIBRARIES
A Literature Guide and Annotated Bibliography

Thomas E. Nisonger

1992
LIBRARIES UNLIMITED, INC.
Englewood, Colorado

*This book is dedicated to my father,
Irvin J. Nisonger,
and the memory of my mother,
Mary C. Nisonger.*

Copyright © 1992 Libraries Unlimited, Inc.
All Rights Reserved
Printed in the United States of America

No part of this publication may be reproduced, stored in a retrieval system, or transmitted, in any form or by any means, electronic, mechanical, photocopying, recording, or otherwise, without the prior written permission of the publisher.

LIBRARIES UNLIMITED, INC.
P.O. Box 6633
Englewood, CO 80155-6633

Library of Congress Cataloging-in-Publication Data

Nisonger, Thomas E.
   Collection evaluation in academic libraries : a literature guide and annotated bibliography / Thomas E. Nisonger.
    xix, 271 p. 17x25 cm.
    Includes indexes.
    ISBN 0-87287-925-9
    1. Libraries, University and college--Collection development--Evaluation--Bibliography. 2. Collection development (Libraries)--Evaluation--Bibliography.   I. Title.
Z675.U5N58   1992
025.2'1877--dc20   92-11037
                                                      CIP

Contents

Acknowledgments vii
Introduction ix
Abbreviations xvii

1 Survey Works 1
  General Survey Works 2
  Overviews from a Special Perspective 10
  Bibliographies 13

2 Methods and Methodology 15
  Methodological Discussions 15
  The Checklist Method 17
  Other Methods 19
  Measurement of Holdings 23
  Measurement of Use 25
  Miscellaneous 27
  Notes 29

3 Case Studies 30
  Collection Evaluation Case Studies in a Single Library 31
  Notes 36

4 Use Studies 37
  General and Miscellaneous Use Studies 38
  Periodical Use 47
  Government Documents Use 54
  The Pittsburgh Study 55
  Notes 60

5 Availability Studies and Document Delivery Tests 61
  Availability Studies 62
  Document Delivery Tests 71
  Notes 72

6 Overlap Studies 74
  Overlap Studies 75
  Collective Evaluations of Two or More Library Collections 79

v

7 Standards...83
Official Statements...85
Other..90
Notes..95

8 Citation Studies..97
General and Miscellaneous..................................99
Case Studies Using Citation Analysis for Collection
　　　Evaluation...106
Structure of Disciplines or Subjects......................111
Notes...119

9 The RLG Conspectus and the National Shelflist Count.....120
The Conspectus — General..................................123
Case Studies of Implementation of the Conspectus in
　　　North America..130
The Conspectus in Europe..................................132
The Conspectus in Australia and New Zealand...............136
The Pacific Northwest Conspectus..........................138
The North American Collections Inventory Project..........142
Verification Studies......................................145
The National Shelflist Count..............................146
Notes...149

10 Evaluation of Serials...................................150
General and Miscellaneous Discussions.....................151
Serials Evaluation Models.................................162
Identification of Core Journals...........................164
Serials Cancellation Case Studies.........................167
Notes...176

11 Journal Ranking..177
Theoretical Discussions...................................179
Journal Rankings in Business..............................185
Journal Rankings in the Social Sciences...................192
Journal Rankings in Other Disciplines.....................202
Notes...207

12 Application of Automation to Collection Evaluation.....209
Automated Systems...210
Software..214
Online Searching..216
Miscellaneous...218
Notes...222

Glossary..223

Author/Title Index..229

Subject Index...255

Acknowledgments

The author is indebted to numerous individuals who assisted in a variety of capacities. I gratefully acknowledge these contributions. Irvin J. Nisonger, my father, gave me the original inspiration to write a book. Claire, Suzanne, and Stanley Nisonger, my wife and children respectively, patiently endured countless hours when my attention was occupied by an article or a computer terminal. Suzanne also photocopied many articles and input some annotations into the word processor, while Claire verified a number of citations. Herbert S. White, former dean of Indiana University's School of Library and Information Science (SLIS), made this book possible by hiring me into a library and information science faculty. Daniel J. Callison, as acting dean of Indiana University's SLIS, arranged a convenient teaching load to allow timely manuscript completion. Judith Serebnick, associate professor of Library and Information Science at Indiana University, and Robert N. Broadus, professor at the School of Information and Library Science, University of North Carolina, Chapel Hill, read preliminary drafts of the manuscript and provided valuable feedback and encouragement. Blaise Cronin, dean, Indiana University's SLIS, provided helpful assistance. David V. Loertscher, senior acquisitions editor of Libraries Unlimited, offered valuable advice throughout this project. Pat Riesenman, a librarian at Indiana University, conducted a DIALOG online search. Karen Fouchereaux, Donna Rhiver, Ben Burck, Anne Fliotsos, and Cathy Zeljak, my graduate assistants over the course of several years, diligently tracked down citations, photocopied innumerable articles, and assisted with inputting. I also thank the Indiana University Office of Research and the University Graduate School for funding $100 of a DIALOG online search. Any deficiencies are the author's own responsibility.

Introduction

This guide's primary objective is to summarize the literature published since 1980 that is pertinent to academic library collection evaluation. The intended audience is anyone interested in collection evaluation in academic libraries. This consists of two broad categories: 1) library practitioners, including full-time collection development specialists, administrators, and librarians with partial collection development responsibilities; and 2) individuals in library science education, including students, faculty, and researchers.

THE BOUNDARIES OF COLLECTION EVALUATION

It is relatively easy to define *collection evaluation*. On the most fundamental level, the term means assessing the intrinsic quality of a library's holdings. On a broader level, the term includes determining how well the collection is serving its purpose and meeting patron information needs. As stated in the Magrill and Corbin textbook, "Collection evaluation is concerned with how good a collection is in terms of the kinds of materials in it and the value of each item in relation to items not in the collection, to the community being served, and to the library's potential users."[1]

Paul Mosher identified several benefits to be derived from conducting a collection evaluation:

1. Understanding the collection's scope, depth, and utility

2. Assisting with collection planning

3. Acting as an aid to writing a collection development policy

4. Measuring a collection development policy's effectiveness

5. Determining collection quality

6. Improving the collection by rectifying deficiencies

x / INTRODUCTION

    7. Focusing human and financial resources on areas requiring attention

    8. Justifying budget increases

    9. Convincing administrators that action is being taken to rectify the "bottomless pit" of library acquisitions.[2]

In recent years there has been increasing interest in the evaluation of innumerable types of library and information services. A keyword search of the term *evaluation* in the *Library Literature* CD-ROM database covering December 1984 through June 1991 revealed 5,538 entries; a similar search in the *Library & Information Science Abstracts* CD-ROM database covering 1969 through March 1991 identified 4,421 entries.

In the *Mission of the Librarian*, Ortega y Gasset observed that a librarian's role is to help patrons filter out from the "torrent of books" the small portion that meets their information needs.[3] In a sense, a bibliography performs the same function, by filtering out from the vast array of published material the portion that seems most relevant to the topic and useful to the reader. Thus, this bibliography seeks to filter out from the vast library and information services evaluation literature the portion most relevant to academic library collection evaluation.

Determining the boundaries encompassed by the collection evaluation concept is much more challenging than defining the term itself. Nevertheless, based on the coverage in textbook chapters on evaluation, the ALA *Guide to the Evaluation of Library Collections* (see entry 1), as well as the work of such authorities as F. Wilfrid Lancaster (see entry 16) and Paul Mosher (see entry 21), one can confidently conclude that collection evaluation embraces use, citation analysis, overlap, and shelf availability studies as well as standards. Each of these categories is represented by a separate section in this literature guide.

A major criterion for separating collection evaluation from other collection development functions that are closely related in practice but analytically distinct in theory concerns whether materials are dealt with at the macro level (that is, in large categories) or the micro level (on an individual, title-by-title basis). Collection evaluation obviously deals with the library's holdings at a macro level, since it focuses on an entire group of materials and sometimes the total collection. In this context, weeding and selection would not be included within the scope of collection evaluation because they normally deal with materials on a title-by-title basis. In some instances, selection is also conducted on the macro level, as when approval plans or blanket orders are used.[4] Nevertheless, the differentiation between evaluation on the one hand and selection on the other remains a valid and generally recognized distinction.

The preceding discussion should not be confused with the distinction between macroevaluation and microevaluation, as explained by Baker and Lancaster, based on work by King and Bryant. *Macroevaluation* is descriptive and measures the overall level of success, whereas *microevaluation* is diagnostic and identifies the reasons for failure.[5]

SCOPE

This annotated bibliography focuses on items pertaining to collection evaluation in academic libraries and published from 1980 to approximately the end of the 1991 calendar year. (The manuscript was submitted in early November 1991, although the final cutoff for adding entries was roughly three months after that date.) "Classic" or extremely important articles published prior to 1980 are also annotated, although a precise definition of *classic* is not readily available. Included are evaluation case studies, research pieces, overviews of the evaluation process, textbook chapters, literature reviews, "how-to" guides and manuals, standards, and methodological and theoretical discussions.

The term *academic* as used here covers universities, colleges, and community colleges. However, a few influential items concerning collection evaluation in public, school, and special libraries were also included. Medical, dental, and law libraries, although commonly classified as special libraries, are covered here because they are frequently affiliated with an academic institution and their collection evaluation literature is highly pertinent to academic librarianship. Non-English items, Ph.D. dissertations, master's theses, ERIC documents, National Technical Information Service documents, in-house library publications, and unpublished speeches or conference presentations were excluded.

This annotated bibliography is neither comprehensive nor highly selective. In other words, even though every identified item has not been included, this list is not limited to the very best contributions. Any work that would warrant the attention of a practitioner or student is included, while items with little substantive value were excluded. The primary selection criteria were the work's intrinsic merit and whether it would be of interest or value to this book's intended audience. Obviously, not every entry will be of equal value to all readers.

Items published before 1980 were included if: 1) they are frequently cited in the post-1980 collection evaluation literature; 2) they are explicitly identified as classic by contemporary authors; 3) their merit or significance warrants inclusion in the judgment of this literature guide's author; or 4) they are necessary for the full understanding of items published after 1980. For the sake of continuity, items published during the late 1970s that follow up or comment on the Pittsburgh Study or Kantor's branching method for analyzing book availability are also included. In the final analysis, the decision to include an item published before 1980 was essentially a subjective judgment for which the author assumes personal responsibility.

Based on advice from the publisher, this work's presumed audience is North American. Nevertheless, an attempt has been made to include relevant English-language material published throughout the world, on the assumption that the principles of collection evaluation are universal rather than limited to a particular geographic location. However, the author freely admits that his survey of internationally published material was limited to items that can be identified through the bibliographic apparatus available in North America.

xii / INTRODUCTION

Selection and weeding are not within this literature guide's scope because they usually deal with materials at the micro rather than the macro level, as previously explained. Also beyond this bibliography's scope are items that primarily discuss other major components of the collection management process, such as collection maintenance, collection development policies, approval plans, and budgeting. Likewise excluded is the evaluation of procedures and issues relating to the collection development and acquisition process, for example, the evaluation of vendors, approval plans, gifts, and the relative merits of faculty selection versus librarian selection.

Items about preservation generally were excluded. Likewise, compilations of library statistics are not included unless they bear a direct application to collection evaluation, such as the National Shelflist Count.

Very little is available concerning nonprint collection evaluation in academic libraries. Most of what has been published about nonprint media, especially the newer formats such as computer software or CD-ROMS, concerns selection on an item-by-item basis rather than evaluation of the entire collection. Hence, this bibliography contains only a few entries pertaining to nonprint materials.

ORGANIZATION

The book is organized into twelve chapters. Chapter 1 concerns overviews of collection evaluation; chapter 2 deals with collection evaluation methods and methodology; chapter 3 annotates collection evaluation case studies; chapter 4 covers use studies; chapter 5 is devoted to shelf availability studies and document delivery tests; chapter 6 focuses on overlap studies; chapter 7 covers standards; and chapter 8 deals with citation analysis. All these topics are obviously considered within the traditional boundaries of collection evaluation.

Chapter 9 concentrates on the RLG Conspectus and its variant form, the Pacific Northwest Conspectus. Earlier evaluation literature did not cover the Conspectus because only within the last half decade has it emerged as a nationally and, in many instances, internationally recognized collection evaluation instrument.

This book heavily emphasizes the evaluation of serials. Chapter 10 covers serials evaluation and chapter 11 is devoted to the closely related concept of journal ranking. Chapter 4 contains a section on periodical use studies. This emphasis reflects the extensive literature on the topic during the last decade. Academic libraries have become especially concerned about their serials collections because of the runaway inflation in serials costs and its effect on stagnant library budgets; thus, a major portion of this literature deals with the evaluation of serials for the purposes of cancellation. One could argue that inclusion of serials evaluation is contrary to the previously noted macro/micro distinction as a criterion for defining the boundaries of collection evaluation, as serials are usually evaluated on a title-by-title basis. However, serials were included because of their major significance to contemporary academic library collection development. Also, most serials evaluation projects take a macro perspective, in that a large group of titles is usually examined. Items relating to serials processing, obviously, were not included.

Finally, chapter 12 covers the use of automation in collection evaluation. Although this topic has often been ignored in previous publications about collection evaluation, it is included here because automation's potential utility for collection assessment is beginning to be recognized both in the literature and in library practice.

The introductory sections to each chapter explain the chapter's scope and organization and briefly summarize the major issues pertinent to the subject. In some cases, they provide background information necessary for full understanding of the chapter's annotations. Some historical information is provided for topics that have a discernible history. These essays are not intended to offer a comprehensive treatment of the topic, but rather a brief introduction. Inevitably, they vary in length depending on the requirements of a particular chapter.

Many entries could have been placed in two or three different chapters or even different sections of the same chapter. Each entry was assigned to a particular location based on the item's primary focus and major contribution to the literature. Thus, an article describing the application of automation in a use study would be placed either in chapter 4 or in chapter 12, according to the criteria listed above.

A separate annotation was usually prepared for each entry. In a few instances, a single annotation was written for two or more entries that contain essentially identical content, such as the draft and final versions of a standard when there were no substantial changes, or two nearly identical reports concerning the same research project. The annotations present information far beyond what is readily apparent from the citation itself. They seek to provide an overview of the item while highlighting the aspects most significant to the collection evaluation literature. For instance, in entries about standards the sections pertaining directly to collections were emphasized. An effort was made to mention especially useful features that could assist collection evaluation, such as a ranked list of journal titles in a particular subject. Annotations range in length from approximately 50 to roughly 200 words, but usually fall between 100 to 150 words. Cross-references are used when an annotation refers to another entry in this bibliography. If an annotation mentions a specific item that is not included because it is beyond the bibliography's scope, an endnote is used. To increase readability, a deliberate variation in the writing style among the various annotations was used. In some instances an explicit commentary is appended, while in others the annotation speaks for itself.

The citation format conforms to *The Chicago Manual of Style* (13th ed. 1982) as well as the policies of Libraries Unlimited. However, prices for monographs were not included. With a few exceptions, most of the monographic entries refer to specific chapters and it is assumed that the reader would not purchase an entire book on the basis of one or two cited chapters.

The glossary defines terms and concepts the meaning of which is necessary for understanding the annotations. Abbreviations for entities that require no definition, such as *ALA* for the American Library Association or *LC* for the Library of Congress, are included in a separate section.

OTHER BIBLIOGRAPHICAL WORK

This work updates and supplements several other bibliographies relevant to collection evaluation and collection development in academic libraries. Signe Ottersen's "A Bibliography on Standards for Evaluating Libraries," published in *College & Research Libraries* in 1971,[6] ostensibly about library standards, is the first general bibliography pertinent to the topic of collection evaluation. It annotates 138 items published between 1933 and 1970. All types of libraries are covered, but the majority of entries concern academic libraries. Ottersen's work is supplemented by Thomas Nisonger's "An Annotated Bibliography of Items Relating to Collection Evaluation in Academic Libraries, 1969-1981," published in *College & Research Libraries*[7] in 1982. It contains 97 items. Godden, Fachan, and Smith's highly selective *Collection Development and Acquisitions, 1970-1980: An Annotated, Critical Bibliography*[8] contains 84 entries (out of 345) in the evaluation section. As in Ottersen's article, all types of libraries are covered, but there is a heavy emphasis on the academic. Godden, Fachan, and Smith cast a broader net than Ottersen and Nisonger, covering use and citation studies.

A number of other pertinent bibliographies should be mentioned. Sam E. Ifidon's "Qualitative/Quantitative Evaluation of Academic Library Collections: A Literature Survey,"[9] which appeared in the 1976 *International Library Review*, annotates nineteen items published worldwide from 1956 to 1974. The American Library Association's *Guide to the Evaluation of Library Collections* (entry 1), published in 1989, contains an unannotated bibliography of approximately 170 items, dating from 1937 through 1987, pertaining to all types of libraries. In 1991 the American Library Association's Reference and Adult Services Division published *Collection Evaluation Techniques; A Short, Selective, Practical, Current Annotated Bibliography 1980-1990* (entry 38) (containing fifty-eight items). The annual bound volumes of the *Social Science Citation Index Journal Citation Reports* contain helpful, unannotated, select bibliographies concerning citation studies. Also, many of the textbook chapters and survey articles cited in chapter 1 and elsewhere contain useful, unannotated bibliographies.

METHODOLOGY

The following methods were used for compiling this bibliography:

1. Searches of CD-ROM databases, such as *Library Literature,* ERIC, and *Library & Information Science Abstracts*

2. Use of *Library & Information Science Abstracts, Information Science Abstracts*, and *Library Literature* in hard copy

Introduction / xv

3. A DIALOG online search of the *Library & Information Science Abstracts* and *Social Science Citation Index* databases

4. Searches of the online catalog of the Indiana University libraries and, through the Internet, the online catalogs of other major research libraries supporting library and information science programs

5. The author's own personal knowledge of the subject area, based on teaching, library practice, and previous research

6. Examination of footnote references and bibliographies in all items identified for inclusion in the bibliography (a technique that frequently led to additional relevant entries)

7. Direct shelf survey of pertinent library and information science journals from 1980 to the present

8. Continuous daily scans of the new serials boxes at Indiana University's School of Library and Information Science library for the last year and a half

9. Suggestions from other individuals, particularly Robert Broadus, Blaise Cronin, and Judith Serebnick.

NOTES

[1] Rose Mary Magrill and John Corbin, *Acquisitions Management and Collection Development in Libraries*, 2d ed. (Chicago: American Library Association, 1989), 234.

[2] Paul H. Mosher, "Collection Evaluation in Research Libraries: The Search for Quality, Consistency, and System in Collection Development," *Library Resources & Technical Services* 23 (Winter 1979): 17.

[3] Jose Ortega y Gasset, *The Mission of the Librarian* (Boston: G. K. Hall, 1961), 22.

[4] Hendrik Edelman, "Selection Methodology in Academic Libraries," *Library Resources & Technical Services* 23 (Winter 1979): 37. Distinguishes between selection at the macro level (i.e., "en bloc") and at the micro level on an item-by-item basis.

[5] Sharon L. Baker and F. Wilfrid Lancaster, *The Measurement and Evaluation of Library Services*, 2d ed. (Arlington, Va.: Information Resources Press, 1991), 8-9.

[6] Signe Ottersen, "A Bibliography on Standards for Evaluating Libraries," *College & Research Libraries* 32 (March 1971): 127-44.

[7] Thomas E. Nisonger, "An Annotated Bibliography of Items Relating to Collection Evaluation in Academic Libraries, 1969-1981," *College & Research Libraries* 43 (July 1982): 300-311.

[8] Irene P. Godden, Karen W. Fachan, and Patricia A. Smith, with Sandra Brug, comps., *Collection Development and Acquisitions, 1970-1980: An Annotated, Critical Bibliography* (Metuchen, N.J.: Scarecrow Press, 1982).

[9] Sam E. Ifidon, "Qualitative/Quantitative Evaluation of Academic Library Collections: A Literature Survey," *International Library Review* 8 (June 1976): 299-308.

Abbreviations

AACSB	American Assembly of Collegiate Schools of Business.
AALL	American Association of Law Libraries.
AALS	American Association of Law Schools.
ABA	American Bar Association.
ABN	Australian Bibliographic Network.
ACM	Associated Colleges of the Midwest (see glossary).
ACML	Association of Canadian Map Librarians.
ACRL	Association of College and Research Libraries.
AEA	American Economic Association.
AECT	Association for Educational Communications and Technology.
ALA	American Library Association.
APA	American Psychological Association.
ARIA	American Risk and Insurance Association.
ARL	Association of Research Libraries.
ASIS	American Society for Information Science.
ASLIB	Association of Special Libraries and Information Bureaux.
ASPA	American Society for Public Administration.
BCL	*Books for College Libraries.*
BLLD	British Library Lending Division (now known as the British Library Document Supply Centre).
BMLA	*Bulletin of the Medical Library Association.*
CALC	Charleston Academic Libraries Consortium.
CASSI	*Chemical Abstracts Service Source Index.*
CD-ROM	Compact-disc read-only memory.
CIS	Computer information systems.
DDC	Dewey Decimal Classification.
FTE	Full-time equivalent.

GMRMLN	Greater Midwest Regional Medical Library Network.
GPO	The U.S. Government Printing Office.
HEGIS	Higher Education General Information Surveys (see glossary).
IAMSLIC	International Association of Marine Science Libraries and Information Centers.
IASLIC	Indian Association of Special Libraries and Information Centres.
IFLA	International Federation of Library Associations and Institutions.
ILL	Interlibrary loan.
ISI	The Institute of Scientific Information (see glossary).
JCR	*Journal Citation Reports* (see glossary).
LC	Library of Congress.
LIBER	Ligue des Bibliothéques Europeénnes de Recherche.
LIRN	Library and Information Resources for the Northwest (see glossary).
LIS	Library and information science.
LLA	Louisiana Library Association.
MARC	Machine-readable cataloging (see glossary).
METRO	Metropolitan Reference and Research Library Agency (see glossary).
MIS	Management information systems.
MPLA	Mountain Plains Library Association.
NCIP	North American Collections Inventory Project (see glossary).
NDLA	North Dakota Library Association.
NHC	National Humanities Center.
NLA	National Library of Australia.
NLM	National Library of Medicine.
NOTIS	Northwestern Online Total Integrated System (see glossary).
OCLC	OCLC Online Computer Library Center.
OPAC	Online Public Access Catalog.
PNLA	Pacific Northwest Library Association.
PSU	Pennsylvania State University.
RLG	Research Libraries Group.
RLIN	Research Libraries Information Network.

RTSD	Resources and Technical Services Division (of the American Library Association now known as ALCTS, or Association for Library Collections and Technical Services).
SAS	Statistical Analysis System (see glossary).
SCI	*Science Citation Index.*
SCONUL	Standing Conference on National and University Libraries (U.K.).
SSCI	*Social Science Citation Index.*
SDLA	South Dakota Library Association.
SLIS	School of Library and Information Science.
SPSS	Statistical Package for the Social Sciences (see glossary).
SuDoc	Superintendent of Documents (of the U.S. Government Printing Office).
SULAN	State University Library Automation Network (Indiana).
SUNY	State University of New York.
VTLS	Virginia Tech Library System (see glossary).
WESS	Western European Studies Section of the ACRL.
WLN	(Formerly Western Library Network).

1

Survey Works

A literature guide logically begins with material presenting an overview of its subject matter. This chapter annotates works that offer broad overviews of the collection evaluation process. Included here are textbook chapters, bibliographies, and survey articles. Individuals who are unfamiliar with collection evaluation terminology should consult the glossary before reading this chapter. Overviews concerning the role of citation analysis in collection development or evaluation are included in chapter 8.

Overview pieces generally introduce or survey collection evaluation techniques. Collection evaluation methods are typically classified according to two schemes: quantitative versus qualitative or collection-centered versus client-centered. Quantitative methods count the number of items held in a collection. Examples are comparative statistics, data on collection size and growth, or formulas such as the Clapp-Jordan Formula (entry 245). Qualitative approaches focus on how good the holdings are. The checklist method, direct examination, and expert opinion are all examples.

A collection-centered method concentrates on the collection itself or compares it to an external standard. Checklists, formulas, the RLG Conspectus, direct examination, and expert opinion are collection-centered methods. A client-centered technique focuses on the use of the collection and how well the collection is meeting patron needs. Use and availability studies are leading examples.

For a concise but excellent description of the various collection evaluation approaches mentioned in this chapter's annotations, along with a summary of uses, benefits, and limitations, the reader is referred to the American Library Association's *Guide to the Evaluation of Library Collections* (entry 1).

This chapter is divided into three sections: survey works or general overviews, overviews from a special perspective, and bibliographies.

GENERAL SURVEY WORKS

1. American Library Association. Resources and Technical Services Division. **Guide to the Evaluation of Library Collections**. Edited by Barbara Lockett. Chicago: American Library Association, 1989. 25p. (Collection Management and Development Guides, no. 2). LC 89-145. ISBN 0-8389-3370-x.

This handy little pamphlet introduces the major collection evaluation approaches to practicing librarians. Using an outline format, a paragraph describes each method and then enumerates its advantages and disadvantages. List checking, direct examination of the collection, compilation of comparative statistics, and applications of standards (classed as collection-centered methods) as well as studies of circulation, in-house use and shelf availability, user surveys, ILL statistics analysis, citation studies, and document delivery tests (classed as client-centered measures) are included. An unannotated bibliography is appended. This work is a quick and convenient reference tool.

2. Baker, Sharon L., and F. Wilfrid Lancaster. "Collection Evaluation: Materials-Centered Approaches." In their **Measurement and Evaluation of Library Services**, 39-78. 2d ed. Arlington, Va.: Information Resources Press, 1991. 411p. LC 91-072908. ISBN 0-87815-061-7.

This entry concerns the first of several chapters from a major evaluation textbook included here. (See also Baker and Lancaster entries 105, 106, and 175; for the first edition see also Lancaster and Joncich entry 16.) The book is extensively revised and rewritten from the first edition, although there is some overlap with Lancaster's *If You Want to Evaluate Your Library* (see also entries 15, 118, 119, 183, and 488). More material is included on nonacademic libraries than in the first edition.

In this chapter, collection-centered evaluation methods are analyzed under seven broad headings: 1) the impressionistic method; 2) standard lists and bibliographies; 3) citation analysis; 4) quantitative standards; 5) the size of subject collections; 6) collection profiling, including Loertscher's collection mapping; and 7) comprehensiveness of the collection, which contains a brief account of the RLG Conspectus. The section on citation analysis is particularly detailed. The various methods are critiqued and numerous studies are synthesized. A useful six-page unannotated bibliography is included at the end. This long-awaited update to Lancaster's seminal 1977 work is a welcome addition to the literature.

3. Bonn, George S. "Evaluation of the Collection." **Library Trends** 22 (January 1974): 265-304.

Although somewhat dated now, this excellent article is without doubt a classic in the collection evaluation literature. While Bonn's and Lancaster's (entry 16) are often considered the two best collection evaluation overviews published up to the 1970s, this piece would probably have offered the best systematic overview to a library practitioner. Numerous approaches are discussed under the following categories: compiling statistics, checking lists, obtaining user opinions, direct observation, applying standards, and total resources (internal and external). The then-current library collection standards from accrediting agencies in art, business, chemistry, law, medicine, optometry, pharmacy, social work, speech pathology, education, and theology are succinctly summarized.

4. Christiansen, Dorothy E., C. Roger Davis, and Jutta Reed-Scott. "Guide to Collection Evaluation through Use and User Studies." **Library Resources & Technical Services** 27 (October/December 1983): 432-40.

Drafted by an RTSD subcommittee consisting of the three authors, these guidelines were approved at the ALA San Antonio Midwinter Meeting on January 11, 1983, by the Resources Section Executive Committee. They use a helpful checklist approach to assist librarians in selecting the most appropriate user-oriented evaluation techniques. The uses, advantages, and disadvantages of circulation studies, user opinion surveys, document delivery tests, shelf availability studies, in-house studies, and citation studies are outlined. A short unannotated bibliography is attached. An updated and expanded version of these guidelines appears in the ALA's *Guide to the Evaluation of Library Collections* (entry 1).

5. Curley, Arthur, and Dorothy Broderick. "Collection Evaluation." In their **Building Library Collections**, 297-307. 6th ed. Metuchen, N.J.: Scarecrow Press, 1985. 339p. LC 84-23665. ISBN 0-81081-776-4.

This work deals as much with collection evaluation in public and school as with academic libraries but is well worth noting because it is a chapter from a standard collection development textbook that has been issued in more editions than any other one. Curley and Broderick stress that collection evaluation requires information about the materials in the collection, the community served, and the collection's purpose. Methods are classified according to evaluation of: 1) current selection, that is, annual and "Best Books" lists; 2) the total collection, measured by standard cumulative lists; and 3) total resources, measured by Orr's Capability Index, which includes document delivery (entry 201). Quantitative approaches are also briefly discussed. The authors make the revealing observation that "the single biggest defect in most library collections is the professional collection."

6. Evans, G. Edward. "Evaluation." In his **Developing Library and Information Center Collections**, 310-30. 2d ed. Littleton, Colo.: Libraries Unlimited, 1987. 443p. LC 87-3224. ISBN 0-87287-463-x; 0-87287-546-6(pbk).

A chapter from one of the best collection development textbooks presents an excellent overview of collection evaluation. A noteworthy feature is a detailed checklist of the reasons for conducting collection evaluation projects: internal reasons include collection development and budgetary needs, while external reasons include local and extraorganizational needs. An evaluative review classifies the available methods by the following categories: impressionistic, checklist, the statistical approach, formulas, and usage methods. In fact, the discussion of formulas is particularly useful because of its detailed descriptions of the California and Washington State versions of the Clapp-Jordan Formula. The chapter concludes by listing eight specific steps for implementing an evaluation project after one has determined the project's goals and objectives.

7. Faigel, Martin. "Methods and Issues in Collection Evaluation Today." **Library Acquisitions: Practice & Theory** 9, no. 1 (1985): 21-35.

A solid introduction to the various collection evaluation approaches available in the mid-1980s is offered, based on the author's professional experience and extensive references to the appropriate literature. Available techniques are discussed under three headings: 1) collection-centered methods, consisting of standards, statistics,

4 / SURVEY WORKS

and list checking; 2) client-centered approaches, including circulation records, ILL statistics, user surveys, document delivery, and shelf availability; and 3) citation studies. A brief, three-page historical sketch of collection evaluation in America, dating from the ALA's 1894 Lake Placid conference, is especially noteworthy because relatively little has been published on the topic.

Faigel concludes that a combination of approaches is preferred because each single method has its "shortcomings." He designates planning as "the most important" element in collection evaluation.

8. Futas, Elizabeth. "Issues in Collection Development: Collection Evaluation." **Collection Building** 4, no. 1 (1982): 54-55.

This short but perceptive piece, part of a series in *Collection Building* from the early 1980s by a well-known authority, introduces collection evaluation to the unsophisticated reader. It stresses that one must first determine the clientele being served and the library's objectives before proceeding with evaluation. The quantitative and qualitative approaches are explained. Since limitations exist in using only one approach, the author argues that a "reasonable solution" is to use both. A noteworthy observation is that student classroom assignments, using both approaches, seldom result in major discrepancies.

9. Gardner, Richard K. "Collection Evaluation and Standards." In his **Library Collections: Their Origin, Selection and Development**, 233-43. New York: McGraw-Hill, 1981. 354p. (McGraw-Hill Series in Library Education). LC 80-23831. ISBN 0-07-022850-7.

Gardner's textbook, although now more than a decade old, offers a solid introduction to several traditional collection evaluation methods. He provides an overview and analytical details concerning using statistics, checking lists, obtaining user opinions, using direct observation, and applying standards. About one-third of the chapter is devoted to a section on standards, including the Clapp-Jordan Formula. The author emphasizes that to be effective a standard must be: 1) based on research, 2) related to a definable and measurable activity, 3) appropriate to the type of institution it deals with, 4) authoritative, and 5) realistic. The chapter concludes by briefly discussing the role of collection use research in the evaluation process.

10. Gleason, Maureen. "The Practice of Collection Development." **Indiana Libraries** 9, no. 2 (1990): 11-17.

Based on both the published literature and the author's experience as the Notre Dame University collection development librarian, this essay presents many philosophical and practical insights into the collection evaluation process. It is argued that "collection evaluation is at the very core of collection development." Gleason stresses that evaluation extends beyond formal measures and reports, requiring "reflection-in-action" whereby the librarian constantly makes ad hoc, informal collection assessments in the performance of daily collection development duties.

11. Gorman, G. E., and B. R. Howes. "Methods of Collection Evaluation." In their **Collection Development for Libraries**, 147-56. London and New York: Bowker-Saur, 1989. 432p. (Topics in Library and Information Studies). LC 85-579. ISBN 0-40830-100-7.

Gorman and Howes, both Australian library and information science educators, have written a collection development handbook that combines textbook narrative with an anthology of previously published readings. This concisely written chapter (chapter 5) analyzes the major collection evaluation methods using the now-traditional dichotomy between user-oriented measures (specifically, use and usage studies, document delivery tests, shelf availability tests, circulation studies, and in-house use studies) and collection-centered measures (verification studies such as list checking and citation analysis). A third approach, user opinion surveys, is strongly recommended. The authors have done a solid job, but their handbook's international perspective is not readily apparent from this chapter alone.

12. Gorman, G. E., and B. R. Howes. "Procedures for Collection Evaluation." In their **Collection Development for Libraries**, 119-29. London and New York: Bowker-Saur, 1989. 432p. (Topics in Library and Information Studies). LC 85-579. ISBN 0-40830-100-7.

Chapter 4 of the handbook described in entry 11 begins by offering three broad reasons for collection evaluation (professional, economic, and administrative) as well as eleven specific aims, including determination of adequacy and budget justification. The authors recommend use and user studies to determine how well the collection is fulfilling its intended purpose—satisfying user needs. Almost half the chapter consists of a step-by-step guide to designing a survey to gather data for collection evaluation. Unlike most collection development textbooks, Gorman and Howes devote two chapters rather than one to the evaluation process.

13. Gorman, G. E., and B. R. Howes. "What Is Collection Evaluation?" and "How Are Collections Evaluated?" In their **Collection Development for Australian Libraries**, 49-83. Wagga Wagga, Australia: Centre for Library Studies, Riverina-Murray Institute of Higher Education, 1988. 564p. (Topics in Australasian Library and Information Studies, no. 1). LC 88-189562. ISBN 0-949060-00-3.

The text of chapters 4 and 5 of this book is identical, except for a few minor changes in wording, to the corresponding chapters of the authors' *Collection Development for Libraries* (entries 11 and 12). Thus, as far as the textual narrative is concerned, no one who has read that book would have any reason to consult this item. Note, however, that about half the supplementary readings in *Collection Development for Australian Libraries* are different.

14. Grover, Mark L. "Collection Assessment in the 1980s." **Collection Building** 8, no. 4 (1987): 23-26.

Grover's short essay concentrates on the purpose, methodology, and value of collection evaluation for academic libraries. Collection assessments have been conducted for three main reasons: to show the adequacy or deficiency of the collection, to decide where growth should take place, and for accreditation purposes. The discussion of considerations in selecting an assessment methodology distinguishes between approaches that provide descriptive data concerning a particular library and analytical approaches that cumulate knowledge pertinent to a discipline or subject. The author points out that value can be measured either by immediate results or by long-term benefits.

6 / SURVEY WORKS

15. Lancaster, F. Wilfrid. "Evaluation of the Collection: Formulae, Expert Judgment, and Use of Bibliographies." In his **If You Want to Evaluate Your Library**, 17-32. Champaign: University of Illinois, Graduate School of Library and Information Science, 1988. 193p. LC 88-91099. ISBN 0-87845-078-5.

This entry refers to the first of several chapters from an important textbook on library evaluation by a well-established authority to be annotated in this literature guide. A brief overview of the available collection evaluation methods is included, along with discussions concerning the Clapp-Jordan Formula, expert opinion, and overlap studies, but most of the chapter concentrates on checking bibliographies against library holdings.

Hypothetical examples as well as numerous cases from the relevant literature are used to illustrate the potential benefits and methodological limitations of various sample sources, including both standard lists and specially prepared lists based on monographs, college textbooks, indexing/abstracting services, selected journals, faculty/student publications, or online bibliographic searches. The author notes that a list can be used to analyze overlap among different libraries. Goldhor's "inductive method" (entry 59) is analyzed and the best available critique of the Lopez method (entries 61 and 62) is presented here. This item is especially valuable because of its sophisticated insight into subtle methodological nuances. (See also entries 118, 119, 183, and 488.)

16. Lancaster, F. Wilfrid, with M. J. Joncich. "Evaluation of the Collection." In their **The Measurement and Evaluation of Library Services**, 165-206. Washington, D.C.: Information Resources Press, 1977. 395p. LC 77-72081. ISBN 0-87815-017-x.

This chapter is devoted to collections from Lancaster's first book on library evaluation, which in 1978 was awarded the ALA's Ralph R. Shaw Award for Outstanding Contribution to Library Literature. Evaluation methods are discussed under three categories: 1) quantitative, including size, formulas, and growth rate; 2) qualitative, embracing the impressionistic approach and evaluation against lists or the holdings of other libraries; and 3) use studies (which receive the greatest emphasis), including circulation and in-house use. Descriptions of various methods for analyzing use cover the advantages and disadvantages of a "collection sample" (in which a portion of the collection's past use is determined) versus a "checkout sample" (studying what is used during a specified time). Jain's "relative use method" (comparing a sample's actual use with expected use) and Trueswell's "last circulation date" approach are explained.

This excellent chapter is especially valuable for its synthesis of prior research. Over eighty previous studies, dating as far back as 1936, are cited, with detailed summaries provided for many. Lancaster and Bonn are frequently mentioned as offering the two best overviews of collection evaluation published before 1980. For the second edition, see Baker and Lancaster entries 2, 105, 106, and 175.

17. Magrill, Rose Mary. "Evaluation by Type of Library." **Library Trends** 33 (Winter 1985): 267-95.

The purpose of this excellent, well-researched article (it contains almost 100 footnotes) is to present an overview concerning how collection evaluation varies from one type of library to another. The choice of technique and the questions that guide the process will vary among types of libraries because of such factors as motivations for conducting the evaluation, the expected benefits, the clientele, the collection's size and purpose, the resources available for the project, the library's governance, and the urgency of the need for information. Separate sections summarize the major evaluation issues and extensively review the pertinent literature for public libraries, school library media centers, large academic libraries, small and medium-sized academic libraries, special libraries in academic settings, special libraries in nonacademic settings, and consortia. The concise summaries of previous collection evaluation research are this contribution's most valuable feature.

18. Magrill, Rose Mary, and Doralyn J. Hickey. "Evaluation." In their **Acquisitions Management and Collection Development in Libraries**, 191-215. Chicago: American Library Association, 1984. 229p. LC 84-9288. ISBN 0-83890-408-4.

19. Magrill, Rose Mary, and John Corbin. "Evaluation of the Collection." In their **Acquisitions Management and Collection Development in Libraries**, 234-61. 2d ed. Chicago: American Library Association, 1989. 285p. LC 89-6784. ISBN 0-8389-0513-7.

These chapters, from a standard acquisitions/collection development textbook, review techniques for generating information useful for evaluation and management of collections, "with emphasis on quantitative techniques." The authors note that automated systems can provide evaluation data. Quantitative collection profiling, list checking, user surveys, inventories, weeding, and studies of overlap, circulation, citation analysis, document delivery, and shelf availability are covered before the chapter concludes by discussing evaluation of the acquisitions process. A helpful bibliography is appended at the end. The chapter's format is essentially the same in the two editions, but the second edition includes a new section on the RLG Conspectus.

20. Mosher, Paul. "Collection Evaluation or Analysis: Matching Library Acquisitions to Library Needs." In **Collection Development in Libraries: A Treatise**, pt. B, edited by Robert D. Stueart and George B. Miller, Jr., 527-45. Greenwich, Conn.: JAI Press, 1980. (Foundations in Library and Information Science, vol. 10). LC 79-93165. ISBN 0-89232-162-8 (pt B).

This work furnishes a helpful overview of the collection evaluation process by one of the preeminent authorities on the topic. The author stresses that evaluation should assess how well the collection is meeting user needs, supporting the parent institution's goals, and implementing the collection development policy. Valuable features include advice on preparation for an evaluation project, a list of thirteen reasons to conduct collection evaluation, and a list of nine types of data to include in the final report, as well as an appendix illustrating a sample evaluation summary form used at Stanford University.

About half the chapter is devoted to brief discussions concerning the uses, advantages, and disadvantages of the most "useful, practical, and economical" methods. In a unique approach, Mosher describes the methods in order from the simple to the complex: surveys and impressions, questioning users, numeric counts, formulas and standards, interlibrary loan analysis, checking lists, checking catalogs of other libraries, use studies, and analysis of machine-readable cataloging data.

8 / SURVEY WORKS

21. Mosher, Paul. "Quality and Library Collections: New Directions in Research and Practice in Collection Evaluation." In **Advances in Librarianship**, vol. 13, edited by Wesley Simonton, 211-38. Orlando, Fla.: Academic Press, 1984. 264p. LC 79-88675. ISBN 0-12-024613-9.

Mosher's excellent contribution begins with a brief history of collection evaluation dating back to 1849, when Charles Coffin Jewett, the Smithsonian Librarian, included an evaluation in his annual report. Based on an extensive literature survey that cites approximately eighty items, detailed summaries of research findings and perceptive commentary are provided regarding the major trends in collection evaluation methodology of the preceding ten to fifteen years. The analysis is organized into the following sections: correlating the shelflist with the courses offered, determining the structure of subject literatures, compiling statistics, profiling collection characteristics, citation studies, overlap studies, and use studies.

The author concludes by predicting that there will be more RLG verification-overlap studies in the future and a greater need for studies to identify "core" collections. This is probably the best state-of-the-art overview of collection evaluation methodology as it existed in the mid-1980s.

22. Nisonger, Thomas E. "Collection Evaluation: Nine Techniques Discussed in the Literature." **Manitoba Library Association Bulletin** 11 (December 1980): 18-20.

The author explains to the uninitiated how to "evaluate a library collection," by summarizing nine of "the most interesting and/or important approaches" reported in the literature. The emphasis is on academic libraries, with a few techniques for public libraries also explained. Included here are list checking, failure studies, Goldhor's inductive method (see entry 59), the Lopez method (see entries 61 and 62), the Clapp-Jordan Formula (see entry 245), and the Voigt current acquisitions model (see entry 251). Nisonger concludes that no single approach "constitutes the ideal or perfect method."

23. Robbins-Carter, Jane, and Douglas L. Zweizig. "Are We There Yet? Evaluating Library Collections, Reference Services, Programs, and Personnel: Lesson Two, Evaluating Library Collections." **American Libraries** 16 (November 1985): 724-27.

A lesson from an American Library Association and University of Wisconsin-Madison continuing education course notes that there are "no standardized, accepted methods" for collection evaluation. Total use, unfilled requests, circulation, and turnover rate are introduced as quantitative methods, followed by the impressionistic approach and list checking as qualitative measures. This article stresses that any evaluation method should measure against a predetermined target figure. Although slanted toward public librarians, this course could also be informative for an academic librarian.

24. Rosenberg, Betty. "Evaluation: Problems of Criteria and Methodology." **California Librarian** 38 (April 1977): 17-21.

Rosenberg's thoughtful essay points out the shortcomings of several standard approaches to collection evaluation, such as formulas, list checking, circulation statistics, etc. Published before this bibliography's 1980 cutoff date, the work does not really qualify as a classic contribution to the collection evaluation literature. However, the author makes one significant point, cited a number of times in other articles, that deserves to be emphasized: the importance of a sense of humor (an observation that applies to life in general as well as collection evaluation). Specifically, the author states, "[T]he only sensible evaluation tool is an intelligent, cultured and experienced librarian—preferably with a sense of humor."

25. Voos, Henry. "Collection Evaluation." **Collection Building** 3, no. 1 (1981): 6-12.

This discussion of evaluation methods employs an interesting dichotomy between input methods and output measures. Although the distinction is not fully elaborated, "input" apparently refers to collection-centered methods, such as list checking, direct examination, or standards, while "output" methods measure effectiveness at meeting patron needs. The author rejects input evaluation methods in favor of the "bibliometric approach," consisting of citation studies, obsolescence studies, and Bradfordian rankings. Each of these methods is summarized and accompanied by references to the appropriate literature. This brief article does not really provide a systematic overview of evaluation methods, as its title might suggest.

26. Wiemers, Eugene, Jr. and others. "Collection Evaluation: A Practical Guide to the Literature." **Library Acquisitions: Practice & Theory** 8, no. 1 (1984): 65-76.

Drafted in preparation for a collection evaluation workshop by the University of Minnesota Libraries, Twin Cities Campus, Collection Development Committee, this article is intended to provide a brief evaluative summary of the most important literature, aimed at an audience of practicing librarians. Following a concise overview of the general literature, the authors discuss the benefits and drawbacks of the major evaluation approaches grouped under the following headings: 1) size and growth factors; 2) checklists, including standard lists, special lists, and the RLG Conspectus verification studies; 3) citation analysis; and 4) use and user studies. More than fifty previous studies are cited in this useful work, which admirably achieves its stated objective.

27. Wortman, William A. "Evaluation and Analysis." In his **Collection Management; Background and Principles**, 101-22. Chicago: American Library Association, 1989. 243p. LC 89-6785. ISBN 0-8389-0515-3.

Wortman stresses that evaluation measures a collection's "intrinsic quality," that is, the holdings' "absolute" caliber, and its "extrinsic effectiveness," defined as the impact on users. The emphasis is on the latter, as more than half of this work focuses on use studies. Wortman explains that the type of material, purpose of use, and material location, as well as the user, must be considered when measuring use. Separate sections deal with circulation, in-house use, Trueswell's "80/20 Rule," and the Pittsburgh Study, which is thoroughly discussed. The RLG Conspectus, standards, overlap studies, and the concept of the "composite collection" (the combined holdings of a group of libraries) are also covered here. This chapter from a 1989 collection management textbook takes a broader perspective than earlier collection development textbooks, which tended to focus more on traditional approaches.

OVERVIEWS FROM A SPECIAL PERSPECTIVE

28. Futas, Elizabeth. "The Role of Public Services in Collection Evaluation." **Library Trends** 33 (Winter 1985): 397-416.

This praiseworthy essay begins by stressing that collection evaluation requires knowledge concerning the collection, the user community, and the collection's purpose in terms of the user community. A useful overview of four qualitative evaluation methodologies is presented: list checking, direct observation, surveys of user opinion, and standards.

The author cogently argues that public service librarians, by virtue of their daily contact with users, are best qualified to conduct qualitative collection evaluations as well as to participate in long-range planning and decision making in regard to the collection. Futas offers the most forceful published statement in favor of strong public-service participation in collection evaluation.

29. Hyman, Ferne. "Collection Evaluation in the Research Library." **Collection Building** 9, no. 3/4 (1989): 33-37. Also issued as "Collection Evaluation in the Research Environment." In **Collection Management: Current Issues**, edited by Sarah Shoemaker, 33-37. New York: Neal-Schuman Publishers, 1989. 74p. LC 89-3258. ISBN 1-555-70034-9.

One of the few overview articles to focus explicitly on the university research library, this essay argues that traditional collection-centered and user-centered evaluation techniques are more appropriate for evaluating a collection's ability to support teaching than its ability to support research. University collections require different assessment techniques because of the emphasis on research, in addition to the usual space and budget problems. The benefits of a basic research-oriented technique, the RLG Conspectus, are outlined, with the first point noting that the Conspectus represents a "standard tool" for assessment.

30. Intner, Sheila S. "Responsibilities of Technical Service Librarians to the Process of Collection Evaluation." **Library Trends** 33 (Winter 1985): 417-33.

This outstanding essay, apparently a companion piece to Futas's article on public services and collection evaluation (entry 28), explains in extensive detail how data derived from technical service functions can be used in the collection evaluation process, while also noting limitations. Separate sections cover acquisitions, cataloging, circulation, interlibrary loan, and preservation. Intner concludes that technical services data is quantitative rather than qualitative; is of value primarily for short-term as opposed to long-term planning; and can assist but not substitute for the evaluator's judgment.

31. Kusnerz, Peggy Ann. "Collection Evaluation Techniques in the Academic Art Library." **Drexel Library Quarterly** 19 (Summer 1983): 38-51.

As promised in the title, Kusnerz discusses the evaluation techniques available to the academic art librarian. Important evaluation studies are summarized according to four headings: list checking, including citation analysis; quantitative analysis; use studies; and review by subject specialists. Kusnerz emphasizes that one must define the evaluation project's goals and recommends the best methods for various objectives. The author makes a conscientious effort to cite examples pertinent to art librarianship. Art librarians in particular will want to look at this article, but much of what is said here applies to any academic library.

32. Richards, Daniel T. "Collection Assessment in Science Libraries: An Overview." In **IAMSLIC at a Crossroads; Proceedings of the 15th Annual Conference**, edited by Robert W. Burkhart and Joyce C. Burkhart, 89-98. N.p.: International Association of Marine Science Libraries and Information Centers, 1990. 200p. (International Association of Marine Science Libraries and Information Centers Conference Series). LC 90-81226. ISBN 0-932939-07-4.

In contrast to the many works emphasizing evaluation methods, Richards provides a much broader perspective of the assessment process in science libraries. In separate sections, he covers the purpose and structure of scientific literature; the functions performed by collection development, collection development policies, and collection evaluation; the assessment planning process; methods; and report writing. The methods section explains the difference between quantitative and qualitative approaches. The textual narrative is effectively enhanced by concise outlines, such as seven steps in the assessment planning process or ten specific topics to be evaluated.

Richards observes that "collection assessment in science libraries does not depart dramatically from the same activity in other types of libraries and ... the underlying principles are the same." Nevertheless, the literature concerning science library collection evaluation is, as stated by the author, "relatively sparse." This paper helps fill the void.

33. Robinson, William C. "Evaluation of the Government Documents Collection: A Step-by-Step Process." **Government Publications Review** 9 (March-April 1982): 131-41.

In a follow-up to the work in entry 34, Robinson offers, as promised in the title, a practical, step-by-step guide to conducting evaluation of government documents collections. He proposes a "continuous revision model" in which segments of the collection are evaluated each year until the entire collection has been evaluated. He explains that problems, importance, demand, obsolescence, and cost should be used to determine which segments are initially evaluated. The segment is then characterized by size, format, age, subject, physical condition, degree of difficulty, special features, completeness, and use. Detailed instructions are provided concerning how to conduct a community survey (defined to include the academic community), including who to contact, what questions to ask, and how to ask them. This advice could apply to any collection evaluation project, not just government documents collections.

34. Robinson, William C. "Evaluation of the Government Documents Collection: An Introduction and Overview." **Government Publications Review** 8a, nos. 1/2 (1981): 111-25.

Robinson's thoughtful essay offers a rare methodological overview of government documents collection evaluation. He begins by listing six categories of evaluation measures: activity, performance, impact, cost, outcome, and benefit. *Collection adequacy* is defined as the ability to meet patron needs. A section explains how the reference, circulation, and interlibrary loan departments can provide

12 / SURVEY WORKS

information that assists the evaluation process. A large portion of the article is devoted to an analysis of the available methods, which are divided into patron-oriented (questionnaires and interviews) and collection-oriented (size, checklists, citation analysis, document delivery capability, use of subject specialists, and direct observation). Government document librarians may wish to examine this essay if for no other reason than that it is one of the few items available on the topic.

35. Sandler, Mark, and Cathryn H. Barling. "Departmental Evaluation and Maintenance of the Library Sociology Collection." **Teaching Sociology** 11 (April 1984): 259-80.

Sandler and Barling's objective is to provide an overview concerning evaluation of the sociology collection for faculty members at small and medium-sized colleges. Under the heading "Quantitative Evaluation Procedures," they recommend: 1) a "baseline" of 1,850 to 3,700 volumes, based on an extrapolation from the ACRL standards; 2) shelflist measurement, to address balance among subareas within a discipline; 3) and consultation of the *American Book Publishing Record* to determine how many books have been published on particular sociology subareas. To assist shelflist measurement, a table sets out the LC class ranges for numerous sociology topics. For qualitative evaluation, the authors recommend various checklists pertaining to the book, reference, and periodical collections. They stress the importance of "customizing" a collection with material of regional and local interest. A concluding discussion advising faculty on how to interact with librarians includes the statement, "[W]e by no means wish to imply that librarians are a pugnacious or uncooperative lot." This work is unusual because the intended audience is faculty rather than librarians.

36. Singer, Loren. "Collection Evaluation in Fine Arts Libraries." In **Current Issues in Fine Arts Collection Development**, 7-15. Tucson, Ariz.: Art Libraries Society of North America, 1984. 36p. (Occasional Papers, no. 3). ISBN 0-942740-03-3. ISSN 0730-7160.

Singer describes "a skeletal plan for collection evaluation" in an art library. Taking "a practitioner's viewpoint," the author explains the major collection evaluation methods. Collection statistics, circulation statistics, interlibrary loan requests, and budget analysis (specifically the ratio of book to serial expenditures) are discussed as examples of quantitative analysis, while the checklist method and citation analysis are described under the heading of qualitative analysis. Eleven tables illustrate the various methods with data used in collection evaluations at Concordia University in such subjects as fine arts, art education, visual arts, photography, and Canadian art. Several of these tables present detailed data on the results of list checking and citation analysis. A rather lengthy, unannotated bibliography is appended. This item offers a useful introduction to collection evaluation for fine arts librarians.

37. Tjoumas, Renee, and Esther E. Horne. "Collection Evaluation: Practices and Methods in Libraries of ALA Accredited Graduate Library Education Programs." In **Advances in Library Administration and Organization**, vol. 5, edited by Gerald B. McCabe and Bernard Kreissman, 109-38. Greenwich, Conn.: JAI Press, 1986. 307p. ISBN 0-89232-674-3.

More than half this piece is devoted to a detailed literature review (more than seventy items are cited) concerning the available approaches to collection evaluation. Separate sections cover fifteen different techniques, including the impressionistic method, checklists, standards, citation analysis, document delivery tests, and automated methods.

A survey of collection evaluation practice in ALA-accredited library and information science schools, as of 1984, is also reported. Only thirteen of forty-six respondents had conducted a collection evaluation; those who did usually did so for accreditation purposes. A table, rank-ordering fifteen standard approaches by frequency of use, reveals that 76.9 percent of respondents employed the impressionistic method and 53.9 percent used checklists and shelflist analysis.

BIBLIOGRAPHIES

38. American Library Association. Reference and Adult Services Division. **Collection Evaluation Techniques; A Short, Selective, Practical, Current Annotated Bibliography 1980-1990**, compiled and edited by Cynthia Stewart Kaag with Sharon Lee Cann and others. Chicago: Reference and Adult Services Division, American Library Association, 1991. 21p. (RASD Occasional Papers, no. 10). ISBN 0-8389-7521-6.

This pamphlet's stated objective is "to assist the planner/evaluator in choosing and implementing techniques for collection evaluation," while emphasizing "practical goals and results." Fifty-eight items published between 1980 and 1990 are annotated. Although material pertinent to public and school librarianship is included, the vast majority of entries are relevant to academic libraries. The bibliography is organized into two sections: articles and chapters, and guidelines and manuals. A brief glossary is appended. This is a useful introduction to some of the most important collection evaluation work published during the 1980s.

39. Godden, Irene P., Karen W. Fachan, and Patricia A. Smith, with Sandra Brug, comps. "The Collection: Evaluation." In their **Collection Development and Acquisitions, 1970-1980: An Annotated, Critical Bibliography**, 15-41. Metuchen, N.J.: Scarecrow Press, 1982. 138p. LC 81-18530. ISBN 0-8108-1499-4.

The authors identified the most "notable" collection development articles and monographs of the 1970s by mailing a questionnaire to 300 library science educators and reviewing the previous 10 years of *Library Literature—The Best of...* plus the 1979 and 1980 annual review articles in *Library Resources & Technical Services*. The twenty-seven-page section concerning collection evaluation annotates eighty-four items, which are grouped into the following categories: 1) "for whom do libraries collect, and how adequate are the collections"; 2) general methods; 3) the Pittsburgh Study; 4) other use studies; and 5) citation studies. The summaries are quite helpful, but because of the authors' selection method a number of important studies were inevitably omitted. Godden, Fachan, and Smith's bibliography may be viewed as a partial forerunner of this annotated bibliography and literature guide.

14 / SURVEY WORKS

40. Nisonger, Thomas E. "An Annotated Bibliography of Items Relating to Collection Evaluation in Academic Libraries, 1969-1981." **College & Research Libraries** 43 (July 1982): 300-311.

Ninty-seven articles, books, and doctoral dissertations pertaining to college and university library collection evaluation and collection standards, published between 1969 and 1981, are annotated. The bibliography includes: case studies, newly proposed techniques, overviews of collection evaluation, attempts to define an adequate collection, commentary on standards, and miscellaneous material.

The short annotations summarize the most important collection evaluation studies from the 1970s. As stated in the introduction, this present volume represents an expanded supplement to the author's 1982 bibliography.

41. Ottersen, Signe. "A Bibliography on Standards for Evaluating Libraries." **College & Research Libraries** 32 (March 1971): 127-44.

This bibliography was prepared for the membership of the Federal Library Committee's Task Force on Acquisition of Library Materials and Correlation of Federal Library Resources. One hundred thirty-eight entries, published between 1933 and 1970, are annotated. Some of the earliest work on collection evaluation is included here. All types of libraries are covered, but a majority of the references pertain to academic libraries. Ottersen states that the entries were "selected because of their contribution to 1) an understanding of the elements of library standards and criteria necessary for subject evaluation, and 2) methodology suitable for application to the evaluation task." This item is the first stand-alone bibliography on collection evaluation.

2

Methods and Methodology

Much of the considerable amount published about general research methodology in library and information science is undoubtedly relevant to collection evaluation methodology. However, this chapter is limited to material that directly addresses collection evaluation. Included here are items dealing with specific techniques to assist the collection evaluation process, such as shelflist measurement methods; newly proposed evaluation methods; discussions of theoretical or methodological issues in collection evaluation; and commentary on specific methods or approaches. This chapter contains items that discuss methods from a theoretical perspective; descriptions of their applications are covered in chapter 3. Items that summarize several different collection evaluation methods are included in chapter 1, while discussions of journal ranking methodology may be found in chapter 11.

This chapter is divided into six sections: methodological discussions, the checklist method, other methods, measurement of holdings, measurement of use, and miscellaneous.

METHODOLOGICAL DISCUSSIONS

42. Futas, Elizabeth, and David L. Vidor. "What Constitutes a 'Good' Collection?" **Library Journal** 112 (April 15, 1987): 45-47.

A study of the Emory University business collection, reported separately in the 1988 *Library Resources & Technical Services*[1] and elsewhere, led to many philosophical thoughts concerning what a good collection is, what a bad collection is, and how the difference can be measured. Employing the Socratic approach, the authors ask, but never explicitly answer, innumerable questions, such as the meaning of *use*, the significance of citation, the difference between want and need, "how much is enough," etc. This short essay provokes thought about fundamental collection evaluation issues.

43. Garland, Kathleen. "Developing a Scale of Comprehensiveness to Serve as a Collection Evaluation Criteria." In **Information Interaction; Proceedings of the 45th ASIS Annual Meeting, Columbus, Ohio, October 17-21, 1982,** vol. 19, edited by Anthony E. Petrarca, Celianna I. Taylor, and Robert S. Kohn, 110-12. White Plains, N.Y.: published for the American Society for Information Science by Knowledge Industry Publications, 1982. 431p. LC 64-8303. ISBN 0-86729-038-2. ISSN 0044-7870.

Garland proposes a new criterion for evaluating a library collection, namely, the degree of subject diversity and relatedness in the holdings. After observing that comprehensiveness is traditionally measured in terms of the number of items held, she proposes "breadth of subject coverage" as an operational definition. A non-normalized Brillouin information measure can be used to calibrate diversity on a 0 to 1 scale. A 0 indicates no diversity and high relatedness; that is, all the holdings are on the same subject. A 1 indicates high diversity and no relatedness; that is, all the books are on different subjects. A test of this approach on 416 science monographs at the Sears Library, Case Western Reserve University, found that diversity/relatedness does not correlate with use, leading the author to conclude that diversity/relatedness represents a separate collection evaluation criterion. This item is quite interesting from the theoretical perspective.

44. Katz, Bill. "By the Numbers: The Fallacy of Formula." **Collection Building** 5 (Spring 1983): 28-30.

This short essay by a well-known expert vehemently argues against the use of quantitative formulas in collection evaluation. Special emphasis is placed on use studies. Katz asserts that these studies presuppose "a mathematical truth which is much closer to speculation than objective formulation." Moreover, they are not used or understood by practitioners, because "the would-be researchers establish laws built upon nothing but air." He argues that the findings of the Pittsburgh Study were not "startling" and that the required time and money would have been better spent elsewhere. This item represents one of the strongest statements against quantification in collection evaluation studies.

45. McGrath, William E. "Circulation Studies and Collection Development: Problems of Methodology, Theory and Typology for Research." In **Collection Development in Libraries: A Treatise,** pt. B, edited by Robert D. Stueart and George B. Miller, Jr., 373-403. Greenwich, Conn.: JAI Press, 1980. (Foundations in Library and Information Science, vol. 10). LC 79-93165. ISBN 0-89232-162-8 (pt B).

Following a discussion of fundamental methodological issues in circulation studies, such as definition, unit of analysis, relationships, variables, generalization, theory, and policy development, the author proposes a five-level hierarchical typology, illustrated in a two-page table, for circulation and collection development research. The "Macrosociological" level focuses on large groups, such as universities, whereas the "Microsociological" concentrates on smaller units, such as departments within universities. The focus of the "Psychological" falls on individuals; the "Bibliographical" on books or articles; and the "Bibliographic" on parts of books, such as paragraphs. This well-thought-out chapter is of considerable theoretical importance for circulation studies.

46. Wainwright, Eric. "Collection Adequacy: Meaningless Concept or Measurable Goal?" In **Collection Management in Academic Libraries: Papers Delivered at a National Seminar, Surfers Paradise, Queensland 16th-17th February, 1984**, edited by Cathryn Crowe, Philip Kent, and Barbara Paton, 1-10. Sydney, Australia: Library Association of Australia, University and College Libraries Section, 1984. 88p. ISBN 0-86804-014-2.

This thought-provoking talk by a prominent Australian librarian elaborates upon the "substantial difficulties" of defining and measuring "collection adequacy." Nine standard collection-centered and client-centered evaluation methods are reviewed and each found, by itself, to be lacking. Wainwright concludes, "While measuring collection adequacy in the true quantitative sense is not possible ... there are now a variety of evaluation methods which, used in combination, allow a library to build up a clear picture of the content of its collections." Although addressed to an Australian audience, this piece helps illuminate a universal collection evaluation problem, the concept of adequacy.

THE CHECKLIST METHOD

47. Comer, Cynthia. "List-Checking as a Method for Evaluating Library Collections." **Collection Building** 3, no. 3 (1981): 26-34.

List checking is one of the oldest and most widely used collection evaluation techniques. The author discusses the approach's benefits—lists are easy to use, flexible, and widely available—as well as its drawbacks—lists are arbitrary and subjective, quickly become outdated, and may not meet the unique needs of a particular library. The pros, cons, and uses of various types of lists are also addressed, including standard lists for the core collection, specialized subject bibliographies for subject collections, Goldhor's inductive method (entry 59) for public libraries, and the citation method for research libraries. Comer stresses that list checking supports collection development by identifying what is lacking. A short "Selective Bibliography" is appended.

48. Devin, Robin B. "Evaluating the Sociology Collection." **Behavioral & Social Sciences Librarian** 4 (Winter 1984/Spring 1985): 1-7.

This article proposes a method for evaluating the sociology journals, monographs, and current monographic acquisitions in academic and research libraries. Primarily aimed at the graduate collection, it is also applicable to undergraduate programs. It recommends that a research library hold 70 percent of the journals indexed in *Sociological Abstracts* and ranked by impact factor in the *Social Science Citation Index Journal Citation Reports*. To evaluate monographic holdings, the author recommends that a research library hold "virtually 100%" of the sociology section in *Books for College Libraries*; less than 90 percent may indicate "significant gaps." Samples of books reviewed in *Contemporary Sociology* can be used to evaluate current acquisitions, with an 80 percent holdings rate the recommended minimum. Although not so indicated in the title, it is obvious that this item depicts the traditional checklist approach to collection evaluation.

49. Heinzkill, Richard. "Retrospective Collection Development in English Literature: An Overview." **Collection Management** 9 (Spring 1987): 55-65.

Although this article offers an overview of retrospective collection development in English literature, the half covering collection evaluation focuses primarily on the checklist method. Heinzkill states that "selective retrospective bibliographies are the principal tools in evaluation." He elaborates upon five criteria in selecting a bibliography to be used as a checklist: comprehensiveness, selectivity, balance, layout, and timeliness. Six uses of checklist bibliographies are enumerated, including comparison with dealer catalogs and creation of a desiderata file. However, the author adds that volumes held, volumes added, and expenditures should also be considered in evaluation. Other sections briefly deal with funding, faculty relations, and report writing. This is the only work annotated here dealing with retrospective collection evaluation in English literature.

50. Lundin, Anne H. "List-Checking in Collection Development: An Imprecise Art." **Collection Management** 11, nos. 3/4 (1989): 103-12.

This well-written essay, quoting numerous sources, covers the history, drawbacks, and benefits of list checking as well as potential sources of lists. Especially useful is a synopsis, based on Katz,[2] of the evaluative factors in list selection: scope, audience, annotations, timeliness, authority, recommendations, and format. The author makes the thought-provoking observation that lists are "more appropriate" for either smaller or specialized libraries. Lundin stresses that list checking is a "heuristic," collection-centered approach to the "imprecise art" of collection development. This article is definitely worth noting because it is one of only a few items to deal exclusively with the list checking method.

51. Porta, Maria A., and F. Wilfrid Lancaster. "Evaluation of a Scholarly Collection in a Specific Subject Area by Bibliographic Checking: A Comparison of Sources." **Libri** 38 (June 1988): 131-37.

To analyze the methodological issues involved in compiling bibliographic samples for list checking, the University of Illinois holdings in irrigation were evaluated by various random samples: 1) 500 items from the 1985 volume of *Irricab*, an abstracting tool; 2) 396 citations taken from items in *Irricab* owned by the library; 3) 269 citations from items in *Irricab* not owned by the library (but obtained on ILL); and 4) 500 citations from the 1985 volumes of three core journals in agriculture. A summary table shows the "widely divergent" results obtained for the different samples. The authors' concluding analysis of these inconsistencies offers valuable theoretical insight into the checklist collection evaluation method.

52. Sandler, Mark. "Quantitative Approaches to Qualitative Collection Assessment." **Collection Building** 8, no. 4 (1987): 12-17.

Sandler's explanation of the methodological issues involved in the checklist evaluation method displays an insightful understanding concerning the approach's complexity. Most of the article is devoted to seven fundamental questions of research design: 1) what is to be learned; 2) the study's scope; 3) the source of the citations; 4) formats to be included in the study; 5) what elements to analyze from each citation, such as language or date; 6) what sampling method to use; and 7) what constitutes a "hit." Unlike many other articles on checklists, the author advocates coding the data and applying statistical packages to test for statistical significance.

Further tabulation of results by categories such as subject or decade, he says, results in "a powerful collection management tool."

53. Winter, Michael F. "Current Social Theory: A Monograph Checklist." **Behavioral & Social Sciences Librarian** 6, nos. 3/4 (1988): 9-37.

Following a brief discussion of the need for a checklist in social theory for evaluating research library collections, because none is available and pertinent LC subject headings can be misleading, an appendix presents a checklist containing approximately 300 monographs. The appendix was compiled by listing every relevant book reviewed or cited in *Contemporary Sociology* and the *Annual Review of Sociology* between 1980 and 1985.

The author states that libraries collecting sociology at RLG Conspectus level 3E or higher should hold most of these items. This approach is unusual in that most checklists are not tied to a specific collecting level. This entry would obviously benefit research libraries in need of a checklist to evaluate their social theory holdings, and Winter asserts that smaller libraries can use it as a comprehensive list.

OTHER METHODS

54. Aquilar, William. "The Application of Relative Use and Interlibrary Demand in Collection Development." **Collection Management** 8 (Spring 1986): 15-24.

Following a review of quantitative, qualitative, and use-oriented approaches, the author proposes an evaluation method whereby the percentage of total ILL requests devoted to a specific subject is compared to the percentage of total holdings on that subject to calculate the "RBH," ratio of borrowings to holdings. Based on the RBH, one determines if a subject area is "overused" or "underused" and applies a decision table to reach one of four options: buy, continue, examine, or do not buy.

The author appears not to have tested his intriguing technique in a library but to have developed it from previously published evaluation literature. Aquilar asserts that his method offers "a powerful analytical tool" utilizing readily available circulation and interlibrary loan data. (See also Lee and Lockway entry 590.)

55. Budd, John, and Mike DiCarlo. "Measures of User Evaluation at Two Academic Libraries: Prolegomena." **Library Research** 4 (Spring 1982): 71-84.

The authors describe a method for evaluating library services, adapted from Chweh's[3] model designed primarily for public libraries, which they jointly administered at the Northeast Louisiana University and Southeastern Louisiana University libraries. Samples of faculty and students at both universities completed a survey instrument rating a series of items on a 1 (low) to 6 (high) scale according to the items' perceived importance and the libraries' performance in the area. The mean differences between the importance and performance ratings were then calculated, although Budd and DiCarlo admit "interpretation of the ratings is a complex task." Two long tables (one for faculty, the other for students) display the combined results from the two universities. At least a quarter of the twenty surveyed items, which included local newspapers, out-of-town newspapers, journals, general books, and the reference collection, were relevant to collection evaluation.

20 / METHODS AND METHODOLOGY

Although ostensibly designed for library services, this method contains an important collection evaluation component. Besson and Sheriff (entry 409) used the approach in serials collection evaluation.

56. Byrd, Gary D., D. A. Thomas, and Katherine E. Hughes. "Collection Development Using Interlibrary Loan Borrowing and Acquisitions Statistics." **Bulletin of the Medical Library Association** 70 (January 1982): 1-9.

The authors describe a fascinating collection evaluation approach predicated on the assumption that the subject distributions of new book acquisitions and ILL requests should parallel each other. The 1980 fiscal year ILL requests and new book data for the University of Kansas Clendening Library (for health sciences), the University of Missouri-Kansas City Health Sciences Library, and the St. Luke's Hospital Library were compared for each library in twenty-seven areas of clinical medicine. A collection balance indicator (CBI) that combined the percentage of ILL requests and the percentage of new acquisitions for each subject was calculated for the three libraries and a combined collection balance indicator (CCBI) was derived for their composite holdings. When the data are plotted on graphs, as illustrated in the article, subject areas that are out of balance become readily apparent. The authors assert that their method is simple and speedy.

57. Chweh, Steven Seokho. "User Criteria for Evaluation of Library Service." **Journal of Library Administration** 2 (Spring 1981): 35-46.

The author's proposed method is not, strictly speaking, a collection evaluation technique because overall library services are evaluated. It is nevertheless mentioned here because a major component concerns collections. In the spring of 1977, 209 library users in the Los Angeles area were asked during interviews to name the 10 most important criteria for a "good" library; the responses resulted in 1,249 named items. A table lists, in rank order, the fifty most frequently mentioned items, along with a weight based on each item's proportion of total responses. "Availability of books" ranked number one, "availability of periodicals" number two, and a "good reference collection" number four. Approximately one-quarter of the fifty evaluation criteria relate to the collection. An appendix exhibits a model questionnaire, oriented towards public and academic libraries, on which library users rate the fifty criteria on a 1 (low) to 5 (high) scale. Chweh stresses that the weighted scoring system constitutes a mathematical model for evaluation of library services based on user-defined criteria.

58. Elzy, Cheryl Asper, and F. Wilfrid Lancaster. "Looking at a Collection in Different Ways: A Comparison of Methods of Bibliographic Checking." **Collection Management** 12, nos. 3/4 (1990): 1-10.

The checklist approach and Goldhor's inductive method (entry 59) were implemented and compared at Illinois State University's Teaching Materials Center. A sample of 434 items from four standard bibliographies was checked against the collection while a 398-item shelflist sample was checked against the same four bibliographies (in other words, the inductive method was used). The library owned 45 percent of the sample from the bibliographies, but 78 percent of the "inductive" sample was not listed in the bibliographies. Further investigation of the inductive sample included checking it against the holdings of four other curriculum centers in Illinois and analyzing it by in-print/out-of-print status and the ten major divisions of the Dewey classification. The authors conclude that "[t]he inductive sample reinforces the other sample" by providing additional information about the collection.

59. Goldhor, Herbert. "Analysis of an Inductive Method of Evaluating the Book Collection of a Public Library." **Libri** 23, no. 1 (1973): 6-17.

Goldhor's famous "inductive method," although obviously oriented towards public libraries, should be brought to the attention of academic librarians. Instead of checking a list to determine how many items a library holds, one begins with a sample from the collection and calculates how many standard bibliographies list each title. Following a sophisticated statistical analysis concerning the technique's application to both fiction and reference in thirteen Minneapolis-St. Paul area library agencies during 1966 (ten tables exhibit the findings), the author concludes that the system "has some merit." The inductive method was tested by Elzy and Lancaster in a university teaching materials collection (see entry 58).

60. Loertscher, David V. "Collection Mapping: An Evaluation Strategy for Collection Development." **Drexel Library Quarterly** 21 (Spring 1985): 9-21.

Although intended for school library media centers, this important and intriguing approach should be noted by academic librarians. A two-step process is employed. First, a collection map is created by calculating the number of collection items per student, based on shelflist data, for three segments of the collection: 1) the total collection; 2) general emphasis areas corresponding to courses, such as travel; and 3) specific emphasis areas corresponding to units of instruction within a course, such as space travel. Next, over the course of several months, the teacher and media specialist evaluate how well the collection responds to demands made upon it, by assigning a 1 (low) to 5 (high) rating system to five criteria and then calculating an overall average. The five criteria are diversity of formats, currency, relevance to need, duplication (i.e., enough materials), and appropriateness of the materials' level.

A collection map is illustrated, a step-by-step guide to creating one is included, and seven potential uses are listed. Although not stated by the author, there are obvious similarities between this approach and that of the RLG Conspectus, the collection is broken down into small segments and a 1-to-5 rating system is used.

61. Lopez, Manuel D. "The Lopez or Citation Technique of In-Depth Collection Evaluation Explicated." **College & Research Libraries** 44 (May 1983): 251-55.

In response to Nisonger's report about experimental testing of the Lopez method in the University of Manitoba library (entry 62), the technique's creator offers some important clarifications concerning the method's use while also describing its actual implementation at the SUNY-Buffalo Library where it was developed. The method is used every five years at Buffalo, in social science areas only, in conjunction with two other approaches: checking the holdings against bibliographical references from dissertations and journals listed in indexes and abstracts. At Buffalo the evaluation begins with 100 references from five sources rather than the 25 references used at Manitoba. A valuable explanation of the method's scoring system is also provided. This is essential reading for anyone interested in the Lopez method.

62. Nisonger, Thomas E. "An In-Depth Collection Evaluation at the University of Manitoba Library: A Test of the Lopez Method." **Library Resources & Technical Services** 24 (Fall 1980): 329-38.

This article describes the first reported implementation of the so-called *Lopez method*, originally proposed in 1969.[4] Intended to measure a collection's depth for research purposes, the method traces citations through four levels. First, citations from a standard bibliography in the subject under evaluation are randomly selected and checked against the collection. The first citation in each item found during the first step is then checked against the holdings. The second citation in each document found at the second level is checked. Lastly, the third citation in each document found at the third level is checked. A 10-20-40-80 scoring system is then applied for items found at the four levels.

The method was tested twice in four subject areas (family therapy, the American novel, modern British history, and medieval French literature) at the University of Manitoba during 1977-1978. Although the author found that the method does measure a collection's depth, result inconsistencies between the two tests, using Lopez's original scheme plus three variations, raised questions concerning the method's reliability.

63. Paskoff, Beth M., and Anna H. Perrault. "A Tool for Comparative Collection Analysis: Conducting a Shelflist Sample to Construct a Collection Profile." **Library Resources & Technical Services** 34 (April 1990): 199-215.

Paskoff and Perrault's outstanding contribution describes a collection profiling method developed at the Louisiana State University Library. A 5 percent random sample of the 785,000-title shelflist, requiring 352 hours of staff time, was tabulated with Stat-Graphics and dBase II software. The data were analyzed by language, publication date, format, LC class, and duplication rate. Several tables display the results and the workform used to gather data is illustrated.

The authors stress that simple shelflist totals are one-dimensional, but their approach provides a multidimensional collection profile that offers more information than a shelflist count or the RLG Conspectus. The data can be used for collection development policies, preservation, cooperative collection development, and completing the RLG Conspectus. It is understood that other libraries are planning to use the collection profiling approach. This article won the prestigious "Best of L.R.T.S." award for 1990.

64. Roeder, Christine S. "Tying the Curriculum to Book Collection Development: The Devry Institute of Technology Learning Resource Center Model." In **Acquisitions '90; Conference on Acquisitions, Budgets, and Collections; May 16 and 17, 1990, St. Louis, Missouri; Proceedings**, compiled and edited by David C. Genaway, 393-99. Canfield, Ohio: Genaway, 1990. 435p. ISBN 0-943970-06-7.

Roeder describes a "curriculum-centered book collection development model" that has been used for the last decade at the DeVry Institute of Technology, described as "a private college with eleven locations in the United States and Canada." The model represents a refinement of a quantitative formula proposed by Allen, Kniesner, and O'Herron in 1981 (entry 242). For nineteen broad subject categories, such as mathematics or computer science, the model specifies a percentage range which that subject should compose of the total holdings, e.g., 3 to 5 percent for mathematics. Actual holdings and current circulation are then compared to the recommended percentage range to evaluate the collection. A table exhibits the recommended percentages for the nineteen categories. The author notes that the model requires precise statistics and modification as the curriculum changes.

65. Tjoumas, Renee, and Virgil L. P. Blake. "Counteracting the Divergence Between Professional Accreditation and the Evaluation of Library Science Collections." **Collection Management** 12, nos. 1/2 (1990): 43-59.

Following their historical review of the American Library Association's standards for accrediting library science programs, which were found to be "qualitative and subjective," the authors propose an "easy," "cost effective," and "accurate" four-step quantitative methodology for evaluating library science collections that could result in guidelines to be used in the accreditation process.

In step one, a faculty research profile is created through analysis of citations in faculty publications for the last five to ten years. A curriculum profile is created in step two by matching course descriptions from the school catalog with the appropriate LC classification number. For step three, shelflist sampling methods are recommended to determine the collection size and profile the holdings by subject, date, language, and country of origin. In step four, an automated method gathers the same data as in step three and the results of the two methods are compared for accuracy and cost-effectiveness. This well-done piece is the only example of a method proposed strictly for library and information science collections.

66. Whaley, John H., Jr. "An Approach to Collection Analysis." **Library Resources & Technical Services** 25 (July/September 1981): 330-38.

Whaley proposes a fascinating method for identifying curricular needs and determining how well a collection can meet them. The technique combines three traditional approaches, list checking, compiling statistics, and obtaining user opinion, each of which is briefly explained. Faculty indicate which classes in the appropriate Library of Congress classification tables support their courses and, if necessary, indicate additional subject terms. The number of times a class number was listed is compared with the class's shelflist holdings to identify deficient areas. The *Library of Congress Subject Catalogs* or the *Library of Congress Shelflist* can then be used to locate potential additions for these areas. The method was tested in the SUNY-Binghamton anthropology department and the University of North Carolina at Charlotte sociology and history departments. The article concludes by explaining the approach's benefits, including evaluation of the collection's ability to support newly proposed courses.

MEASUREMENT OF HOLDINGS

67. Belgum, Kathie. "Volume Equivalents of Microforms—A Question." **Law Library Journal** 76 (Spring 1983): 345-56.

This work addresses the issue of how legal material in microform holdings is converted to bibliographic volume equivalents. Based on a detailed count of United States and Iowa documents in the University of Iowa Law Library microform holdings, the eight-to-one conversion ratio suggested in 1975 by the AALS, AALL, and ABA is rejected in favor of a newly proposed six-to-one ratio. The author reports that separate calculations using the two ratios resulted in a 25 percent difference regarding the Iowa Law Library's total holdings (although this is hardly a profound finding, as different ratios must logically produce different results). Numerous figures illustrate the mathematical calculations, with data on specific law sets presented in the appendix. Belgum's article would be of most value for shelflist measurement to any library collecting legal materials in microform.

68. Black, George W., Jr. "Estimating Collection Size Using the Shelf List in a Science Library." **Journal of Academic Librarianship** 6 (January 1981): 339-41.

This article should be of considerable practical value to librarians still interested in shelflist measurements (although traditional shelflist measurement with a ruler is undoubtedly on the wane in the era of automation). Based on data from the Southern Illinois University at Carbondale Science Division collection, the method is illustrated with a calculation of the number of volumes per shelflist inch for the Dewey 500s' ten divisions (general science, mathematics, astronomy, physics, chemistry, etc.). Black's contribution is important for its point that the number of volumes represented by an inch of shelflist will vary significantly among subject areas.

69. Black, George W., Jr. "Statistical Determination of Bound Volume Journal Holdings in a Science Library." **Serials Librarian** 5 (Winter 1980): 31-39.

Black explains a method used at the Southern Illinois University at Carbondale Library's Science Division to gather statistical data on back periodical holdings. Every tenth Science Division title from the 1975 *Periodical List* and its 1976 *Supplement* was sampled. After analysis using the Statistical Package for the Social Sciences, data were generated concerning total periodical holdings, bound volumes, periodical reels, current and inactive titles, complete runs, predominant language, and country of publication arranged by Dewey numbers. The data are presented in five tables.

Total holdings were within 4.5 percent of data calculated by another method, directly sampling the shelves themselves, leading to the conclusion that the figures "should be of value." The author believes that the collection's statistical profile may be of interest to other science librarians, but the description of a relatively quick method for tabulating bound periodical holdings is this article's main contribution.

70. Lauer, Joseph J. "A Methodology for Estimating the Size of Subject Collections, Using African Studies as an Example." **College & Research Libraries** 44 (September 1983): 380-83.

Although shelflist measurement is a standard method for calculating the titles held in a subject area, a problem is posed by the fact that many subjects, such as African studies, are dispersed throughout the classification table. Lauer's research note explains the methodology used in deriving a formula to calculate total African Studies holdings, based primarily on an analysis of the distribution of African holdings throughout the various LC classes in the Michigan State and Indiana University supplementary African shelf lists. This piece's most useful feature is the formula itself: to include North Africa in the total, one multiplies 2.8 times the titles held in the "DT" (i.e., African history) section of the LC classification; for sub-Saharan Africa only, one multiplies by 3.

The author asserts that his methodology can be applied to other subject areas as well. This item would be of most use in large research libraries.

71. Saunders, Stewart, Harriet Nelson, and Priscilla Geahigan. "Alternatives to the Shelflist Measure for Determining the Size of a Subject Collection." **Library Research** 3 (Winter 1981): 383-91.

The authors' purpose is to demonstrate that shelflist measurement to determine the size of holdings in a subject "may be highly inaccurate" and to suggest alternate techniques. Samples of books reviewed in standard anthropology, philosophy, political science, history, and sociology journals were compared to their officially assigned Dewey and LC classification numbers. The fact that 30 percent to 80 percent were classed outside their subject schedules indicates that shelflist measurement is unreliable. Two tables display the results.

Two alternate methods are proposed. In the first, one measures the shelflist and uses a reciprocal figure, derived from the tables, to extrapolate a total figure. Alternately, one takes a thousand-title sample from the catalog and projects the results onto the entire collection. Libraries needing to calculate the size of subject holdings may wish to consult this study.

MEASUREMENT OF USE

72. Bremer, Thomas A. "Assessing Collection Use by Surveying Users at Randomly Selected Times." **Collection Management** 13, no. 3 (1990): 57-67.

Bremer describes a method for randomly selecting time intervals to interview patrons concerning their use of library materials. The methods for calculating sample size and the survey instrument itself are described in detail. This approach was implemented during forty-one randomly selected hours in the spring quarter of 1984 at the Montana State University Library (to resolve a dispute between the library and the chemistry department concerning the physical location of *Chemical Abstracts*).

Bremer claims that his method is unique among use studies because it presents a random sampling methodology based on time intervals rather than physical units. He also believes that this methodology could be used by other libraries wishing to assess the use of noncirculating material.

73. Broadus, Robert N. "The Measurement of Periodicals Use." **Serials Review** 11 (Summer 1985): 57-61.

Broadus offers an admirable overview of the available methods for conducting a periodical use study. While conceding that formal use studies can be costly and misleading, the author argues that a well-designed study provides better information for periodical decision making than mere observation. He briefly addresses major questions concerning how well usage studies predict future use, their applicability to other libraries, and what type of study to use. More than half the essay is devoted to explaining four formal methods and discussing examples of their use cited in the literature: the sweep method (counting items left on tables, etc.), the questionnaire, direct observation, and citation data. Librarians contemplating a periodical use study may wish to read this article.

74. Konopasek, Katherine, and Nancy Patricia O'Brien. "Undergraduate Periodicals Usage: A Model of Measurement." **Serials Librarian** 9 (Winter 1984): 65-74.

Konopasek and O'Brien offer a detailed description of a "simple and inexpensive" method for measuring periodical use, which was implemented at the University of Illinois Undergraduate Library during a sixteen-week period in the spring of 1980. Green dots were attached to bound volumes being reshelved and patrons were asked to sign sheets stapled to current periodicals. The data were manually coded and tabulated.

Uses of the methodology included: 1) ranking titles by frequency of use, 2) determining total bound volume use by title and year, 3) comparing use of current issues and bound volumes, and 4) identifying the titles required to satisfy 90 percent of demand. The authors believe that this methodology could be used "in another library setting."

75. Rooke, Su. "Surveying Non-Usage of Serials." **Serials Librarian** 18, nos. 1/2 (1990): 81-96.

Librarians contemplating periodical cancellation are really interested in nonusage rather than use. A method, developed at the Plymouth Polytechnic Library, United Kingdom, for monitoring nonuse of serials through the dislocation of slips attached to the volumes is explained here. The data were gathered between January 1984 and July 1986 and again in the fall of 1987 for expensive and supposedly seldom-used titles. Then a formula, based on uses, days surveyed, and length of the backrun, was used to calculate an index value for each surveyed title. The index-to-price ratio represents the average cost per journal consultation.

The library's experience with this approach was "very positive." Rooke asserts that the method is "easy to administer," "reliable," and does not depend on the user's cooperation. Nevertheless, "it cannot cope accurately with heavily used titles."

76. Shaw, W. M., Jr. "A Practical Journal Usage Technique." **College & Research Libraries** 39 (November 1978): 479-84.

After a discussion of the deficiencies of traditional techniques for measuring journal usage (time-consuming and "of doubtful practical utility"), a method developed and used at the Case Western Reserve University Libraries is explained. When reshelving the first time, a label is attached to a bound volume's spine or the shelf by a current issue, so the collection can easily be divided into two categories: used and not used. There is no set time period for applying the technique, but when the used portion of the collection reaches a "constant fraction," unused volumes will probably "not experience significant use in the foreseeable future." Then a formula, considering subscription, binding, and storage costs, is proposed for "assessing the relative liability of unused titles." Shaw's method has often been used by other libraries and is frequently cited in the literature.

MISCELLANEOUS

77. Budd, John. "The Utility of a Recommended Core List: An Examination of **Books for College Libraries**, 3rd Ed." **Journal of Academic Librarianship** 17 (July 1991): 140-44.

Books for College Libraries is often used as a collection evaluation checklist. To test its utility, this sophisticated research study checked a sample of 283 titles, with imprint dates of 1980 or later, from the U.S. history, American literature, and English literature sections of the *BCL*'s 1988 third edition against the holdings of 713 institutions, using OCLC. Tables displaying, for each subject, the percentage of the sample held on average by four size categories of institutions, ranging from research universities to liberal arts colleges, reveal "a progressive, substantial decline in average holdings percentage as schools decrease in size." Moreover, a survey revealed that collection development officers from all four institutional types felt that their collections should hold a higher percentage than they actually did, with the discrepancies greatest for smaller institutions. Checking a stratified random sample of 383 titles against *Books in Print Plus* indicated that 42.8 percent were out-of-print.

Budd concludes that "one must adopt a cautionary attitude in using *BCL3* to assess the collections of academic libraries." Librarians using *BCL3* should ponder the implications of these findings.

78. Hacken, Richard D. "Statistical Assumption-Making in Library Collection Assessment: Peccadilloes and Pitfalls." **Collection Management** 7 (Summer 1985): 17-32.

This thoughtful essay warns against sloppy, misleading applications of statistics, as they may result in false conclusions and flawed collection assessments that could haunt a library for years. Writing in layman's terms, Hacken explains with easily comprehensible illustrations some common errors in the use of statistics, including inaccurate sampling, faulty survey designs, false assumptions, misleading percentages and averages, and imprecise definitions. In a somewhat lighthearted vein, he hopes that librarians will never use "statistics as a drunken man uses lampposts—for support rather than illumination." This item will be especially useful to those who are unsophisticated in statistics.

79. Hall, Blaine H. **Collection Assessment Manual for College and University Libraries.** Phoenix, Ariz.: Oryx Press, 1985. 212p. LC 85-13694. ISBN 0-89774-148-x.

As the titles imples, Hall offers a practical, "how-to" guide to collection assessment in academic libraries. This easy-to-use, well-organized manual covers planning an assessment, selecting and applying an appropriate method, analyzing the results, and reporting the findings. Advantages, disadvantages, procedures, and data analysis advice are listed for the standard collection-centered measures (compiling statistics, list checking, direct observation, applying standards) and client-centered methods (user, availability, citation, circulation, in-house use, and periodical use studies).

Nearly half the book is devoted to five appendixes, which present much useful information. Appendix A contains a short bibliography; B presents advice on sampling, including a sample size table at the 95-percent confidence level and a table of random numbers; C lists the names and addresses of accrediting bodies; D illustrates sample survey instruments; and E reprints the then-current ACRL standards for university, college, and two-year college libraries.

80. Hall, Blaine H. "Writing the Collection Assessment Manual." **Collection Management** 6 (Fall-Winter 1984): 49-61.

The importance of a collection assessment manual, a recommended evaluation planning process, and the techniques such a manual should include are highlighted in this work concerning how to write a collection assessment training manual. Numerous references are made to the Brigham Young University manual, which resulted from a 1978-1979 ARL Collection Analysis project. The planning process should address the collection to be assessed, a review of the collection development policy, assessment objectives, techniques to be used, and required resources. In accordance with the author's assertion that the manual's "heart" should be a discussion of the recommended techniques, about half this article is devoted to list checking, compiling statistics, standards, and "opinionnaires," as well as availability, circulation, and periodical usage studies.

Hall stresses that writing a manual is well worth the considerable effort required because it can result in better collection evaluation decisions. This article will be most valuable for large academic libraries contemplating the creation of a collection evaluation manual.

81. McGrath, William E. "Collection Evaluation: Theory and the Search for Structure." **Library Trends** 33 (Winter 1985): 241-66.

The purpose of this article is "to review the meaning and theory of collections and what is meant by structure" and "to enumerate some of the ways that data on collections can be organized to reveal underlying global structure—the links and connections between collections, parts of collections, and the users." Eight proposed models for data collection are explained: 1) "the subject structure model," which examines how subject areas are related; 2) "the user structure model," which examines the relationship among users; 3) "the subject/user model," which explores how subject areas and users are related; 4) "the user/formats model," which explores the relationship between users and formats; 5) "the subject/format model," which examines the relationship between subject area and format; 6) "the network model I," which addresses title overlap; 7) "the network model II," which addresses shared subject areas among libraries; and "the network model III," which addresses the extent to which libraries use each other's holdings. McGrath's highly abstract essay is one of the few works that seeks to provide a theoretical underpinning for collection evaluation.

82. Pedersen, Wayne A. "Graphing: A Tool for Collection Development." **Bulletin of the Medical Library Association** 74 (July 1986): 262-64.

Pedersen explains how a two-dimensional bar graph can present data concerning three variables: number of books, their subject, and their age. Employing shelflist data from a branch of the University of Texas Health Science Center Library at San Antonio, the number of books was displayed on the x-axis, while their subject content (based on the National Library of Medicine classification) and age (using different shadings for books published prior to and after 1980) were presented on the y-axis. The method is explicitly recommended for small- to medium-sized hospital libraries, but could be adapted for small academic libraries as well.

83. Stelk, Roger Edward, and F. Wilfrid Lancaster. "The Use of Shelflist Samples in Studies of Book Availability." **Collection Management** 13, no. 4 (1990): 19-24.

Two different methods of selecting samples to measure shelf availability are compared based on tests at the University of Illinois at Urbana-Champaign Undergraduate Library: a random shelflist sample and a systematic sample of recently circulated books, termed a "previously used" sample. Both samples contained 450 items. The former was drawn from the shelflist using a computer-generated list of random numbers, while the latter was systematically selected from items that circulated during a five-week period in September and October 1988. The shelf availability of the two samples was checked in April and May of 1989. The results, broken down by broad subject category, are compared.

Because circulation is concentrated on a small number of frequently used items, the authors conclude that a "previously used" sample offers a better indication of availability for "an item likely to be sought by a user." This piece would be useful for libraries considering which sampling method to use in a shelf availability study.

NOTES

[1] David L. Vidor and Elizabeth Futas, "Effective Collection Developers: Librarians or Faculty?" *Library Resources & Technical Services* 32 (April 1988): 127-36.

[2] William Katz, *Collection Development: The Selection of Materials for Libraries* (New York: Holt, Rinehart & Winston, 1980), 150-51.

[3] Steven S. Chweh, "A Model Instrument for User-Rating of Library Service," *California Librarian* 39 (April 1978): 46-55.

[4] Manuel D. Lopez, "A Guide for Beginning Bibliographers," *Library Resources & Technical Services* 13 (Fall 1969): 462-70.

3

Case Studies

Although case studies are sometimes deprecated as "how we do it good in our library" pieces (and sometimes deservedly so), the case study is recognized as a legitimate social science research method. Library case studies often provide guidance to practitioners and can serve as a foundation for further research.

Perhaps the earliest known collection evaluation study in North American library history was conducted by Charles Coffin Jewett in the mid-nineteenth century, using the now-familiar checklist approach. In his 1848 report as the Smithsonian Institute's assistant secretary, Jewett revealed that he had checked 139 citations in Wheaton's *History of International Law*, 251 references from the *History of Commerce* by Hoefer, 204 items in J. A. Bartlett's study of ethnology, and 38 references in a chemistry report by Berzelius against the holdings of many leading American libraries. Jewett concluded that these holdings were inadequate, especially compared to the European libraries of the period.[1]

The educational value of most collection evaluation case studies lies in the techniques or methodology used rather than the precise statistical results obtained for a particular library. Accordingly, the annotations in this chapter generally focus on how the evaluation was carried out.

This chapter annotates case studies reporting collection evaluation projects in a single library. Case studies concerning the evaluation of multiple libraries are discussed in chapter 6. Case studies dealing exclusively with serials are included in chapter 10, while chapter 8 contains case studies of evaluation projects based primarily on citation analysis. Because of the relatively small number of entries, this chapter is not subdivided.

COLLECTION EVALUATION CASE STUDIES IN A SINGLE LIBRARY

84. Alt, Martha S., and Richard D. Shiels. "Assessment of Library Materials on the History of Christianity at the Ohio State University: An Update." **Collection Management** 9 (Spring 1987): 67-77.

This follow-up report covers the second year of the History of Christianity assessment project at Ohio State University (see Shiels and Alt entry 97). After a review of the first year's evaluation procedures, a large part of this article is devoted to describing what follow-up actions were taken, such as fund allocation and creation of a written collection development policy. During the second year, emphasis was placed on evaluating the reference collection, serials, and holdings concerning Europe by checking standard lists against the collection. Also, newly available National Shelflist Count data for 1985 were used to compare OSU's Christianity holdings with those of Indiana, Michigan, Michigan State, and Wisconsin.

85. Association of Research Libraries. Office of Management Studies. **Collection Description and Assessment in ARL Libraries**. Washington, D.C.: Association of Research Libraries, Office of Management Studies, 1983. 117p. (SPEC Kit, 87). ISSN 0160-3582.

SPEC kits are usually of considerable practical value because they present a collection of in-house documents from several libraries to illustrate how a particular function is performed. This kit contains the second edition of the *RLG Collection Development Manual*, the planning section from the Brigham Young University library's *Collection Assessment Manual*, and a description of the Stanford University library's collection evaluation program, as well as actual collection assessment reports from Arizona State University, the University of California at San Diego, DePauw, the University of Illinois at Chicago Circle, and Notre Dame.

86. Byrne, Elizabeth Douthitt. "University of Cincinnati Design, Architecture, and Art Library Collection Evaluation Project." **Art Documentation** 1 (May 1982): 67-69.

Byrne briefly describes an art evaluation project at the University of Cincinnati based on an adaptation of a simple method developed at Yale University. Library Committee members, in consultation with faculty who relied on their library use experience plus subject expertise, completed a form (illustrated in an appendix). The entire collection as well as specific subject areas were ranked in one of fifteen categories, ranging from "marginal or scattered" to "comprehensive." The author is "aware that this elementary type of evaluation is necessarily subjective and superficial."

87. Coale, Robert Peerling. "Evaluation of a Research Library Collection: Latin-American Colonial History at the Newberry." **Library Quarterly** 35 (July 1965): 173-84.

Correctly deemed a classic by Mosher (see entry 21), this important study reports in considerable detail one of the earliest published applications of the checklist method. To evaluate the Newberry Library's Latin-American colonial history collection, one approach was separately applied to Mexico, Peru, Chile, and Colombia and Venezuela (the latter two combined into one category).

The books and articles from bibliographies in several scholarly works were checked against the Newberry's collection. Then the books from the two bibliographies that produced the best and worst results were checked against the Texas, California-Berkeley, and Hispanic Society of America catalogs for comparative purposes. To assess whether "the library has kept up with the acquisition of the current scholarly output," the history sections in the *Handbook of Latin American Studies* for 1936, 1940, 1945, 1950, 1959, and 1962 were checked, although these findings were not compared with other libraries. The statistical results were displayed in twelve tables.

88. Gallagher, Kathy E. "The Application of Selected Evaluative Measures to the Library's Monographic Ophthalmology Collection." **Bulletin of the Medical Library Association** 69 (January 1981): 36-39.

Nine different methods were used to evaluate the monographic ophthalmology collection at the Washington University (in St. Louis) Medical Library. In an interesting classification, the techniques were divided into either "retrospective measures" or "current measures." Retrospective measures included the "recommended titles" technique; the "classic text" technique, whereby citations are checked against holdings; monetary expenditures; size; and use. Current measures included ILL analysis and checking against holdings, book reviews, publishers' fliers, and suggestions-for-purchase cards. The publishers' fliers method was "worthless," while monetary expenditures, size, and use were "difficult to interpret." The main value of this article lies in its comparison of different approaches.

89. Gyeszly, Suzanne D., Jeanne Harrell, and Charles R. Smith. "Collection Growth and Evaluation at Texas A & M University, 1978 and 1988: A Comparative Statistical Analysis." **Collection Management** 12, nos. 3/4 (1990): 155-72.

In addition to describing the organization of collection development at Texas A & M, this case study illustrates how easily obtained data concerning holdings, faculty, students, and expenditures can be used for collection evaluation. Shelflist data from 1978 and 1988 were used to calculate the percentage growth rate for broad ranges of the LC classification (e.g., A, B, C-F, etc.). The same data were reconfigured, by assigning LC class numbers to the corresponding program, to ascertain the growth rate for books supporting the university's eight major colleges. The serials expenditures breakdown was evaluated by a chart comparing each college's percentage of total serials costs, undergraduate enrollment, graduate enrollment, and faculty. The authors observe that their approach can be used to plan for future growth as well as to assess current holdings.

90. Herubel, Jean-Pierre V. M. "The Philosophy Collection: An Experiment in Evaluation." **Southeastern Librarian** 39 (Fall 1989): 107-10.

An evaluation, which the author terms experimental, of the philosophy collection at the University of Mississippi library is reported here. The reference collection was evaluated by the checklist method. Checklists based on indexes and standard lists, as well as citations from masters theses and five major philosophy journals, were used to assess periodical holdings. Monographs were evaluated through shelflist measurement, circulation statistics, and on-site observation. This case study is noteworthy because it incorporates a variety of methods and focuses on three major collection components (monographs, periodicals, and reference) for a single subject.

91. Kehoe, Kathleen, and Elida B. Stein. "Collection Assessment of Biotechnology Literature." **Science & Technology Libraries** 9 (Spring 1989): 47-55.

The authors describe the evaluation of the current English-language monographic holdings in biocatalysis and applied molecular biology at Columbia University Library's Science Division in 1987. A bibliography of books published since 1982, compiled from publishers' advertisements and a search of LC subject headings and keywords in RLIN, was used as a checklist to evaluate the holdings. Next, the cost of the books not held was calculated.

This process was undertaken to identify gaps, gain understanding of the subject, and justifiy additional funding. The detailed description of how the checklist was compiled is this item's most useful aspect.

92. Kelland, John Laurence. "An Evaluation of the Vertebrate Zoology Collection at the R. M. Cooper Library, Clemson University." **Collection Management** 7 (Spring 1985): 33-45.

The author describes his own evaluation of the Clemson University library's Q600 to Q740 range of the LC classification, covering vertebrate zoology, ichthyology, herpetology, ornithology, and mammalology. Systematic shelf and shelflist samples were evaluated by either direct examination, yearly circulation between 1974 and 1981, or analysis of copyright date to determine age. Circulation data corresponded to a Bradfordian distribution, as 37 percent of the sample did not circulate, while "small numbers circulated frequently." Several tables compare the results for the five areas included in the study and display distribution of the sample titles throughout twenty-six minute segments of the LC classification. Kelland's study is notable for applying an intense evaluation effort to a small area of the collection.

93. Lee, Ching-Tat. "Subject Collection Evaluation, Quantitative and Qualitative." **Australian Academic & Research Libraries** 17 (June 1986): 73-83.

Lee describes the evaluation of the Western Australian Institute of Technology's (WAIT) social work collection. A list of 1,294 social work monographs, published in 1980, was compiled from national and trade bibliographies in Australia, the United States, the United Kingdom, New Zealand, and Canada and was checked against the WAIT holdings. The items held were deemed to represent the library's "collecting intensity," while the list itself was identified as the subject "publishing intensity." The results are tabulated by country.

In a unique twist to the checklist method, teaching faculty were then asked to evaluate the usefulness of the publications not acquired as well as the entire collection's adequacy, although the low response rate (seven of twenty) was "disappointing." Finally, circulation and ILL statistics from 1980 through 1984 were also examined.

94. Lincoln, Tamara, and C. Eugene West. "The Research Value of Siberia Content Monographs in Polar Collections of the University of Alaska-Fairbanks." **Collection Management** 8 (Summer 1986): 31-47.

The authors describe an evaluation of the Siberiana monographic holdings in the University of Alaska-Fairbank's Alaska Collection, employing an RLG Conspectus format. After an introductory section about the geographic, economic, and political divisions of Siberia, the evaluation methodology is addressed. The authors apparently developed their own Conspectus worksheets based on segments of the LC classification pertaining to Siberia. Holdings data (exhibited in two tables) were then analyzed by LC class and language (e.g., Russian, English, or other). A notable feature is a table comparing the University of Alaska's total Siberiana holdings with those of the Library of Congress, the Scott Polar Research Institute at Cambridge, England, and the Universities of Hawaii, Hokkaido, Washington, California-Berkeley, Stanford, Oregon, British Columbia, and Melbourne.

Although a Conspectus format was used, this study's primary focus is on the evaluation of Siberiana rather than the RLG Conspectus itself. (See also West and Lincoln entry 101.)

95. O'Connell, John Brian. "Collection Evaluation in a Developing Country: A Mexican Case Study." **Libri** 34 (March 1984): 44-64.

The monographic engineering collection at the University of Guanajuato was evaluated by direct examination of all 3,037 volumes. Holdings data were tabulated by language, publication date, and thirteen broad Dewey subject categories. Acquisitions data indicated that 43 percent of the volumes were purchased at least seven years after publication. This type of analysis is seldom used in traditional collection evaluation. Loan records revealed that 44 percent of the circulating collection had not circulated between 1976 and 1982.

O'Connell concluded that the collection's problem is "not necessarily ... lack of quantity" but lack of quality, a generalization he extends to other Mexican and developing countries' libraries. Because this case study illustrates some collection evaluation problems of developing countries' libraries, it will be of primary value to those interested in comparative librarianship.

96. Olaosun, Adebayo. "Materials Provision Survey at the University of Ife Library, Nigeria." **College & Research Libraries** 45 (September 1984): 396-400.

The author recounts a study of the library's ability to support the French program at the University of Ife in Nigeria. The primary focus falls on a comparison of the holdings with the French department's course outline, although teacher and student surveys are briefly noted. The results are summarized in three tables. One of the study's most noteworthy features is the table listing seventy-nine authors covered in the curriculum as well as the number and percentage of their original works held by the library.

The article concludes with a concise discussion of the study's implications for such issues as selection and user education, while also enumerating six specific recommendations (e.g., the library should purchase all French novels needed for courses). This is not an outstanding item, but it is worth mentioning.

97. Shiels, Richard D., and Martha S. Alt. "Library Materials on the History of Christianity at Ohio State University: An Assessment." **Collection Management** 7 (Summer 1985): 69-81.

The authors describe a three-part evaluation, completed in the spring of 1984, of the Ohio State University library's History of Christianity collection. In part one,

National Shelflist Count 1977 data were used to compare Ohio State's total volumes in pertinent religious areas with holdings at Indiana, Michigan, Michigan State, and Wisconsin. Ohio State's religious holdings as a percentage of the total collection are tabulated for 1975, 1977, 1979, and 1984. In the second part of the evaluation, selected bibliographies, emphasizing Christianity in the Third World, were checked against the holdings. Third, a faculty survey was conducted concerning use of an interest in Christianity materials by time period, geographic area, and disciplinary approach. The paper concludes with nine specific recommendations, including creation of a collection development policy. (See also Alt and Shiels entry 84.)

98. Snow, Marina. "Theatre Arts Collection Assessment." **Collection Management** 12, nos. 3/4 (1990): 69-89.

A variety of methods were employed in an evaluation, completed in 1987, of the California State University at Sacramento's theatre arts collection. Separate sections discuss each method used. The collection-centered methods were: 1) a comparison of total theatre arts holdings with *National Shelflist Count* 1985 data for nine other universities offering a master's degree in the subject; 2) a check against basic lists of periodicals and reference books; 3) approval plan analysis; and 4) a questionnaire responded to by six other universities in the California State system concerning their periodical and book holdings (results are displayed in two tables naming the universities). As a client-centered measure, the faculty were surveyed concerning how well the collection supported the curriculum and faculty research.

99. Taranto, Cheryl, and Anna H. Perrault. "An Evaluation of the Music Collection at Louisiana State University." **LLA Bulletin** 51 (Fall 1988): 89-92.

This entry reports a three-year checklist-method evaluation, begun in 1984, of the Louisiana State University library's music collection. The project focused on scores and monographs. Most of the article is devoted to describing the six basic music reference books (three pertaining to the overall collection, three focusing on piano) that were used as checklists and explaining how they were used. A table displays the percentage of items held by subject and format categories from one of the six books, the ALA's *A Basic Music Library*. This case study sheds light on some of the methodological issues involved in evaluating a music collection.

100. Webb, William. "Project CoEd: A University Library Collection Evaluation and Development Program." **Library Resources & Technical Services** 13 (Fall 1969): 457-62.

Deservedly termed a classic by Mosher (see entry 21), Webb's report on the Collection Evaluation and Development Program at the University of Colorado is one of the more frequently cited examples of the checklist method (although the term *survey* rather than *checklist* is used). In Phase I of the project, the monographic, serials, and reference collections in five subject areas (medieval studies, art history, political science, physics, and Slavic studies) were evaluated by checking samples from bibliographies against the library holdings. The results for Slavic studies are displayed in a table. In Phase II, still in process at the time of writing, an attempt was made to fill gaps in English and American literary and social history by acquiring virtually every title listed in the third edition of Spiller's standard bibliography, *Literary History of the United States*.

36 / CASE STUDIES

The article is especially useful for its reporting, from first-hand experience, of some of the problems (e.g., deciding which bibliographies and sampling methods to use) and benefits (e.g., "meaningful quantitative data" and "much less work than anticipated") of the checklist approach based on sampling.

101. West, C. Eugene, and Tamara Lincoln. "A Critical Analysis and Evaluation of Russian Language Monographic Collections at the University of Alaska-Fairbanks." **Collection Management** 10, nos. 1/2 (1988): 39-51.

This case study report, based on the same four-year assessment project that was partially described by Lincoln and West in 1986 (entry 94), analyzes the Russian-language and subject monographic holdings, including in-process titles, at the University of Alaska-Fairbanks Library. The RLG Conspectus format, which is briefly explained, was used. Also, this item presents tables breaking down total holdings by broad LC class number and language and comparing the size of the library's Siberiana holdings with those of the Library of Congress and ten other major Pacific Rim Libraries.

The authors state that their evaluation procedures may "have utility" for other libraries. The data on Russian and Siberian holdings could be of interest to libraries collecting in those areas.

102. Whitehead, Derek. "Catching Up on Collection Evaluation." **Australian Academic & Research Libraries** 20 (March 1989): 38-46.

After briefly describing the library's history, Whitehead focuses on a collection evaluation project carried out at the State Library of Victoria from September 1983 through April 1984 as the groundwork for writing a collection development policy. The evaluation concentrated on 52 major subdivisions and 200 smaller units of the DDC. Up to fifteen "elements," listed in outline format, were entered in the report for each area, including volumes held, serial titles, publishing output, etc. Four evaluation approaches, each of which is analyzed in the project's context, were applied to every subject: statistics, qualitative evaluation, use data, and comparison with other libraries. The author concludes by stressing the importance of comparison with other libraries as a means of understanding one's own collection—a point with universal applicability beyond Australia.

NOTES

[1]C. C. Jewett, "Report of the Assistant Secretary Relative to the Library, Presented December 13, 1848," in *Third Annual Report of the Board of Regents of the Smithsonian Institution to the Senate and House of Representatives* (Washington, D.C.: Tippin & Streeper, 1849), 39-47.

4

Use Studies

Robert N. Broadus defines *use studies* "as those that start with a group of library materials, then try to determine what use, or how much use, they receive. A user study, on the other hand, begins with people and asks whether, or how much, they use library materials, and perhaps what kind of resources."[1] This chapter's primary focus is on use studies. However, it covers some user studies that also address the question of what materials are being used. Studies that analyze the use of scholarly materials outside a library setting or deal with the general information needs of scholars are not included in this literature guide.

Methodological controversies abound concerning what constitutes use of library materials. The ALA's *Guide to the Evaluation of Library Collections* lists circulation studies, in-house use studies, and surveys of user opinion under the use category.[2] Most of the works annotated in this chapter deal with circulation, requested items, browsing, or some type of in-house use. Citation analysis is often considered a type of use study, on the assumption that if an author has cited a work, he or she has used it. However, citation studies are discussed separately in chapter 8.

A valuable historical summary of major use studies is provided by Stanley J. Slote in his treatise on weeding,[3] a topic beyond this bibliography's scope. He noted the existence of over 1,000 use studies dating as far back as a 1902 article in *Library Journal* by Charles W. Eliot, president of Harvard, concerning the library's division into "books in use" and "books not in use."[4] Charles B. Osburn noted that use studies "came into some degree of prominence" during the 1960s and 1970s.[5]

Use studies typically address such questions as:

1. What proportion of material is used, or what proportion is required to satisfy a certain percentage of total uses?

2. Which periodical titles are heavily used (sometimes to identify the core collection)?

3. Which periodical titles are lightly used (to assist cancellation or weeding)?

4. Are there use patterns by subject or age?

A number of studies also determined an average cost per use.

Major issues regarding use studies concern whether past use predicts future use, whether findings in one library can be generalized to other libraries, and whether in-house use correlates with circulation. In conducting a use study, the length of the study and the method of recording use are significant issues.

Specific criticisms of use studies vary, depending upon the type of study. However, general criticisms applicable to most use studies stress that: 1) they reflect what was found on the shelf rather than what was wanted or needed; 2) only successes are recorded, while failures are ignored; and 3) a recorded or observed usage does not indicate how much benefit the patron derived from the item.

Perhaps the best-known use study was conducted by Kent and colleagues at the University of Pittsburgh in the 1970s, the so-called "Pittsburgh Study." The circulation histories of more than 35,000 books acquired by Pittsburgh's Hillman Library in 1969 were traced for seven years, while samples were taken of in-house book use and periodical use in six branch libraries. The study's major conclusion—that a large proportion of a research library's collection is seldom, if ever, used—generated much controversy throughout the library community. The Pittsburgh Study was criticized both for its methodology and for its implication that research libraries are wasting scarce financial resources by acquiring material that is not used.

This chapter's entries are organized into four sections: general and miscellaneous use studies, studies of periodical use, government documents use, and the Pittsburgh Study.

GENERAL AND MISCELLANEOUS USE STUDIES

103. Agnew, Grace, William E. Meneely, and Lyn Thaxton. "Faculty Audiovisual Materials Use and Collection Planning at Georgia State University." **Collection Management**, 11, no. 1/2 (1989): 151-74.

A survey concerning faculty use of audiovisual materials, conducted at Georgia State University in May 1985 by a media committee charged with developing a collection policy, is described in this well-done article. Major findings from the 307 faculty responses were: 1) 37.5 percent did not use audiovisuals; 2) of the twenty-one standard formats surveyed, videocassettes were the most used (by 56.2 percent) and considered the most important (41.7 percent rated them "very important"); 3) media were most often used for required course instruction (by 66.7 percent); and 4) most faculty considered books and periodicals more important for library acquisitions than audiovisuals.

Five tables present the data, which is often broken down either by faculty subject specialty or by the twenty-one formats. The authors consider the survey "very enlightening" and recount its practical benefits. This report is especially valuable because it is one of the few items to focus on collection evaluation of audiovisuals in an academic library.

104. Arrigona, Daniel R., and Eleanor Mathews. "A Use Study of an Academic Library Reference Collection." **RQ** 28 (Fall 1988): 71-81.

Use of the Iowa State University library reference collection by both reference staff and patrons was studied during four weeks of the 1986 spring semester. Tally sheets tabulated resources consulted by staff and books that patrons left on tables. A "use index" (the number of uses divided by volumes held) was calculated for approximately fifty broad LC class numbers. All the data are presented in a table rank-ordering the LC classes according to total combined uses by staff and patrons. Further analysis compares patron and staff use patterns by LC class and type of material.

As stated by the author, a use study is "an essential step in the evaluation of reference service." Although there are a number of studies concerning use of reference collections in public libraries, this is the only identified item dealing with use of an academic library reference collection.

105. Baker, Sharon L., and F. Wilfrid Lancaster. "Collection Evaluation: Use-Centered Approaches." In their **Measurement and Evaluation of Library Services**, 79-121. 2d ed. Arlington, Va.: Information Resources Press, 1991. 411p. ISBN 0-87815-061-7. LC 91-072908.

Baker and Lancaster begin by noting that research libraries are "ambivalent about use studies," an attitude they attribute to the controversy generated by the Pittsburgh Study. The authors explain that the two types of recorded data most frequently utilized in use studies are ILL statistics, which reflect unmet demand, and circulation statistics, which reflect met demand. More than a third of their book chapter is devoted to a discussion of factors that help identify which materials are most likely to be used, with the focus on age, language, popularity of author or title, subject, degree of subject specificity, and quality. The role of use studies in identifying core collections and materials for weeding and remote storage is also addressed. A helpful eight-page unannotated bibliography is included at the end. This chapter is particularly valuable for its detailed analyses of numerous use studies at all types of libraries. (See also Baker and Lancaster entries 2, 106, and 175.)

106. Baker, Sharon L., and F. Wilfrid Lancaster. "Evaluation of In-House Use." In their **Measurement and Evaluation of Library Services**, 123-42. 2d ed. Arlington, Va.: Information Resources Press, 1991. 411p. ISBN 0-87815-061-7. LC 91-072908.

This textbook chapter provides a valuable overview of in-house use studies, including material pertaining to public libraries. Following a discussion of the methodological issues involved in defining *in-house use*, four methods for measuring in-house use are explained: the table count method, the slip method, patron questionnaires, and patron interviews. Several questionnaires are exhibited. Next, the significant findings from twenty in-house use studies dating from 1960 are analyzed. The authors found that: 1) the level of in-house use varies widely among libraries, 2) circulation and in-house usage correlate with each other, and 3) older material receives less in-house use. A useful but unannotated bibliography is appended. (See also Baker and Lancaster entries 2, 105, and 175.)

107. Britten, William A. "A Use Statistic for Collection Management: The 80/20 Rule Revisited." **Library Acquisitions: Practice & Theory** 14, no. 2 (1990): 183-89.

Britten's well-done article, based on data generated by the Geac automated system, uses the entire 1982 to 1989 circulation record of the University of Tennessee at Knoxville's 1.5-million-item collection to test Trueswell's 80/20 Rule. Overall, the 80/20 Rule was confirmed, as 20 percent of the items represented "slightly more" than 80 percent of circulation. However, when the analysis was limited to items that circulated at all, 44 percent accounted for the 80 percent figure.

Study of twenty selected LC classes indicated wide variation among them. The percentage of the collection accounting for 80 percent of circulation ranged from a low of 1.5 percent for J (political science) to a high of 40 percent for RG (gynecology and obstetrics). Further analysis of specific classes revealed similar variation among their subclasses. The author quite correctly concludes that his findings have collection management implications.

108. Broadus, Robert N. "Information Needs of Humanities Scholars: A Study of Requests Made at the National Humanities Center." **Library & Information Science Research** 9 (April-June 1987): 113-29.

This excellent scholarly study analyzes 10,981 requests for materials by 79 visiting scholars at the National Humanities Center, Research Triangle Park, North Carolina, during 1982-1983 and 1983-1984. Analysis of the requests by format found that 59.7 percent were for monographs and 30.7 percent for serials. Ten percent of the requested items were less than three years old, while 23.7 percent were published prior to 1950. Eighty-six percent of the requests were in English, 6.1 percent in German, and 5.1 percent in French, with 16 other languages also identified. The requests were fairly evenly distributed among thirty-five LC classes, with the most (7.5 percent) in philosophy. The data were further analyzed in numerous ways, including comparing data from the study's first and second years and separating out requests by scholars specializing in humanities projects.

Extensive comparisons with many citation and circulation studies in the humanities revealed that the scholars requested a larger proportion of serials, more recent publications, and more English-language items than indicated by those previous studies. As stressed by Broadus, this approach offers a valuable new perspective because circulation and citation studies include only what was found and checked out, while requests reflect what was wanted.

109. Broadus, Robert N. "The Range of Subject Literatures Used by Humanities Scholars." **Collection Management** 12, nos. 1/2 (1990): 61-68.

A total of 10,760 requests for library materials by scholars at the National Humanities Center at Research Triangle Park, North Carolina, during the 1982-1983 and 1983-1984 academic years were analyzed according to 207 LC classification ranges. Each scholar requested an average of 26.3 subjects, reduced to 14.9 when subjects with only one request were eliminated. More than half the scholars (45 out of 79) requested material in each of five major areas: general, humanities, history, social sciences, and science. The author concludes that materials needed by humanists are even more widely dispersed than suggested by earlier research and argues that his data support the concept of centralized humanities collections.

110. Broadus, Robert N. "Use by Humanists of University Press Publications." **Scholarly Publishing** 19 (October 1987): 43-48.

The proportion of university press publications among more than 5,000 items requested by scholars at the National Humanities Center during 1983 and 1984 confirms "the value of university presses in providing materials considered useful by high-ranking scholars." About a third (36.5 percent) of the requested twentieth-century, English-language monographs were from university presses. The percentage of requests for university press material as a proportion of total requests was highest for recently published items and the humanities and lowest in the sciences. Two tables exhibit the data.

A total of 107 different university presses were requested. A table rank-orders the top twenty-six, headed by Oxford and Cambridge, and displays rankings from two other studies. This article constitutes the only work in this bibliography to focus exclusively on the use of materials by a particular type of publisher.

111. Broadus, Robert N. "Use Studies of Library Collections." **Library Resources & Technical Services** 24 (Fall 1980): 317-24.

A top-notch review of library use studies emphasizes five conclusions: 1) "in many libraries ... there are miles of books that are not borrowed for years and years"; 2) in-house use of material is proportional to circulation; 3) "past use predicts future use"; 4) recent material is the most heavily used; and 5) Americans do not use foreign-language materials. Major studies supporting each conclusion are analyzed.

Broadus then notes some limitations of use studies, such as the problem of measuring in-house use and the fact that these studies determine what has been used rather than what should have been used. He concludes that "in spite of these difficulties use studies are valuable."

112. Burrell, Quentin L. "The 80/20 Rule: Library Lore or Statistical Law?" **Journal of Documentation** 41 (March 1985): 24-39.

To test Trueswell's 80/20 Rule, a simple stochastic model (an advanced statistical technique explained in the article's appendix) was applied to circulation data from the Wishart Library of Cambridge University, the Pittsburgh and Sussex University Libraries, and two British public lending libraries. Burrell concludes that Trueswell's identification of a core collection based on the 80/20 Rule "is not so clear cut." When noncirculating items are eliminated, 43 percent to 58 percent of the collection is required to account for 80 percent of circulation. Burrell stresses that the investigation's time period is "of crucial importance," as one can reduce the collection's portion necessary to account for 80 percent of circulation by increasing the time period studied.

113. Eyman, David H. "Liberal Arts College Library Acquisitions: Are Past Practices Appropriate for the Future?" In **Building on the First Century; Proceedings of the Fifth National Conference of the Association of College and Research Libraries, Cincinnati, Ohio, April 5-8, 1989**, edited by Janice C. Fennell, 211-17. Chicago: Association of College and Research Libraries, 1989. 353p. ISBN 0-8389-7289-6.

Eyman describes a circulation analysis at Skidmore College (a liberal arts institution in Saratoga Springs, New York) that was quite similar to the Pittsburgh Study, although not a precise replication. Three years of circulation data were analyzed for a random sample of 584 circulating books, representing 10.8 percent of the monographs acquired between July 1983 and June 1984. It was found that 33.2 percent never circulated, whereas only 3.4 percent circulated six or more times. An analysis of the time interval before initial circulation revealed that 41.4 percent of the sample circulated within the first six months. Comparisons are made with other circulation studies. An appended table plus a figure illustrate use by twenty-one broad LC class ranges. Eyman concludes, "[T]his study reinforces the idea that a substantial portion of the books acquired for the circulating collection in a smaller academic library does not circulate."

114. Fussler, Herman H., and Julian L. Simon. **Patterns in the Use of Books in Large Research Libraries**. Chicago: University of Chicago Press, 1969. 210p. ISBN 0-226-27556-6. LC 72-79916.

This frequently quoted seminal work is without doubt a major classic. It was originally published in a small preliminary edition by the University of Chicago Library in 1961. The study's objective was the development of a procedure "to predict with reasonable accuracy ... which groups of books ... are likely to be used in a research library." The authors used a "cross-sectional approach" in which they analyzed the circulation of large samples (approximately 1,000 items each) of Teutonic languages and literatures and economics books during a five-year period, 1954 to 1958, in the University of Chicago library. Circulation was analyzed by publication date and language. A number of smaller samples for other subject areas was also studied. They concluded that "the best predictor of the future use of a title is its past use." After obtaining comparative circulation data from Yale, Northwestern, and the University of California, Berkeley, Fussler and Simon concluded, "For low-use titles held by a pair of libraries, past use at one institution predicts almost as well for the future at another institution as it does for the original institution." After an examination of questionnaires inserted in books, it was found that browsing behavior would not "substantially" alter patterns based on recorded use only. This sophisticated study is still of interest.

115. Hayes, Robert M. "The Distribution of Use of Library Materials: Analysis of Data from the University of Pittsburgh." **Library Research** 3 (Fall 1981): 215-60.

This rigorous study by a prominent LIS researcher uses "a mixture of Poisson distributions" to test and describe circulation, in-house use, and ILL data gathered in the Pittsburgh Study between 1969 and 1975. Eight specific statistical tests were applied and are described in extensive detail in this article. Twenty-seven tables and figures illustrate the findings. Hayes asserts that "the key point is that circulation data do not adequately represent the total use of a research collection." He thus concludes that circulation data alone should not be used to relegate material to remote storage, as up to 25 percent of in-house usage would be "adversely affected." This article is most appropriate for sophisticated, advanced-level scholars, but the findings have implications for many collection management and evaluation decisions.

116. Holicky, Bernard H. "The Collection Use Survey: The Purdue University Calumet Experience." **College & Research Libraries News** 44 (May 1983): 154.

A three-phase use study is reported. "Daily pickups" of bound and unbound periodicals during 9 two-day survey periods between 1978 and 1982 recorded 2,495 uses for 404 titles, with only 260 used more than once. Another sample during the summer of 1981 of 420 bound periodical volumes containing 74 titles revealed an average circulation per volume of 1.3, but 63 percent of the titles never circulated. For phase three, in the summer of 1982, a sample of 1,000 monographs found an average total circulation of 3.1 since 1973 (or the date of the book's acquisition), with 29.8 percent never circulating. Holicky's one-page piece is useful for both the data and the brief description of the methodology used.

117. Lancaster, F. Wilfrid. "Evaluating Collections by Their Use." **Collection Management** 4 (Spring/Summer 1982): 15-43.

A nationally recognized authority offers a valuable overview concerning the application of use studies to collection evaluation. Separate sections cover studies of circulation records, in-house use, document delivery, and shelf availability. These approaches are explained and subjected to detailed methodological critiques, and important earlier studies are analyzed.

Lancaster observes that a major limitation to these approaches is their focus on the "expressed demands" of actual users, while neglecting the "needs" of nonusers. He also notes that the potential of automated systems for generating use data "has not been widely recognized." This item is recommended to those interested in use studies from both the theoretical and practical perspectives.

118. Lancaster, F. Wilfrid. "Evaluation of the Collection: Analysis of Use." In his **If You Want to Evaluate Your Library,** 33-51. Champaign: University of Illinois, Graduate School of Library and Information Science, 1988. 193p. LC 88-91099. ISBN 0-87845-078-5.

This chapter concentrates on the use of circulation data for collection evaluation. It is explained that circulation follows a hyperbolic distribution, that is, a small number of items circulate a lot, while most books seldom circulate. Many earlier use studies are summarized and there is a fairly extensive discussion of the Pittsburgh Study. A major portion of the chapter is devoted to "relative use," defined as a subject's proportion of circulation compared to its proportion of the holdings. The implications of "underused" and "overused" segments of the collection are analyzed. The concept of "shelf bias" (the books available on the shelf are there because no one wants to borrow them) is introduced here.

Several methods for investigating use are explained, including Jain's collection sample (analyzing the total circulation history for a sample of the collection) and checkout sample (determining which books circulate during a specific time period) methods as well as Trueswell's last circulation date method (recording the date of the last previous circulation for items circulating within a set time frame and then extrapolating usage patterns). The chapter ends with sections covering interlibrary loan analysis and methods that compare the collection with the curriculum. (See also Lancaster entries 15, 119, 183, and 488.)

119. Lancaster, F. Wilfrid. "In-House Use." In his **If You Want to Evaluate Your Library**, 52-59. Champaign: University of Illinois, Graduate School of Library and Information Science, 1988. 193p. LC 88-91099. ISBN 0-87845-078-5.

The next chapter from Lancaster's evaluation textbook begins by noting that in a research library in-house use "may greatly exceed circulation." Several previous studies of in-house use are summarized, from which it is concluded that in-house use will be "more or less the same" as circulation. Several methods for measuring in-house use are critiqued, with the primary focus on "table counts." "Observation periods," the "dotting method," survey forms, and interviewing are discussed to a lesser extent. Again, Lancaster offers an outstanding overview. (See also Lancaster entries 15, 118, 183, and 488.)

120. Metz, Paul. **The Landscape of Literatures: Use of Subject Collections in a University Library**. Chicago: American Library Association, 1983. 143p. (ACRL Publications in Librarianship, no. 43). LC 83-15511. ISBN 0-8389-3286-x.

Metz's meticulously researched study analyzes the 58,457 books charged to 10,126 borrowers on May 24 and 25, 1982, at the Virginia Tech Library, utilizing data from the VTLS online circulation system. Unlike most circulation studies, which are based on an archival circulation record over a set time period, this author took a "snapshot" of circulation at a specific moment. To determine who is using which subject collections, he analyzed the departmental affiliation of faculty and students and the books they checked out in eighty-one segments of the LC classification. It was found that patrons use books outside their department's area to a greater extent than indicated by citation studies. Astute comparisons are made with numerous other circulation and citation studies. Much detailed data is contained in seventy-five tables.

To test the stability of the findings, circulation data were also taken from VTLS on October 28, 1982. Metz reports that the correlation between the May and October data is "extremely high" and would "justify a high degree of confidence" in snapshot data. This major circulation study is extremely important for revealing a high level of interdisciplinarity in the use of subject collections.

121. Metz, Paul, and Charles A. Litchfield. "Measuring Collections Use at Virginia Tech." **College & Research Libraries** 49 (November 1988): 501-13.

This outstanding, methodologically sophisticated report, based on a use study at the Virginia Tech library, addresses use by subject, over time, and by kind of use (i.e., in-house versus circulation). The Virginia Tech Library System software generated monthly circulation data in thirty subject categories for January through May 1987, which were compared with 1982 data from Metz's monographic study (see entry 120). In-library use of bound volumes and current periodicals was calculated, based on reshelving, for May 1987. A table summarizes all types of use (circulation, in-house, reshelving current periodicals, etc.) for twenty-eight LC class ranges during May 1987. The data were analyzed in numerous ways.

The most important conclusions are: 1) in-house use of bound materials correlates highly with circulation; 2) current periodicals account for 30 percent of in-house usage, but the pattern is "qualitatively different" from other use categories; 3) a three-day circulation sample will usually be sufficient; and 4) circulation statistics were remarkably stable from 1982 to 1987 and from month to month in 1987.

122. Peasgood, Adrian N., and Peter J. Lambert. "Multi-User Subjects, Multi-Subject Users: Reader-Defined Interdisciplinarity in Journals Use at the University of Sussex." **British Journal of Academic Librarianship** 2 (Spring 1987): 20-36.

This fascinating journal analysis is a spin-off from a 1985 serials review project conducted at the University of Sussex, in which each faculty member distributed 100 votes among the university's journals. (See also Horwill entry 463 plus Horwill and Lambert entry 464.) Analysis of the vote distribution by thirty-eight departmental affiliations revealed significant interdisciplinarity. For example, for two-thirds of the subjects at least 20 percent of the voters were from outside the discipline. Several bar charts and tables illustrate the results in a variety of ways. The authors distinguish between "exported" interdisciplinarity, in which political scientists vote for journals in other subject areas, and "imported" interdisciplinarity, whereby academics from other disciplines vote for political science journals. The authors conclude by discussing their findings' practical implications, including the necessity for wide consultation during journal cancellation projects.

The interdisciplinarity of journal usage patterns has been demonstrated by circulation and citation studies. This study employs a unique approach to illustrate the same phenomenon.

123. Ross, Johanna. "Observations of Browsing Behavior in an Academic Library." **College & Research Libraries** 44 (July 1983): 269-76.

Following an introductory methodological discussion concerning previously used research techniques and the definition of *browsing*, an unobtrusive study at the University of California at Davis Physical Sciences Library is reported. Patron browsing behavior was observed during 520 randomly selected 15-minute intervals over 13 weeks. A sophisticated statistical analysis of the results indicated that each patron removed between 6.26 and 7.2 books from the shelf, replaced between 5.02 and 6.0 books, and browsed from 12.99 to 14.77 minutes. All data are at the 95 percent confidence level.

The article's most interesting aspect from a collection evaluation perspective is a table, organized into thirty LC class ranges mostly in science, that tabulates the books, browsers, circulation, books removed, and books replaced, as well as other data, for each class. The description of the methodology would be useful for anyone wishing to analyze browsing behavior.

124. Sridhar, M. S. "Subject and Longitudinal Use of Books by Indian Space Technologists." **Collection Management** 8 (Spring 1986): 101-15.

This circulation study at the Indian Space Research Centre Library in Bangalore is intriguing, but some of the conclusions are questionable. The loan record for a 20-percent stratified sample of the collection was analyzed by subject and date from 1972 through most of 1983. Between 1972 and 1983, 27 percent of the sample never circulated, while 20.6 percent of the books accounted for 82.7 percent of circulation. The use per linear foot of shelf space was calculated for twenty-four subject areas and presented in a table. It was found that year of acquisition "has a stronger effect on total use" than year of publication. However, the conclusion, "Use did not clearly correlate with age," is contrary to most other studies and methodologically suspect because it was based on cumulative circulation rather than circulation within a limited time frame.

125. Stiffler, Stuart A. "Core Analysis in Collection Management." **Collection Management** 5 (Fall/Winter 1983): 135-49.

The circulation of 164 "quality-core" religion books, determined by inclusion in both *BCL2* and another basic list, was compared to a random sample of 151 noncore religion titles at Cornell College in Iowa. In a twenty-one year period (1962 to 1982), the annual circulation rate for core titles was .43, contrasted with .17 for the noncore. Further analysis indicated that this difference was not due to total shelflife years or the "recent-addition-to-collection" factor, but, in the author's viewpoint, to the "effective promotional effort by teaching faculty." Stiffler also found that 40.4 percent of the noncore titles satisfied 81 percent of circulation, while 45.8 percent of the core titles accounted for 80 percent. A significant feature is a table explaining six methods for determining the number of titles in the core religion collection.

126. Trochim, Mary Kane. "Measuring Academic Library Use: The ACM Model." In **ALA Yearbook; A Review of Library Events 1980**, vol. 6, edited by Robert Wedgeworth, 26-28. Chicago: American Library Association, 1981. 377p. LC 76-647548. ISBN 0-8389-0335-5.

This entry describes the "ACM Library Collection Use Study," a pilot project conducted in early 1980 at the St. Olaf, Lake Forest, and Knox College Libraries. Four percent samples were taken with three different methods (circulation, stack, and shelflist), resulting in an 11 to 12 percent total sample for each library. It was found that foreign-language materials were used less than their proportion of holdings, while "use of materials, in general, corresponded to their age." An interesting feature is a table that reports the percentage of the collection required to meet 80 percent of circulation in 22 broad subject areas. The results ranged from 18 percent for geology to 67 percent for anthropology. Trochim comments that the 80/20 Rule should "be modified to read 80/40ish." A second table displays the distribution of use among the twenty-two subject categories. A manual was developed as an outgrowth of this project (see entries 127 and 128).

127. Trochim, Mary Kane. **Measuring the Circulation Use of a Small Academic Library Collection: A Manual**. Chicago: Associated Colleges of the Midwest, 1980. 91p.

128. Trochim, Mary Kane, with Arthur Miller, Jr., and William M. K. Trochim. **Measuring the Book Circulation Use of a Small Academic Library Collection: A Manual**. Washington, D.C.: Office of Management Studies, Association of Research Libraries, 1985. 73p.

These manuals provide an extremely practical, "cookbook" approach concerning how to conduct a book circulation study in a small academic library. A thirteen-week process is recommended. The procedures were tested in pilot projects at Lake Forest, St. Olaf, and Knox Colleges (see entry 126) and a draft manual was further tested at Tuskegee Institute, Dillard University, Atlanta College of Art, and Tougaloo College.

The format of the two manuals is essentially the same. Major sections cover preparation for the project, actual implementation, follow-up, data collection, and data analysis. Detailed, step-by-step guidance is provided for each stage. Instructions are provided for three types of samples: shelf, circulation, and stack. The 1985 manual contains a brief description of the pilot project at Lake Forest College.

Short bibliographies are appended to each. Either manual would be valuable for librarians wishing to conduct a circulation study.

129. Trueswell, Richard W. "Some Behavioral Patterns of Library Users: The 80/20 Rule." **Wilson Library Bulletin** 43 (January 1969): 458-61.

This classic article by an industrial engineer at the University of Massachusetts introduced to the library community the now-famous Trueswell's 80/20 Rule: approximately 20 percent of a library's holdings will account for about 80 percent of circulation. (The concept logically evolved from a series of research papers published by Trueswell during the 1960s.) Line graphs of journal circulation data from an unnamed biomedical library and monographic circulation data from the Air Force Cambridge Research Laboratory Library and the Northampton, Massachusetts Public Library are used to illustrate that the rule applies to all types of libraries. As a corollary, 50 percent of holdings will be responsible for 90 percent of circulation, while 60 percent will represent 99 percent of circulation. The similarity to business inventory is stressed, and the potential utility of this information for libraries is briefly explained. Trueswell's often-cited rule has become part of collection development's conventional wisdom.

PERIODICAL USE

130. Advani, N., and M. G. Gupta. "Readers Utilization of Journals in Maulana Azad Medical College Library (University of Delhi)." **Library Herald** 22 (January 1984): 201-6.

Following the presentation of data and a short discussion concerning the "spiralling" cost of serials, Advani and Gupta recount a use study, based on reshelving counts of unbound journals, conducted at the University of Delhi Medical College library from June to August 1979. Journals not utilized during this period were examined further in September and included in the final data. A table displaying usage patterns for the 278 journals, organized into twenty-two medical subject categories, reveals that fourteen were used more than one hundred times, while sixty-four were not used at all. Another table rank orders the top 103 journals (the vast majority of which appear to be published in North America or Europe) by the number of times used.

131. Alldredge, Noreen S. "The Non-Use of Periodicals: A Study." **Serials Librarian** 7 (Summer 1983): 61-64.

This article reports an investigation, based on attaching marked adhesive labels to current periodical issues when reshelving, at Texas A & M University to identify titles unused during two full calendar years, 1977 and 1978. The unused titles—734 of 6,327 (11.6 percent)—cost about $65,000, were primarily English-language publications (85.9 percent) in the sciences (73.4 percent), and were available at the Center for Research Libraries (73.6 percent). About 85 percent were initially published before 1970.

The author concludes that this approach's main benefits are identification of cancellation candidates and titles to be sent to faculty for review. She also observes that it is easier to implement than a regular use study because a single usage removes a title from further investigation.

132. Ambia, Golam. "Use of Periodicals in Physics in Delhi University Science Library, IIT Library, NPL Library: A Comparative Study." **Libri** 41 (June 1991): 98-108.

The use of physics periodicals at three libraries in Delhi, India, was analyzed for one month in late 1986 in this rather haphazardly presented study. Based on counting items left on tables and book carts, 43.15 percent of ninety-five periodicals in the Delhi University Science Library, 82.75 percent of fifty-eight in the IIT Library, and 53.03 percent of sixty-six in the NPL Library were used during a month. (The initials are never explained.)

A table displays how frequently patrons of the three libraries used physics journals, based on a survey. Most of the entry's data are contained in a conclusions section that lists twenty specific points, many of which are not addressed in the text itself. This article would have benefited by more careful editing.

133. Broadus, Robert N. "Use of Periodicals by Humanities Scholars." **Serials Librarian** 16, nos. 1/2 (1989): 123-31.

The 3,403 periodical requests by fellows at the National Humanities Center (NHC) during two academic years (1982-1984) form the basis of this study. A total of 1,154 titles were requested, with 11.7 percent of them accounting for 49.0 percent of the requests. To test the relationship between citation and use, the top-ranked titles were compared to 1980 and 1981 lists of the fifty humanities titles most frequently cited by source journals in the *Arts & Humanities Citation Index*. After analyzing the data in a number of ways, the author concludes that, despite "differences" in the rankings, "enough of a harmony" was found to justify use of citation rankings in journal collection development decisions. An appendix names the forty-eight most frequently requested periodicals at the NHC plus the number of requestors.

134. Chrzastowski, Tina E. "Journal Collection Cost-Effectiveness in an Academic Chemistry Library: Results of a Cost/Use Survey at the University of Illinois at Urbana-Champaign." **Collection Management** 14, nos. 1/2 (1991): 85-98.

135. Chrzastowski, Tina E. "Where Does the Money Go? Measuring Cost Effectiveness Using a Microcomputer to Analyze Journal-Use Data." In **Building on the First Century: Proceedings of the Fifth National Conference of the Association of College and Research Libraries, Cincinnati, Ohio, April 5-8, 1989**, edited by Janice C. Fennell, 201-4. Chicago: Association of College and Research Libraries, 1989. 353p. ISBN 0-8389-7289-6.

These items report a six-month journal-use study, beginning in January 1988, at the University of Illinois at Urbana-Champaign Chemistry Library. A total of 31,703 uses were recorded, including circulation, in-house use determined by reshelving, and ILL loans and borrowings. Statistics were tabulated with an in-house, custom-created database using spreadsheet software. The findings were: 1) 24 percent of 529 active titles received 2 or fewer uses, while 9 percent were not used at all; 2) the average cost per use was $3.53; 3) Trueswell's 80/20 Rule was "verified," as 26 percent of active subscriptions accounted for 80 percent of use; and 4) 61 percent of the 529 journals would meet 90 percent of demand. Comparisons are made with journal data from the Pittsburgh Study.

136. Clarke, Ann. "The Use of Serials at the British Library Lending Division in 1980." **Interlending Review** 9 (October 1981): 111-17.

Serials requests to the BLLD during a ten-day working period in May 1980 were tabulated and compared to a 1975 study. In 1980, 10 percent of the titles satisfied 50 percent of requests, whereas 9 percent had done so in 1975. The proportion of titles required to satisfy a given percentage of requests was smallest for science, followed by social sciences, then the humanities. Overlap between the 1975 and 1980 top-ranked title lists decreased from 60 percent for the leading 100 to 52 percent for the top 5,000, casting "doubt on the value of core lists." Numerous tables and figures illustrate further analysis of requests by subject, date, and user category. An appendix rank-orders the fifty most frequently requested titles, based on post-1974 holdings only. (For a critique, see Urquhart entry 495.)

137. Evans, Josephine King. "Tracking Periodical Usage in a Research Library." **College & Research Libraries News** 51 (November 1990): 958-59.

Evans concisely describes a procedure for monitoring serials use at the University of South Florida's Florida Mental Health Institute. Beginning in 1987, the sweep method (counting journals left on tables by users), along with data on ILL requests and misshelved volumes, was employed to tabulate journal use. Each month the data were entered into a LOTUS 1-2-3 spreadsheet, which calculated use for the year-to-date. This information was used for serials cancellation and subscription decisions.

138. Fjällbrant, N. "Rationalization of Periodical Holdings: A Case Study at Chalmers University Library." **Journal of Academic Librarianship** 10 (May 1984): 77-86.

Bound and unbound periodical use was surveyed for a four-month period at Chalmers University of Technology in Gothenburg, Sweden, by counting items placed on book trolleys. The major findings included: 1) 10 percent of the held titles met 72 percent of demand; 2) about 70 percent of the journals used more than ten times were in English; 3) multiple-copy journals (jointly held by branch libraries) were used more than single-copy titles; 4) more than 70 percent of the totally unused titles were acquired by gift and exchange; and 5) more than 80 percent of the unused journals were available in other Swedish research libraries or from the British Library Lending Division. Appendixes present rank-order displays of the fifty most frequently used titles and the fifty-two most frequently used non-Swedish periodicals.

139. Franklin, Hugh. "Comparing Quarterly Use Study Results for Marginal Serials at Oregon State University." **Serials Librarian** 16, nos. 1/2 (1989): 109-22.

The use of 145 serial titles (selected on the basis of presumed low usage) was surveyed by student reshelvers during three academic quarters in 1982 and 1983 at the Oregon State University Library. Franklin offers a detailed account of the methodology, which included the use of gold slips to bring the selected titles to the attention of reshelvers, and of the techniques for checking the recorded data's accuracy. In the results section, two tables display the quarterly and total use for each title as well as the cost per use (although the periodicals are not identified by name). Use varied considerably between quarters, leading to the significant conclusion that a minimum of one continuous year is required to survey low-use titles. Cost per use ranged from $0.15 to $253.37.

140. Goldblatt, Margaret A. "Current Legal Periodicals: A Use Study." **Law Library Journal** 78 (Winter 1986): 55-72.

Goldblatt recounts a study, based on counting checkout cards, of unbound legal periodicals at the Washington University (in St. Louis) Law Library conducted from March 29, 1982, to March 28, 1983. Ten percent of the 770 titles accounted for 50 percent of the total uses, while 37.8 percent were never used. A table names, in rank order, the thirty-four most frequently used titles. Another table, organizing the subscriptions into six major categories (e.g., foreign law journals, interdisciplinary journals, etc.), indicates that general U.S. law school reviews were most likely to be used (83.5 percent). Further analysis revealed that faculty evaluation and cost did not correlate with use. Indexed titles were used more often than nonindexed ones (90 percent contrasted with 39 percent). A four-page section analyzes the use of second-copy subscriptions. This detailed article is the only item in this guide dealing with use of a law library.

141. Gordon, Martin. "Periodical Use at a Small College Library." **Serials Librarian** 6 (Summer 1982): 63-73.

The use of bound, microfilm, and current periodicals at the Franklin & Marshall College Library was studied for the entire 1979 calendar year, based on observation of items needing to be reshelved. Findings included: 1) ranking by frequency of use confirmed Bradford's Law for the upper 90 percent of use; 2) 77.1 percent of all uses were of retrospective material; 3) 27.6 percent of the titles accounted for 90 percent of the usage, but 58.3 percent of all titles were used; 4) July was the lowest use month (1.5 percent of all uses) and November the highest (16.4 percent of total uses); 5) foreign-language titles received 26 percent of total use; and 6) local bibliographic instruction in a title's subject, indexing, and prominent display correlated with higher usage. Tables present a breakdown by subject and the thirty-five most frequently used titles. Gordon states that comparisons with other libraries are impossible because natural and life science periodicals were not included in his study.

142. Guy, Wendell A. "Pharmacy Faculty Members' Exposure to Current Periodicals." **Science & Technology Libraries** 4 (Fall 1983): 79-84.

Guy reports a study of the periodicals routed to and personally subscribed to by faculty members at the Arnold and Marie Schwartz College of Pharmacy, in Brooklyn, New York. For purposes of analysis, both routed and subscribed journals were considered to be "seen." A table rank-orders the twenty-six "most seen" journals by the entire faculty, while another table lists the ten journals "most seen" by three different faculty categories, specializing in pharmacy practice, pharmacy-related sciences, and pharmaceutical science. Data on the average number of journals seen by the various faculty categories are also reported. This, the only item dealing with pharmacy journals, is also noteworthy for its utilization of data from the library routing system as a measure of use.

143. Hansen, Inge Berg. "Use of the Danish Veterinary and Agricultural Library by Direct Library Users and Uses of an Online Documentation Service." **Quarterly Bulletin of the International Association of Agricultural Librarians & Documentalists** 26, no. 3 (1981): 89-96.

The 2,839 loans and photocopy requests at the Danish Veterinary and Agricultural Library during November 1979 were analyzed by Hansen. Her primary focus falls on the 71 percent of the requests that were for serials rather than the 29 percent for books. It was found that: 1) about 13 percent of the 4,400 current serials subscriptions fulfilled 100 percent of need; 2) about 7 percent filled 85 percent of the requests; 3) about 20 percent of the requested items were more than 15 years old. A table lists the fifty most frequently requested serial titles, most of which belong to what Hansen terms "a core of international journals." The second half of the article reports an evaluation of a document delivery service conducted between September 1979 and February 1980. This entry reveals that serials usage patterns in a Danish veterinary library are basically similar to those that would be found in a North American library.

144. Irvine, Betty Jo, and Lyn Korenic. "Survey of Periodical Use in an Academic Art Library." **Art Documentation** 1 (October 1982): 148-51.

Irvine and Korenic report a use study, conducted during a two-year period (1978-1980) and based on reshelving data, of the 160 current periodical subscriptions in Indiana University's Fine Arts Library. It was found that 35 percent of the titles accounted for 75 percent of use. The indexing of these titles was checked in four major indexes, such as *Art Index*. Eighty-one percent of the titles were indexed, while 23 percent were indexed in all four sources. A comparison of the usage data with indexing indicated that "indexing access may be less important than local needs" in influencing usage. A table summarizes the usage and index coverage for the 160 titles, arranged in alphabetical order. Although the study was determined to be "a valuable tool," the authors conclude that "other variables" must also be considered in cancellation decisions. The authors assert that this is the first use study of fine arts periodicals.

145. Mankin, Carole J., and Jacqueline D. Bastille. "An Analysis of the Differences Between Density-of-Use Ranking and Raw-Use Ranking of Library Journal Use." **Journal of the American Society for Information Science** 32 (March 1981): 224-28.

Mankin and Bastille compare journal rankings based on total use with rankings based on density-of-use (usage divided by occupied shelf space), employing data gathered in their use study of the Massachusetts General Hospital's 647-title collection in 1977. (See also Bastille and Mankin entry 406.) A significant difference "above random chance" between the two ranking methods is demonstrated. Moreover, Trueswell's 80/20 Rule applies to ranking by raw use, but not to density-of-use ranking.

The authors conclude that "using density-of-use ranking rather than raw-use ranking is a better approach" to making journal collection management decisions. This article would have theoretical relevance for libraries concerned about shelf space shortages when reaching journal deselection decisions.

146. Merry, Karen, and Trevor Palmer. "Use of Serials at the British Library Lending Division in 1983." **Interlending & Document Supply** 12 (April 1984): 53-56.

Requests for serials at the British Library Lending Division were surveyed for ten days in May 1983. The study analyzed concentration of demand on core titles and the stability of the top-ranked title list when compared to earlier studies. About

52 / USE STUDIES

12 percent of the titles satisfied 50 percent of demand, but "substantial differences in the content of core lists clearly reduce [the lists'] value." For example, there was only a 60 percent overlap between the top-ranked lists (considering the leading 100 through 5,000 titles) of 1983 and 1980 and a 55 percent overlap between lists for 1980 and 1975. Data are also presented about requestors. Merry and Palmer's study has significant theoretical implications for the core periodical concept.

147. Miller, Naomi. "Journal Use in a Clinical Librarian Program." **Bulletin of the Medical Library Association** 72 (October 1984): 395-96.

Miller's brief report analyzes the journals used to answer patient-related questions in clinical medicine at the Medical College of Pennsylvania during 1983. Her unique approach is not used by other items annotated in this section. A total of 191 journals with 904 pertinent articles were used to answer 144 questions. The top 18 journals, identified in a table, provided 47.6 percent of the articles. Another table, tabulating articles by date, reveals that 64.4 percent of the articles were published within the last five years.

148. Naylor, Maiken. "Assessing Current Periodical Use at a Science and Engineering Library: A dBASE III+ Application." **Serials Review** 16 (Winter 1990): 7-19.

Current periodical usage at the SUNY-Buffalo Science and Engineering Library for the year beginning in October 1987 was assessed by the sweep method and resulted in the cancellation of 223 titles costing about $49,000. Data concerning identification number, fund, location, status, and monthly and total use were maintained in dBASE III+. Comparison of the ninety-six most frequently used titles with their total citation ranking in the 1988 *SCI JCR*, displayed in a two-page table, found "citation frequency in *SCI* would not have been a good indicator of use for over half of our high use journals." Additional findings were: 1) usage "fluctuates markedly" during the year; 2) a six-month study is preferable to a three-month; 3) only 4.8 percent of the titles were unused; and 4) 40 percent of the titles accounted for 81 percent of usage.

149. Riordan, Paul J., and Nils Roar Gjerdet. "The Use of Periodical Literature in a Norwegian Dental Library." **Bulletin of the Medical Library Association** 69 (October 1981): 387-91.

Riordan and Gjerdet offer a brief but well-done study of periodical use at the University of Bergen School of Dentistry library, based on loans and photocopy requests between March 1, 1980, and February 28, 1981. One hundred nineteen titles received 2,242 uses. The twenty-one most frequently used titles are listed in a table. A Bradfordian distribution was observed, with twelve titles accounting for half the uses. Further analysis by age, subject, and language (illustrated in graphs) indicates that a majority of uses were in English, with Scandinavian literature becoming obsolete more quickly.

150. Sauer, Jean S. "Unused Current Issues: A Predictor of Unused Bound Volumes?" **Serials Librarian** 18, nos. 1/2 (1990): 97-107.

During the fall semester of 1987 at the SUNY-New Paltz Library, a use survey was conducted of bound volumes and microform holdings, based on patrons marking attached slips, for 268 periodical titles whose current issues had been completely unused during the autumn of 1986. Fifty percent of the titles and 95 percent of the 7,765 volumes remained unused, leading to the conclusion that "current issues of periodical titles which are not used will continue to show little or no use after binding or replacement by microfilm." Tables tabulate the results by broad subject area and date of volume holdings. Sauer was unable to find any other study of this question in the reported literature.

151. Siemaszkiewicz, Wojciech. "The Readership of the Current Periodical and Newspaper Collection in the Slavic and Baltic Division of the New York Public Library." **Serials Librarian** 20, nos. 2/3 (1991): 131-49.

The use of Slavic newspapers and periodicals in the New York Public Library was analyzed by tabulating call slips submitted by patrons in the Slavic and Baltic Division between 1985 and September 1988. Only requests for items published since 1970 were considered. Sixty-two titles, of which forty-four were in Russian, were requested five or more times. The 452 titles used at least once, from a total of 1,370, are listed in rank order by 1987 usage (although the number of uses is also reported separately for 1985, 1986, and January through September 1988) in an extremely lengthy table. Six shorter tables use the same format to report the most frequently requested titles from the following languages: Polish; Ukrainian; Byelorussian; Czech and Slovak; Serbo-Croatian, Macedonian, and Slovenian; and English. The author attempts to correlate the findings to current events in the Soviet Union since 1985. This report would be of primary value to libraries with Russian or Eastern European periodical holdings.

152. Veenstra, Robert J. "A One-Year Journal Use Study in a Veterinary Medical Library." **Journal of the American Veterinary Medical Association** 190 (March 15, 1987): 623-26.

This entry recounts a journal use study conducted at Auburn University's Veterinary Medical Library from March 1985 through February 1986, based on reshelving data for current and bound issues. Veenstra found that 64.5 percent of the titles accounted for all 8,790 recorded uses during the year, a statistic that he compares to 11 earlier journal usage studies published between 1963 and 1983. That 19.8 percent of the titles accounted for 80.1 percent of total usage was deemed "surprisingly close" to Trueswell's findings. A table names, in rank order, the fifty most frequently used titles. Although Veenstra's investigation is one of only a few items to address collection evaluation in veterinary medicine, his findings are generally consistent with those of other journal usage studies.

153. Veenstra, Robert J., and James C. Wright. "A Review of Local Journal Use Studies: An Investigation of Possible Broader Applications." **Collection Management** 10, nos. 3/4 (1988): 163-73.

Applying a meta-analysis approach (although this term is not used), the authors combined the results of fifteen journal usage studies from the United States, the United Kingdom, and Norway. The studies were based on actual data counts of at least three months' duration, mostly in academic libraries, but also in a few hospital, dental, and public libraries. The mean number of recorded uses per journal per month ranged from 0.31 to 11.29. On average, 59 percent of the journal titles accounted for 100 percent of use, but the figure ranged from 20 percent to 86 percent. A table summarizes the key data for the fifteen studies.

54 / USE STUDIES

An inverse relationship was found between size of holdings and percentage of titles used. In other words, the larger the collection, the smaller the proportion actually used. Veenstra and Wright provide a useful synthesis of previous research.

GOVERNMENT DOCUMENTS USE

154. Alabi, G. A., and L. O. Aina. "Government Documents Usage in an Academic Library: The Case Study from Ibadan University Library." **Government Publications Review** 7A, no. 4 (1980): 333-36.

The authors describe a government docoments use study carried out at Ibadan University, Nigeria, in the 1970s, based on counting requests filed by users. Analysis by six types of documents (such as gazettes, statutes, or commission reports) during peak usage periods in 1975 and 1978 revealed that statistical sources were the most heavily used category (33.8 percent in 1975 and 36.4 percent in 1978). The proportion of government document uses to total uses of research materials was calculated for each year from 1974 to 1978, ranging between 9.4 and 11.2 percent. Although this is not the definitive article on the subject, few studies are available concerning the use of government documents.

155. Cook, Kevin L. "Circulation and In-Library Use of Government Publications." **Journal of Academic Librarianship** 11 (July 1985): 146-50.

After concisely reviewing some major use studies and the difficulties inherent in measuring use of government documents (because they often do not circulate), Cook describes a government documents use study at Arkansas State University, a GPO depository. Total circulation was calculated for three years, beginning June 1, 1980. In-house use data, based on reshelving, were gathered on thirty-nine randomly selected days between August 1982 and July 1983. Cook found that 19 SuDoc subject classes, out of approximately 5,500, accounted for one-third of the circulations, while 2 titles made up almost 20 percent of the in-house uses. "Some association" (a .48 correlation) between circulation and in-house use appeared when broken down by subject. He also notes that "circulation is not constant over time," as the subject correlation between the last twelve months and the first twenty-four months was .40. A table summarizing the date of items used in the library indicates that about 80 percent were less than 10 years old.

156. Cook, Kevin L. "Gathering Useful Circulation Data in the Documents Department." **RQ** 25 (Winter 1985): 223-29.

This companion piece to entry 155 analyzes data concerning the circulation of government documents at the Arkansas State University library between June 1980 and July 1983. The author explains how the data can easily be compiled with a manual checkout system. The emphasis is on user category, such as undergraduates, faculty, etc., rather than the material being used. The study nevertheless is relevant to collection management, as a table breaks down 2,054 circulations according to 13 SuDoc classification numbers. It was found that only three out of sixty agencies (the U.S. Congress plus the Health and Human Services and Commerce Departments) accounted for 44.8 percent of total circulation, confirming, in Cook's viewpoint, the 80/20 Rule.

157. Sears, Jean L., and Marilyn K. Moody. "Government Documents Use by Superintendent of Documents Number Areas." **Government Publications Review** 11 (March/April 1984): 101-12.

The in-house use and circulation of U.S. federal government documents, based on circulation statistics and reshelving counts, during a one-year period from July 1, 1981, through June 30, 1982, at Miami University (in Ohio) is analyzed in this study. The major findings were that: 1) total uses amounted to 14,247; 2) 2.9 percent of the 480,000-item print collection and .48 percent of the 75,000 microfiche pieces were used; 3) in-house use of documents amounted to 80 percent of total use; 4) excluding the Census collection, 1.2 percent of the documents accounted for 61.2 percent of total use; and 5) less than 1 percent of the documents collection circulated, contrasted to 24.66 percent of the main library book collection during the same period. Tables list the twenty-three most frequently used individual documents and the twenty-four most frequently used series. Another table breaks down usage by sixty-three broad SuDoc number areas. Type of use (in-house, faculty, or student) is also analyzed. The authors conclude by stressing the implications of their findings, including the need for "active weeding" and better user education. This is the most detailed of the relatively small number of government documents use studies.

158. Watson, Paula D., and Kathleen M. Heim. "Patterns of Access and Circulation in a Depository Document Collection Under Full Bibliographic Control." **Government Publications Review** 11 (July-August 1984): 269-92.

This outstanding study is based on a questionnaire completed by 150 government documents patrons at the University of Illinois at Urbana-Champaign and the circulation record of post-1979 government documents during a two-and-one-half-month period in the spring of 1983. Congressional documents received the "greatest use," accounting for 52.9 percent of the questionnaire sample and 42.7 percent of circulation. The publications of various agencies circulated "in almost direct proportion to their numbers in the collection." The ratio of circulation to volumes held was 22 percent, compared to 12 percent for the general stacks circulating collection during 1982 and 1983. Tables exhibit usage statistics by SuDoc class number, issuing agency, and congressional committee. Two pie charts compare the breakdown of holdings and circulation by SuDoc class. The investigation also analyzes the types of users, their reasons for using government documents, and how they identified documents for use. This item represents the most scholarly government documents usage study identified for this bibliography.

THE PITTSBURGH STUDY

159. Borkowski, Casimir, and Murdo J. MacLeod. "A Faculty Response from the University of Pittsburgh." **Journal of Academic Librarianship** 5 (May 1979): 63-65.

Two University of Pittsburgh faculty members quote extensively from a reply, dated February 15, 1978, to the Pittsburgh Study, drafted by a group of faculty representatives plus a librarian and approved by a full faculty representatives meeting. The study is termed "a highly subjective and political document." Furthermore, "As a piece of policy analysis, it is remarkably superficial and unidimensional. It fails to comprehend seriously ... what a university is."

56 / USE STUDIES

160. Borkowski, Casimir, and Murdo J. MacLeod. "Report on the Kent Study of Library Use: A University of Pittsburgh Reply." **Library Acquisitions: Practice & Theory** 3, nos. 3/4 (1979): 125-51.

One of the most detailed and penetrating critiques of the Pittsburgh Study originates from the chairperson and another member of the University of Pittsburgh Senate Library Committee. The study's footnotes, recommendations, and conclusions are critiqued, but the primary focus falls on the study's methodology, which Borkowski and MacLeod believe consistently underestimated actual usage. Books requested on ILL, placed on reserve, or in reference were not counted as used, while in-house use was based on extrapolation from a thirty-day sample and did not consider volumes reshelved by library patrons. Journal use was likewise underestimated by exaggeration of the number of titles and flaws in the sample design and projection technique. (For a response by Kent and his colleagues, see entry 168.)

161. Broadus, Robert N. "The Use of Serial Titles in Libraries with Special Reference to the Pittsburgh Study." **Collection Management** 5 (Spring/Summer 1983): 27-41.

The author argues that the Pittsburgh Study overestimated serials use (both titles used and total uses) because of methodological errors. The sample was biased towards periods of heavy use. The multiplier (the factor the sample time is multiplied by to cover all hours the library is open) failed to consider that the test libraries were open fewer hours during the summer trimester. A thorough review of similar studies indicated lower usage than reported by the Pittsburgh Study. Finally, the author points out problems involved in the logarithmic method of projecting the percentage of titles used.

Broadus concludes: "The fault lies not merely with the particular application to the Pittsburgh collections; the basic method itself has not been validated." (See also Flynn entry 163.)

162. De Klerk, Ann, and Roger Flynn. "A Comparative Periodical Use Study." In **The Information Community: An Alliance for Progress; Proceedings of the 44th ASIS Annual Meeting, Washington, D.C., October 25-30, 1981**, vol. 18, edited by Lois F. Lunin, Madeline Henderson, and Harold Wooster, 15-18. White Plains, N.Y.: published for the American Society for Information Science by Knowledge Industry Publications, 1981. 401p. LC 64-8303. ISBN 0-914236-85-7. ISSN 0044-7870.

A year-long periodical usage study, replicating the Pittsburgh Study's methodology for serials, was conducted at the three library units of the Carnegie-Mellon University from September 1979 through the summer of 1980. The major findings were: a small portion of the collection accounts for most of the use, a large portion is not used, and recent titles are the most heavily used. (The data cannot readily be summarized because they are reported separately for the different library units.) The results are compared to two earlier studies, based on total periodical usage rather than sampling, at Carnegie-Mellon in 1975-1976 and 1977-1978.

This item's most useful part is the concluding section, which compares the Pittsburgh methodology, based on interviewing and observing patrons during sampling periods, with the methodology used in an earlier Carnegie-Mellon study, based on circulation and recording bound volumes left on tables. It concludes that the Pittsburgh method is harder to administer, but produces more information.

163. Flynn, Roger R. "The University of Pittsburgh Study of Journal Usage: A Summary Report." **Serials Librarian** 4 (Fall 1979): 25-33.

Analysis of journal usage during one or two semester periods at six University of Pittsburgh libraries (Physics, Engineering, Life Sciences and Psychology, Chemistry, Computer Science, and Mathematics) led to two major conclusions. First, a small portion of the titles account for the majority of use; second, "usage is primarily of more recently published volumes." The average cost per use, based on subscription price, ranged from $2.25 to $7.54 in the six libraries, and from $3.30 to $10.07 when all costs, including processing and storage, were considered. The criteria to be used in journal acquisition, cancellation, and weeding decisions are discussed. A decision table, incorporating cost, usage, and subjective value judgment, is appended.

164. Galvin, Thomas J., and Allen Kent. "Use of a University Library Collection: A Progress Report on a Pittsburgh Study." **Library Journal** 102 (November 15, 1977): 2317-20.

Although termed "preliminary," the major findings of the Pittsburgh Study, along with a brief description of the project's objectives, are provided to the library community by the principal investigator and his dean. The reported findings include: 1) 40 percent of the 36,869 books acquired in 1969 never circulated in 7 years; 2) based on a thirty-day sample, 74 percent of the books used in-house circulated; 3) the overall average cost per book use was $11.75; 4) samples of journal use in three departmental libraries indicated that from 8.4 to 37 percent of the titles accounted for all the use; and 5) the average cost per journal use ranged from $3.00 to $6.70. Galvin and Kent conclude that "the hard facts are that research libraries invest very substantial funds to purchase books and journals that are rarely, or never, called for." This short summary article still offers a useful overview of the Pittsburgh Study.

165. Hardesty, Larry. "Use of Library Materials at a Small Liberal Arts College." **Library Research** 3 (Fall 1981): 261-82.

The Pittsburgh Study was replicated at DePauw University in Indiana by examining the five-year circulation history of 1,904 books acquired between December 1972 and June 1983. This sophisticated and well-documented report (more than fifty references are cited) validated the Pittsburgh findings, although DePauw books circulated even less than those at Pittsburgh. About 37 percent of DePauw's books did not circulate during the five-year study, while approximately 44 percent failed to circulate in the first three years. Over the five-year period, 30 percent of the books accounted for 80 percent of total circulation, confirming "in general" Trueswell's 80/20 Rule. It is significant that a steep decline in circulation was observed after three years, with books uncirculated then unlikely to circulate during years four or five. Several graphs illustrate comparisons of DePauw's circulation patterns with those of Pittsburgh. (See also entry 166.)

166. Hardesty, Larry. "Use of Library Materials at a Small Liberal Arts College: A Replication." **Collection Management** 10, nos. 3/4 (1988): 61-80.

Hardesty replicated the Pittsburgh Study a second time (see also entry 165) in a methodologically rigorous study. The circulation of 1,398 books purchased during the 1982-1983 fiscal year for the circulating collection at Eckerd College in Florida was monitored from time of acquisition through October-November 1985. Moreover, in-house use was compared with circulation during a two-month period (December 1983 to January 1984). The Pittsburgh Study and its earlier replication at DePauw University were confirmed, as approximately a third of Eckerd's collection did not circulate. A high correlation (.83) was found between in-house use and recorded circulation. A five-page table displays circulation and internal use data by subject, using nearly seventy LC classification ranges.

It is concluded that "recorded circulation is a good indicator of the total use of books, and a large portion of the books remain unused." The author speculates that the latter fact is due to the faculty's inability to select appropriate undergraduate material. The major significance of Hardesty's research is to demonstrate that the Pittsburgh Study's usage patterns also apply to smaller collections.

167. Kent, Allen. "A Rebuttal." **Journal of Academic Librarianship** 5 (May 1979): 69-70.

Kent's rebuttal to Schad's critique (see entry 171) focuses on issues concerning the Pittsburgh Study's data. Among the main points, he responds to the missing data charge by asserting, "[W]e have taken the conservative approach, so that circulations were computed on the basis of books after shrinkage." Also, "to the best of our knowledge the circulation figures are accurate as reported." In regard to limiting the study to external use, Kent asserts "external circulation data can be utilized with a high degree of confidence to measure total book use *in terms of books used at least once.*" The question concerning prediction of future use can be answered by "tracking use over time."

168. Kent, Allen, and others. "A Commentary on 'Report on the Study of Library Use at Pitt by Professor Allen Kent et al.' The Senate Library Committee, University of Pittsburgh, July 1969." **Library Acquisitions: Practice & Theory** 4, no. 1 (1980): 87-99.

Kent and three co-authors of the Pittsburgh Study respond to the Pitt Senate Library Committee's critique published in the 1979 *Library Acquisitions: Practice & Theory* (entry 160). The authors begin by asserting that their critics' misinterpretations "suggested to us a less than careful reading" of the full report. They also note that the Executive Committee for Libraries of the University of Pittsburgh asked them not to carry out their study because "the results might fall into the wrong hands" and be used to cut library budgets.

Most of this article is devoted to refuting specific criticisms by the Library Committee. The authors organize their "fundamental differences" with the committee under seven headings covering evidence, inference, measurement, conduct of research, reporting of research, the method of criticizing research, and policy recommendations. This is Kent's most detailed published response to his critics.

169. Kent, Allen, and others. **Use of Library Materials; The University of Pittsburgh Study**. New York: Marcel Dekker, 1979. 272p. (Books in Library and Information Science, vol. 26). LC 79-11513. ISBN 0-8247-6807-8.

This book is the published version of the Pittsburgh Study. Chapter 1 presents the background of the study. Chapter 2 covers the circulation and in-house use of books. It was found that 39.8 percent of the 36,892 books cataloged in 1969 had never circulated by the end of 1975. Based on thirty-day samples of in-house use and examination of ILL and reserve room data for an eighty-six-month period, it was concluded that "external circulation data can be utilized with a high level of confidence to measure total book use in terms of books used at least once." Chapter 3 reports the study of journal use, based on observation plus questionnaire and interview techniques, during one or two semester sampling periods in six regional science libraries on the University of Pittsburgh campus. Data too numerous to summarize are presented on sample usages, projected yearly usage, age, photocopying, patron status, and alert method, that is, what directed a user to a specific title. In general, usage was "low" and "primarily of current journals." Chapter 4 addresses the methodological issues involved in calculating cost per use. It presents cost-per-journal-use data at the six regional libraries covered by the study plus cost-per-book use by LC class. The remaining three chapters discuss various implications of the study.

The Pittsburgh Study generated extreme controversy. The official published version is obviously important because it includes the complete results and full description of the methodology.

170. Peat, W. Leslie. "The Use of Research Libraries: A Comment about the Pittsburgh Study & Its Critics." **Journal of Academic Librarianship** 7 (September 1981): 229-31.

On the premise that circulation data measures course-related rather than "research" use, Peat advocates that the citations from Pittsburgh faculty publications and Ph.D. dissertations be entered into a machine-readable database and then compared to acquisitions and circulation statistics. He believes "the 40 percent non-use figure would shrink dramatically."

171. Schad, Jasper G. "Missing the Brass Ring in the Iron City." **Journal of Academic Librarianship** 5 (May 1979): 60-63.

In his introduction to a symposium on the Pittsburgh Study (entries 159, 167, 172, and 173), the author argues that "no accurate conclusions can be drawn" from the data because data are missing: stolen books were not considered; circulation transactions were underreported, in large part because of a new automated system; and the study was limited to external use. Moreover, instructional use, which intensively uses a small number of items, must be differentiated from research use, "characterized by much less intensive use of a vast body of material." Finally, Schad distinguishes use from need and stresses that research use is subject to change and unpredictable.

172. Trueswell, Richard W. "Balancing Library Objectives with Book Circulation." **Journal of Academic Librarianship** 5 (May 1979): 68-69.

Trueswell points out that his own research plus that of others support the empirical findings of the Pittsburgh Study: a large proportion of books is rarely, if ever, used; and a small core accounts for the majority of circulation. He found an almost identical circulation pattern between Pittsburgh and Mt. Holyoke College. "What needs to be done is to use the results ... to meet ... the needs of library users."

173. Voigt, Melvin J. "Circulation Studies Cannot Reflect Research Use." **Journal of Academic Librarianship** 5 (May 1979): 66.

Voigt argues that the Pittsburgh Study statistics are "hopelessly distorted by the intensive use of relatively few volumes by undergraduates." Data concerning circulation and books left on tables and shelves cannot measure research use by scholars. He also questions whether the serials portion of the study considered multiple uses.

NOTES

[1]Robert N. Broadus, "Use Studies of Library Collections," *Library Resources & Technical Services* 24 (Fall 1980): 317.

[2]American Library Association, Resources and Technical Services Division, *Guide to the Evaluation of Library Collections* (Barbara Lockett, ed.) (Chicago: American Library Association, 1989), 9-11.

[3]Stanley J. Slote, *Weeding Library Collections*, 3d ed. (Englewood, Colo.: Libraries Unlimited, 1989), 45-78.

[4]Charles William Eliot, "The Division of a Library into Books in Use, and Books Not in Use, with Different Storage Methods for the Two Classes of Books," *Library Journal* 27 (July 1902): 51-56.

[5]Charles B. Osburn, "Non-Use and Loser Studies in Collection Development," *Collection Management* 4 (Spring/Summer 1982): 48.

5

Availability Studies and Document Delivery Tests

As the name implies, an *availability study* tests the actual shelf availability of library materials. This approach is closely related to a concept often termed *performance measurement*, as the question of whether a patron can find a book on the shelf when it is wanted serves as an obvious measure of how well a library is performing.

Ciliberti traced the origin of performance measurement to the 1930s.[1] The earliest availability study reported in Mansbridge's survey dates to 1934.[2] The terms *satisfaction study, frustration study, failure study*, or *shelf availability study* are often used as synonyms for *availability study*.

These studies have been conducted in a variety of ways. Normally one begins with a sample of patron self-reports, usually collected on forms or slips, concerning their success or failure at finding material and then calculates an overall availability rate. Theoretically, an availability study may also be structured around a preselected sample of citations. According to the ALA collection evaluation guidelines, a shelf availability study presumes that an item is held in the collection and tests the patron's ability to locate it on the shelf.[3] However, most academic library availability studies also consider whether the item was owned by the library, as well as other factors.

During the 1970s, Paul B. Kantor developed a so-called "branching technique" for analyzing the results of an availability study. The four branches are: 1) acquisitions—the item must have been acquired by the library; 2) circulation—the item must be available on the shelf rather than checked out; 3) library operations—the item cannot be in technical services processing or on a book cart; and 4) the user—the patron must be able to find the item in the catalog and on the shelf. Later refinements of Kantor's technique have added additional branches. Lack of success in any one branch results in total failure, but for an item to be located on the shelf, success must be achieved in all branches. Several of these branches (acquisitions plus circulation and library operations to a lesser extent) have obvious implications for collection evaluation or collection management. Branches are further divided into subcategories. For instance, acquisitions failure can result from a book never having been ordered, being on order but not yet received, or having been weeded.

According to the official ALA guidelines, the advantages of a shelf availability study are that it "reports the failures of real users," "identifies noncollection development reasons" for failure, and can be repeated to measure change over time. The listed disadvantages are: the cooperation of users is required, the studies may be time-consuming and difficult to implement, nonusers are ignored, and users may forget items they could not find.[4]

Also included in this chapter are items dealing with a closely related concept, the document delivery test. This method was developed during the 1960s by Dr. Richard H. Orr, a medical doctor. A document delivery test calculates the portion from a list of citations either owned by the library or which the library can provide, typically by ILL or from another external source, within a set time period. It usually tests both the ability to supply a document and the speed of delivery. This test clearly addresses the issue of access versus ownership.

The fairly significant number of studies that focus on patron success in using the catalog and evaluations of the ILL function were not included here, as they generally do not contain a collection management or evaluation component. Likewise, the substantial literature concerning performance measurement in public libraries is beyond this book's scope. This chapter is divided into sections on availability studies and document delivery tests.

AVAILABILITY STUDIES

174. Bachmann-Derthick, Jan, and Sandra Spurlock. "Journal Availability at the University of New Mexico." In **Advances in Serials Management**, vol. 3, edited by Jean G. Cook and Marcia Tuttle, 173-212. Greenwich, Conn.: JAI Press, 1989. 265p. ISBN 0-89232-965-3.

As noted by its authors, this is one of the few availability studies to address serials. Kantor's approach was implemented in the University of New Mexico library during November 1986, based on 483 journal searches reported by patrons on survey forms. The overall success rate was 56 percent, but only 85.2 percent of the sought items had been acquired by the library (the lowest performance factor). Circulation performance (96.7 percent) was much higher than reported in book availability studies. Against Kantor's personal recommendation, "immediate assistance" was offered to unsuccessful patrons, a modification that the authors justify.

The entry constitutes the longest account of an availability study contained in this bibliography, with the methodology described in detail. Particularly notable is a six-page flowchart of the procedure. Other features include a literature review, description of the pilot study, and specific recommendations. Bachmann-Derthick and Spurlock conclude that "the model was easy to implement and its results were immediately useful."

175. Baker, Sharon L., and F. Wilfrid Lancaster. "Evaluation of Materials Availability." In their **Measurement and Evaluation of Library Services**, 143-80. 2d ed. Arlington, Va.: Information Resources Press, 1991. 411p. ISBN 0-87815-061-7. LC 91-072908.

This textbook chapter begins with a description and nearly full-page illustration of Kantor's branching technique. About a third of the item is then devoted to the conduct of availability studies, with separate sections for studies that are citation-based (use a predetermined set of citations) and patron-based (use patrons' actual searches). Much attention is paid to sample selection. Next, the results of nine previously reported studies from 1976 to 1984 are subjected to detailed scrutiny. Separate sections analyze failures in these studies due to acquisition, circulation, library error, and patron error. A table exhibits the data. The chapter concludes by discussing variations on traditional availability studies, such as analysis by type of user or availability over time. A useful bibliography is appended. This detailed analysis also includes material pertaining to availability studies in school and public libraries. (See also Baker and Lancaster entries 2, 105, and 106.)

176. Broadbent, Marianne. "Who Wins? Who Loses? User Success and Failure in the State Library of Victoria." **Australian Academic & Research Libraries** 15 (June 1984): 65-80.

A user and "stock failure" survey was conducted by interviewing 2,160 visitors on a systematic, random-sample basis as they left the State Library of Victoria during 12 days in April and May 1983. The success rate was 80.9 percent for 2,821 known-item searches. The stock failure rate was 13.6 percent, that is, the library did not own the item, there were not enough copies, or the book was misplaced. Furthermore, 47.9 percent of the unsuccessful known-item searches were due to the library not owning the book.

For 751 subject searches, the success rate was 79.9 percent. Although a majority of subject search failures were due to cataloging problems, 15.8 percent of such failures were attributed to "not enough items" and 13 percent failed because the material was "unsuitable." Although the terminology is somewhat different, this research is quite similar to a North American availability study.

177. Ciliberti, Anne C., and others. "Material Availability: A Study of Academic Library Performance." **College & Research Libraries** 48 (November 1987): 513-27.

Following a brief historical sketch of availability studies, the authors describe a methodologically sophisticated availability study, employing a modification of Kantor's model, conducted at the William Patterson College library. The analysis was based on 402 self-report forms by patrons and 34 observations by library staff (to check the accuracy of patron self-reports) gathered during randomly selected half-hour intervals throughout the fall semester of 1985. The overall success rate was 54 percent: 47 percent of the observed and 50 percent of the self-reported known-item searches were successful, while the corresponding figures were 53 and 50 percent for subject searches. The data were further analyzed by source of failure, patron status, and longitudinal changes throughout the semester. Overall, 25 percent of all failures were because the book was in circulation and 19 percent because the item was not owned. This study can be distinguished from most others in this chapter because it uses two different methodologies and covers both known-item and subject searches.

178. Ferl, Terry Ellen, and Margaret G. Robinson. "Book Availability at the University of California, Santa Cruz." **College & Research Libraries** 47 (September 1986): 501-8.

The authors describe an availability study conducted at the University of California, Santa Cruz library, based on the methodology outlined in Kantor's manual *Objective Performance Measures for Academic and Research Libraries* (see entry 181). Throughout the month of November 1984, survey forms were distributed to 145 participating library users. The success rate was 61.3 percent for the 408 items sought. Of the 38.7 percent not located, 35.5 percent were circulating, while 24.6 percent had never been owned by the library. A table displays twenty-three reasons why items were not found. Figures illustrate the user survey forms, the tracer forms to determine why a book was not found, and the availability analysis form in which Kantor's branching technique is applied.

179. Frohmberg, Katherine A., Paul Kantor, and William A. Moffett. "Increases in Book Availability in a Large College Library." In **Communicating Information; Proceedings of the 43rd ASIS Annual Meeting; Anaheim, California, October 5-10, 1980**, vol. 17, edited by Alan R. Benenfeld and Edward John Kazlauskas, 292-94. White Plains, N.Y.: published for the American Society for Information Science by Knowledge Industry Publications, 1980. 417p. LC 64-8303. ISBN 0-914236-73-3. ISSN 0044-7870.

During a two-year period (1978-1979 and 1979-1980), six availability surveys based on Kantor's method and six questionnaires concerning perceptions of availability, mailed to random samples of students, were used to assess the impact of installing an automated circulation system in the Oberlin College library. It was found that the automated system increased availability of materials and that this phenomenon was noticed by library patrons. However, there was a greater difference in objective availability than perceived availability, leading to the conclusion that it is easier to change performance than patron attitudes. A table exhibiting the results for five availability tests (one study's results were unusable) indicates that a book was owned from 82.3 to 96.8 percent of the time, whereas overall availability ranged from 47.7 to 71.6 percent.

180. Kantor, Paul B. "Availability Analysis." **Journal of the American Society for Information Science** 27 (September-October 1976): 311-19.

In this important article, Kantor explains his branching technique for availability analysis. A number of subtle methodological points are elaborated upon. For example, possible sources of error, which Kantor feels should not exceed 4 to 5 percent, are discussed. Data from availability studies conducted at Case Western Reserve University in 1972 and 1974 are briefly reported. (For a more detailed report, see Saracevic, Shaw, and Kantor entry 193.) A major section of Kantor's paper is devoted to a retrospective application of the branching technique to data from about half-a-dozen previously published availability studies dating as far back as 1957.

Kantor stresses that if library procedures are reducing the availability rate, "management analysis of policies" rather than "statistical analysis" is required. He concludes with suggestions for future research. Individuals with a theoretical interest in Kantor's technique will want to read this article.

181. Kantor, Paul B. "Measurement of Availability Using Patron Requests and Branching Analysis." In his **Objective Performance Measures for Academic and Research Libraries**, 43-56. Washington, D.C.: Association of Research Libraries, 1984. 76p. ISBN 0-918006-09-0.

This chapter from a "how-to" manual, written specifically for the ARL, is intended to assist academic libraries in implementing Kantor's technique. It was tested, along with the manual's other performance measures not relating to collection evaluation, in 1982 at the Emory, Pennsylvania, Virginia, York, and University of Massachusetts at Amherst libraries. Kantor recommends a minimum sample size of 400 and explains why genuine patron searches are preferable to a shelflist sample (mainly because books not owned by the library will be included). Much practical information is contained in this chapter, which employs an outline format and includes tracing of books, data analysis, and result interpretation. Twenty-five steps for completing a data analysis worksheet are illustrated, followed by a practice data-analysis exercise with answers. Bachmann-Derthick and Spurlock (entry 174) note that this manual was especially useful in implementing their serials availability study at the University of New Mexico.

182. Kolner, Stuart J., and Eric C. Welch. "The Book Availability Study as an Objective Measure of Performance in a Health Sciences Library." **Bulletin of the Medical Library Association** 73 (April 1985): 121-31.

The authors recount an availability study, modeled on Kantor, conducted during ten randomly selected days in April 1983 on the Chicago, Rockford, and Peoria campuses of the University of Illinois Health Sciences Center and based on nearly 900 self-reports from patrons. The article begins with a useful checklist outline of the advantages and disadvantages of a capability measure (here a document delivery test) versus an availability measure. A pilot study indicated that it was not feasible to include serials or consider the branches "as an integrated whole," as originally planned. The overall success rate was 59 percent on the Chicago campus, 54 percent for Peoria, and 73 percent at Rockford. Separate tables analyze the causes of failure at each campus, while another table compares the results to sixteen findings of earlier availability studies, dating back to 1961. Kolner and Welch conclude, "The results suggest that book availability in academic health science libraries may be no better and no worse than in the average academic library."

183. Lancaster, F. Wilfrid. "Shelf Availability." In his **If You Want to Evaluate Your Library**, 90-103. Champaign: University of Illinois, Graduate School of Library and Information Science, 1988. 193p. LC 88-91099. ISBN 0-87845-078-5.

This chapter from a library evaluation textbook offers an excellent synthesis of the methodological issues involved in conducting an availability study. An analysis of simulated studies, based on citations to documents, focuses on sample selection and scoring methods. Much valuable advice, both practical and theoretical, is provided regarding user surveys of availability. The concept of *latent need*—the patron needs an item but never seeks it at the library—is briefly introduced. Lancaster concludes with an enlightening discussion of the factors that affect availability, such as demand level, number of copies, and loan period.

Numerous previous studies are cited throughout Lancaster's chapter. This is the best overview of availability studies published to date. (See also Lancaster entries 15, 118, 119, and 488.)

184. Mansbridge, John. "Availability Studies in Libraries." **Library & Information Science Research** 8 (October-December 1986): 299-314.

Forty availability studies published during the previous fifty years are compared with each other in terms of study samples, data-gathering methods, categories of availability, and data analysis. Tables listing the sample size and availability rates for the reported studies are particularly beneficial. Sample sizes ranged from 87 to 5,392, with a 437 median, resulting in availability rates for 21 comparable studies between 8 percent and 89 percent, with an average of 61 percent.

Orr's document delivery test, De Prospo's use of availability probabilities,[5] and Kantor's branching technique are considered landmarks in the evolution of availability studies. This top-notch work not only reviews the literature, but also places previous studies in an analytical framework.

185. Metz, Paul. "Duplication in Library Collections: What We Know and What We Need to Know." **Collection Building** 2, no. 3 (1980): 27-33.

Metz provides a well-done synthesis of numerous studies concerning book availability and user behavior, which reveals that most patrons know what titles they seek but often are frustrated because the titles are unavailable. Hence, duplication of popular titles will increase user satisfaction. Although never explicitly stated by the author, the article leads to the obvious conclusion that some duplication is desirable. Questions for future research are proposed. Although not an availability study per se, this item is included here because it provokes thought concerning fundamental issues relating to availability.

186. Murfin, Marjorie E. "The Myth of Accessibility: Frustration & Failure in Retrieving Periodicals." **Journal of Academic Librarianship** 6 (March 1980): 16-19.

An experiment to test periodical availability, carried out in 1972 in an unnamed "large academic library of a million volumes" is reported. A class of thirty-one undergraduates attempted to retrieve, within one hour, 155 articles cited in the *Readers' Guide*. Their success rate was 55 percent; 15 percent of the cases resulted in failure due to user error and 30 percent represented library operations failure. The causes of failure are analyzed and tabulated in two tables, while the results are compared to Saracevic, Shaw, and Kantor's availability study of books (entry 193).

Library acquisitions policy was not tested, as citations not held in the collection were removed from the sample. Nevertheless, there are important collection management implications in the fact that 30 percent of the cases were failures because articles were torn out (9 percent), received issues were missing (8 percent), volumes were at the bindery (5 percent) or missing from the shelf (5 percent), or issues were never received (3 percent).

187. Palais, Elliot. "Availability Analysis Report." In Association of Research Libraries. Office of Management Studies. **User Surveys and Evaluation of Library Services**, 73-82. Washington, D.C.: Association of Research Libraries, Office of Management Studies, 1981. 107p. (SPEC Kit, 71). ISSN 0160-3582.

An availability study conducted at the Arizona State University library during two test periods in the spring and summer of 1980 resulted in an overall success rate of 60.4 percent from a sample of 1,097 books. A detailed breakdown, based on Kantor's method, revealed that 5.5 percent of the books were not owned by the library; 7.8 percent were in circulation; and 14.3 percent were missing from the proper shelf. Twenty percent of the time the patron lacked the skill to find an item in the catalog or on the shelf. Measures are proposed to improve the overall success rate to 75 percent, a level claimed never to have been previously obtained by a library.

188. Radford, Neil A. "Failure in the Library: A Case Study." **Library Quarterly** 53 (July 1983): 328-39.

Radford's study interviewed patrons about their known-item searches at the University of Sydney library during seven weeks spaced throughout the winter and spring of 1981, in contrast to the majority of availability or failure studies, which are based on questionnaires. Failures were analyzed according to two broad categories: catalog failures and shelf failures.

The results showed that 9.9 percent of 2,497 known-item searches failed because the library did not own the book, while 37.8 percent of catalog failures were for that reason. Books "on loan" accounted for 18.4 percent of shelf failures, while 12.8 percent were due to an owned item being unavailable for other reasons. The overall failure rate was 35.9 percent, with user mistakes accounting for the largest number of both catalog and shelf failures.

189. Rashid, Haseeb F. "Book Availability as a Performance Measure of a Library: An Analysis of the Effectiveness of a Health Sciences Library." **Journal of the American Society for Information Science** 41 (October 1990): 501-7.

This study, based partially on the author's doctoral dissertation, employed an expanded version of Kantor's branching technique for investigating book availability at the Cleveland Health Sciences Library of Case Western Reserve University. Seven categories instead of Kantor's original four were used to analyze nonavailability. Collection development policy was added as a new category and user failure was subdivided into three categories. A sample of 1,000 patron book requests was gathered between February 15 and March 30, 1984, and between March 27 and May 20, 1985.

The total availability rate was 63.5 percent with a librarian's assistance and 59.6 percent without it. A detailed breakdown revealed that acquisitions performance—funds were lacking or a selected book had not been ordered—was the largest cause of nonavailability, accounting for 24.5 percent of failures without assistance. Collection development policy failure (the desired item was not covered by the policy or was not selected) and operations performance failure (the book was lost, misshelved, etc.) caused 12.4 percent and 12.1 percent, respectively. A table, in which the initial seven categories are further subdivided, presents data concerning twenty-three specific reasons for failure, with and without a librarian's help.

190. Revill, D. H. " 'Availability' as a Performance Measure for Academic Libraries." **Journal of Librarianship** 19 (January 1987): 14-30.

After a remarkably detailed but not always accurate review of several earlier availability studies, Revill reports the implementation of Kantor's method at the nine site libraries of the Liverpool Polytechnic Library Service in the United Kingdom. On February 17, 1986, patrons entering these 9 libraries were asked to complete forms, resulting in 1,458 known-item requests. The composite availability rate was 69 percent, ranging from 58 percent to 87 percent for the nine system libraries. Overall, 35.3 percent of failures were due to circulation and 24.3 percent were acquisitions failures. Branching diagrams illustrate the composite findings for the

68 / AVAILABILITY STUDIES AND DOCUMENT DELIVERY TESTS

system and an appendix presents the separate data for the nine locations. The author concludes by recommending the adoption of a similar availability study as a performance measure for British academic libraries.

191. Revill, D. H. "An Availability Survey in Co-operation with a School of Librarianship and Information Studies." **Library Review** 37, no. 1 (1988): 17-34.

Revill describes a repetition of the Liverpool Polytechnic availability study (entry 190) conducted almost exactly one year later, on February 16, 1987. Except for a few inconsequential modifications, the identical methodology was employed. Before reporting the results, the author analyzes both the use of library and information studies students to implement the project and a survey of patron reactions to the study. Based on 2,064 known-item searches, overall availability was 75 percent, ranging from 72 to 89 percent at the nine sites. In a novel approach, the percentage of respondents found to be successful in all their searches was 69 percent (most availability studies analyze the findings on an item-by-item basis only). Numerous tables display a variety of pertinent data for the nine locations. Copies of the forms used in the study, as well as procedural outlines, appear in the appendix.

Revill speculates on reasons for the increase in availability. This item is this bibliography's only follow-up article reporting a second availability study in the same library system.

192. Rinkel, Gene E., and Patricia McCandless. "Application of a Methodology Analyzing User Frustration." **College & Research Libraries** 44 (January 1983): 29-37.

The authors term their modification of Kantor's approach a "satisfaction" study, defined as the patron obtaining a known item within one hour. On fifteen randomly selected days in November 1980, University of Illinois at Urbana-Champaign library patrons seeking specific titles were asked to complete a questionnaire, resulting in 509 cases reported on 379 forms. The overall satisfaction rate of 71.91 percent is deemed "relatively high."

The Statistical Package for the Social Sciences was used for a sophisticated analysis of frustration by source of failure as well as by user category. A fifth cause of failure was added to Kantor's original four: the user's failure to obtain the correct call number from the catalog.

193. Saracevic, T., W. M. Shaw, Jr., and P. B. Kantor. "Causes and Dynamics of User Frustration in an Academic Library." **College & Research Libraries** 38 (January 1977): 7-18.

The first library application of Kantor's branching technique to be published is contained in this often-cited and methodologically sophisticated article. After discussing the concept of library performance and presenting a literature review, the authors describe two implementations conducted at Case Western Reserve University's Sears Library (one of two on campus). To test the effect of a change in loan policy, the results of a six-day availability study in April 1972 (when charged items were not due until the semester's end) were compared with the results from a nine-day study in November 1974 (when a four-week loan was in effect). The tests were based, respectively, on 423 and 437 known-item searches. Between 1972 and 1974, total availability increased from 48 to 56 percent. The complete results are presented in tables and branching diagrams. Separate sections discuss each of Kantor's four branches (acquisitions, circulation, library operations, and user performance) and their implications for overall library effectiveness.

This article is especially important, not only for illustrating an application of Kantor's frequently replicated branching technique, but also for discussing the theoretical relevance of availability studies to library performance measurement.

194. Shaw, W. M., Jr. "Longitudinal Studies of Book Availability." In **Library Effectiveness: A State of the Art; Papers from a 1980 ALA Preconference, New York, New York, June 27 & 28, 1980**, edited by Neal K. Kaske and William G. Jones, 337-49. Chicago: Library Administration and Management Association, American Library Association, 1980. 414p.

Six "experimental" studies of book availability conducted at the two main libraries of Case Western Reserve University between 1973 and 1979 are analyzed by Shaw, using Kantor's branching technique framework. He isolates management decisions and external factors that affect availability over time. For instance, the decline in the book budget, illustrated in a table, is identified as the cause of an increase in acquisitions failures, because the desired books were not owned by the library. Furthermore, his conclusion that replacing missing books will have a greater impact on library performance than an equivalent expenditure on new books has significant collection management implications. An appendix presents the acquisitions, circulation, library, and user performance rate data and overall book availability for studies in 1972, 1973, 1974, 1975, 1978, and 1979. (See also Saracevic, Shaw, and Kantor entry 193.)

195. Smith, Rita, and Warner Granade. "Undergraduate Library Availability Study 1975-1977." In Association of Research Libraries. Office of Management Studies. **User Surveys and Evaluation of Library Services**, 83-90. Washington, D.C.: Association of Research Libraries, Office of Management Studies, 1981. 107p. (SPEC Kit, 71). ISSN 0160-3582.

The authors discuss an availability study conducted at the University of Tennessee Undergraduate Library in the spring of 1977, based on patron-submitted forms reporting 2,375 title searches for books listed in the catalog (thus, the investigation did not address whether desired items had been acquired, but the findings still have collection management implications). A quarter of the paper describes a two-year effort to perfect the methodology by revising the questionnaire.

The total success rate was 53.8 percent: 13.9 percent of items were available but not found by the patron, whereas 34.9 percent were actually unavailable. Of the unavailable items, 71.1 percent were in circulation and 20.3 percent were lost. In a unique feature, a table displays availability according to twenty broad divisions of the LC classification.

196. Thompson, Ronelle K. H. "How Are We Doing? Using a Materials Availability Survey in an Academic Library." In **Libraries and the Literacy Challenge: The Frontier of the 90's; Proceedings of the Mountain Plains Library Association Academic Library Section Research Forum; MPLA/NDLA/SDLA Joint Conference, September 23-26, 1987, Bismarck, North Dakota**, edited by V. Sue Hatfield, 17-30. Emporia, Kan.: Emporia State University, 1987. 116p. ISBN 0-934068-04-6.

70 / AVAILABILITY STUDIES AND DOCUMENT DELIVERY TESTS

The Augustana College library director recounts an availability study based on public library performance measures. The survey was administered at randomly selected times to 857 library patrons during the 1986 National Library Week and to 585 patrons during the 1987 National Library Week, using self-reporting forms. The *title file rate* (the percentage of occasions on which patrons located specific titles) was 71 percent in 1986 and 81 percent in 1987. The combined author-subject file rates were 78 percent in 1987, contrasted to 75 percent in 1987. The browser file rate was 69 percent in 1986 and 65 percent in 1987. Thompson asserts that these findings demonstrate the success of the Augustana College bibliographic instruction program.

This entry is interesting because it illustrates the application in an academic library of performance measures developed for public libraries. Unlike Kantor's method, the reasons for nonavailability are not analyzed.

197. Van House, Nancy A., Beth T. Weil, and Charles R. McClure. "Materials Availability and Use." In their **Measuring Academic Library Performance; A Practical Approach**, 54-76. Chicago: American Library Association, 1990. 182p. plus 17 survey forms in pocket. LC 89-77253. ISBN 0-8389-0529-3.

Two of *Output Measures for Public Libraries*'[6] five authors (Van House and McClure) prepared, at the ACRL's behest, a similar manual for academic libraries. This chapter's primary focus is on availability studies, although circulation, in-library use, total materials use, and requested materials delay (e.g., time required to receive an ILL request) are also covered. Each topic is dealt with in distinct units entitled "Definition," "Background," "Data Collection," "Data Analysis," "Discussion," and "Further Suggestions."

Materials availability is defined as "the proportion of actual user searches for library materials that is successful at the time of the user's visit." Much basic, practical guidance is provided. Librarians wishing to analyze causes of failure are referred to Kantor. Several forms and worksheets are illustrated, with examples included in a pocket. A table presents the number of observations needed at the 95 percent confidence level. Academic librarians will find this chapter, and other manual sections that do not directly address collection evaluation, to be quite useful.

198. Watson, William. "A Periodicals Access Survey in a University Library." **College & Research Libraries** 45 (November 1984): 496-501.

Two surveys to assess periodical shelf availability at the University of British Columbia library are reported. The first, conducted in November 1983, had hired searchers attempt to locate 5,392 randomly selected periodical issues less than ten years old and currently subscribed to. The results indicated that 78.45 percent were immediately available; 7.62 percent were accessible with staff assistance; 5.84 percent became available within two weeks, after return from the bindery, for example; and 8.09 percent were unavailable, because they were declared missing, the subscription had lapsed, etc. A second survey in March 1984 focused on 200 heavily used science issues, evenly divided between 1974-1983 and 1983 only. For the 1974-1983 category, 85.5 percent were immediately available; 7 percent were available with staff assistance; 6.5 percent became available within two weeks; and only 1 percent were totally unavailable. In contrast, only 39 percent of the 1983 set were immediately available; 24.5 percent were available with staff aid; 30 percent were accessible within two weeks; and 6.5 percent were not available at all. Watson's data could be of interest to other libraries assessing periodical shelf availability.

199. Whitlatch, Jo Bell, and Karen Kieffer. "Service at San Jose State University: Survey of Document Availability." **Journal of Academic Librarianship** 4 (September 1978): 196-99.

Whitlatch and Kieffer describe an availability study conducted during "various hours" in April 1976 at the San Jose State University library. Every fifth patron seeking a known item was asked to complete a questionnaire, resulting in a 1,441-item sample reported on 999 survey forms. The results were diagrammed using Kantor's branching method, which the authors believe provides "a more meaningful picture of library performance than can be achieved by merely measuring one aspect of service." The overall success rate was 58.9 percent. Emphasis is placed on analyzing failure at the catalog and in the stacks. It was found that 42 percent of user failures resulted from the book being in circulation or on reserve. This is one of the earliest studies to report the use of Kantor's method.

200. Wulff, Yvonne. "Book Availability in the University of Minnesota Bio-Medical Library." **Bulletin of the Medical Library Association** 66 (July 1978): 349-50.

The earliest published report concerning the application of Kantor's technique in a medical library is offered in this short item. For thirty hours during a week in April 1977 at the University of Minnesota Bio-Medical Library, exiting patrons deposited forms reporting their search results. The overall success rate for the 388-book sample was 63 percent. A table summarizing the causes of failure reveals that 17 percent were due to the book not being owned, 27 percent because the book was in circulation, and 32 percent attributed to library operations performance (e.g., the item was missing or misshelved).

DOCUMENT DELIVERY TESTS

201. Orr, Richard H., and others. "Development of Methodologic Tools for Planning and Managing Library Services: II. Measuring a Library's Capability for Providing Documents." **Bulletin of the Medical Library Association** 56 (July 1968): 241-67.

Orr and his associates here propose the now-famous and frequently cited document delivery test that bears Orr's name. The authors begin by stressing that the traditional checklist approach does not consider the library as part of a larger system that can supply information from external sources, or the time required for the patron to obtain an item. Therefore, they propose a test to evaluate how quickly a library can provide a sample of documents. The results are measured in terms of a "capability index," which would be 100 if every test document were immediately available on the shelf. Exploratory trials at the Wayne State University College of Medicine and the SUNY-Upstate Medical Center are described. The results from full-scale trials in nine unnamed libraries (seven academic and two nonacademic), using a 290-item sample from a "local citation pool," are then reported. Next, the results of a "reservoir document delivery test" (testing a library's capacity to provide documents needed by other libraries rather than individual patrons) are reported for a 244-item sample from "a national citation pool," tested in seven medical libraries including Wayne State College of Medicine, the New York Academy of Medicine, and the National Library of Medicine. The authors assert that their approach, although developed for medical libraries, could also be used in other types of libraries.

202. Orr, Richard H., and Arthur P. Schless. "Document Delivery Capabilities of Major Biomedical Libraries in 1968: Results of a National Survey Employing Standardized Tests." **Bulletin of the Medical Library Association** 60 (July 1972): 382-422.

This long article explains in great detail the results of implementation of Orr's document delivery test, using a 300-item sample, in 92 unnamed U.S. medical libraries during 1968. A library's "capacity" is analyzed in terms of the mean time that would be required for a user to obtain documents from the sample. The test results are analyzed at a highly technical level. Orr and Schless present a mathematical model that distinguishes between a library's "virtual" capacity, which includes items that can be provided to patrons from external sources, and its "basic" capacity, which is limited to items actually held in the collection. The model can be used to calculate the benefit derived from "coupling with other resources," that is, use of ILL borrowing. Although somewhat difficult to read, this is an extremely important article. The document delivery test clearly foreshadows the present emphasis on access versus ownership in academic library collection development thought.

203. Penner, Rudolf Jacob. "Measuring a Library's Capability." **Journal of Education for Librarianship** 13 (Summer 1972): 17-30.

The application of Orr's document delivery test in the field of library and information science is described. Much of the article is devoted to recounting how the 296-item test sample was generated. The deans of six Canadian LIS schools listed twenty "primary journals" in the field, resulting in a "Consensus List" of twenty-four journals, which are named in a table. The references in the last full year of these titles (1968 or 1969) were used to create a citation pool from which the final sample was randomly selected. The document delivery test was administered, using this sample, in two unnamed Canadian LIS libraries, but the complete results of one were lost in a mail strike. Consequently, the library was retested using a 300-item sample from the 1969 *Annual Review of Information Science and Technology*. Several tables summarize the results. Penner observes that a library's capability index is "closely related" to the number of sample items it owns and concludes that the document delivery test is "applicable" to library and information science as well as biomedicine.

NOTES

[1] Anne C. Ciliberti and others, "Material Availability: A Study of Academic Library Performance," *College & Research Libraries* 48 (November 1987): 516.

[2] John Mansbridge, "Availability Studies in Libraries," *Library & Information Science Research* 8 (October-December 1986): 312-14.

[3]American Library Association, Resources and Technical Services Division, *Guide to the Evaluation of Library Collections* (Barbara Lockett, ed.) (Chicago: American Library Association, 1989), 11.

[4]Ibid., 12.

[5]Ernest R. De Prospo, Ellen Altman, and Kenneth E. Beasley, *Performance Measures for Public Libraries* (Chicago: Public Library Association, American Library Association, 1973).

[6]Nancy A. Van House and others, *Output Measures for Public Libraries; A Manual of Standardized Procedures*, 2d ed. (Chicago: American Library Association, 1987).

6

Overlap Studies

As implied, overlap studies analyze the titles held in common by two libraries or among a group of libraries. These studies also generate data concerning uniqueness and gaps. A *unique* title is defined as one held by only a single library among the group under investigation. *Gaps* represent titles not held by any library. According to William Potter (entry 214), whose literature review traces overlap studies back to the 1940s, these studies have been conducted for a variety of purposes, including investigating the feasibility of centralized processing, cooperative collection development, and pure research. They have also been used for other purposes, such as planning the merger of two libraries. Overlap studies are important for collection evaluation because they:

1. Indicate the potential for cooperative collection development;

2. Reveal the composite strength of a group of libraries;

3. Identify strengths of individual libraries by revealing unique holdings; and

4. Indicate collective collecting patterns.

Overlap and uniqueness are frequently analyzed by subject, language, and publication date, thus adding to the data's value for collection analysis purposes. Overlap by size and type of library has been addressed in theoretically oriented research studies.

Most overlap studies have traditionally been based on samples, although automated technology now offers the opportunity for analysis of all the holdings for which records have been converted to machine-readable form. RLG Conspectus verification studies (see chapter 9) sometimes analyze overlap in holdings.

This chapter also annotates items concerning the collective evaluation of two or more library collections. These investigations normally do not analyze overlap. In fact, they are not a recognized category, as are use, citation, availability, and overlap studies. Nevertheless, numerous studies that simultaneously evaluate multiple collections have been published and are often noteworthy because of their methodology or because they deal with library collections in a particular geographical region. These studies are included here because, like overlap studies, they analyze the collections of a group of libraries rather than a single library. However, entries that describe use of the RLG Conspectus by library consortiums are contained in chapter 9. The fairly extensive literature concerning the universal availability of publications is not within the scope of this literature guide.

OVERLAP STUDIES

204. Bentley, Stella. "Overlap and Description of Psychology Collections in Research Libraries." In **Building on the First Century; Proceedings of the Fifth National Conference of the Association of College and Research Libraries, Cincinnati, Ohio, April 5-8, 1989**, edited by Janice C. Fennell, 192-200. Chicago: Association of College and Research Libraries, 1989. 353p. ISBN 0-8389-7289-6.

This well-done overlap study, termed "exploratory" by the author, is based on 5-percent proportionate random samples of pre-1983 psychology monographs from the shelflists of three unnamed universities with doctoral programs in the discipline. In the sample of 1,243 items, 24.6 percent were unique to a single library, 75.6 percent were held by two or more libraries, and 50.7 percent were contained in all three.

Further analysis by language, publication date, and subject area within psychology revealed that "unique titles were more likely to be non-English, older, and in the special aspects subject category." The greatest overlap with the total sample was found in the largest of the three collections (86.2 percent contrasted with 71.0 percent and 68.3 percent). The various findings are illustrated in ten bar charts appended at the end of the article. Frequent comparisons are made to the findings of earlier overlap studies. Bentley stresses that her investigation of a specific subject found much higher overlap than earlier studies of entire research collections.

205. Buckland, Michael K., Anthony Hindle, and Gregory P. M. Walker. "Methodological Problems in Assessing the Overlap Between Bibliographical Files and Library Holdings." **Information Processing & Management** 11 (August 1975): 89-105.

This important article focuses on the methodology for calculating overlap among library collections or the coverage of abstracting and indexing services. Examples from overlap studies conducted during the early 1970s in the United Kingdom by the University of Lancaster Library Research Unit and in Indiana based on the OCLC database are used for illustration. After describing the concept of overlap and its significance for libraries, three methods for assessing overlap are explained: 1) comparison of segments of catalogs, i.e., the letter "O" from the author catalog; 2) sampling from external lists; and 3) what is termed the "direct statistical approach," whereby statistical sampling methods are employed (here explained at a fairly technical level). The article concludes with practical advice at an advanced technical level concerning sampling, checking, and statistical analysis. This rigorous entry is significant from both the theoretical and practical perspectives.

206. Cairns, Paul M. "Crerar/Chicago Library Merger." **Library Resources & Technical Services** 30 (April/June 1986): 126-36.

This entry focuses on a sample survey taken in the summer of 1980 to estimate overlap between the John Crerar Library's collection and the University of Chicago library's science holdings, as part of the planning process for the merger of the two collections. Much of the article describes the technical details of implementing the survey. The items housed on a stratified sample of 466 of the Crerar Library's 31,729 shelves were checked against the University of Chicago files. It was estimated that in September 1980 the Crerar Library contained about 237,000 duplicate and approximately 352,000 bound volumes, including both monographs and serials. (Percentages are not presented.) A two-page table summarizes the findings by eight classes and twenty divisions of the DDC for both serials and monographs. This is the only identified item to analyze overlap for the purpose of merging two libraries.

207. Johnston, Christine. "Automated Collection Assessment: CASSI as a Tool." **Technical Services Quarterly** 8, no. 2 (1990): 43-54.

208. Johnston, Christine. "CASSI and Collection Assessment: New Uses for an Old Tool." In **Building on the First Century; Proceedings of the Fifth National Conference of the Association of College and Research Libraries, Cincinnati, Ohio, April 5-8, 1989**, edited by Janice C. Fennell, 218-23. Chicago: Association of College and Research Libraries, 1989. 353p. ISBN 0-8389-7289-6.

These two items provide essentially the same report on an identical study. The titles are somewhat misleading, as these items describe an overlap study, but unlike most published overlap studies the focus falls on serials rather than monographs. The overlap in current chemistry serial subscriptions during the late 1980s between the University of Texas libraries, on the one hand, and the MIT and UC-Berkeley libraries, on the other, was analyzed based on customized *CASSI* printouts. (*CASSI*, or the *Chemical Abstracts Service Source Index*, is an online union list of 69,000 serials and conference proceedings maintained by Chemical Abstracts.) Of 7,228 current titles owned by either Texas or Berkeley, 2,810 (38.9 percent) were held by both, while there was a 37.5 percent overlap (1,764 of 4,707) in the titles held by either Texas or MIT. The titles owned by MIT and Berkeley but not Texas were broken down by subject and country of origin. These articles are fascinating because they represent a slightly new approach to overlap analysis.

209. Knightly, John J. "Library Collections and Academic Curricula: Quantitative Relationships." **College & Research Libraries** 36 (July 1975): 295-301.

This frequently cited overlap study used a sample of 845 titles in 19 subject areas from the *American Book Publishing Record* to analyze holdings and duplication among 22 state-supported senior universities or colleges in Texas. The results were related to the curriculum by classifying the institutions into four categories for each subject, supporting: 1) no degree, 2) a bachelor's degree, 3) a master's degree, or 4) a doctoral degree. It was generally found that for each subject the holdings and duplication rates "progressively" increased at institutions with higher levels of curricular support. Two tables present the findings. It was also discovered that books were more likely to be duplicated if they were reviewed in *Choice*.

Knightly states, "[I]t may be inferred from the data that curriculum is a major controlling influence on collections." The author then concludes by speculating on variables other than the curriculum that could account for differences among collections. He focuses on five variables: equivalency of titles (libraries may select different titles with the same subject content); vagaries of the selection process; budget; maturity of collections; and differences in teaching styles.

210. Miller, Ruth, and Martha W. Niemeier. "A Study of Collection Overlap in the Southwest Indiana Cluster of SULAN." **Indiana Libraries** 9, no. 2 (1990): 45-54.

A random sample of 497 titles from *Books for College Libraries*, third edition, was checked against the Indiana State University, Southern Indiana University, Rose-Hulman Institute of Technology, and St. Mary-of-the-Woods Library holdings (all part of Indiana's State University Library Automation Network) to analyze overlap, uniqueness, and gaps. It was found that 34.1 percent of the sample was held by at least two libraries. Detailed statistics are provided, including comparisons among the four libraries and with the findings of earlier studies. A breakdown by publication date revealed the greatest percentage of overlap during the 1960s. Analysis by subject found the highest overlap in arts and humanities. As a second aspect of the investigation, the holdings of Indiana State and Southern Indiana were compared for seven LC classification segments from *BCL3*. Six charts illustrating the results are appended.

211. Moore, Barbara, Tamara J. Miller, and Don L. Tolliver. "Title Overlap: A Study of Duplication in the University of Wisconsin System Libraries." **College & Research Libraries** 43 (January 1982): 14-22.

OCLC archival tapes from July 1, 1977, to June 30, 1979, were used for overlap analysis among the library collections of the eleven degree-granting institutions in the University of Wisconsin system. Overlap comparisons for all titles regardless of imprint date and for 1976-1979 imprints were made: 1) among the eleven libraries, 2) between the two doctoral and nine nondoctoral university libraries, and 3) among the nondoctoral university libraries. Overlap was less than anticipated, as 18.16 percent of all titles were in two or more locations, whereas 31.99 percent of current imprints were. A table displaying the percentage of unique titles among total holdings and current acquisitions for the eleven universities is especially interesting. Further analysis revealed that English-language, university-press books cataloged by the Library of Congress tended to have high overlap, although no subject pattern was found.

212. Mowat, Ian R. M. "EGOS: A Study of Stock Overlap in the Libraries of the Universities of Glasgow and Edinburgh." **Catalogue & Index**, no. 69 (Summer 1983): 1-3.

Mowat briefly describes an overlap study conducted to assess the potential for a shared retrospective cataloging effort between the Universities of Glasgow and Edinburgh in Scotland. The overlap in pre-1950 monographic holdings was calculated by checking a random sample of 1,713 entries from the Edinburgh guardbook catalog against Glasgow's collection. The data were analyzed according to eight categories, based on date and place of publication (United Kingdom or foreign). The total overlap was 31 percent, ranging from 14 to 50 percent for the eight categories. The overlap was higher for the United Kingdom than for foreign material, leading to the conclusion that cooperative retrospective cataloging for older United Kingdom publications was "worth further investigation."

213. Potter, William Gray. "Collection Overlap in the LCS Network in Illinois." **Library Quarterly** 56 (April 1986): 119-41.

After concisely reviewing four types of overlap studies (see entry 214 for details), Potter describes an overlap study of twenty-one academic libraries in Illinois, begun in July 1983, based on a 1 percent random sample of the Library Computer System network database. Separate sections cover the methodology, sample construction, and record matching before the results are analyzed in detail. Seven tables exhibit the data, including overlap between named pairs of libraries as well as total overlap by date, language, and subject. The major findings were: 1) the percentage of titles held by one library only was 69.46, falling to 66.5 percent when the largest library, the University of Illinois at Urbana-Champaign, was dropped; 2) the percentage of titles unique to one library ranged from 6.1 to 68.4; 3) the percentage of unique titles was highest for older and non-English material; 4) for ordered pairs of libraries, "the extent that one library is duplicated by another library increases with the size of the second library"; and 5) generally, larger libraries have a higher percentage of unique titles.

214. Potter, William Gray. "Studies of Collection Overlap: A Literature Review." **Library Research** 4 (Spring 1982): 3-21.

Potter provides an extremely useful, although now somewhat dated, literature review of overlap studies. The author begins by commenting that inconsistent objectives and methodologies make comparisons difficult. Consequently, twenty major studies, dating back to 1942, are described under four headings: studies concerning union catalogs, studies to determine the feasibility of centralized processing, investigations conducted for cooperative collection development, and research studies. The purpose, methodology, and results of the specific studies are examined. A concluding section observes that: 1) overlap depends on the age, size, and type of library; 2) a large proportion of titles will be unique to one library; 3) cooperative collection development often need only formalize existing patterns; and 4) computers will allow studies based on larger samples.

215. Rochester, Maxine K. "The ABN Database: Sampling Strategies for Collection Overlap Studies." **Information Technology & Libraries** 6 (September 1987): 190-96.

Three methods for sampling the Australian Bibliographic Network (ABN) to determine overlap among Australian libraries are analyzed. The first approach, a random sample of 200 items taken from the ABN microfiche catalog in March 1985, is deemed the "cheapest and easiest" method. The second, a random sample of 400 items from ABN online, taken in October 1985, is called the "preferred option." The third technique, a monographic sample of 142 items from a subject bibliography checked against ABN online in October 1985, is considered the preferred method for analyzing a particular subject area.

Rochester asserts that no conclusions can be reached about overlap in Australian libraries because of the limited number of participants and retrospective records in the ABN. However, she believes "the study has confirmed the ease of carrying out collection overlap studies using an online database."

216. Shaw, Debora. "Overlap of Monographs in Public and Academic Libraries in Indiana." **Library & Information Science Research** 7 (July-September 1985): 275-89.

This rigorous research project was done for the author's doctoral dissertation. A .03 percent shelflist sample of pre-1980 monographs from 20 academic and 20 public libraries in Indiana, resulting in 3,073 titles, was checked against the holdings of the largest 26 libraries to analyze overlap. A positively skewed distribution was observed, with many books in a few libraries and few books in many libraries. Library type, collection size, publication date, and subject were found to predict overlap. The greatest overlap was observed in books published in the 1960s and, for academic libraries, in the social sciences. A lengthy appendix contains nine tables and four figures displaying the results.

217. Stroyan, Sue. "Collection Overlap in Hospital Health Sciences Libraries: A Case Study." **Bulletin of the Medical Library Association** 73 (October 1985): 358-64.

Stroyan analyzed overlap in two small, unnamed community hospital libraries in Illinois by studying seventy-six randomly selected monographs from each library's shelflist and comparing their respective serials lists. As the author expected, monographic overlap between the two collections was low. (The first library held 19.7 percent of the second's sample; the second had 26.3 percent of the first's.) Serials overlap was much higher (45 percent and 57.7 percent). A breakdown of the monographic sample into five broad subject categories (medicine, nursing, hospital, science, and general) revealed that medicine, followed by nursing, displayed the highest overlap. Analysis of the sample by publication date led to the unexpected finding that books published between 1976 and 1980 showed greater overlap than those published between 1981 and 1984.

COLLECTIVE EVALUATIONS OF TWO OR MORE LIBRARY COLLECTIONS

218. Dorn, Knut. "The Representation of German Social Science Titles in Australian Libraries." **Australian Academic & Research Libraries** 17 (March 1986): 14-24.

A representative of the German book dealer, Harrassowitz, examines the number of German social science titles his company sold to major Australian and U.S. libraries. In 1983 the National Library of Australia's approval plan received 383 German social science monographs, compared to approximately 1,700 for the Library of Congress and about 900 for other U.S. research libraries. A select list of 200 titles received on approval by the Texas, Arizona State, and Columbia libraries was checked against the Harrassowitz order records from the University of Melbourne, La Trobe University, the University of Sydney, and the University of New South Wales. Dorn's paper describes an intriguing but infrequently utilized approach: use of vendor records for multilibrary, cross-national collection evaluation.

219. Flesch, Juliet. "German Collecting in the Social Sciences in Australian Libraries." **Australian Academic & Research Libraries** 17 (March 1986): 25-28.

To assess the result of cutbacks by the National Library of Australia, 2,056 titles in law, public administration, politics, sociology, business, labor, and statistics from 12 issues of *Das Deutsche Buch* for 1982 and 1983 were checked against the Australian Bibliographic Network database, as of June 1985. Only 20.8 percent were held by any Australian library. Of these, only 11.7 percent were held only by a library other than NLA, indicating that library's "importance." Flesch's case study is noteworthy for two reasons: a methodology for evaluating the holdings of an entire country is described, and some collecting problems of Australian libraries are illustrated.

220. Makino, Yasuko. "An Evaluation of East Asian Collections in Selected Academic Art Libraries in the United States." **Collection Management** 10, no. 3/4 (1988): 127-36.

Makino reports a collective evaluation of eight major East Asian art collections in the United States, stating that no previous qualitative studies have been undertaken in this subject. Three checklists—Chinese- and Japanese-language citations from five standard scholarly works, a randomly selected list from the Illinois shelflist, and "important" titles—were compared against the holdings of Berkeley, Chicago, Columbia, Harvard, Michigan, Princeton, Yale, and Illinois. Six tables summarize the results, including analysis by language and by date, but the eight institutions are referred to by code rather than explicitly identified. A larger percentage from the randomly generated list was held by all libraries than from the other lists.

221. Makooi, Aref. "Distribution of Middle Eastern Periodicals in the UK Libraries: A Statistical Analysis." **INSPEL** 24, no. 3 (1990): 107-13.

In an unusual approach to serials collection evaluation, three union catalogs of Persian, Arabic, and Turkish periodicals were used to assess the serials holdings in these languages from the Middle East and Afghanistan in United Kingdom libraries. A total of 2,369 titles were analyzed by holdings location, language, date, and broad subject area. Moreover, 67.9 percent of the titles were uniquely held by a single library. Makooi concludes that union catalogs can be "helpful to obtain bibliographical information on the strengths and weaknesses of holdings."

222. Olden, Anthony, and Spencer S. Marsh. "An Evaluation of the Extent to Which the Holdings of Four United States Research Libraries Would Have Supported the Writing of Award-Winning Books on Africa." **International Journal of Information & Library Research** 2, no. 3 (1990): 177-93.

A total of 636 citations randomly selected from twenty-two 1965 to 1985 annual award-winning books on Africa were checked against the African holdings of the Illinois, Indiana, Yale, and Northwestern University libraries in this fairly sophisticated checklist study. The holdings data are reported separately for two categories: items published in Africa and items published elsewhere. It was found that 55 percent of the total sample was owned by all four libraries, while 11 percent was not held by any. A table displays the number of books not owned by each library and the proportion of those that the other three libraries did own. Investigation by format indicated that a higher percentage of serials (60 percent) than books (55 percent) was collectively owned.

Analysis of the sample itself, displayed in three tables, revealed that 61 percent were books, and 52 percent were dated between 1960 and 1979. A breakdown by place of publication found that the cited items had been published in twenty-seven African countries, headed by Ghana with 19 percent of the African citations, and at least eight non-African countries, topped by the United States and the United Kingdom at 33 percent each. This well-done report will be of value for African specialists.

223. Seavey, Charles A. "Ranking and Evaluating the ARL Library Map Collections." **College & Research Libraries** 53 (January 1992): 31-43.

Seavey analyzes the map holdings of eighty-eight ARL libraries—all ARL libraries except Canadian institutions and American libraries for which map data was unavailable. Six tables name and present the data for the "top twenty" and "bottom twenty" libraries according to the following criteria: 1) total size of the map collection in 1989; 2) absolute increase in map holdings between 1984 and 1989; 3) percentage increase in map holdings, 1984 to 1989; 4) total cartographic holdings in 1989, including maps, aerial photographs, and remote sensing images; 5) absolute increase in cartographic holdings, 1984 to 1989; and 6) percentage increase in cartographic holdings between 1984 and 1989. A final table names the top eighty-seven libraries in rank order based on composite size and growth rankings.

A low or weak (0.31) correlation was found between these map rankings and the overall ranking by the ARL Index, leading the author to conclude that "little consensus about the importance of the cartographic format exists within the ARL libraries." The author defends the use of a strictly quantitative approach in his investigation. This well-done study is the only entry to deal exclusively with maps.

224. Urbancic, Frank R. "University Library Collections of Accounting Periodicals." **Accounting Review** 58 (April 1983): 417-27.

A Youngstown State University accounting professor's fascinating study concerning the accounting periodical subscriptions of U.S. university libraries was based on a questionnaire mailed to reference librarians at universities: 1) offering a Ph.D. degree in accounting, 2) not offering a Ph.D. but with an accredited business school, and 3) offering an accounting degree without having a Ph.D. or accredited business school. One hundred sixty-two responded. A table tank-orders the twenty responding universities, in each of the three categories, holding the most accounting periodical subscriptions. Another table indicates the percentage of libraries from the three categories that held each title in a "recommended" list of fifteen accounting periodicals, based on inclusion in two of four core lists (Daniels, Katz, the American Institute of Certified Public Accountants, and Price Waterhouse). Finally, an appendix presents the holdings data for ninety-one accounting periodicals (every title held by at least seven respondents).

The methodology is exceptional because it reverses the usual evaluation procedure: instead of determining what titles a library holds, the author ascertains how many libraries hold specific titles. The wealth of holdings data would obviously be of value for comparative purposes to libraries evaluating their accounting periodicals.

82 / OVERLAP STUDIES

225. Walcott, Rosalind. "A Survey of Major Library Collections in the Geosciences in the State of Victoria, Australia." In **Roles and Responsibilities in Geoscience Information; Proceedings of the Eighteenth Meeting of the Geoscience Information Society, Oct. 31-Nov. 3, 1983**, edited by Unni Havem Rowell, 231-42. N.p.: Geoscience Information Society, 1984. 243p. (Proceedings of the Geoscience Information Society, vol. 14).

A librarian from SUNY-Stony Brook describes her evaluation of the geosciences collections of fourteen major libraries in Victoria during her sabbatical leave from December 1981 through April 1982. Checklists of 1,542 serials, derived from a variety of sources, and 506 monographs, reviewed in *Choice* between 1974 and 1980, were used to evaluate the general geosciences holdings. Additional monographic and serials checklists were utilized to focus on oceanography. The results are reported collectively rather than for individual libraries, but the author does offer candid observations on specific collections based on her personal visits to ten libraries to examine the holdings directly. Walcott concludes by recommending sabbaticals to other librarians—perhaps the most inspiring idea in this article.

7

Standards

For at least the last half century, authoritative library organizations have promulgated innumerable sets of standards for almost all types of libraries. Standards have now been provided for university, college, and community college libraries, not to mention public, school, special, and state libraries. These standards typically address all components of library support, including staff, finance, space, facilities, and collections. Obviously, the annotations in this chapter focus on the sections pertinent to collections.

Analysis of a particular collection in terms of an external standard represents one of the traditional approaches to collection evaluation. In fact, the initial collection evaluation bibliography by Ottersen was entitled "A Bibliography on Standards for Evaluating Libraries."[1]

Qureshi[2] traced the first use of the word *standard* in a library context to 1894, while noting that in 1929 the American Library Association adopted a plan for budgets, classification, and compensation in college and university libraries.[3] According to Wallace, the first standards for two-year college libraries were jointly issued in the early 1930s by the American Council on Education and the American Association of Junior Colleges, and quickly followed by the American Library Association standards published in 1932, both of which contained quantitative figures for minimum collection size.[4] Collections are also covered in "Standards" or "Guidelines" for what are variously termed community, two-year, or junior college libraries. These have been issued by the ACRL in 1960[5]; the American Library Association, the American Association of Community and Junior Colleges, and the Association for Educational Communications and Technology (jointly) in 1972,[6] supplemented by a quantitative statement in 1979[7]; and the ACRL and the Association for Educational Communications and Technology in 1982 (entries 237 and 238) and 1990 (entry 239).

84 / STANDARDS

Kaser and Brown both trace the movement for college library standards to the late 1920s.[8] Draft standards proposed by Carl Milam in 1930[9] and William M. Randall in 1932[10] were never adopted. In 1943 the officially adopted ALA standards for academic libraries contained minimum quantitative figures for collection size and book expenditures.[11] ACRL standards specifically for college libraries, which contained sections about the collections, were adopted in 1959[12] and official revisions were promulgated in both 1975[13] and 1986 (entry 231).

The 1943 ALA standards for academic libraries applied to university libraries. However, the first standards specifically for university libraries were officially issued by the ACRL and ARL in 1979[14] and were later replaced by the ACRL standard of 1989 (entry 236). Each of these contains provisions for the collection.

Standards have also been adopted for off-campus services (entry 232), branch libraries (entry 226), and audiovisuals (entry 228) and proposed for the academically disadvantaged (entry 229). It should also be noted that numerous regional accrediting agencies and foreign countries have issued standards for academic libraries, although these are beyond the scope of this bibliography.

A perennial issue regarding standards concerns whether they should be *quantitative*, specifying a definite number of items a collection must contain and/or acquire within a year, or *qualitative*, based on prescriptive statements. Quantitative standards frequently include a formula. Other important issues concern:

1. Whether a standard should realistically describe library practice or represent a high ideal towards which to strive

2. The degree to which library administrators are aware of and influenced by standards

3. The extent to which libraries actually meet the requirements set forth in standards

4. Whether a standard takes into consideration the provision of information resources from beyond the library collection

5. Whether standards should be based on subjective judgment or scientific evidence

6. Whether a standard should signify a level of adequacy or excellence

7. Whether standards represent mere guidelines or should be enforced.

Qualitative standards are often criticized for being vague or meaningless. Quantitative standards have frequently been criticized for not considering a collection's quality and encouraging libraries to pad their numbers by not weeding irrelevant or obsolete material.

Standards can be used for evaluation of a collection's adequacy, comparison with other libraries, budget justification, goal setting, and long-range planning.

Included here are drafts of standards as well as their final versions, the history of standards, newly proposed standards, and commentary on standards. Items pertaining to "Guidelines," "Formulas," and "Model Mission Statements" are also included, as these phenomena represent types of standards. Public, school, and special library standards were excluded. Note that the various guidelines and standards issued by the American Library Association or the Association of College and Research Libraries have usually been published as separate documents as well as in *College & Research Libraries News*. For convenience, *College & Research Libraries News* is cited here.

OFFICIAL STATEMENTS

226. Association of College and Research Libraries. "ACRL Guidelines for Branch Libraries in Colleges and Universities." **College & Research Libraries News** 52 (March 1991): 171-74.

227. Association of College and Research Libraries. University Libraries Section. Committee on Guidelines for Branch Libraries, Stella Bentley, Chair. "Guidelines for Branch Libraries in Colleges and Universities: A Draft." **College & Research Libraries News** 50 (May 1989): 392-94.

One of the few available items pertaining to branch libraries, these guidelines were approved by the ACRL Board of Directors on June 26, 1990. They are divided into four sections: programs, resources, communications, and evaluation. The resources section includes collections (in addition to personnel, staffing, and facilities), while the evaluation section addresses the question of collection size.

Avoiding the quantitative approach in favor of qualitative guidelines, the ACRL states that a collection "should ideally provide for a significant part of the literature and information needs of its primary constituents." When focusing on collection size and growth rate, the evaluation process should consider: 1) data from "comparable branches at comparable institutions," 2) whether the requirements of accrediting agencies are met, and 3) whether the collection matches "the academic programs as described in the collection policy." The importance of access and preservation is also stressed by these guidelines. No notable differences in format or the sections dealing with collections are apparent between the draft and final versions.

228. Association of College and Research Libraries. Audiovisual Committee, Margaret Ann Johnson, Chair. "Guidelines for Audiovisual Services in Academic Libraries." **College & Research Libraries News** 48 (October 1987): 533-36. Draft statement in **College & Research Libraries News** 47 (May 1986): 333-35.

Very little has been published with an exclusive focus on audiovisual collection evaluation in academic libraries. Consequently, the official ACRL guidelines concerning audiovisual services are well worth noting. Employing an outline format, the text is organized into ten sections: planning, budget, personnel, facilities, equipment and supplies, collection development, acquisitions, cataloging, collection maintenance, and service. The five points under collection development call for: 1) assignment of collection development responsibility to a designated librarian; 2) a "clear" collection development statement; 3) consideration of the curriculum, research needs, an item's quality, an item's life expectancy, and an item's intended use as selection criteria; 4) review of material prior to purchase; and 5) evaluation of "the existing collection frequently in order to determine subject areas that need to be strengthened or deemphasized." The sixth point of the collection maintenance section recommends "regular evaluation of the condition of materials and equipment."

These guidelines were approved by the ACRL board at the 1987 ALA Annual Conference. They replace the first ACRL audiovisual *Guidelines*, published in 1968. Comparison of the final version to the draft indicates that only minor editorial changes were made in the sections pertaining to collection development and collection maintenance. However, the document's foreword was significantly expanded to stress, among other things, that the guidelines are a "framework for development," not a "manual for practitioners."

229. Association of College and Research Libraries. Community and Junior College Libraries Section. Committee on Services to the Disadvantaged, Madison Mosley, Chair. "Library Services to the Academically Disadvantaged in the Public Community College: A Draft." **College & Research Libraries News 48** (April 1987): 189-91.

This "position paper" addresses the library's role in providing services to academically disadvantaged community college students, termed "basic skills" students throughout the document. Following an introduction that states "[L]ibrarians must take an active role in the education process which will bring basic skill students up to appropriate levels," separate sections composed of narrative paragraphs cover staff development, collection development, programs and services, and visual accessibility. The collection development paragraph urges a materials budget allocation for the special skills area and integration of the materials into the regular collection. It goes without saying that this subject is seldom addressed in the collection development literature of academic librarianship.

230. Association of College and Research Libraries. Library Standards Committee, Jacquelin M. Morris, Chair. "Standards for College Libraries, 1985." **College & Research Libraries News 46** (May 1985): 241-52.

231. Association of College and Research Libraries. Library Standards Committee, Jacquelin M. Morris, Chair. "Standards for College Libraries, 1986." **College & Research Libraries News 47** (March 1986): 189-200.

This revision of the 1975 ACRL College Library Standards received final approval by the ACRL board in January 1986, at the ALA's Midwinter meeting. The document is composed of preliminary material plus separate "standards" covering objectives, "the collections," organization of materials, staff, service, facilities, administration, and budget. The standards consist of several prescriptive statements with commentary on each. The three statements of the collections standard call for "all types of recorded information," provision of "a high percentage" of needed materials "as promptly as possible," and use of a quantitative formula. Starting with a basic collection of 85,000 volumes, the formula adds allowances for factors such as

FTE faculty, FTE students, undergraduate majors, and graduate degrees. Audiovisual items and resource-sharing activities count toward meeting the number of volumes required by the formula, which is used to calculate an A through D grade for the collection. It is stated that collections should grow at a rate of 5 percent per year until they receive an A and then grow at 2 to 5 percent annually.

The 1986 version has two notable changes from the 1985 draft in regard to the collection standard. It was explicitly added that library collections obtaining lower than an A on the formula should grow at a 5 percent annual rate until an A is achieved. Also, online database searches are no longer counted toward meeting the formula requirements. (For follow-up studies, see Faulkner entry 246 and White entry 253.)

232. Association of College and Research Libraries. Standards and Accreditation Committee. "Guidelines for Extended Campus Library Services." **College & Research Libraries News** 43 (March 1982): 86-88.

The final guidelines approved by the ACRL board on January 26, 1981, are different enough from the draft version (entry 233) to warrant a separate annotation. A sixth major section, "Planning," was added, while the "Evaluative Checklist" was completely dropped. The "Resources" section calls for "access to library materials in sufficient number" to support student course work needs and instructional preparation needs.

Moreover, programs should provide access to collections that meet the standard for the appropriate degree level, e.g., "Guidelines for Two-Year Learning Resources Programs" and the "Statement on Quantitative Standards" for associate degrees; "Standards for College Libraries" for bachelor's and master's degrees; and "Standards for University Libraries" for doctoral degrees.

233. Association of College and Research Libraries. Standards and Accreditation Committee. "Guidelines for Library Services to Extension/Noncampus Students: Draft of Proposed Revisions." **College & Research Libraries News** 41 (October 1980): 265-72.

A proposed revision to the 1967 guidelines was reviewed at the January 1981 ALA Midwinter meeting in Washington, D.C. The guidelines are divided into five sections, using an outline format: finances, personnel, facilities, resources, and services. The two points under resources state: 1) "all the resources" needed for student course preparation should be "available either through cooperative arrangement with other libraries or systematic collection development"; and 2) the rate of collection development for noncampus programs should be "comparable to the main campus"—a strong statement that was removed from the final version.

Next appears a draft of an "Evaluative Checklist," organized under five "components": budget, staff, facilities, resources, and services. A 1-to-12 rating system is applied to a series of statements that describe aspects of the program. For example, under resources, statements concerning "provision of resources" and "rate of collection development" are rated.

234. Association of College and Research Libraries. Undergraduate Librarians Discussion Group, Wilma Reid Cipolla, Chair. "The Mission of a University Undergraduate Library: Draft Model Statement." **College & Research Libraries News** 48 (April 1987): 192-94.

235. Association of College and Research Libraries. Undergraduate Librarians Discussion Group and University Libraries Section Steering Committee. "The Mission of a University Undergraduate Library: Model Statement." **College & Research Libraries News** 48 (October 1987): 542-44.

A replacement for the ACRL 1979 model mission statement for separate undergraduate libraries within a larger university, the 1987 statement is organized into seven sections: environment, users, information services, collection, staff, study facilities, and development. The five narrative paragraphs dealing with the collection prescribe: 1) a reference collection; 2) purchase of multiple copies of high-demand items; 3) provision of the "best materials of historical or research value" plus "introductory" and "overview" items; 4) a periodical reference collection based on "the more standard and interdisciplinary periodical indexes"; 5) emphasis on collecting the periodicals included in these indexes; 6) a supply of nonprint material with bibliographic access; 7) "sufficient comprehensiveness and depth" so that the collection is a "starting point" to find the basic information needed for undergraduate instruction; and 8) development of the collection for the "cultural, career, and recreational interests" of undergraduates.

Most of what is included in this statement would apply to any college library. However, a few recommendations, such as the observation that undergraduates should be referred to the graduate collection for their advanced needs, recognize the unique character of a separate undergraduate library. Although the model statement's final version, approved by the ACRL board at the 1987 Annual Conference, added the University Libraries Section Steering Committee's name as a sponsoring body, the section dealing with collections appears to be identical to the draft version.

236. Association of College and Research Libraries. University Library Standards Review Committee, Kent Hendrickson, Chair. "Standards for University Libraries: Evaluation of Performance." **College & Research Libraries News** 50 (September 1989): 679-91. Draft statement in **College & Research Libraries News** 49 (June 1988): 343-50.

Replacing the 1979 "Standards for University Libraries," this final version was approved by the ACRL board at the 1989 ALA Midwinter Conference. Both the quantitative and qualitative approaches are rejected. Instead, these standards "set forth the process by which expectations may be established, and enumerate the topics that should be addressed." Employing an outline format, the standards are organized into four major sections, covering: A) setting goals, B) factors in developing goals, C) measuring achievement, and D) evaluative criteria. Section B(3A) lists six points under collection management, the first of which calls for providing access to material as well as purchase for retention. Section D(4) lists ten general evaluative criteria for determining collection adequacy, such as, "Does the current collecting reflect an appropriate level of program support?" A "standards" bibliography is appended, followed by a short, annotated bibliography on "supporting materials" that includes six items pertaining to collections.

A number of changes were made between the draft and final versions. Section D2, criteria for collection adequacy, was expanded from eight to ten. However, section 3A concerning collection management was unchanged.

Official Statements / 89

237. Association of College and Research Libraries and Association for Educational Communications and Technology. "Guidelines for Two-Year College Learning Resources Programs (Revised), Part I." **College & Research Libraries News** 43 (January 1982): 5-10.

238. Association of College and Research Libraries and Association for Educational Communications and Technology. "Guidelines for Two-Year College Learning Resources Programs (Revised), Part II." **College & Research Libraries News** 43 (February 1982): 45-49.

Approved by the ACRL Board of Directors on June 30, 1981, this document replaces the previous guidelines published in 1972. The introduction states that these guidelines are "designed to provide criteria for information, self-study, and planning, not to establish minimal (or accreditation) standards." Using an outline format, part 1 covers objectives and purposes, organization and administration, and budget; part 2 covers instructional system components, services, and interagency cooperative activities.

The instructional system components are further subdivided into staff, facilities, instructional equipment, and materials. Under the materials heading, fifteen points are elaborated upon. Point one stresses that material should be selected on the basis of instructional objectives, while point five states that "high caliber" material should be included even if it does not meet "curricular needs." Other points cover gifts, the reference collection, newspapers, government documents, pamphlets, recorded material, conservation, and archival items.

239. Association of College and Research Libraries and Association for Educational Communications and Technology. "Standards for Community, Junior and Technical College Learning Resources Programs." **College & Research Libraries News** 51 (September 1990): 757-67.

240. Association of College and Research Libraries and Association for Educational Communications and Technology. AECT-ACRL Joint Committee, J. O. Wallace and Dan Koenig, Co-chairs. "Standards for Two-Year College Learning Resources Programs: A Draft." **College & Research Libraries News** 50 (June 1989): 496-505.

This document, intended for two- or three-year academic institutions awarding an associate degree, replaces the 1982 "Guidelines for Two-Year College Learning Resources Programs (Revised)" (entries 237 and 238) and the 1979 "Quantitative Standards for Two-Year Learning Resources Programs." It is composed of seven separate standards covering objectives, organization, administration and staff, budget, services, collections, and facilities. The collection section consists of seven specific statements with appended commentary, dealing with the collection development policy, selection, weeding, the reference collection, access, and the institution's history. It advocates "diversified forms of information" as well as support of the curriculum and student and faculty information needs. Two tables, for a minimum and an "excellent" collection, list the number of recommended volumes, current serial subscriptions, videos and films, "other items" (defined as microforms, maps, etc.), and total collection size for various increments of FTE students, ranging from "less than 200" to "17,000 to 19,000." Instead of recommending an annual growth rate, "an annual replacement rate of 3 to 5 percent is anticipated" for volumes and "other items."

The most significant change regarding collections between the draft and final versions is an increase in the required "films and videos," "other items," and total collection size for both a minimum and an excellent collection.

241. International Federation of Library Associations and Institutions. Section of University Libraries and Other General Research Libraries. **Standards for University Libraries**, edited by Beverly P. Lynch. The Hague, Netherlands: International Federation of Library Associations, 1986. 38p. (IFLA Professional Reports, no. 10). ISBN 90-70916-13-4. ISSN 0168-1931. Also published in **IFLA Journal** 13 (May 1987): 120-25.

These qualitative standards are intended to serve as "guidelines" and "general principles" to be used "to evaluate the university library" and serve as "a framework within which various countries or regions could develop their own statements of standards." Quantitative measures are explicitly rejected. After a brief introduction and statement of purpose, ten standards cover purpose, organization and administration, services, collections, staff, facilities, budget and finance, technology, preservation and conservation, and cooperation.

Four points in section 4 state that a collection should: 1) "be of sufficient size ... to support ... instructional needs"; 2) include "required and assigned" materials for students; 3) contain all formats; and 4) be "reviewed systematically." Another two points advocate a collection development policy and interlibrary cooperation. These two items are identical except that the separately published document contains the statement in English, French, German, and Spanish.

OTHER

242. Allen, William R., Daniel L. Kniesner, and Virginia O'Herron. "Developing a Quantitative Formula for the Book Collection in Small Academic Technical Libraries." **Science & Technology Libraries** 2 (Fall 1981): 59-68.

The authors describe the development, during the early 1980s, of a book collection formula for the libraries in the Bell & Howell Education Group, seven proprietary, postsecondary technical institutes throughout the United States. Based on a faculty questionnaire and the holdings of the Ohio Institute of Technology in Columbus, a committee recommended a minimum total collection of 2,000 books, subdivided with minimum figures for 10 subject categories, such as 200 books for mathematics, etc. In an interesting tactic, a "copyright age limit," ranging from five to fifteen years, was imposed for each category, so that none of the books used to meet the minimum figure could be older than the limit. The complete committee recommendations are exhibited. Although this standard applies to only seven libraries, almost nothing else has been published concerning collections in this type of library. (See also Roeder entry 64.)

243. Carpenter, Raymond L. "College Libraries: A Comparative Analysis in Terms of the ACRL Standards." **College & Research Libraries** 42 (January 1981): 7-18.

HEGIS data for 1977 from 1,100 colleges and universities were used to determine how well the 1975 ACRL "Standards for College Libraries" were being fulfilled in the areas of collections, staff, budget, and service. The section concerning collections contains tables tabulating collective data on book collection size, volumes per faculty, volumes per student, number of periodical subscriptions, volumes added per year, and percentage growth rate for four categories of colleges (public undergraduate and graduate; private undergraduate and graduate). The section also constructs a hypothetical model of book collection size (123,100 volumes), since HEGIS does not provide enough data to calculate required size on a college-by-college basis. It was found that the mean and median collection size for both private and public undergraduate institutions fall below this hypothetical minimum requirement. Also, the median figure for books added per year is below 5 percent of collection size as stipulated in this standard. An inverse relationship was found between student body size and volumes per capita, but a strong positive relationship exists between staff and collection size.

244. Carpenter, Raymond L. "Two-Year College Libraries: A Comparative Analysis in Terms of the ACRL Standards." **College & Research Libraries** 42 (September 1981): 407-15.

Applying the approach in entry 243 to two-year college libraries, 1977 HEGIS data from 1,146 two-year colleges, representing 95 percent of the U.S. total, were compared to the 1979 ACRL quantitative standards for staff, collections, budget, and service. Tables arranged by institutional size and affiliation (public or private) display the percentage of colleges that had obtained the "minimum" and "good" standards for periodicals, books, and audiovisuals. The majority of colleges were below minimum in all these categories, but generally came closest to the standard for audiovisuals, followed by books, then periodicals. Finally, 41 percent of private colleges and 69 percent of public ones met the standard of annually adding 5 percent of their total book holdings.

245. Clapp, Verner W., and Robert T. Jordan. "Quantitative Criteria for Adequacy of Academic Library Collections." **College & Research Libraries** 26 (September 1965): 371-80. Reprinted in **College & Research Libraries** 50 (March 1989): 154-63.

Having been chosen a *College & Research Libraries* "Classic Reprint" to appear in the journal's fiftieth anniversary volume is sufficient to prove this article's enduring value. In it the authors propose the "Clapp-Jordan Formula," undoubtedly the most influential and perhaps most controversial formula in the history of academic librarianship. Challenging the viewpoint that quantitative measures cannot measure adequacy, the authors propose that the minimum required holdings for an academic library can be calculated by adding to 50,750 (for the undergraduate collection): 100 volumes for each FTE faculty member; 12 volumes for each FTE student; 12 volumes for each undergraduate in honors or independent study; 345 volumes for each undergraduate "major" subject field; 3,050 volumes for each master's degree offered; and 24,500 volumes for each doctoral degree offered.

The number of volumes contained in four standard lists of books for college libraries published between 1931 and 1965 (the Shaw, Lamont, Michigan, and California lists) are cited to justify the 50,750 volumes required for a basic undergraduate collection. Finally, tables illustrate the Clapp-Jordan Formula's application to the collections at Oberlin, Swarthmore, Antioch, Illinois, Michigan, UCLA, and two junior colleges, in addition to numerous unnamed institutions. The Clapp-Jordan Formula has been used, misused, and modified many times, but the original article remains indispensable for interested librarians.

92 / STANDARDS

246. Faulkner, Ronnie W. "West Virginia Public Colleges and the Latest ACRL Standards." **West Virginia Libraries** 39 (Summer 1986): 30-34.

Faulkner's short piece applies the 1986 ACRL College Library Standards' (entry 231) staffing and collection-size formulas to the eight public colleges in West Virginia plus Marshall University (to which the standards also apply). Collectively the 9 institutions held 101.8 percent of the 1,762,044 volumes required by the collection formula. Eight received a grade of "A" for collection size, while one received a "C." A table lists the volumes held, volumes required, fulfillment rate, and grade for the nine institutions. The work is modeled after White's application of the same standards to the University of California system (entry 253), although White offers more detail in illustrating how the required-volume figures for each institution were derived.

247. Ifidon, Sam E. "Establishment of Standards for Bookstock in West African University Libraries." **Libri** 33 (June 1983): 92-106; **African Journal of Academic Librarianship** 2 (December 1984): 54-60.

The article's text in the two journals is identical. After reviewing university library collection standards in the western democracies as well as tentative efforts towards standards in Nigeria that "produced little results," ten factors that influence collection size are discussed:

1. Student body size

2. Faculty size

3. Library staff size

4. The curriculum

5. Instruction methods

6. Proximity of other libraries

7. Bookshop services

8. Annual acquisitions rate

9. Financial support

10. Library organization.

A proposed quantitative collection standard for West African universities, based on data from 26 universities in the region, calls for a basic collection of 50,000 plus 30 books per reader, and relates the weight for a curricular program to its duration. Ifidon's proposed standard is unique in that a maximum rather than a minimum figure is derived. This article will be of most use to individuals interested in standards from a theoretical perspective.

248. Kaser, David. "Standards for College Libraries." **Library Trends** 31 (Summer 1982): 7-19.

The author begins with a brief historical survey of college library standards since the 1920s, followed by a discussion of the quantitative-versus-qualitative issue. The primary focus falls on the 1975 ACRL "Standards for College Libraries," as the author traces their history from 1972. Seven specific ways in which the 1975 standards differ from those of 1959 are listed, e.g., legal ownership of material provided to students is no longer required and a library can assume a "no-growth" posture once the required number of volumes has been obtained. Developments subsequent to adoption of the 1975 standards, including impact, acceptance level, misunderstandings, future prospects, and the 1979 "An Evaluative Checklist for Reviewing a College Library Program," are also discussed. This item is especially authoritative and insightful because Kaser is the individual primarily responsible for writing the 1975 standards.

249. Lynch, Beverly P. "University Library Standards." **Library Trends** 31 (Summer 1982): 33-47.

The twelve-year history of the 1979 ACRL and ARL "Standards for University Libraries" is reviewed. The Downs and Smith Committees, instrumental in the standards' development, are discussed at considerable length. Lynch explains that the Carnegie Commission classification was used to define a "university library," while qualitative principles rather than quantifiable measures were developed. A major portion of this item analyzes an October 1981 survey responded to by eighty-eight ARL library directors concerning the standards' usefulness. It was found that 54 percent "did not use the standards at all." A two-page table displays the survey results.

The author concludes that the standards provide a "framework" or "outline" for evaluation, but no "bench marks." Thus, "the standards are much less useful as a tool for evaluation than are the standards developed for other types of academic libraries."

250. Stubbs, Kendon. "University Libraries: Standards and Statistics." **College & Research Libraries** 42 (November 1981): 527-38.

In light of the fact that the 1979 university library standards avoided any quantitative formulas, Stubbs applied sophisticated statistical analysis to 1978-1979 data for 196 U.S. and Canadian libraries at Ph.D.-granting universities, to derive characteristic data that describe university libraries. An extremely interesting feature is a table that names and ranks the 196 libraries according to a Principal Component Score, derived from ten variables: volumes held, volumes added, microforms, current serials, expenditures for materials and binding, salaries, other operating expenses, and staff (professional and nonprofessional). Empirical criteria characteristic of university libraries in 1978 and 1979 that "represent the lowest permissible standard thresholds" have been calculated, such as 600,000 volumes held, 24,000 volumes added per year, and 6,000 serial subscriptions. The author stresses "these are not standards in the sense of goals that most libraries should strive to achieve," as 75 percent of university libraries had already surpassed these levels.

94 / STANDARDS

251. Voigt, Melvin J. "Acquisition Rates in University Libraries." **College & Research Libraries** 36 (July 1975): 263-71.

Voigt proposes a formula (he uses the term *model*) for determining how many current book and journal volumes a large university library supporting many Ph.D. programs should acquire in a year. Beginning with a base acquisitions rate of 40,000, one adds additional volumes in increments of 1,000 for specific graduate or professional programs, the number of undergraduate students, sponsored research on campus, and lack of access to other research libraries. For example, 1,000 volumes are added for a library science program; 1,000 volumes for every 2,000 undergraduate students over 5,000; 1,000 volumes for every $15 million in sponsored research at the university; and 10,000 volumes if the nearest major research library is one to two hours away in travel time. The model's application to the University of California, San Diego, and three other unnamed institutions is illustrated in a table.

Voigt's numbers may seem unduly high from the perspective of the 1990s, but his formula is worth noting because it complements the better-known Clapp-Jordan Formula that addresses total size of the collection. Also, unlike most standards' authors, Voigt analyzes growth rate in terms of fundamental factors rather than as a percentage of total holdings.

252. Wallace, James O. "Two-Year College Learning Resources Standards." **Library Trends** 31 (Summer 1982): 21-31.

This essay focuses on developments regarding two-year college library standards from 1972 to 1981. Wallace states that the 1972 "Guidelines for Two-Year College Learning Resources Programs," based strictly on qualitative standards, have "received general acceptance." Research pertaining to their use is reviewed. The author chaired the ACRL ad hoc subcommittee that drafted the supplementary quantitative standards published in 1979. Innovative concepts in the quantitative 1979 standard are discussed, including five levels against which a library can evaluate itself and the consideration of all resources on campus when calculating collection size. It is noted that the 1972 guidelines and 1979 quantitative statement were reaffirmed, with some revisions, by the ACRL in 1981.

253. White, Phillip M. "College Library Formulas Applied." **College & Research Libraries News** 47 (March 1986): 202-7.

Formulas A (for total collection size) and B (for staff size) from the 1986 ACRL "Standards for College Libraries" (entry 231) are applied to the nineteen California State University System libraries. A table names the universities and mathematically depicts how the ratings were derived. It is noteworthy that 89 percent (17 of 19) received an A for collection size, while all 19 received an A for volumes added per year. Collectively the nineteen libraries required 10,714,655 volumes, but actually held 13,193,420 volumes, for a 123 percent fulfillment rate. While representing a significant investigation in its own right, this item would also be particularly useful for anyone wishing to see a graphic illustration of how formulas are applied.

NOTES

[1] Signe Ottersen, "A Bibliography on Standards for Evaluating Libraries," *College & Research Libraries* 32 (March 1971): 127-44.

[2] Naimuddin Qureshi, "Standards for Libraries," in *Encyclopedia of Library and Information Science*, vol. 28, ed. Allen Kent, Harold Lancour, and Jay E. Daily (New York: Marcel Dekker, 1980), 473.

[3] American Library Association, Committee on Classification of Library Personnel, *Budgets, Classification and Compensation Plans for University and College Libraries* (Chicago: American Library Association, 1929).

[4] James O. Wallace, "Two-Year College Library Standards," *Library Trends* 21 (October 1972): 221-22.

[5] Association of College and Research Libraries, Committee on Standards, "Standards for Junior College Libraries," *College & Research Libraries* 21 (May 1960): 200-206.

[6] American Library Association, American Association of Community and Junior Colleges, and Association for Educational Communications and Technology, "Guidelines for Two-Year College Learning Resources Programs," *College & Research Libraries News* 33 (December 1972): 305-15.

[7] Ad Hoc Subcommittee to Develop Quantitative Standards for the "Guidelines for Two-Year College Learning Resources Programs," "Draft: Statement on Quantitative Standards for Two-Year Learning Resources Programs," *College & Research Libraries News* 40 (March 1979): 69-73. The final version was issued separately by the ACRL, but never appeared in *College & Research Libraries News*.

[8] David Kaser, "Standards for College Libraries," *Library Trends* 31 (Summer 1982): 8; Helen M. Brown, "College Library Standards," *Library Trends* 21 (October 1972): 204-6.

[9] Kaser, "Standards for College Libraries," cites Carl H. Milam, "Suggestions for Minimum College Library Standards," *ALA College & Reference Library Yearbook* 2 (1930): 90-92.

[10] Kaser, "Standards for College Libraries," cites William M. Randall, *The College Library* (Chicago: University of Chicago Press, 1932).

96 / STANDARDS

[11] Kaser, "Standards for College Libraries,' cites American Library Association, Salaries, Staff and Tenure Board, Subcommittee on Budgets, Compensation, and Schemes of Service, *Classification and Pay Plans for Libraries in Institutions of Higher Education, Vol. 2: Degree-Conferring Four-Year Institutions* (Chicago: American Library Association, 1943).

[12] Association of College and Research Libraries, Committee on Standards, "Standards for College Libraries," *College & Research Libraries* 20 (July 1959): 274-80.

[13] Association of College and Research Libraries, "Standards for College Libraries," *College & Research Libraries News* 36 (October 1975): 277-79, 290-95.

[14] Association of Research Libraries and Association of College and Research Libraries, "Standards for University Libraries," *College & Research Libraries News* 40 (April 1979): 101-10.

8

Citation Studies

The use of statistical data to analyze patterns of book production and scholarly communication is termed *bibliometrics*. The dominant branch of bibliometrics has been citation studies, an analysis of references in and citations to documents such as books and articles. Citation studies have been used for innumerable purposes. To name only the most obvious, they include:

1. Identifying the most productive authors, departments, universities, and nations

2. Identifying a core literature

3. Analyzing a discipline's structure in terms of format, language, and age

4. Depicting research fronts

5. Evaluating funded versus nonfunded research.

Robert Broadus considers the counting of scrolls held by the ancient library of Alexandria in the third century B.C. to be the forerunner of modern bibliometrics.[1] A count of publications in comparative anatomy between 1543 and 1860, published by F. J. Cole and Nellie B. Eales[2] in *Science Progress* in 1917, is often identified as the first bibliometric study. The term *statistical bibliography* was applied to this area in 1923 by E. W. Hulme[3] and used until Alan Pritchard[4] introduced the term *bibliometrics* in 1969.[5]

Charles Coffin Jewett's 1848 Smithsonian annual report, discussed in the introduction to chapter 3, was identified by Broadus as the "first organized citation study."[6] Others credit Gross and Gross's landmark analysis of chemistry journals in 1927 as the first citation study.[7] A major impetus was provided by the founding of the *Science Citation Index* in 1961, the *Social Science Citation Index* in 1973, and the *Arts & Humanities Citation Index* in 1978 by Eugene Garfield's Institute for Scientific Information.[8]

Citation analysis is based on the assumption that documents cited by a researcher have been used in the research process. Consequently, this approach helps clarify both the information needs of researchers and what should be contained in a research library collection. Major uses of citation analysis pertinent to collection evaluation include identifying the core collection, using citations as a checklist, ranking journals, and analyzing a discipline's structure to assist collection management decision making.

A number of limitations to citation studies must be acknowledged. A citation may be negative, with the author cited as an incompetent or the methodology as an example of the way not to do it—although research tells us this seldom occurs. When evaluating journals, numerous factors other than scholarly merit can result in high citation counts, including the journal's circulation, the reputation of its authors, its cost, the journal's availability in library collections, the availability of indexing, the controversiality of its subject matter, and national research priorities.[9] Other criticisms of the application of citation analysis to collection development include:

1. It indicates the obvious

2. It is not clear what the act of citation means

3. It tabulates what is easy to count rather than what is significant.

A technical distinction is sometimes made between a reference study, which analyzes the bibliographic items cited by an author, and a citation study, which considers every single footnote. If a work was cited five times in a source article, it would be counted once in a reference study but five times in a citation study. Alternately, an item cited in an article is often termed a *reference*, while an item citing an article is called a *citation*. Investigators have been inconsistent in the use of these terms and in how they count citations or references. In this bibliography, the term *citation* is generally used for either a citation or a reference contained within an article or book, unless the author of the annotated item has explicitly used the term *reference*. Most studies for collection development purposes (and hence the ones contained in this bibliography) are concerned with what books or articles cite rather than what cites them.

The preceding discussion is not intended to serve as a comprehensive summary of citation analysis. Rather, the purpose is to provide background information that facilitates understanding of this chapter's entries. It should be understood that this bibliography contains only that fraction of the vast citation analysis literature which is most relevant to academic library collection evaluation. This chapter is organized into three sections: general and miscellaneous discussions of citation analysis, case studies that used citation analysis for collection evaluation, and the structure of disciplines and subjects (specific topics within a subject area generally have not been included). The reader is also referred to chapter 11, which contains many entries concerning the use of citation analysis for journal ranking.

GENERAL AND MISCELLANEOUS

254. Adewole, Segun. "Selecting Livestock Periodicals through Citation Analysis Technique." **Information Processing & Management** 23, no. 6 (1987): 629-38.

Adewole's objective is to apply citation analysis to the journal literature of livestock science. Citations during the years 1980 through 1983 in the 125 periodicals on the National Animal Production Research Institute's (in Nigeria) 1983 subscription list to the same set of journals form the basis of this study. One hundred fourteen journals, rank-order listed in a long table, received more than 34,000 citations. Applying Bradford's law, the leading eighteen journals, representing 32.3 percent of the total citations, are considered the core. The study concludes that "citation study is a useful means of measuring the use of materials and of utilizing scarce resources."

255. Aina, L. O. "The Use of Government Documents by Researchers in Agricultural Economics and Agricultural Extension in Nigeria: A Research Note." **Government Publications Review** 15 (January/February 1988): 61-64.

A citation analysis was based on fifty-six source articles dealing with agricultural economics and agricultural extension in the 1974 through 1977 volumes of the *Nigerian Agricultural Journal*, the *Journal of Rural Economics & Development*, and *Agricultural Administration*. Nearly 30 percent of the 640 total citations were journals; nearly 20 percent books; and about 18 percent government documents. The government document citations (70 percent of which were technical reports) were approximately equally divided among international agencies, including foreign governments (37.6 percent); Nigerian state governments (35 percent); and the Nigerian federal government (27.4 percent).

256. Bobick, James E. "Citation Data for Selected Journals in Reproductive Biology." **Fertility & Sterility** 35 (February 1981): 126-30.

This study, commissioned by the editor of *Fertility & Sterility*, supplies citation data from the *JCR* for a dozen journals in the areas of obstetrics and gynecology, andrology, and reproductive biology, as well as for two general medical journals. Total citations, impact factor, and immediacy index plus overall ranking by these three measures are presented for the fourteen journals for each year between 1974 and 1979. Although not an outstanding article, this is the only identified item concerning journal evaluation in reproductive biology.

257. Bowman, Michael. "Format Citation Patterns and Their Implications for Collection Development in Research Libraries." **Collection Building** 11, no. 1 (1991): 2-8.

This article is built around a long, three-page table that summarizes the format patterns revealed by citation studies in thirty-four disciplines. Grouping the studies by discipline, the table indicates the source citations' timeframe and sample size before revealing the percentage distribution for books, journals, conference proceedings, government documents, theses, and reference works.

Over 100 cases are reported, some dating as far back as the late nineteenth century and many from hard-to-locate master's theses and Ph.D. dissertations. Bowman correctly believes that his literature search can serve as a guide to research librarians evaluating their acquisitions budget breakdown. In some disciplines the varying results between reported studies were surprising, but the author attributes this to changing patterns over time and the small sample size for some cases.

258. Broadus, Robert N. "On Citations, Uses, and Informed Guesswork: A Response to Line." **College & Research Libraries** 46 (January 1985): 38-39.

In this short piece, Broadus responds to Line's commentary (entry 269) on his prior work (entry 259). Broadus reiterates his contention that utilizing the *SSCI Journal Citation Reports* to identify little-cited periodicals that are candidates for cancellation is less expensive and nearly as effective as a formal use study. Citation analysis could simplify procedural difficulties with Line's proposal for faculty review by reducing the number of titles to be examined.

259. Broadus, Robert N. "A Proposed Method for Eliminating Titles from Periodical Subscription Lists." **College & Research Libraries** 46 (January 1985): 30-35.

Broadus cogently advocates use of the *SCI* and *SSCI Journal Citation Reports* to identify periodicals with low citation counts as candidates for cancellation. After analyzing previous research comparing the results of journal usage and citation studies, the author concludes that *JCR* citation count data is "almost as good" as local use studies in predicting use. He proposes that a library compare its current periodicals list with the *JCR* and examine the 20 percent receiving the fewest citations. However, it is emphasized that a little-cited periodical might be retained for a variety of reasons, including heavy local use, a low price, value for purposes other than research, political considerations, or the fact that it is a young journal (which has not had time to be cited). Broadus stresses that using this method is much more economical than conducting an "expensive" local use study. (For Line's commentary, see entry 269.)

260. Budd, John. "A Citation Study of American Literature: Implications for Collection Management." **Collection Management** 8 (Summer 1986): 49-62.

Based on analysis of the same data used in his 1986 *Library & Information Science Research* article (entry 297), Budd asserts, "The use of citation studies in the practice of collection management in the humanities is still something of a question mark." Budd concludes that references to books are very "diffuse," as 4,573 citations refer to 3,850 titles. A total of 497 journals were cited, with the top 30 (listed in a table) accounting for 38.6 percent of the periodical citations. The author divided the journal citations into Bradfordian zones. The most frequently cited primary monographs and secondary monographs are identified and compared with standard lists and other citation studies.

Budd stresses that "small clusters of frequently-cited materials" were identified, but that the citation analysis was less successful in dealing with "fringe" areas.

261. Crissinger, John D. "The Use of Journal Citations in Theses as a Collection Development Methodology." In **Keeping Current with Geoscience Information: Proceedings of the Fifteenth Meeting of the Geoscience Information Society, November 16-20, 1980**, edited by Nancy Jones Pruett, 113-24. N.p.: Geoscience Information Society, 1981. 214p. (Proceedings of the Geoscience Information Society, vol. 11).

This paper's objective "is to determine the value of citation analysis in theses as a journal collection development methodology." The journal citations (3,562 out of 6,443 total) in eighty-one master's theses and twenty-one doctoral theses completed at Virginia Tech's geology department between 1970 and 1979 were analyzed. The author asserts that local publications, popular journals, and newspapers were seldom cited, in contrast to abstracts, which were heavily cited. Three tables list the leading twenty-five journals cited in M.S. theses, Ph.D. dissertations, and overall. The top twenty-five overall accounted for 67 percent of the journal citations and 37 percent of all citations.

Although he admits that the results "are what basically would be expected," the author feels this approach is worth pursuing by other libraries because of eleven "unexpected conclusions," such as better knowledge of local research. These conclusions are enumerated in a summary section.

262. Devin, Robin B. "Who's Using What?" **Library Acquisitions: Practice & Theory** 13, no. 2 (1989): 167-70.

Speaking at the 1988 Charleston Conference (an annual meeting on library acquisitions), Devin asks what is the appropriate percentage of a materials budget to expend on serials. Stating that no standard or formula addresses the question, she argues that citation analysis can offer a "guideline." A table summarizes the proportion of citations to serials in twenty-four citation studies, published between 1931 and 1980, from all major branches of knowledge. The author advocates that libraries use this data "to determine whether their serial/monographic [expenditure] ratios are in-line." This item appears to be a preliminary version of the study by Devin and Kellogg (entry 263).

263. Devin, Robin B., and Martha Kellogg. "The Serial/Monograph Ratio in Research Libraries: Budgeting in Light of Citation Studies." **College & Research Libraries** 51 (January 1990): 46-54.

After discussing the impact of escalating serials cost on research libraries, the authors advocate that research librarians consult citation studies to provide guidance in allocating their materials budgets between monographs and serials. For instance, for a particular subject, the percentage of citations to serials and the proportion of the budget devoted to serials should be approximately equal. A table exhibits the percentage of citations to serials in sixty-six reported cases (including theses and dissertations), dating back to 1931, for forty-one disciplines, subdisciplines, or broad subject areas. Unlike the Bowman article (entry 257), which observed discrepancies in the data among different studies of the same discipline, Devin and Kellogg assert, "One of the most striking results of these various studies is the consistency of the data they provide."

264. Fuseler-McDowell, Elizabeth. "Collection Evaluation and Development Using Citation Analysis Techniques." In **IAMSLIC at a Crossroads; Proceedings of the 15th Annual Conference**, edited by Robert W. Burkhart and Joyce C. Burkhart, 99-108. N.p.: International Association of Marine Science Libraries and Information Centers, 1990. 200p. (International Association of Marine Science Libraries and Information Centers Conference Series). LC 90-81226. ISBN 0-932939-07-4.

This generally useful piece provides an overview of how citation analysis can be used in collection evaluation and collection management. Most of the article is devoted to a worthwhile literature review. An especially handy feature is a two-page table that succinctly compares fourteen previously reported citation studies (e.g., the Lopez method) in terms of such factors as the data source, method of analysis, and uses for the findings. Fuseler-McDowell concludes by suggesting that librarians wishing to utilize citation analysis begin by selecting a single locally relevant journal and using the *JCR* to create a "collection linkage map" to show how it is related to other journals. A figure illustrates such a map, but the mechanics of creating it or its potential uses are not explained.

265. Griscom, Richard. "Periodical Use in a University Music Library: A Citation Study of Theses and Dissertations Submitted to the Indiana University School of Music from 1975-1980." **Serials Librarian** 7 (Spring 1983): 35-52.

Sixty-seven theses and dissertations, containing 3,789 citations, were used to analyze periodical use in music research at Indiana University. Exactly 58 percent of these citations were to books, compared with 29.8 percent to periodicals. Two hundred fifty-six periodical titles were cited, but only seventy-nine (about 30 percent) were cited more than once. A figure illustrates the citation pattern by date for the fifty most cited journals (53.5 percent were dated between 1965 and 1978) and a table names, in rank order, the fifty most cited journals. Corresponding figures and tables are presented for the areas of music education, musicology, and music theory. The author believes that his finding—that music researchers use only a small number of journals that become obsolete with age—would apply to other institutions.

266. Gross, P. L. K., and E. M. Gross. "College Libraries and Chemical Education." **Science** 66 (October 28, 1927): 385-89.

The first recorded use of citation analysis for journal evaluation dates to this now-classic article. To help determine which chemistry periodicals "are needed in a college library," Gross and Gross, chemistry professors at Pomona College, tabulated 3,633 citations from the 1926 volume of the *Journal of the American Chemical Society*. A table lists the top twenty-eight journals, based on gross citations, while also indicating distribution by date. Seven of the 247 cited journals received more than 15 references, but 99 were cited only once. A language breakdown for the non-U.S. publications shows that a majority of citations were in German (52.5 percent), followed by 35.2 percent in English.

267. Hanson, David J. "Core Literature of the Two Social Psychologies." **Psychological Reports** 63 (August 1988): 225-26.

The core literatures of psychologically oriented social psychology and sociologically oriented social psychology were identified through items cited in common in five textbooks in the former (59 or 7,164 for 0.8 percent) and three textbooks in the latter (9 of 2,502 for 0.4 percent). Comparison of the two core literatures revealed the sociologically oriented social psychology core is smaller, older, more oriented toward monographs, and more likely to cite its own subarea.

268. Hardesty, Larry, and Gail Oltmanns. "How Many Psychology Journals Are Enough? A Study of the Use of Psychology Journals by Undergraduates." **Serials Librarian** 16, nos. 1/2 (1989): 133-53.

The journals cited in the 105 senior psychology theses written at Indiana University and DePauw University, a liberal arts college, between 1974 and 1980 were analyzed to identify a core of psychology periodicals. Because the rankings at the two schools differed, "[a] readily identifiable core list of journals heavily cited by psychology students at both institutions does not emerge from this study." Two separate three-page tables rank-order the thirty-eight journals cited three or more times by Indiana University students and the forty-two cited at least three times at DePauw. Bradford's law applied at both institutions, as about twenty periodicals accounted for approximately 80 percent of the citations.

Roughly a third of the article is devoted to an extensive review of an ongoing controversy in the *American Psychologist* concerning the validity of citation analysis for ranking psychology journals. This well-done study would be of value to anyone interested in the core concept or psychology periodicals.

269. Line, Maurice B. "Use of Citation Data for Periodicals Control in Libraries: A Response to Broadus." **College & Research Libraries** 46 (January 1985): 36-37.

Line disputes Broadus's contention concerning the utility of *SSCI Journal Citation Reports* citation count rankings for periodical collection management decisions. (See Broadus entry 259.) Noting instability in journal rankings at the BLLD, Line argues that the observed correlation between local journal usage and citation count data applies mainly to core journals. However, most periodical addition and cancellation decisions involve "titles at the fringe of use" where the chance of receiving a few citations can "dramatically" affect rankings. Line asserts that "librarians may as well rely on what their users say they want."

270. Magrill, Rose Mary, and Gloriana St. Clair. "Undergraduate Term Paper Citation Patterns by Disciplines and Level of Course." **Collection Management** 12, nos. 3/4 (1990): 25-56.

The citations in 1,775 undergraduate term papers from 13 departments at East Texas Baptist University, Oregon State University, Texas A & M, and Westmar College (a liberal arts college in LeMars, Iowa) were analyzed by format, age, discipline, number of citations, and student grade level for this long, detailed, sophisticated study. Composite data is presented by broad subject category. Separate sections analyze six disciplines in detail: biology, English, history, philosophy, religion, and sociology.

The finding that the humanities use the largest proportion of books (68 percent), followed by the social sciences (57 percent) and the sciences (21 percent), confirms other citation studies. However, the common assertion that English and history use more library resources than the sciences was not supported. Undergraduates were generally found to cite a larger proportion of books than advanced-level researchers. This unique application of citation analysis to the undergraduate

104 / CITATION STUDIES

level has important implications for college library collection development. (See also St. Clair and Magrill entry 276.)

271. McCain, Katherine W., and James E. Bobick. "Patterns of Journal Use in a Departmental Library: A Citation Analysis." **Journal of the American Society for Information Science** 32 (July 1981): 257-67.

The 3,739 citations to 336 journals cited in faculty publications, doctoral dissertations, and qualifying papers by students entering the Ph.D. program at Temple University's Biology Department from 1975 to 1977 were exhaustively analyzed in this rigorous paper. The citation patterns for the three user groups are analyzed separately, with composite data also presented. In a Bradfordian distribution, sixty titles (18 percent) accounted for 80 percent of the total citations. These sixty titles are rank-ordered in a table, while another table presents citations to these titles by date. Because 80 percent of the citations were to volumes published after 1960, for fifty-one of the top sixty journals, 1960 was established as a new cutoff date for back journal holdings in the biology library. The findings are compared with those of earlier studies.

272. McGinty, Stephen. "Political Science Publishers: What Do the Citations Reveal?" **Collection Management** 11, nos. 3/4 (1989): 93-101.

This interesting investigation is based on the 7,166 citations to monographs in the *American Political Science Review* and the *Journal of Politics* from 1974 to 1975 and from 1984 to 1985. An examination of the two tables that list, in rank order, the top twenty-five publishers by total citations in 1974-1975 and 1984-1985 reveals "a strong degree of volatility" as seventeen publishers changed position by three or more places during the decade. Additional findings indicated the following: 1) foreign language citations accounted for 4.6 percent of the total in 1974-1975 and 5.1 percent in 1984-1985; 2) "nontraditional" channels, that is, conference proceedings and papers, increased from 2.3 percent in 1974-1975 to 7.3 percent in 1984-1985; 3) G.P.O. publications declined from 4.5 to 2.7 percent; and 4) the share of total citations received by the top twenty-five publishers increased from 53.8 percent to 69.2 percent. In contrast to the extensive literature concerning journal ranking, this is one of only a few studies that ranks monographic publishers.

273. Metz, Paul. "Bibliometrics: Library Use and Citation Studies." In **Academic Libraries: Research Perspectives**, edited by Mary Jo Lynch and Arthur P. Young, 143-64. Chicago: American Library Association, 1990. 271p. (ACRL Publications in Librarianship, no. 47). LC 90-32120. ISBN 0-8389-0532-3.

Metz provides an exceptionally good survey of the significant citation, circulation, and in-house use studies of the last half century while also clarifying major issues. The highlighted topics include obsolescence, concentration and scattering, Bradford's law, the Pittsburgh Study, factors predicting usage, and relationships among disciplines.

The author concludes with five specific recommendations for future research: 1) previously ignored data should be exploited; 2) one-time studies should be supplemented by ongoing analysis; 3) more citation studies at the disciplinary and interdisciplinary level should be done; 4) studies should be brought closer to the user; and 5) greater exploitation of electronic media should be attempted.

274. Neeley, James D., Jr. "The Management and Social Science Literatures: An Interdisciplinary Cross-Citation Analysis." **Journal of the American Society for Information Science** 32 (May 1981): 217-23.

Neeley's sophisticated analysis of interdisciplinarity between management and the social science disciplines is based on the cross-citations patterns among nineteen core journals, identified by citations and expert subjective evaluation, in management, economics, psychology, sociology, and political science. Data were gathered from *SSCI* tapes covering 1976 and 1977. The author distinguishes between "dependent interdisciplinarity," in which one discipline uses another's journals, and "general interdisciplinarity," in which two disciplines use the same journals regardless of which discipline the journals actually belong to.

Several hypotheses were tested. The major findings were that management core journals cite the social sciences more than the social sciences core journals cite management or each other. For example, about 25 percent of the management citations were to economics, psychology, or sociology journals. Several tables exhibit the cross-citation data. Neeley quite correctly observes that his findings have implications for library collection management.

275. Smith, Thomas E. "The **Journal Citation Reports** as a Deselection Tool." **Bulletin of the Medical Library Association** 73 (October 1985): 387-89.

This "brief communication" advocates use of the *SCI Journal Citation Reports* for serials deselection decisions, while also explaining how the tool works. Smith believes the *JCR* should be used for the final decision after other methods have identified prospective candidates for deselection. He describes how to locate in the Journal Ranking Package (a part of the *JCR*) the impact factor as well as the characteristics of other journals a title cites and is cited by. The author feels "it is probably sound" to cancel titles that do not rank in the top 60 to 80 percent of their subject area by impact factor.

After a preliminary test in the George Washington University Health Sciences Library, the *JCR* was deemed "a helpful objective tool." This useful introduction to the *JCR* would also benefit specialists in nonmedical subject areas.

276. St. Clair, Gloriana, and Rose Mary Magrill. "Undergraduate Term Paper Citations." **College & Research Libraries News** 51 (January 1990): 25-28.

Based on the same research project reported by these authors in the 1990 *Collection Management* (see entry 270), this paper compares the term-paper citation patterns of undergraduate students at liberal arts colleges (using 614 papers from East Texas Baptist University and Westmar College) with those at universities (analyzing 1,161 papers from Oregon State University and Texas A & M). The major findings were that liberal arts college students cite "slightly older books," "slightly newer journal articles," and fewer sources (5.6 compared to 8.5) than do university students. Detailed comparisons between liberal arts and university undergraduate citations are also made for junior-level business and freshman-level religion and sociology courses.

The authors express a wish that their study be replicated in other types of institutions. Readers who found the authors' other article useful will also wish to consult this shorter companion piece.

277. Subramanyam, Kris. "Citation Studies in Science and Technology." In **Collection Development in Libraries: A Treatise**, pt. B, edited by Robert D. Stueart and George B. Miller, Jr., 345-72. Greenwich, Conn.: JAI Press, 1980. (Foundations in Library and Information Science, vol. 10). LC 79-93165. ISBN 0-89232-162-8 (pt B).

An excellent introductory overview of citation analysis, with special emphasis on science and technology, is offered here. Following an informative historical sketch, the basic principles, methods, assumptions, and limitations of citation analysis are reviewed, as are recent developments. Finally, the application of citation studies to collection development, including serials selection, determination of core book collections, and obsolescence studies, is discussed. A notable feature, although now dated, is a ranked list of sixty-five core computer science journals, based on citations in the 1970 and 1971 *IEEE Transactions on Computers*. Many previous citation studies pertinent to science are briefly summarized and approximately 100 items are cited altogether. The author concludes, "Like any other evaluation tool, citation frequency should not be used in isolation."

CASE STUDIES USING CITATION ANALYSIS FOR COLLECTION EVALUATION

278. Basak, Nanda Dulal, and Binod Bihari Das. "Organization of Periodicals Collection Based on Citation Analysis." **Indian Library Association Bulletin** 21 (April 1985): 1-13.

A citation analysis evaluation of the statistics periodical collection at the Indian Statistical Institute Library is discussed by Basak and Das. The holdings were checked against the most frequently listed titles in the 1984 *Statistical Theory & Methods Abstract* (technically not a citation method) as well as the journals most cited in the 1984 volumes of *Biometrika* and the *Journal of the American Statistical Association*. Separate tables list, in rank order, the fifty most frequently cited titles from these three sources. Further analysis of citation dates indicated that to achieve 80 percent coverage, twenty years of back volumes should be retained.

279. Bland, Robert N. "The College Textbook as a Tool for Collection Evaluation, Analysis and Retrospective Collection Development." **Library Acquisitions: Practice & Theory** 4, nos. 3/4 (1980): 193-97.

Checking textbook citations against library holdings is advocated as a collection evaluation method for small- and medium-sized college libraries. The author argues that if locally used textbooks are selected, relevance to local teaching needs may be presumed. The study is based on twenty-five textbooks (named in an appendix) used at Western Carolina University, equally divided among mathematics, philosophy, physics, psychology, and sociology. Bland believes that an average of 472 citations per text answers the criticism that textbooks contain few citations, while the fact that only 32 percent of a 250-citation sample was found in *Books for College Libraries* refutes the contention that the method would merely duplicate items on a standard list. The sample was also checked against the library holdings.

Bland's work is significant for demonstrating the applicability of citation analysis to entities other than large research libraries. (See also Stelk and Lancaster entry 293.)

280. Buzzard, Marion L., and Doris E. New. "An Investigation of Collection Support for Doctoral Research." **College & Research Libraries** 44 (November 1983): 469-75.

To evaluate support for doctoral research, the citations in twelve recent, randomly selected dissertations in the sciences, social sciences, and humanities were checked against the holdings of the University of California, Irvine Library. The hypothesis that the collection would contain 90 percent of the material was verified for the entire list of 1,384 citations. Based on further statistical analysis, the authors assert the 90 percent hypothesis was confirmed for the humanities and social sciences, but not the sciences. A table indicates the checklist results for the twelve dissertations, with separate data for monographs and serials.

This investigation in notable because, as mentioned by the authors, the citation approach is applied exclusively to Ph.D.-level research. Buzzard and New conclude that citation analysis is "a valuable tool for evaluating collection support for doctoral research" and can be used in all disciplines.

281. Currie, William W. "Evaluating the Collection of a Two-Year Branch Campus by Using Textbook Citations." **Community & Junior College Libraries** 6, no. 2 (1989): 75-79.

Currie's case study at Firelands College, a two-year branch of Bowling Green State University, is one of only a few studies to address collection evaluation in this type of library. For every course at Firelands College, a textbook was randomly chosen in the bookstore. Eighty citations from each textbook (or all the citations for those with less than eighty) were then checked against the holdings of both Firelands College and Bowling Green State University, using target figures of 30 percent and 75 percent respectively. This approach is called a "cost-effective" way to evaluate the collection's quality.

282. Dombrowski, Theresa. "Journal Evaluation Using **Journal Citation Reports** as a Collection Development Tool." **Collection Management** 10, nos. 3/4 (1988): 175-80.

Inspired by Thomas Smith's paper in the 1985 *Bulletin of the Medical Library Association* (entry 275), the embryology and anatomy and morphology periodical subscriptions at the SUNY/Buffalo Health Sciences Library were evaluated by use of citation data contained in the 1980 and 1984 *SSCI Journal Citation Reports*. This article's contribution lies in its sophisticated description concerning how *JCR* can be used for journal evaluation. The evaluation's starting point was the *JCR*'s lists of the two subjects' leading journals, ranked by impact factor, which were checked against the library's holdings. Then, unlike most other reported uses of *JCR* for journal evaluation, the "cited journal listing" was employed to identify which titles most frequently cited the ones under evaluation, leading to the observation that the two fields were "very tight" and had a small core of journals. However, it is not explained what further use was made of the information concerning citing journals. Citation analysis "will not provide all the answers," but it was concluded to be a "helpful tool."

283. Gleason, Maureen L., and James T. Deffenbaugh. "Searching the Scriptures: A Citation Study in the Literature of Biblical Studies: Report and Commentary." **Collection Management** 6 (Fall/Winter 1984): 107-17.

108 / CITATION STUDIES

Gleason and Deffenbaugh describe a citation analysis in Biblical studies conducted at the University of Notre Dame to validate RLG Conspectus collecting level assessments, as part of an ARL pilot project. A citation base of 1,235 items was created by a 10-percent sample of articles in the 1977-1981 volumes of *Journal of Biblical Literature, Catholic Biblical Quarterly*, and *Biblische Zeitschrift*. This sample was then checked against the holdings. Numerous methodological issues concerning citation studies and collection evaluation are discussed. The authors are convinced "that citation studies are a potentially valuable tool for collection development in the humanities" and are optimistic about their use for Conspectus validation purposes, but feel more studies are required.

284. Haas, Stephanie C., and Kate Lee. "Research Journal Usage by the Forestry Faculty at the University of Florida, Gainesville." **Collection Building** 11, no. 2 (1991): 23-25.

A list of 263 Forestry Department faculty publications, randomly selected from 532 items published between 1984 and 1989, was checked against the University of Florida library holdings. More important, the 248 separate journal titles, cited in 80 randomly selected articles by faculty, were used as a checklist to evaluate the journal collection. Ten percent of these titles accounted for 50 percent of the faculty citations to journals. A table names, in rank order, the twenty-four most cited journals. This brief report is noteworthy primarily because it is the only entry to address collection evaluation in the subject area of forestry.

285. Herubel, Jean-Pierre V. M. "Philosophy Dissertation Bibliographies and Citations in Serials Evaluation." **Serials Librarian** 20, nos. 2/3 (1991): 65-73.

The bibliographies in the fifty-one philosophy dissertations completed at Purdue University between 1950 and 1978 were examined, resulting in 4,751 citations. Of these, 28.7 percent were to serials and 71.3 percent to monographs. The approximately 120 serials and journals cited at least twice (listed in a long, three-page table) were used as a checklist to evaluate the Purdue periodical collection. Herubel asserts, "This simple procedure is both effective and easily performed." Similar in concept to the study conducted at UC-Irvine (see Buzzard and New entry 280), this article would have benefited by providing clearer and more detailed data concerning the citations.

286. Herubel, Jean-Pierre V. M. "Simple Citation Analysis and the Purdue History Periodical Collection." **Indiana Libraries** 9, no. 2 (1990): 18-21.

As an experiment in the use of bibliometric techniques, citations were drawn from three core interdisciplinary history journals (the *Journal of Social History*, the *Journal of Interdisciplinary History*, and the *Journal of the History of Ideas*) during three two-year periods (1972 to 1973; 1979 to 1980; and 1986 to 1987) to evaluate Purdue's history periodical collection. Although a statistical breakdown is not presented, history was the most cited field and English the predominant language among the resulting 4,349 citations from 1,464 journals. Journals cited twenty or more times were checked against the holdings. Herubel believes his approach represents "a viable evaluation measure ... for the hard-pressed subject bibliographer or serials librarian."

287. Joshi, Y. "Rationalizing Library Acquisitions Policy: A Case Study." **Quarterly Bulletin of the International Association of Agricultural Librarians & Documentalists** 30, no. 1 (1985): 7-13.

A current subscription evaluation project, structured around citations in staff research papers at the Central Plantation Crop Research Institute in Kasaragod, India, is depicted. The 114 papers published during 1983 and 1984 were analyzed, resulting in 689 citations to 213 journals. A table lists, in rank order, the fourteen most cited journals, which accounted for 38 percent of the citations. In an unusual approach, the percentage distribution of citations among twenty-two subject areas collected by the Institute was compared with the distribution of serial subscriptions and staff among the twenty-two subjects. Areas of strength and weakness (i.e., where the number of subscriptions was disproportionate to the total citations or staff) are discussed by the author. There might be some practical problems with this approach, but it is certainly worth mentioning.

288. Lewis, D. E. "A Comparison between Library Holdings and Citations." **Library & Information Research News** 11 (Autumn 1988): 18-23.

At Loughborough University in the United Kingdom during the late 1980s, 1,300 citations from recent dissertations and faculty-published books and articles were used as a checklist to evaluate the library's ability to meet patron needs. Numerous short tables provide a detailed breakdown of the percentage the library held according to various combinations of broad subject area, format, and publication date. Next, as a significantly unusual follow-up method not used by any other checklist evaluation in this bibliography, ILL records were analyzed for a two-year period (August 1985 to July 1987) to determine if cited material not contained in the collection had been borrowed by the author. However, only 3.9 percent of the unheld cited items had been.

289. Moulden, Carol M. "Evaluation of Library Collection Support for an Off-Campus Degree Program." In **The Off-Campus Library Services Conference Proceedings; Charleston, South Carolina, October 20-21, 1988**, edited by Barton M. Lessin, 340-46. Mount Pleasant, Mich.: Central Michigan University, 1989.

To evaluate library support for the nontraditional off-campus program run by the National College of Education, located in Evanston, Illinois, the 2,465 citations in the sixty-five master's theses submitted for the Management/Development of Human Resources program during 1984 were analyzed by format and used to develop a checklist. Initially, 56.9 percent of the citations were to periodicals and 37.6 percent to books. After adjustments for unverifiable citations, periodicals and books accounted for 94.2 percent of the adjusted total. The 52 books and 131 journals cited in more than one thesis were considered "essential" and checked against the library's holdings. This is one of the few collection evaluation studies that addresses the issue of support for off-campus programs.

290. Neal, James G., and Barbara J. Smith. "Library Support of Faculty Research at the Branch Campuses of a Multi-Campus University." **Journal of Academic Librarianship** 9 (November 1983): 276-80.

This investigation had two objectives: 1) to ascertain how well the Pennsylvania State University libraries were supporting the research needs of branch campus faculty, and 2) to determine how branch campus faculty obtained their research materials. To answer the first question, 1,836 citations from 149 journal articles published by branch campus faculty members during the 1979-1980 fiscal year were checked against the library system holdings. A table summarizes the results by format and broad subject area. As for the second issue, the results of a questionnaire to the faculty who authored the articles indicated that their personal collections and the PSU libraries were the major sources of their research materials.

291. Nisonger, Thomas E. "A Test of Two Citation Checking Techniques for Evaluating Political Science Collections in University Libraries." **Library Resources & Technical Services** 27 (April/June 1983): 163-76.

After reviewing the citation checking technique's history, two methods of evaluating university political science collections were developed: 1) randomly selecting one citation from each article in the *American Political Science Review* during a three-year period, 1977 through 1979; and 2) randomly selecting one citation from each article in the most recent volume (1977 or 1978) of five other leading political science journals, selected to cover all the discipline's subareas. Analysis of the citations from these sampling methods revealed that 62 percent referred to monographs, 93.5 percent were in English, 40.5 percent dated from 1970-1974, and 46.4 percent were classed in political science according to the LC system.

Two samples were drawn using each method and checked against the holdings of the Georgetown, George Washington, Howard, Catholic, and George Mason university libraries. Based on consistency in results, the author asserts that these are reliable and valid methods for evaluating political science research collections.

292. Saye, Jerry D., and Belver C. Griffith. "Monograph Support Provided by the National Library of Medicine and Its Regional Medical Libraries in the Medical Behavioral Sciences." **Bulletin of the Medical Library Association** 76 (October 1988): 295-305.

A sophisticated research project, funded by the National Institute of Health, evaluated the monographic holdings in the medical behavioral sciences (e.g., psychiatry, medical sociology, etc.) of the NLM and ten other large medical libraries, including Johns Hopkins, UCLA, North Carolina, and the Cleveland Health Sciences Library. Two hundred thirty-nine monographic citations from sixty-one named "core," "general," and "slice" (only partially dealing with the subject) source journals, determined by a rather complex process using "expert judgment" and *JCR* data, were used as a checklist.

The methodology, composition of the sample, and results are analyzed in meticulous detail. The overall hit rates plus the hit rates in psychology, the social sciences, medicine, and internal medicine for the eleven libraries are summarized in two tables. Overlap and uniqueness in holdings between the NLM on the one hand and the ten other libraries on the other are also addressed. It is interesting that the Library of Congress, although not included in the detailed analysis, held a higher percentage of the sample than did the NLM.

293. Stelk, Roger Edward, and F. Wilfrid Lancaster. "The Use of Textbooks in Evaluating the Collection of an Undergraduate Library." **Library Acquisitions: Practice & Theory** 14, no. 2 (1990): 191-93.

The authors describe a pilot study follow-up to an evaluation method proposed by Bland in 1980 (entry 279), namely, the use of college textbook references as a checklist. The citations in five undergraduate core-course religious studies textbooks (world religions, Judaism, Catholicism, Protestantism, and New Testament) at the University of Illinois at Urbana-Champaign were checked against the holdings of the undergraduate library and the university library. Stelk and Lancaster's thoughtful conclusion, based on examination of the results, places this approach in proper perspective: it is a "useful component" of undergraduate library collection evaluation and "potentially valuable in identifying subject areas requiring a more in-depth analysis."

STRUCTURE OF DISCIPLINES OR SUBJECTS

294. Alafiatayo, Benjamin O. "The Research Literature of Agricultural Economics." **International Library Review** 21 (October 1989): 465-79.

A bibliometric study of sub-Saharan African agricultural economics was based on analysis of the 1,450 citations in a single monograph, a "critical survey" published by Michigan State University in 1982. The citations tended to be monographic (57.8 percent), in English (93.1 percent), and published between 1975 and 1979 (44.6 percent). Nigeria was the most productive of forty-one African countries, followed by Kenya and Ghana. The forty-six most frequently cited journals are listed, the top eight of which are identified as the core, based on Bradfordian distribution.

295. Baughman, James C. "A Structural Analysis of the Literature of Sociology." **Library Quarterly** 44 (October 1974): 293-308.

Baughman's frequently cited article deserves to be considered a classic. His citation analysis of sociology was based on 446 articles in 71 different journals listed under 52 sociology subject headings in the *Social Sciences & Humanities Index's* 1970/71 volume. This search produced 11,130 citations, resulting in 8,926 separate bibliographic items to be studied. More than half the items were books (51.7 percent compared to 38.5 percent serials) and 95.2 percent were in English. Both serials and nonserials age at approximately the same rate, with 7.5 years the median for the former and 8.5 years for the latter. Concentration of cited journal titles followed a Bradfordian distribution. A core of ten periodicals (five from disciplines other than sociology) was identified based on the number of their articles cited at least twice. Further analysis indicated "the core is heavily cited by the core."

296. Brill, Margaret S. "Government Publications as Bibliographic References in the Periodical Literature of International Relations: A Citation Analysis." **Government Information Quarterly** 7, no. 4 (1990): 427-39.

This analysis was based on a systematic sample of three international relations journals (*World Politics, Journal of International Affairs*, and *Orbis*) for the years 1964, 1974, and 1984, resulting in 3,784 citations. The citations to government publications (19 percent of the total) received detailed scrutiny: 46 percent of these were to U.S. government publications and over 90 percent were English-language. U.S. and international organization citations were broken down by issuing agency (with the Central Intelligence Agency leading the former, and the United Nations the latter), while foreign government citations were tabulated by country of origin (headed by China, then the United Kingdom and Japan). The twelve most frequently cited series or titles are also listed.

297. Budd, John. "Characteristics of Written Scholarship in American Literature: A Citation Study." **Library & Information Science Research** 8 (April-June 1986): 189-211.

A 10-percent random sample of English-language items from the 1981 MLA *International Bibliography*'s American literature section resulted in 7,149 references. Sixty-four percent of the references were to books; 99.5 percent were in English; 22.7 percent were to items more than fifty years old. A breakdown by broad subject category shows that 72.1 percent were from American literature; 18.6 percent from "other humanities," and 5.9 percent "other literatures." The data were further analyzed by type of source (e.g., books, book articles, journal articles, and dissertations) as well as by citation function (e.g., argumentation, background information, etc.). Finally, the format and age findings were compared with other citation studies from the sciences, social sciences, and humanities.

298. Cauchi, Simon, and Roderick Cave. "Citations in Bibliography: Characteristics of References in Selected Journals." **Journal of Librarianship** 14 (January 1982): 9-29.

Cauchi and Cave report a detailed citation analysis in the field of bibliography (defined as "the grammar of literary investigation") conducted with the assistance of library science students at the Victoria University of Wellington in New Zealand. A total of 15,983 references in 3 or 4 volumes from the late 1970s of 12 journals (such as *Book Collector, Printing History*, etc.) were analyzed. The results indicated that 47.0 percent of the citations were to secondary books, while 15.9 percent were to primary books. A breakdown of secondary materials by country of origin revealed that 36.0 percent were published in the United Kingdom and 31.0 percent in the United States, with thirty other countries represented. Eight hundred eighty-four journals were cited, with 25 percent of them accounting for 73.63 percent of the citations. A table lists, in rank order, the leading fifty journals by total times cited, while another table rank-orders the top fifty according to the number of journals citing them. Other tables display the findings by country of publication and date and by format and date.

299. Cullars, John. "Characteristics of the Monographic Literature of British and American Literary Studies." **College & Research Libraries** 46 (November 1985): 511-22.

More than 22,000 references in 15 prizewinning and 15 nonprizewinning monographs were analyzed and the citation patterns compared. As one might expect, the prizewinning books contained 15,838 citations, contrasted with 6,302 from the nonprize books. Cullars's article differs from earlier studies in the humanities by using monographs rather than journals as the source and by counting every citation within a work, including implicit ones. The findings of previous humanities studies were generally confirmed. When the prizewinning and nonprize citations were combined, the majority were to books (65.7 percent) published between 1950 and

1980 (61.7 percent). In contrast to previous research, manuscripts were quite significant, accounting for 20.7 percent of the references.

300. Cullars, John. "Citation Characteristics of French and German Literary Monographs." **Library Quarterly** 59 (October 1989): 305-25.

This detailed investigation employs 579 randomly selected citations from 89 French and 78 German literary monographs listed in the 1984 *MLA International Bibliography*. The author asserts that this project differs from most humanities citation studies because books rather than journals were used as the source. Of the 327 French citations, 80.7 percent were books, 61.2 percent were primary sources, 84.4 percent were in French, and 57.2 percent were published between 1950 and 1980. The 252 German citations were 76.6 percent books, 48.8 percent primary sources; 75 percent were in German and 56.7 percent were published from 1950 to 1980. Numerous comparisons are made with earlier citation studies, including Cullars's own. Manuscripts were cited less frequently (5.2 percent of both the French and German citations) than in Cullars's study of American and British literature (entry 299); the reasons for this are speculated upon.

301. Cullars, John. "Citation Characteristics of Italian and Spanish Literary Monographs." **Library Quarterly** 60 (October 1990): 337-56.

Another outstanding bibliometric study by Cullars is based on a random sample of 472 citations from 160 Spanish and Italian literary study monographs identified through the *MLA Bibliography* online, 1981 to 1986—an adaptation of the methodology from Budd's 1986 study (entry 297). The findings are consistent with other humanities studies: 71.5 percent of the Italian and 75.5 percent of the Spanish citations were to books, while 76.5 percent of the Spanish citations and 64.9 percent were published since 1950. Analysis by language showed that 65.7 percent of the Italian citations were to Italian, whereas 83.7 percent of the Spanish citations were to Spanish. Overall, 10.6 percent of all the citations were to languages other than that of the author or topic. Extensive comparisons to earlier studies are a major strength of this article.

302. Delendick, Thomas J. "Citation Analysis of the Literature of Systematic Botany: A Preliminary Survey." **Journal of the American Society for Information Science** 41 (October 1990): 535-43.

This rigorous citation analysis of systematic botany (plant taxonomy) was based on 3,143 citations in the 1986 volumes of three leading journals in the field, *Brittonia, Systematic Botany*, and *Taxon*. Data are tabulated separately for all papers and taxonomy papers as well as for the three journals on which the study is based. As expected, the taxonomy literature is old, with nearly 25 percent of the citations predating 1900 in two of the three journals. For all papers, 34 percent of the cited journals accounted for 80 percent of the citations, but in taxonomy 60 percent did so. The twenty-six journals most frequently cited in taxonomy papers are tabulated for each of the three source journals.

303. Fitzgibbons, Shirley A. "Citation Analysis in the Social Sciences." In **Collection Development in Libraries: A Treatise**, pt. B, edited by Robert D. Stueart and George B. Miller, Jr., 291-344. Greenwich, Conn.: JAI Press, 1980. (Foundations in Library and Information Science, vol. 10). LC 79-93165. ISBN 0-89232-162-8 (pt B).

114 / CITATION STUDIES

The author's objective is to summarize social science citation studies and their application to collection development in large research libraries. Following an outstanding introductory overview and historical sketch of citation analysis, Fitzgibbons analyzes 119 previous citation studies, published between 1938 and 1978, in general social science, business and management, economics, education, library and information science, political science, psychology, and sociology. Separate sections for each subject summarize the findings concerning such topics as the format, age, language, and subject dispersion of the citations; core journals; important authors; and comparison of citation studies with use studies or readership patterns.

The examined studies are listed in a bibliography. A nine-page appendix provides a useful synopsis, concisely listing author, date, citation source, number and date of the citations, purpose of the study, and subject focus. This is a well-organized (a system of headings makes it easy to quickly locate what one is looking for) and meticulously researched review.

304. Forney, Christopher D. "The Acquired Immune Deficiency Syndrome: A Bibliometric Analysis, 1980-1984." **Science & Technology Libraries** 10 (Summer 1990): 45-90.

Six National Library of Medicine bibliographies on AIDS were used to carry out a citation analysis of the periodical literature from 1980 to 1984 concerning the disease. Almost 91 percent of the 2,122 articles were in English, while 63.2 percent were published in the United States. A table lists the eighteen titles cited twenty or more times, which are considered to constitute the core. An appendix lists all 420 cited journal titles. This is a useful bibliometric study of a very important topic and the first to analyze the structure of the AIDS literature.

305. Heinzkill, Richard. "Characteristics of References in Selected Scholarly English Literary Journals." **Library Quarterly** 50 (July 1980): 352-65.

Heinzkill's meticulously detailed study is based on 9,556 citations from every article appearing in 24 bibliographical volumes, published between 1972 and 1974, of 15 literary journals, such as *English Studies* and *Modern Language Review*. Seventy-five percent of the citations were to books and 20 percent to journals. The 33 most frequently cited journals, of an estimated 580 total, are listed in a table. These thirty-three journals accounted for 61.2 percent of the journal citations, although the distribution of citations among journals is non-Bradfordian. A useful table summarizes the proportion of citations to journals from twenty-six other studies in all knowledge areas. Additional tables tabulate the results by format and date according to eight literary periods, such as Anglo-Saxon, Victorian, etc. Ninety-one percent of all the citations were in English, while 44 percent of the foreign citations were in Latin. The author concludes that his findings confirm the "folklore" about humanities scholars.

306. Herubel, Jean-Pierre V. M. "Materials Used in Historical Scholarship: A Limited Citation Analysis of the **Journal of Garden History**." **Collection Management** 14, no. 1/2 (1991): 155-62.

This study is based on the 962 citations in the 1989 volume of the *Journal of Garden History*. Herubel found that 40.95 percent of the citations were to primary materials. Analysis by format revealed that 45.21 percent were to monographs and 11.64 percent to serials. After comparison with a few earlier citation studies in history, the author concludes that garden history displays the citation patterns found "in the humanities in general." This article might be of some interest for collection development in art history and landscape architecture.

307. Hitchcock, Eloise R. "Materials Used in the Research of State History: A Citation Analysis of the 1986 **Tennessee Historical Quarterly**." **Collection Building** 10, no. 1/2 (1991): 52-54.

Hitchcock's short article is based on a systematic sample of every eighth citation (99 of 794) in the 1986 *Tennessee Historical Quarterly*. She found that 61.6 percent of the citations were to primary sources. A break-down by format found that 37.4 percent were to archives and 20.2 percent to monographs. Publication dates ranged from 1829 to 1985 with 1942 being the median date. A few references are made to previous studies. This somewhat simplistic citation study is the only one pertaining to state history that fell within this literature guide's parameters.

308. Jones, Clyve, Michael Chapman, and Pamela Carr Woods. "The Characteristics of the Literature Used by Historians." **Journal of Librarianship** 4 (July 1972): 137-56.

This frequently cited citation study of English history is based on three original studies (concentrating on the medieval, early modern, and later modern periods) completed for the master of arts degree in librarianship at the University of Sheffield. The investigation is based on 7,127 references in 119 English history articles in the 1968 and 1969 volumes of 7 leading British history journals, such as *English Historical Review* and *Historical Journal*. It was found that: 1) 59.8 percent of the citations were to non-serials, with 34.1 percent to monographs; 2) 86 percent were to items published in the United Kingdom or Ireland, with 57.9 percent of the foreign citations published in the United States; and 3) 92.4 percent were in English. The data concerning citation age do not lend themselves to easy summary, but the authors conclude that serials and secondary monographs age rapidly, while primary sources "retain their value over time." Approximately fifteen of the top, most frequently cited journals for each period are displayed in a table.

Comparisons are made with numerous citation studies from other disciplines, leading to the conclusion that history is situated between the sciences and social sciences in its citation patterns. This well-done report represents one of a very few citation studies in history.

309. Kelland, John Laurence. "Biochemistry and Environmental Biology: A Comparative Citation Analysis." **Library & Information Science Research** 12 (January-March 1990): 103-15.

Kelland's methodologically sophisticated research uses 839 biochemistry citations and 1,992 environmental biology (ecology) citations in randomly selected articles from the 1986 *Biological Abstracts* to compare the two disciplines. The median age of ecology citations was one year older than biochemistry citations, but the difference was not statistically significant. Kelland rejects Taylor's assertion in the 1981 *Canadian Field Naturalist* (entry 492) that field sciences, such as ecology, cite older material than laboratory sciences, such as biochemistry. Analysis by format showed that 74.6 percent of biochemistry citations were to serials, compared to 70.0 percent for ecology. A number of sophisticated statistical tests indicate that ecology cites a more diverse subject literature, not simply in the number of subjects cited, but also in the distribution of citations among subjects.

310. Line, Maurice B. "The Structure of Social Science Literature as Shown by Large-Scale Citation Analysis." **Social Science Information Studies** 1 (January 1981): 67-87.

A total of 59,000 citations (11,000 from 300 monographs and 48,000 from 140 serial titles) were analyzed in this first-rate study. The exhaustive and sophisticated statistical breakdowns include: concentration, scatter, and ranking of serial titles; links between selected subjects; country and language analysis; and date and format of cited material. Lists of top-ranked psychology and economics journals, as well as the most frequently cited monographic authors, are presented. Twelve figures illustrate the data, including various linkages among subjects, formats, and countries. Line found that monographs and serials displayed different citation patterns, as did forty-seven top-ranked journals compared to forty-seven randomly selected ones.

This entry is remarkable for the large number of source citations and the rigor of the analysis. The author was formerly Librarian of Bath University during the 1970s, where he directed the well-known DISISS project (Design of Information Systems in the Social Sciences), which included analysis of social science citation patterns.

311. Mahapatra, M., and S. K. Musib. "Subject Dispersion Studies in Agricultural Economics." **Libri** 34 (December 1984): 341-49.

A subject analysis of the 7,701 citations from research articles published in the *American Journal of Agricultural Economics* and the *Indian Journal of Agricultural Economics* between 1970 and 1980 forms the basis of this study. Overall, 68 percent of the citations were to the social sciences and 27.2 percent to the humanities. A breakdown by Dewey class number indicated that 53.2 percent of references were to economics and 17.4 percent to agriculture, with sociology, statistics, management sciences, and commerce ranging from 2 to 5 percent. Numerous comparisons are made between the two journals. Several tables analyze citations by date, but they are awkward to interpret or summarize.

312. McCain, Katherine W. "Citation Patterns in the History of Technology." **Library & Information Science Research** 9 (January-March 1987): 41-59.

313. McCain, Katherine W. "Cross-Disciplinary Citation Patterns in the History of Technology." In **ASIS '86; Proceedings of the 49th ASIS Annual Meeting, Chicago, Illinois, September 28-October 2, 1986**, vol. 23, edited by Julie M. Hurd, 194-98. White Plains, N.Y.: published for the American Society for Information Science by Knowledge Industry Publications, 1986. 376p. LC 64-8303. ISBN 0-938734-14-8. ISSN 0044-7870.

These two publications report the same research project, although more detail is presented in the first, upon which this annotation concentrates. A rigorous citation analysis concerning the history of technology is based on the secondary sources cited in a systematic sample of twenty-seven historical and historiographic articles published in *Technology & Culture* between 1967 and 1977. Of 711 secondary source citations, 65 percent were to books and 35 percent to serials. Analysis by date found the median citation age was 14.8 years, with 15 percent less than 5 years old. A subject breakdown revealed that book citations fell in all but two main LC classes. Several tables report the data separately for historical and historiographic articles. Three core books and six core journals are identified. Detailed comparisons of these findings are made with earlier reported citation studies, although the author appreciates the subtle nuances in how previous studies might have counted citations differently.

314. Miwa, Makiko, Shuichi Ueda, and Kazuhiko Nakayama. "Characteristics of Journal Citations in the Social Sciences: Comparisons of SSCI Data of 1972 and 1977." **Library & Information Science**, no. 18 (1980): 141-55.

This investigation, published in a Japanese journal, compares the 1972 and 1977 citation patterns in economics, education, law, politics, psychology, and sociology, using more than 700,000 citations contained on magnetic tapes of the *SSCI* database purchased from the ISI. Numerous tables and graphs present format, date, self-citation, and subject dispersion data for the six disciplines. The study's major findings include the following: 1) from 1972 to 1977, the proportion of citations to journals increased for all subjects but law; 2) except for law, 90 percent of all citations were less than twenty-four years old; 3) between 1972 and 1977 the age of citations increased in all subject areas, a phenomenon attributed by the authors to a greater lag time between acceptance and publication; and 4) economics displays the least subject dispersion in the social sciences. An appendix lists the twenty most frequently cited journals for 1972 and 1977 in the six disciplines. This entry is remarkable for the vast number of citations analyzed.

315. Musib, S. K. "Forms of Literature Studies in Agricultural Economics." **Herald of Library Science** 25 (July-October 1986): 185-89.

A companion piece to the work by Mahapatra and Musib (entry 311), this article analyzes the format of 9,475 citations published in the *American Journal of Agricultural Economics* and the *Indian Journal of Agricultural Economics* from 1970 to 1980. Eleven different formats were represented, with 41.6 percent of the citations referring to journals and 35.3 percent to books. Tables present the total findings, compare the two journals, and offer some selective data on the distribution of citations by date. The two articles could easily have been combined into one.

316. Nisonger, Thomas E. "The Sources of Canadian History: A Citation Analysis of the **Canadian Historical Review**." **Manitoba Library Association Bulletin** 11 (June 1981): 33-35.

Although it appeared in a fairly obscure publication, this is the only citation analysis of Canadian history. Every reference in the 1979 *Canadian Historical Review* — a total of 1,152 — was analyzed. The fact that almost half the citations (49.7 percent) were to archival documents, a format that would not normally be found in most library collections, was an especially noteworthy finding. The vast majority of citations to nonarchival sources were to sources in English (82.6 percent, with 17.1 percent in French) and published in Canada (79.3 percent). Nearly half the nonarchival citations (48.7 percent) dated from 1960 to 1979, while 14 percent predated 1900.

317. Peritz, Bluma C. "Citation Characteristics in Library Science: Some Further Results from a Bibliometric Survey." **Library Research** 3 (Spring 1981): 47-65.

Peritz's sophisticated study, based on her doctoral dissertation, analyzed 5,334 citations from 716 research papers published in 39 core library science journals in 1950, 1960, 1965, 1970, and 1975. Numerous tables present the citation patterns at the corresponding five-year intervals, thus allowing longitudinal comparison. Overall, the vast majority of citations were from the field of library and information science (78 percent), followed by business and economics (3 percent, although 8 percent of the articles had at least one citation from this area). Journals accounted for 47 percent of total citations, books for 28 percent, and reports for 14 percent. Exactly one-quarter of all the citations were at least seven years old. The article concludes with comparisons to several other citation studies from other disciplines.

318. Stern, Madeleine. "Characteristics of the Literature of Literary Scholarship." **College & Research Libraries** 44 (July 1983): 199-209.

Three authors (Milton, James, and Auden) and three literary movements (Symbolism, Existentialism, and Structuralism) were analyzed through 7,020 citations from 679 sources in the *Arts & Humanities Citation Index*, 1976 through 1980. Comparison of studies of authors and literary movements found that both were heavily oriented towards monographs (82.7 percent and 78.8 percent, respectively), but that the literature about authors used more primary sources (47.4 percent, contrasted with 22.3 percent) and was older (21.6 percent published within the last ten years, compared to 30.3 percent). Four tables summarize the finding, while a fifth displays the percentage of citations ten years old or less in seventeen other citation studies from the three major branches of knowledge.

A noteworthy finding concerns the importance of book reviews to literary scholarship. Stern concludes that her results support the contention that humanistic scholarship is "distinctive and unique" compared to the sciences or social sciences.

319. Yitzhaki, Moshe. "Determining the Mutual Dependence between Two Disciplines by Means of Citation Analysis: The Case of Biblical Studies and Ancient Near-East Studies." **Libri** 36 (September 1986): 211-23.

Approximately 9,000 citations in Biblical studies and 5,000 citations in Ancient Near-East studies from the 1923, 1948, 1971, and 1981 editions of *Elenchus Bibliographicus Biblicus*, the field's major index, were examined to determine how frequently the two areas cite the same sources, and, by implication, how closely related they are. A large portion of the study is devoted to the author's hypotheses concerning why the two fields were found to cite each other very infrequently.

From the collection development perspective, this article's most interesting attribute is the appendix, which tabulates 2,685 citations in Biblical studies and 1,453 in Ancient Near-East studies. Most of the Biblical studies citations were to monographs (42.9 percent, compared with 27.2 percent to serials), in German (39.4 percent, with another 32.6 percent in English), and published in Germany (37.1 percent, with 16.0 percent published in the United States). For Ancient Near-East studies, most of the citations were to serials (43.0 percent, while 37.6 percent were to monographs), in English (42.1 percent, with 23.8 percent in German), and published in Germany (19.5 percent, with 19.4 percent published in the United States). It would seem that the strong German influence probably reflects the use of a German index as the citation source.

NOTES

[1] Robert N. Broadus, "Early Approaches to Bibliometrics," *Journal of the American Society for Information Science* 38 (March 1987): 127.

[2] F. J. Cole, and Nellie B. Eales, "The History of Comparative Anatomy," *Science Progress* 11 (April 1917): 578-96.

[3] E. W. Hulme, *Statistical Bibliography in Relation to the Growth of Modern Civilization* (London: Grafton, 1923).

[4] Alan Pritchard, "Statistical Bibliography or Bibliometrics?," *Journal of Documentation* 25 (December 1969): 48-49.

[5] The last two sentences are based on Emilie C. White, "Bibliometrics: From Curiosity to Convention," *Special Libraries* 76 (Winter 1985): 35-36; Francis Narin and Joy K. Moll, "Bibliometrics," in *Annual Review of Information Science and Technology*, vol. 12, ed. Martha E. Williams (White Plains, N.Y.: Knowledge Industry Publications for American Society for Information Science, 1977), 35-38.

[6] Broadus, "Early Approaches," 128.

[7] White, "Bibliometrics," 39.

[8] Ibid.

[9] *Social Science Citation Index Journal Citation Reports; 1987 Annual* (Philadelphia: Institute for Scientific Information, 1988), 6A.

9

The RLG Conspectus and the National Shelflist Count

The Research Libraries Group (RLG), founded in 1974 as a consortium of Harvard, Yale, Columbia, and the New York Public Library, began development of the Conspectus in the late 1970s as a tool to assess research library collections in order to lay the groundwork for cooperative collection development. In 1983 the Association of Research Libraries adopted the Conspectus for the North American Collections Inventory Project, under which the more than 100 ARL member libraries are using the Conspectus to analyze their collections. The American Library Association's *Guide for Written Collection Policy Statements* (entry 321), published in 1989, recommends use of the Conspectus format for drafting a collection development policy. Although many librarians have had criticisms and reservations concerning the RLG Conspectus (and some still do), the Conspectus has achieved international recognition. It has been used in Australia, New Zealand, Canada, Scotland, and England and plans are under way to implement it in continental European libraries as well.

The RLG Conspectus is organized into a three-tier subject hierarchy composed of Divisions, Subject Categories, and Subject Groups. There is a separate worksheet for each of the twenty-four Divisions, which correspond to broad areas of knowledge such as art and architecture, library and information science, or natural history and biology. The Conspectus is usually completed one worksheet at a time. Divisions are divided into components called Subject Categories, of which there are approximately 100. For example, the Art and Architecture Division is organized into seven Subject Categories: "Visual Arts in General"; "Architecture"; "Sculpture"; "Drawing, Design, Illustration"; "Painting"; "Graphic Arts"; and "Decorative Arts." Subject Categories are in turn divided into approximately 7,000 Subject Groups, the basic unit of analysis. "Economic Theory" or "Agricultural Economics" are examples of Subject Groups in the "Economics" Subject Category of the "Economics and Sociology"

Division. (Various versions of the RLG Conspectus, such as the Pacific Northwest Conspectus, use slightly different terminology for the three tiers.) Also, the literature concerning the Conspectus is not consistent in the usage of this terminology. Subject Groups are sometimes referred to as subject descriptors or subject headings.

The RLG Conspectus uses an assessment from 0 to 5 (0 = Out of Scope; 1 = Minimal Level; 2 = Basic Information Level; 3 = Study or Instructional Support Level; 4 = Research Level; and 5 = Comprehensive Level). An assessment number is assigned to each Subject Group for the existing collection strength and the current collecting intensity, the latter defined as the library's collecting activity during the last year or two. A set of language codes is also used to indicate collections predominantly in English [E]; with selected non-English material [F]; with a wide selection of languages [W]; and predominantly in a single non-English language [Y]. The worksheets usually indicate the Library of Congress classification range that corresponds to a Subject Group and contain an area for comments. Conspectus collecting levels assigned by participating libraries have been included in a number of online databases, such as RLIN.

A modified version, known as the Pacific Northwest Conspectus, was introduced through the Library and Information Resources for the Northwest (LIRN) Program. The RLG's original six collecting levels were expanded to ten, with levels 1, 2, and 3 divided into a and b sublevels. Moreover, assessment levels are assigned for a third category, the intended goal, in addition to total strength and current acquisitions. Unlike the RLG version, which is limited to the Library of Congress classification system, alternate versions of the Pacific Northwest Conspectus are available in Dewey or LC. As responsibility for the Pacific Northwest Conspectus was transferred from the Oregon State Library Foundation to the WLN in 1990, the latter's promotional brochures now refer to it as the WLN Conspectus, although this term has yet to appear in the professional literature.

A variety of methods can be employed to reach the assessments, including direct examination, shelflist measurement, checking bibliographies, and faculty consultation. One considers such factors as size of holdings, representation of major authors and important works, the research sets and serials contained in the collection, and, if appropriate to the subject, whether the necessary audiovisual materials are held.

The Association of Research Libraries is developing a system of "verification studies" to verify the consistency in assigning collecting levels among different libraries. An appropriate bibliography is compiled and checked against the holdings of the participating libraries to be certain the comparative percentage of items held can be reconciled with the assigned collecting levels. A verification study would identify inconsistencies such as a library that holds 60 percent assigning a level 4 while another library that holds 70 percent assigns a 3. Verification studies have also been used to analyze overlap among the holdings of large research libraries.

The collecting levels assigned by libraries participating in the NCIP can be accessed through the Conspectus Online database, maintained by RLIN. The online database of assigned collecting levels created through the Pacific Northwest Conspectus was transferred to the WLN in 1990.

Although ostensibly developed as an instrument to facilitate cooperative collection development, the RLG Conspectus is by its intrinsic nature a collection evaluation tool, as it attempts to ascertain areas of strength and weakness in a collection. It has been or can be used for:

1. Collection evaluation

2. Writing collection development policies

3. Setting priorities for preservation decisions

4. Budgeting decisions

5. Grant proposals

6. Overlap studies and

7. Both internal and external communication of a library's collecting priorities.

Numerous criticisms or reservations about the Conspectus concern its suitability for medium-size or small libraries as well as nonacademic libraries and its applicability to nonbook formats. It has also been accused of a North American bias. Errors and inconsistencies on the worksheets have been noted, as well as the subjective nature of the collecting level assessments and the ability of bibliographers to apply them correctly. Further, critics who decry the cost and time required to implement the Conspectus think the effort of implementing it might be better placed in alternate endeavors.

The existence of a few newsletters published by library consortiums, such as the *Conspectus in Scotland Newsletter*, the *Pacific NW Collection Assessment & Development Newsletter*, or *NCIP News*, concerning the basics of implementing the Conspectus, should be mentioned. However, these newsletters were not included in this literature guide because they generally do not contain substantive articles and are not readily accessible.

The bulk of this chapter deals with the RLG Conspectus itself, but a separate section annotates a few items concerning the National Shelflist Count. The National Shelflist Count gathered data, organized into approximately 500 subdivisions of the Library of Congress classification system, on the holdings of major research libraries, and may thus be viewed as a forerunner of the Conspectus. Items dealing primarily with cooperative or coordinated collection development are not included.

Because of the controversiality of the RLG Conspectus, this chapter's annotations highlight subjective opinions, often based on direct experience, criticizing or praising the Conspectus approach. The chapter is divided into eight sections: general, case studies of the Conspectus's implementation in North America, the Conspectus in Europe, the Conspectus in Australia and New Zealand, the Pacific Northwest Conspectus, the North American

Collections Inventory Project, verification studies, and the National Shelflist Count.

THE CONSPECTUS—GENERAL

320. Abell, Millicent D. "The Conspectus: Issues and Questions." In Association of Research Libraries, **NCIP: Means to an End; Minutes of the 109th Meeting, October 22-23, 1986, Washington, D.C.**, 26-30. Washington: Association of Research Libraries, 1987. 127p. ISSN 0044-9652.

The author addresses the Conspectus's potential role in collaborative collection development at the national level in this speech given the 1986 ARL annual meeting. She mentions the viewpoints, expressed by her colleagues, that Conspectus collecting level assignments "are not data, but expressions of opinion," and that the Conspectus structure does not accommodate formats such as archives, manuscripts, and video. Abell stresses that the Conspectus is "a tool, not a panacea" and expresses concern that too much energy will be focused on perfecting the tool itself rather than using it effectively. Abell concludes that there is "abundant evidence" concerning the Conspectus's "local utility" and sees "reasoned optimism" about its utility for national efforts.

321. American Library Association, Resources and Technical Services Division. **Guide for Written Collection Policy Statements**. 2d ed. Edited by Bonita Bryant. Chicago: American Library Association, 1989. 29p. (Collection Management and Development Guides, no. 3). LC 89-6955. ISBN 0-83893-371-8.

This revision of the 1979 *Guidelines for the Formation of Collection Development Policies* is included here because it "strongly" recommends that all sizes of libraries use either the RLG or Pacific Northwest Conspectus subject breakdown and collecting level codes as a framework for their collection development policies. The appendix contains much useful information about the Conspectus, including worksheet samples for the RLG, Pacific Northwest Library of Congress, and Pacific Northwest Dewey versions, as well as listing the twenty-one RLG divisions as of 1989 and the twenty-four Pacific Northwest divisions. A glossary defines many terms relevant to use of the Conspectus.

322. Association of Research Libraries. Office of Management Studies. **Qualitative Collection Analysis; The Conspectus Methodology**. Washington, D.C.: Association of Research Libraries, Office of Management Studies, 1989. 119p. (SPEC Kit 151). ISSN 0160-3582.

This SPEC kit is organized into four sections covering Conspectus implementation planning and procedures, collection assessment with the Conspectus, uses of the Conspectus, and Conspectus project reports. Documents are reproduced from numerous university libraries, including Harvard, Yale, Emory, Virginia, Missouri-Columbia, Washington, Toronto, Indiana, Oklahoma, UCLA, Alberta, and British Columbia. An attached summary sheet, termed a "SPEC flyer," indicates that approximately 50 percent of the ARL libraries responding to a 1988 questionnaire about the North American Collections Inventory Project had used the Conspectus. Like most SPEC kits, this entry provides useful, practical examples illustrating actual library experience.

323. Ferguson, Anthony W. "Internal Uses of the RLG Conspectus." In Association of Research Libraries, **NCIP: Means to an End; Minutes of the 109th Meeting, October 22-23, 1986, Washington, D.C.**, 21-25. Washington, D.C.: Association of Research Libraries, 1987. 127p. ISSN 0044-9652.

324. Ferguson, Anthony W., Joan Grant, and Joel Rutstein. "Internal Uses of the RLG Conspectus." **Journal of Library Administration** 8 (Summer 1987): 35-40.

As acknowledged in both, these two articles cover the same set of points. It is convincingly argued that the Conspectus represents an important library management tool, especially for allocating resources effectively. Ten areas where it can be of assistance are elaborated upon: 1) collection development policies, 2) space and storage, 3) setting preservation priorities, 4) staffing allocation, 5) fund requests, 6) accreditation agencies, 7) faculty liaison, 8) selector training, 9) establishing processing priorities, and 10) grant proposals.

325. Ferguson, Anthony W., Joan Grant, and Joel Rutstein. "The RLG Conspectus: Its Uses and Benefits." **College & Research Libraries** 49 (May 1988): 197-206.

Three members of the RLG Collection Management and Development Committee discuss uses of the Conspectus at three levels: national, international, and internal to a specific library. National uses include establishing Primary Collecting Responsibilities to protect "endangered species" areas and Primary Preservation Responsibilities for cooperative preservation purposes. NCIP and state efforts in Colorado, Alaska, New York, and Indiana are also mentioned. At the international level, the Conspectus's application in Canada and Western Europe is briefly noted. The second half of the item, which focuses on internal benefits, covers essentially the same points delineated in the preceding article. The articles conclude that "the Conspectus is not in and of itself a plan," but "a useful planning document."

326. Gwinn, Nancy E. "Cooperative Collection Development—National Trends and New Tools." **Art Documentation** 4 (Winter 1985): 143-47.

Following an overview of cooperative collection development, Gwinn explains how the Conspectus works and summarizes its use throughout North America up to 1985, with close attention paid to art and architecture. An especially notable feature is a discussion of the RLG Conspectus Online, a database that became available in 1982 of Conspectus collecting level assessments by North American research libraries. A figure illustrates how a Conspectus Online subject group from the Art and Architecture Division appears on a terminal screen, while the search strategies for accessing the database are explained. In an interesting analogy, Gwinn believes the Conspectus will be to collection development what the MARC format is to cataloging, a framework for presentation and access of data through automation.

327. Gwinn, Nancy E., and Mosher, Paul H. "Coordinating Collection Development: The RLG Conspectus." **College & Research Libraries** 44 (March 1983): 128-40.

This excellent, award-winning article originally helped bring the Conspectus to the library community's attention and still ranks among the best general overviews of the topic. The Conspectus's early historical development is traced from the 1978 ALA Annual Conference, when a new national collection plan was first broached, through the early 1980s. The authors elaborate upon the anticipated benefits of using the Conspectus for: 1) drafting local collection development policies; 2) collection rationalization, whereby certain libraries agree to assume "primary collecting responsibility" for "endangered" fields; 3) backup for the reference and interlibrary loan functions; and 4) collection planning at the regional and national level.

The Conspectus Online Database, the development of "verification studies," and the testing of the worksheets for religion and philosophy, chemistry, and economics in the Iowa State, Notre Dame, Manitoba, Cincinnati, and Wisconsin university libraries are also described. Gwinn and Mosher conclude that the Conspectus project has "gone a long way toward realizing the dream of many librarians for a description of existing research collections nationwide." They hope it "will give to librarians and scholars a bibliographic research tool on a grand scale."

328. Lein, Edward. "Suggestions for Formulating Collection Development Policy Statements for Music Score Collections in Academic Libraries." **Collection Management** 9 (Winter 1987): 69-89.

In order to draft a collection development policy for music scores in academic libraries, Lein recommends use of the 1979 RTSD Guidelines[1] and the RLG Conspectus. Separate sections of the paper describe both. It is noted that the Conspectus music worksheet "is similar in structure and purpose" to the "detailed analysis of collection development policy" advocated in the RTSD Guidelines, but it offers the advantage of a ready-made tool that is fast gaining acceptance. The author recommends that the Conspectus format be supplemented with a list of composers, arranged by chronological categories, to remedy some organizational deficiencies on the worksheet.

He concludes that use of the Conspectus worksheet and collecting codes for music scores will fit into a general collection development policy that is "comprehensible" and will allow comparison with other institutions. Note that the 1989 ALA *Guidelines* (entry 321) explicitly recommend use of the Conspectus for collection development policies.

329. McGrath, William E., and Nancy B. Nuzzo. " 'Existing Collection Strength' and Shelflist Count Correlations in RLG's Conspectus for Music." **College & Research Libraries** 52 (March 1991): 194-203.

McGrath and Nuzzo investigate the correlation between the assigned "Established Collection Strength" (ECS) and actual shelflist counts for 138 class ranges on the Music Conspectus in 17 RLG libraries (which are identified in several tables). In this quantitatively rigorous study, innumerable correlations are calculated across libraries and within a single library. Correlations within a library ranged from 0.36 to 0.89, while across-library correlations ranged from -0.34 to 0.94. The negative across-library correlations led to the conclusion that "cross-library comparisons [based on ECS] should not be trusted and are probably not intended by RLG." The authors attribute the negative correlations to the fact that libraries interpret and apply collecting levels differently. The meaning of assigned Conspectus collecting levels in terms of statistical theory is also analyzed. Many individuals have questioned the consistency of Conspectus collecting level assignments, this study addresses the issue with empirical data.

330. Nisonger, Thomas E. "Editing the RLG Conspectus to Analyze the OCLC Archival Tapes of Seventeen Texas Libraries." **Library Resources & Technical Services** 29 (October/December 1985): 309-27.

The Conspectus was edited in 1984 by the Association for Higher Education of North Texas, a consortium of Dallas-Fort Worth area libraries, so that the Conspectus subject breakdown could be used in an analysis of overlap among their collecting patterns, based on data generated from OCLC archival tapes. Problems encountered on the Conspectus worksheets are discussed here, including typographical and other errors, incomplete LC classification numbers, and organizational discrepancies between the Conspectus headings and the LC classification schedule. Editorial attention was required by roughly three-fifths of the 2,682 Conspectus subject groups on the 13 worksheets available at the time of this project.

The author concludes that "the Conspectus is definitely appropriate for overlap studies." However, because of the extensive specificity in the Conspectus subject breakdown, its suitability for medium-sized libraries must "remain open."

331. Reed-Scott, Jutta, preparer. **Manual for the North American Inventory of Research Library Collections**. Rev. ed. Washington, D.C.: Association of Research Libraries, Office of Management Studies, 1988. 98p.

This manual, the third and best one prepared by the author for the Association of Research Libraries, is intended to be used as a "guide" by libraries implementing the Conspectus, especially those taking part in NCIP. Earlier versions were tested at the Indiana, Purdue, and Notre Dame university libraries. The manual is organized into ten chapters covering topics such as NCIP, the Conspectus format, the Conspectus Online, training, completing the worksheets, and local implementation issues. A final chapter provides an overview of collection assessment methods. Nearly a dozen appendixes contain much useful information, including a selected bibliography on the Conspectus and collection evaluation, sample worksheets, and a list of available verification studies. This item admirably achieves its intended objective.

332. Scott, Marianne. "The National Plan for Collections Inventories." **Canadian Library Journal** 44 (October 1987): 289-90.

This entry is based on the National Librarian of Canada's presentation about the Conspectus at a June 1987 workshop on the National Plan for Collections Inventories—a project, similar in concept to NCIP, in which Canadian libraries implement the Conspectus in order to inventory their holdings. Scott relates that the Conspectus is being used to identify strengths of Canadian libraries for purposes of resource sharing, collection development, and preservation. Assigned collecting levels are available through the Canadian Conspectus Search Service, coordinated at the National Library of Canada. She notes that the National Library of Canada and the Canadian Association of Research Libraries have adapted the Conspectus for Canadian use by translating documentation into French, expanding coverage of Canadian subjects, and revising the language codes.

333. Stam, David H. "Collaborative Collection Development: Progress, Problems, and Potential." **Collection Building** 7, no. 3 (1986): 3-9. Also published in **IFLA Journal** 12 (February 1986): 9-19.

Stam's paper, delivered at the August 1985 IFLA conference, was published in both *Collection Building* and the *IFLA Journal*. It begins with a discussion of the Conspectus's history through 1985. Stam stresses that in planning for collection development, U.S. research libraries have historically had to deal with the contradictory forces of autonomy and interdependence. The testing of the Conspectus in non-RLG libraries and its use in NCIP are seen as particularly significant phases in its development.

About half the article is devoted to an illuminating discussion of the leading problems and issues that arose during development of the Conspectus and what progress has been made in attempts to resolve them. The questions covered include: 1) subjective judgment versus objective shelflist data in assigning collecting levels; 2) use of the LC classification; 3) the handling of area studies, collections based on format, language codes, and current collecting intensity; 4) implementation logistics; and 5) local political considerations.

334. Stam, David H. "Development and Use of the RLG Conspectus." In Association of Research Libraries, **NCIP: Means to an End; Minutes of the 109th Meeting, October 22-23, 1986, Washington, D.C.**, 7-10. Washington, D.C.: Association of Research Libraries, 1987. 127p. ISSN 0044-9652.

In contrast to his presentation at the 1985 IFLA meeting (see entry 333), Stam terms this somewhat humorous talk, prepared for an ARL meeting, "an informal secret history of the Conspectus." While discussing a number of personalities involved in the Conspectus's early development, he states that "the real secret ... is that the Conspectus was developed by a group of subversives—collection development officers." He concludes by stressing that the Conspectus is not "a panacea for all of our woes." Individuals who wish to read comprehensively about the Conspectus's history may wish to consult this item.

335. Stam, David H. "Think Globally—Act Locally: Collection Development and Resource Sharing." **Collection Building** 5 (Spring 1983): 18-21.

This short article by the Chair of the RLG Collection Management and Development Committee (which played a vital role in the Conspectus's early historical development) is worth noting because it is frequently cited and offers one of the earliest published descriptions of the Conspectus, albeit a brief one. Beginning with the ditty, "Too much information ... Driving me insane," this well-written discussion of resource sharing, replete with literary allusions, makes the important point that "all libraries are linked in a great chain of access and that what each has and does will have importance for the whole universe of libraries." Moreover, the Conspectus will be a tool for libraries to communicate their collection development decisions to each other.

336. Stielow, Frederick J., and Helen R. Tibbo. "Collection Analysis and the Humanities: A Practicum with the RLG Conspectus." **Journal of Education for Library & Information Science** 27 (Winter 1987): 148-57.

The authors describe a 1986 project in which advanced MLS students in a humanities course at the University of Maryland College of Library and Information Services participated in a practicum to test the RLG Conspectus at the University of Maryland, College Park. Student teams, focusing on subfields within art, English literature, music, and history, interviewed faculty, surveyed the curriculum, and checked bibliographies to assign intended and desired RLG collecting levels.

The project was "jolted" when the students had difficulty relating the university catalog or faculty views of the collection to the Conspectus collecting levels. It was thus concluded that the collecting levels "while valuable ... do not reflect the reality of a university setting." (See also Stielow and Tibbo's companion piece, entry 337.)

337. Stielow, Frederick J., and Helen R. Tibbo. "Collection Analysis in Modern Librarianship: A Stratified, Multidimensional Model." **Collection Management** 11, nos. 3/4 (1989): 73-91.

Following a useful five-page historical review of collection evaluation, the authors propose a model, structured on the RLG Conspectus, for collection assessment in university libraries. Because their earlier research (entry 336) led to the conclusion that the Conspectus "does not encompass ... [the university's] joint teaching/research mission," the collecting levels are redefined as "basic," "survey," "advanced," "research," and "comprehensive," using a cumulative Guttman scale approach. These five levels are applied to six categories—monographs, serials, reference material, government documents, primary sources, and media—resulting in a thirty-cell framework which the authors believe "begins to capture the complexity of the activities involved" in collection evaluation. Stielow and Tibbo note that a wide range of specific techniques can be used to gather data for their approach. This entry serves as an interesting example of a theoretical evaluation framework based on the Conspectus.

338. Tezla, Kathy E. "Reference Collection Development Using the RLG Conspectus." **Reference Librarian** no. 29 (1990): 43-51. Simultaneously issued in **Weeding and Maintenance of Reference Collections**, edited by Sydney J. Pierce, 43-51. New York: Haworth Press, 1990. 173p. LC 90-30910. ISBN 1-56024-001-6.

Tezla describes the role the Conspectus can play in collection evaluation and policy writing for both the reference and general collections. She envisions a collection development policy consisting of a narrative description, shelflist counts, and a summary of strengths and weaknesses, using the RLG Conspectus plus other evaluation methods as "guides." The author also explains that the addition of a third Conspectus collecting level, "desired collecting intensity," can serve as a basis for communication with faculty. Although not based on actual library experience, this entry is noteworthy for recognizing that the Conspectus can be applied to a reference collection.

339. Treadwell, Jane, and Charles Spornick. "Translating the Conspectus: Presenting Collection Evaluation Results to Administrators." **Acquisitions Librarian** 3, no. 6 (1991): 45-49. Simultaneously issued in **Evaluating Acquisitions and Collection Management**, edited by Pamela S. Cenzer and Cynthia I. Gozzi, 45-49. New York: Haworth Press, 1991. 162p. LC 91-15299. ISBN 1-56024-160-8.

Based on their experience at the Emory University Library, the authors explain how Conspectus findings can be made "comprehensible" and "useful." More than 1,000 pages of worksheets were reduced to an "executive summary" of less than 50 pages. Bar graphs were used to illustrate the collection's current level, the desired level, and the difference between the two for condensed subject groups. Also, a "cost-summary" was calculated for broad disciplines through the following method:

1. The size of the desired collection was calculated by determining the mean holdings of four or five institutions collecting at the desired Conspectus level, using the National Shelflist Count and the Conspectus online.

2. The average cost per title in the discipline was multiplied by the number of volumes required to obtain the target level.

This is the most explicitly detailed explanation available concerning how Conspectus findings can be summarized.

340. Walker, Gay. "Preservation Planning and the Conspectus at Yale University." **Conservation Administration News**, no. 31 (October 1987): 8-9.

This short piece, written in the first person plural, describes another use of the RLG Conspectus: setting preservation priorities. The Yale University Preservation Planning Task Force, appointed in December 1985, decided to take a subject approach to identifying material for preservation. As a starting point, they received from the RLG a list of Yale's subject areas collected at Conspectus levels 4 or 5, so their effort could be concentrated on strong areas of national importance. Walker asserts, "The Conspectus is not absolutely perfect—yet ... [it] was for us an extremely valuable tool, providing a great advantage to preservation planners."

341. Whaley, John H., Jr. "Groping toward National Standards for Collection Evaluation." **Show-Me Libraries** 37 (March 1986): 25-28.

This perceptive essay is one of the few published items that focuses primarily on the Conspectus's potential role as a national collection evaluation standard. Following a brief review of post-World War II efforts at developing a national collection plan, the Conspectus itself is addressed. Problems with the Conspectus include lack of benchmarks for achieving a standard and difficulty defining appropriate code levels for smaller libraries. Although standards promote rational planning of resources, the necessity of uniform standards for unique institutions is questioned. Whaley suggests that perhaps only two standard collection levels are necessary: research collection or not. "Attempting to identify the numerous gradations of collections below the research level" may be "an endless task."

CASE STUDIES OF IMPLEMENTATION OF THE CONSPECTUS IN NORTH AMERICA

342. Gilman, Lelde B. "Evaluating Research Library Collections in Psychology: Beyond the Conspectus." **Behavioral & Social Sciences Librarian** 10, no. 2 (1991): 27-56.

The eight University of California system libraries plus Stanford had completed the Psychology Conspectus as part of NCIP, Phase I, between 1983 and 1985. Between 1986 and 1988, Gilman chaired a "pilot" committee, containing representatives from the nine institutions, charged with further analysis and exploration of the possibilities of cooperative collection development in psychology. The article describes the committee's charge, issues and problems, process, and recommendations. Although no formal cooperative agreements were reached, it was decided to continue meeting once a year. Useful information is contained in a lengthy appendix that lists the nine participating libraries' collecting levels and language codes for fifty-one subject groups on the psychology worksheet and presents an alternative psychology subject breakdown developed at UC-Riverside, which the committee believed describes contemporary psychology better than the Conspectus terminology. Many articles recount implementation of the Conspectus, but this entry describes what happens afterwards.

343. MacEwan, Bonnie. "The North American Inventory Project: A Tool for Selection, Education and Communication." **Library Acquisitions: Practice & Theory** 13, no. 1 (1989): 45-50.

This reflective analysis, based on the author's participation in the ongoing implementation of the Conspectus at the University of Missouri-Columbia (UM-C) Libraries as part of the North American Collections Inventory Project, emphasizes the practical value derived from applying the Conspectus. Somewhat facetiously, MacEwan mentions two approaches: "get-the-darn-thing-done" and "work through the sheets slowly." UM-C opted for the latter and is spending five years on the project. Benefits include greater knowledge of the collection, better communications with faculty, attention addressed to touchy issues such as branch-central library relationships, and attention focused on the collection itself. A table illustrating how the worksheets were modified by the UM-C Libraries is particularly interesting.

344. Millson-Martula, Christopher A. "The Greater Midwest Regional Medical Library Network and Coordinated Cooperative Collection Development: The RLG Conspectus and Beyond." **Illinois Libraries** 71 (January 1989): 31-39.

This entry offers a detailed description concerning use of the RLG Medical and Health Sciences Conspectus worksheets in the GMRMLN Conspectus Project, during 1987-1988, to analyze forty-two academic and hospital library collections in a ten-state area. The worksheets were modified by the addition of ten new subject descriptors dealing with the socioeconomic aspects of medicine, while separate collecting level assessments were assigned for both serials and monographs. Data on current and retrospective serial holdings, total monographs, and current monographic acquisitions were compiled to help evaluators assign collecting levels. Millson-Martula lists seven perceived benefits derived from the project, including staff training and better control of operating costs. The last half of the article explains how the gathered data are being used for implementing cooperative collection development activities (a task still in progress).

345. Newby, Jill, and Patricia Promis. "Collection Assessment Using the RLG Conspectus." **Collection Management** 13, nos. 1/2 (1990): 1-14.

This entry's title is a slight misnomer. A locally devised Conspectus approach, but not the RLG Conspectus itself, was used to evaluate the general ecology and plant ecology collection at the University of Arizona. LC subject headings and class numbers were assigned to courses and faculty research interests, while the undergraduate, core, reference, journal, graduate student, faculty research, and specialized topic collections were assessed by various checklists. To obtain a single document that would integrate information concerning the curriculum, faculty research, and library holdings, the findings were summarized in a worksheet similar in format to the RLG Conspectus. Much detailed information concerning the model's implementation is contained here.

The authors assert that the "uniqueness of this approach" is that other categories of information can be added. Additionally, they believe that their model "can be replicated to good effect elsewhere."

346. Stark, Marilyn M. "Evaluating the Geoscience Collection." In **Maps in the Geoscience Community; Proceedings of the Nineteenth Meeting of the Geoscience Information Society, Nov. 5-8, 1984,** edited by Claren M. Kidd, 91-108. N.p.: Geoscience Information Society, 1985. 209p. (Proceedings of the Geoscience Information Society, vol. 15).

Stark describes the evaluation of the Colorado School of Mines geoscience collection, using a modified form of the RLG Conspectus, during 1983 and 1984 as part of a Colorado Alliance of Research Libraries cooperative project and to assist the writing of a collection development policy. She stresses the procedures used as well as both the "positive results" (e.g., involvement of faculty) and "negative results" (e.g., subjectivity of evaluation). Three-fourths of the article is devoted to an appendix that displays the Conspectus workforms and materials pertinent to the collection development policy. This is not an especially well-written contribution, but it offers one of the earliest examples of applying the Conspectus in a specific library.

347. Stubban, Vanessa L. "Use of the RLG Conspectus as a Tool for Analyzing and Evaluating Agricultural Collections." **Quarterly Bulletin of the International Association of Agricultural Librarians & Documentalists** 33, no. 3 (1988): 105-10.

The Kansas State University agricultural collection was quickly analyzed using the Conspectus in September and October 1986 to provide data to the National Agricultural Library. A major portion of the article focuses on the four data-gathering methods used: 1) compiling statistics on circulation, ILL, and holdings; 2) checking standard lists and bibliographies; 3) user and staff opinion; and 4) direct examination. However, assigning collecting codes was the "most difficult portion."

Stubban observes that "[t]he RLG Conspectus can be a useful tool in analyzing agricultural collections." She notes that other libraries needing to complete the Conspectus with minimal time or staff could be interested in these methods, while advising them to set timetables and delegate responsibility.

348. Triplehorn, Julia, and Dennis Stephens. "Evaluation of a Geoscience Library Collection." In **Micros, Minis, and Geoscience Information; Proceedings of the Twentieth Meeting of the Geoscience Information Society, Orlando, Florida, October 27-31, 1985**, 107-12. Alexandria, Va.: Geoscience Information Society, 1987. 176p. (Proceedings of the Geoscience Information Society, vol. 16).

Triplehorn and Stephens relate, in a first-person narrative, the Conspectus' use in the Geophysical Institute library of the University of Alaska-Fairbanks as part of the Alaska Project, whereby major Alaskan libraries are implementing the Conspectus. They perceive five separate steps to the implementation: worksheet preparation, selection of the evaluation team, the actual collection evaluation itself, compilation of the information gathered, and analysis of the results. The authors conclude by listing six specific benefits of the Conspectus methodology, including its suitability for a small special library and the observation that it is inexpensive and requires "minimal time" (in contrast to what many others have observed). Finally, the Conspectus is recommended for other geoscience libraries.

349. Wood, Richard. "The Conspectus as a Collection Development Tool for College Libraries and Consortia." In **Acquisitions '90; Conference on Acquisitions, Budgets, and Collections; May 16 and 17, 1990, St. Louis, Missouri; Proceedings**, compiled and edited by David C. Genaway, 413-34. Canfield, Ohio: Genaway, 1990. 435p. ISBN 0-943970-06-7.

The use of the Conspectus by the Charleston Academic Libraries Consortium (CALC) during the late 1980s is appraised by the director of one of the participating libraries, the Citadel. After describing the Conspectus itself, the CALC efforts are analyzed, concentrating on an ARL training workshop in September 1987, the consortium objectives, results achieved, obstacles, and perceived benefits. A notable feature is a review of the problems encountered in various techniques for collection level assessment, including list checking, shelflist counts, shelf scanning, expert opinion, and client-centered statistical techniques relating to circulation, ILL, etc. Throughout the presentation the author is quite positive about the Conspectus, concluding that "most institutions should find the Conspectus methodology very valuable."

THE CONSPECTUS IN EUROPE

350. Hanger, Stephen. "Collection Development in the British Library: The Role of the RLG Conspectus." **Journal of Librarianship** 19 (April 1987): 89-107.

Between March and October 1985, the British Library was the initial institution in the United Kingdom to implement the Conspectus, in the first analysis of its collection since the one conducted by Panizzi in the 1840s. Hanger analyzes the implementation and the difficulties encountered. An "Exclusions Policy" was developed to deal with material not covered by the Conspectus, such as manuscripts, art works, and telephone directories. Numerous problems are discussed, including the collecting level codes, which seemed more appropriate to a university than a national library, and "anomalies" in the LC classification breakdown. Appendixes list the Conspectus collecting level and language codes as well as the slightly revised language codes devised by the British Library.

The author attributes the difficulties to the British Library itself as much as to the Conspectus, while stating, "Despite the limitations of the RLG Conspectus ... the British Library remains optimistic about the scheme." (See also Holt and Hanger entry 352.)

351. Heaney, Henry. "Western European Interest in Conspectus." **Libri** 40 (March 1990): 28-32.

The activities of a Conspectus Working Group, appointed by LIBER (Ligue des Bibliothéques Europeénnes de Recherche) to conduct long-range planning for its implementation in continental Europe, are recounted. Important tasks include revising worksheets to counter translation bias, developing a model training program, and rewriting the manual "probably into several language versions." The creation of an international database indicating collection strengths is a major aim. Much has been written about the Conspectus in the United States, the United Kingdom, Canada, and Australia; Heaney's short piece helps fill a void in regard to continental Europe.

352. Holt, Brian G. F., and Stephen Hanger. **Conspectus in the British Library; Collection Development Review; A Summary of Current Collecting Intensity Data as Recorded on RLG Conspectus Worksheets with Completed Worksheets on Microfiche**. London: British Library, 1986. 60p. plus 9 microfiche in pocket. ISBN 0-7123-0123-2.

Although in-house library publications were excluded from this literature guide and bibliography, this item is a published book available for commercial sale. The results of using the Conspectus to analyze the British Library collection in 1985 are displayed. (See also Hanger entry 350.) As stated in the preface, it is hoped to "demonstrate how, in the British context, the Conspectus methodology ... can be implemented."

Most of the document is devoted to summaries, using the Conspectus format, of the British Library's selection policy. The completed Conspectus worksheets themselves are contained on nine supplementary microfiche. Appendixes include the collecting level and language code definitions, as well as the Exclusions Policy that concerns materials not covered by the Conspectus. Beyond its obvious value to anyone interested in the British Library's collection, this item offers a detailed illustration of the Conspectus's application in a specific library.

353. Matheson, Ann. "The Conspectus Experience." **Journal of Librarianship** 22 (July 1990): 171-82.

The Keeper of Printed Books at the National Library of Scotland describes the Conspectus's application by a consortium of eleven Scottish research libraries (the first use by a European consortium) in the ten months from October 1986 to August 1987. They used a "fast-track" approach, that is, getting it done quickly. The cost, data seldom revealed in the Conspectus literature, was 35,000 British pounds. Uses of the Conspectus by a single library, a group of geographically close libraries, and a consortium are fairly extensively discussed. The Scottish participants believe the Conspectus was "well worth undertaking," despite lingering concerns about its methodology and reliability. (See also Matheson entry 356.)

354. Matheson, Ann. "Conspectus in the United Kingdom." **Alexandria** 1 (May 1989): 51-59.

Apart from the British Library, eleven Scottish research libraries, and the National Library of Wales (all of which will have completed the Conspectus when the latter finishes the task in 1989), Matheson declares that the Conspectus's reception in the United Kingdom has been "generally cool." There have been no more than "some minor flirtations" with the Conspectus "in a few English libraries." Matheson attributes this "caution" to a number of factors, including fear that Conspectus information will be used for "cost-cutting" in the United Kingdom's "adverse ... funding climate" for research libraries and concerns about the staffing implications, as well as the system's "imprecisions."

355. Matheson, Ann. "Co-operative Approaches in Scotland." In **Collection Development: Options for Effective Management; Proceedings of a Conference of the Library and Information Research Group, University of Sheffield, 1987**, edited by Sheila Corrall, 119-31. London: Taylor Graham, 1988. 155p. ISBN 0-947568-25-5.

This selection discusses the Conspectus in the context of cooperation among Scottish research libraries dating from the 1970s. Matheson attributes some of the Conspectus's biases to "the particular interests of individual academics" on the North American committees that devised the various sections. Four benefits of having used the Conspectus are elaborated upon: advancing collaboration, gathering "raw data" about a collection, giving an indication of a collection's strengths and weaknesses, and understanding what other libraries are currently collecting. An appended synopsis of the discussion following Matheson's presentation includes the statement that the Conspectus "worked better" in the humanities than the sciences.

356. Matheson, Ann. "The Planning and Implementation of Conspectus in Scotland." **Journal of Librarianship** 19 (July 1987): 141-51.

Preparation for application of the Conspectus in eleven Scottish research libraries is narrated. Following the unanimous "go ahead" decision in May 1986, the worksheets were adapted by reducing the North American bias and expanding subject areas pertinent to Scotland. A two-day workshop was held in October 1986 to explain the theoretical and practical aspects of applying the Conspectus. A coordinator was appointed and the chief conspectors from each library arranged to meet regularly with a steering group established to monitor and guide the project. This article, finished in February 1987, emphasizes the planning process for a project completed in August 1987. For a final report, see Matheson entry 353.

357. Milne, Ronald. "Conspectus at the Coal-Face." **British Journal of Academic Librarianship** 3 (Summer 1988): 89-98.

Milne recounts the Conspectus's implementation at the Glasgow University Library between November 1986 and the autumn of 1987, as part of the Scottish Conspectus Project described by Matheson (entries 353 and 356). Problems were posed by worksheet flaws, application of the supplemental guidelines for natural history and biology, and Glasgow's use of classification schemes other than LC. The author believes the "fast-track" approach, relying primarily on qualitative assessment (i.e., impressionistic "informed gut reaction"), "almost certainly" produced as reliable results as more time-consuming methods. In summary, he states that the Conspectus "worked tolerably well," but "some skepticism remains."

358. Pringle, R. V. "Conspectus in Scotland: Report to SCONUL." **LIBER News Sheet**, no. 23 (1988): 5-17.

After briefly describing the Conspectus process, a librarian from St. Andrews University reports that, as of September 1987, several libraries, including his, were "weeks or even months" behind schedule in implementing the Scottish Conspectus. He states that the Scottish Studies Update requires more time to complete than the other worksheets. Following discussion of numerous problems involving the worksheets, such as inaccurate LC class numbers and omission of some subjects, it is estimated that 6 percent of the headings required revision. Upon adoption, the Conspectus was viewed "with varying degrees of enthusiasm and cynicism," but "all of us ... learned a great deal more about our libraries." Pringle considers the scheme "workable."

359. Reed-Scott, Jutta. "The Conspectus in North America and Western Europe: A Report on the Program Session at the ACRL/WESS." **LIBER News Sheet**, no. 24 (1988): 14-20.

The author summarizes the presentations at a session devoted to the Conspectus in North America and Western Europe at an ACRL Western European Studies Section conference held in Florence, Italy, in April 1988. Gardner offered an overview of the Conspectus's historical development and use in North America. Reed-Scott discussed the implications of the Conspectus for Western European Studies, noting that fifty Primary Collecting Responsibilities had been assigned in Western European Studies in North America. Matheson recounted use of the Conspectus in Scotland. Simonot's presentation from the French perspective noted that the Conspectus "seemed to fit the French university libraries" despite a number of difficulties, including the North American bias, the LC classification, and the lack of subject specialists in French academic libraries. Finally, Heaney addressed Conspectus planning in Europe, terming the Conspectus the "best vehicle" for resource sharing and preservation.

360. Van Heijst, Jacob. "Dutch Cooperative Collection Development and the Conspectus Method." **LIBER Bulletin**, no. 30 (1988): 33-36.

The National Librarian of the Netherlands describes use of the Conspectus in his country. In April 1987, a Dutch Association of Research Libraries committee recommended that Dutch research libraries analyze their collecting patterns by assigning Conspectus "Current Collecting Intensity" codes and that every title added to the Dutch national union catalog contain the applicable Conspectus descriptor (to facilitate computerized verification studies). The Dutch were also considering use of the Conspectus classification in their online shared subject catalog, so that subject searches could be conducted by Conspectus category. Van Heijst observes that the "Conspectus can save time and money." This is the only item in this bibliography that deals with the Conspectus in the Netherlands.

THE CONSPECTUS IN AUSTRALIA AND NEW ZEALAND

361. Allen, G. G. "A Case against Conspectus." **Australian Library Journal** 38 (August 1989): 211-16.

As the title promises, this essay is vehemently critical of the Conspectus and its proponents. Initial statements that the Conspectus has achieved a "mystical status" and the pertinent literature is "self-congratulatory" indicate the author's tone. Allen's argument against the Conspectus may be summarized as follows: it has "inherent logical weaknesses"; is not accurate; will not produce relevant results; is not worth the required cost and labor even if it did produce results; and, in any case, is irrelevant to the needs of most Australian libraries. His comment that the Conspectus "is the outcome of an outmoded concern for the ownership of massive, comprehensive collections" might be questioned by many observers.

362. Campbell, Judith. "Conferences: The RLG Conspectus and Collection Evaluation." **Australian Academic & Research Libraries** 19 (December 1988): 235-36.

A seminar on the Conspectus at the University of South Wales in August 1988 is briefly reported. Campbell stresses that the "firm belief" of keynote speaker Paul Mosher in the Conspectus "gave confidence even to those with sceptical tendencies." This entry is of value because of the rather short summaries of the presentations by Mosher,[2] Wainwright (entry 370), Cameron,[3] Schmidt (entry 368), Henty (entry 365), and Whitehead (entry 102), which were published in the March 1989 issue of *Australian Academic & Research Libraries*.

363. Clayton, Peter. "Conspectus Reconsidered." **Australian Academic & Research Libraries** 21 (September 1990): 179-86.

Responding to recommendations to adopt the Conspectus for Australian libraries made in 1988 by the Australian Libraries Summit and a special task force, Clayton suggests consideration of alternatives, such as greater use of the Australian Bibliographic Network or conducting a Conspectus cost-benefit analysis before final commitment. After briefly listing ten benefits (e.g., resource sharing, preservation priorities, budget requests), he elaborates at considerably greater length upon ten problems with the Conspectus, including the large amount of required work, its North American bias, and the tendency to measure size rather than quality in the Conspectus assessment process. In a "Dear Peter" rejoinder, Margaret Henty asserts that the question "is not so much one of 'can we afford it?' as 'can we not afford it?' "

364. Henri, James. "The RLG Conspectus Down Under: Report on an Australian Seminar, 'The RLG Conspectus and Collection Evaluation.' " **Library Acquisitions: Practice & Theory** 13, no. 1 (1989): 73-80.

The presentations at an August 29, 1988, seminar sponsored by the Library Association of Australia, concerning the suitability of the RLG Conspectus for Australian academic libraries, are thoroughly summarized, including Mosher's[4] keynote address and papers by Wainwright (entry 370), Cameron,[5] Schmidt (entry 368), Henty (entry 365), and Whitehead (entry 102). These items were also published in the March 1989 *Australian Academic & Research Libraries* and are individually annotated in this bibliography. This piece will clearly be useful to American readers wishing a quick introduction to the use of the Conspectus in Australia.

365. Henty, Margaret. "Library Acquisitions Policy by Consultation Out of Conspectus." **Australian Academic & Research Libraries** 20 (March 1989): 47-50.

This paper describes the process of drafting the collection development policy, modeled on the format of the RLG Conspectus, for the Australian National University Library during 1987. The Conspectus language codes were modified by the addition of two new codes: "A" for Asian vernacular languages and "C" for Asian colonial languages. Henty stresses that the fact that the Law and East Asian vernacular holdings were not classed in the LC system presented a problem. The ALA has recommended use of the Conspectus format for writing collection development policies and it is interesting to observe that the Conspectus has been used for that purpose in Australia.

366. Horacek, John. "The Victorian Chemistry Conspectus Pilot Project." **Australian Academic & Research Libraries** 21 (December 1990): 252-60.

Horacek describes a pilot project in which the Chemistry Division of the Pacific Northwest Conspectus was tested in eleven college, university, and public sector special libraries in the Australian state of Victoria during late 1989-early 1990. The CASSI list of "1,000 journals most frequently cited" was checked against the library holdings to assist completion of the worksheets. Horacek notes "the methodology, as such, was found interesting by the participants, but not all were convinced of its cost-effectiveness." The Dewey classification posed problems because either several participating libraries did not classify their serials (the most important format for Chemistry) in Dewey or much useful Chemistry material lies outside the 540 Dewey range covered on the worksheet. The article ends with seven specific conclusions, including the astute observation that although the Conspectus is perceived as time-consuming the same could be said of other collection evaluation methods.

367. Powell, Nancy, and Margaret Bushing. "Collection Evaluation Workshops Project: Consultants Report." **New Zealand Libraries** 46 (September 1991): 9-12.

The authors, who acted as consultants, describe several national and regional Conspectus training workshops for New Zealand librarians held in Wellington, Auckland, and Chrishchurch, New Zealand in November 1990, after the New Zealand Library Association adopted the Pacific Northwest Conspectus as a model for collection evaluation. The participants, representing academic, public and special libraries, returned for follow-up workshops after implementing a Conspectus Division in their libraries. The workshop objectives, the type of data gathered to assist assessment, and the potential uses of the assessment information are listed in bullet style. A figure illustrates ILL, a spreadsheet for circulation, and acquisitions data used to help librarians identify strengths and weaknesses in their collections. While not essential reading for North American librarians, this item has value for describing the status of the Conspectus in New Zealand.

368. Schmidt, Jannie. "Collection Evaluation and the Conspectus." **Australian Academic & Research Libraries** 20 (March 1989): 29-37.

Schmidt argues that the Conspectus may not be suitable for the Australian environment because of the small number of Australian research libraries. Moreover, a less detailed subject breakdown based on Dewey and the diversion of potential Conspectus implementation costs to the Australian Bibliographic Network might be preferable. Additional pertinent observations include: 1) many evaluation techniques "measure" rather than evaluate, 2) evaluation of a library program is more useful than evaluating the collection per se, and 3) the success of library cooperation is determined more by commitment than collection evaluation.

369. Shaw, J. Margaret. "Conspectus as a Tool for Art Libraries in Australia." **Australian Academic & Research Libraries** 21 (March 1990): 33-38.

After briefly reviewing use of the Conspectus by major North American art libraries and conceding that they "have been generally enthusiastic about the Conspectus," Shaw offers a biting critique from the Australian perspective. Based on a "Conspectus-type analysis" of several art collections in Canberra, she observes that the Conspectus is of "no particular value" to Australian art libraries, because of the costs of implementation and verification studies, problems in the subject breakdown, and difficulties in comparing different types of libraries. The author concludes with a quote from Nancy Gwinn, "There is the tendency to fall in love with the process of data gathering," meaning that the Conspectus implementation process can become an end in itself.

370. Wainwright, Eric. "Conspectus and the National Library of Australia." **Australian Academic & Research Libraries** 20 (March 1989): 16-22.

The National Library of Australia's Deputy Director-General offers an overview of the Conspectus in Australia and the National Library's role in promoting it. In December 1987 the National Library of Australia adopted the Conspectus for revision of its collection development policy. He explains that "geographic collecting levels," whereby every country in the world was assigned a level, were added to the Conspectus. Wainwright states that the general collecting levels are not useful for pictorial material, oral history, and manuscripts. Wainwright asserts that if the Conspectus is universally adopted in Australia, the worksheet areas covering Australian history, literature, and law will need to be revised and the supplementary guidelines "Australianized." The author concludes that the National Library believes the Conspectus is "worth it."

THE PACIFIC NORTHWEST CONSPECTUS

371. Bradley, Kate. "Science Collections in Community College Libraries." **College & Research Libraries News** 50 (July/August 1989): 579-82.

Bradley's piece is notable for appraising the Conspectus's use in a community college library. Bellevue Community College in Washington belatedly entered the LIRN project, evaluating its science holdings with the Conspectus. The author believes that the methodology was successful in assessing the collection's adequacy to support the curriculum, but the Conspectus emphasis on resource sharing does not address community college needs. Because of interdisciplinarity in the social sciences, its usefulness for evaluating these subjects in community colleges is questioned.

372. Fedunok, Suzanne. "Collection Assessment in a Regional Consortium: METRO's Use of the Conspectus." In **Acquisitions '90; Conference on Acquisitions, Budgets, and Collections; May 16 and 17, 1990, St. Louis, Missouri; Proceedings**, compiled and edited by David C. Genaway, 147-58. Canfield, Ohio: Genaway, 1990. 435p. ISBN 0-943970-06-7.

After discussing a number of cooperative collection development efforts in New York State throughout the 1980s, the Metropolitan Reference and Research Library Agency (METRO) Collection Inventory Project, in which seventy-two Greater New York City Libraries are implementing the Pacific Northwest Conspectus, is analyzed. The Conspectus is completed for three subjects (representing science, the social sciences, and the humanities) each year. Twelve of the twenty-four Divisions have been finished so far. Fedunok emphasizes the improvements the METRO project made in the implementation process. She lists nine specific examples, including revising the training workshops and manual and redefining some collecting level code definitions. The author concludes that the Conspectus has been used more internally than externally, because collaboration is both a political and psychological process. (For an earlier report on METRO's use of the Conspectus, see Grimes entry 375.)

373. Forcier, Peggy J. "Building Collections Together: The Pacific Northwest Conspectus." **Library Journal** 113 (April 15, 1988): 43-45.

The Pacific Northwest Conspectus and its implementation through the LIRN Project (Library and Information Resources for the Northwest), a consortium of libraries in Alaska, Idaho, Montana, Oregon, and Washington, are described in this concisely written piece covering the Conspectus structure, creation of an online database, reports, benefits, and training. As of February 1988, 211 libraries had entered 98,000 assessments online. This article will be especially useful to anyone wishing a short, quick overview concerning the Pacific Northwest Conspectus and its implementation.

374. Forcier, Peggy J., and Nancy Powell. "Collection Assessment in the Pacific Northwest: Building a Foundation for Cooperation." In **Advances in Library Automation and Networking**, vol. 3, edited by Joe A. Hewitt, 87-121. Greenwich, Conn.: JAI Press, 1989. 269p. ISBN 0-89232-966-1.

A long and detailed overview of the Pacific Northwest Conspectus is presented, including training, the Conspectus structure, the assessment process, validation studies, the Pacific Northwest Conspectus Database, and potential uses. This paper contains much practical information concerning the assignment of collecting levels. A checklist of points for examining the collection, quantitative guidelines for assigning levels, and data on publishing output in the Conspectus divisions are particularly useful features.

375. Grimes, David. "Assessing Assessment: A Researcher's Evaluation of 'Conspectus.'" **Catholic Library World** 60 (May/June 1989): 259-61, 274.

Beginning in June 1987, the twenty Greater New York academic libraries in METRO conducted a pilot Conspectus collection assessment project modeled after LIRN. The author, who participated at St. John's University (Jamaica, New York) in the areas of art, education, and chemistry, reflects on the Conspectus's value in this short essay. He comments that the Conspectus "standardizes evaluation" and that St. John's used it to evaluate the speech subject area outside the METRO project. Grimes concludes that, despite "imperfections," the Conspectus is "well-rounded, well-organized, and well-supported," as well as "excellent" for its intended purposes. (For a later report concerning the METRO project, when seventy-two libraries rather than just twenty had participated, see Fedunok entry 372.)

376. Haley, Anne, and Douglas K. Ferguson. "The Pacific Northwest Collection Assessment Project." **Resource Sharing & Information Networks** 2 (Spring/Summer 1985): 185-97. Simultaneously issued in **Coordinating Cooperative Collection Development: A National Perspective**, edited by Wilson Luquire, 185-97. New York: Haworth Press, 1986. 253p. LC 85-24847. ISBN 0-86656-543-4.

Haley and Ferguson provide a useful overview of the Library and Information Resources for the Northwest (LIRN) Program. Separate sections of the article cover the project's history, design of the assessment process, training for the library staffs, the Pacific Northwest Conspectus Database (into which the assessments will be entered), the expected timetable, financial aspects, and anticipated outcomes of the project. The Conspectus will also be used to create a directory of special collections. The authors note that over 90 percent of the largest libraries in the region are committed to participating in the assessment process.

377. Oberg, Larry R. "Evaluating the Conspectus Approach for Smaller Library Collections." **College & Research Libraries** 49 (May 1988): 187-96.

The application of the Pacific Northwest Conspectus during the late 1980s at the Albion College library is described. The LIRN project, the Pacific Northwest Conspectus's structure, assessment of the collection, assignment of collecting levels, the validation process, and staff costs are covered in this outstanding article. Three figures illustrate Conspectus worksheets and a comparative report.

Oberg concludes that the Conspectus's benefits outweigh its flaws and that it "is the best instrument we have" for evaluating collections. His assertion that the Conspectus is a "valuable tool" for small academic and public libraries is especially significant, as some observers have disputed that point.

378. Powell, Nancy, comp. and ed. **Pacific Northwest Collection Assessment Manual**. 3d ed. Salem: Pacific Northwest Collection Development Program, Oregon State Library Foundation 1990. 1v. (various pagings). ISBN 1-878609-00-9.

This well-done manual contains a wealth of information about the Pacific Northwest Conspectus and its implementation. It is intended to serve as a "reference tool" for librarians already trained in the Pacific Northwest Conspectus method and a "beginning point" for others. After introducing the Conspectus framework, much attention is paid to the assessment process. Five techniques are outlined: shelflist measurement, shelf scanning, list checking, evaluation by an outside expert, and citation analysis. Examples of LC and Dewey worksheets, as well as various data-gathering worksheets, are included. A particularly useful section covers such assessment issues as uncataloged or special collections, the relationship to collection development policies, audiovisual materials, government documents, and validation studies. An appendix recommends "field tested" bibliography checklists in more than two dozen subject areas.

379. Stephens, Dennis. "The Conspectus in Alaska and How We're Using It." **PNLA Quarterly** 53 (Spring 1989): 15-16.

A brief discussion of the Conspectus's use in Alaska is offered in this first-person narrative. Stephens dates Alaska's "Conspectus effort" to a 1982 Alaska State Library grant and a consultant's report by Paul Mosher. The fact the Pacific Northwest Conspectus Database (in which Alaskan libraries are participating) cannot generate reports mixing LC and Dewey class ranges represents a "substantial difficulty." Examples of Conspectus decision making in three categories are elaborated upon: "easy," "difficult enough to warrant putting them off forever," and those leading to "satisfactory resolution." An appendix displays Conspectus collecting levels for several Alaskan libraries.

380. Stephens, Dennis. "A Stitch in Time: The Alaska Cooperative Collection Development Project." **Resource Sharing & Information Networks** 2 (Spring/Summer 1985): 173-84. Simultaneously issued in **Coordinating Cooperative Collection Development: A National Perspective**, edited by Wilson Luquire, 173-84. New York: Haworth Press, 1986. 253p. LC 85-24847. ISBN 0-86656-543-4.

Stephens describes the Conspectus's role in an Alaskan cooperative collection development project, begun in 1982, involving all types and sizes of libraries. One major long-term goal was the creation of an "Alaska Conspectus" in which the participating Alaskan libraries enter their assessments online. The RLG Conspectus collecting levels 1, 2, and 3 were modified by the addition of sublevels a and b. The author notes "problems fitting in the time" to complete the Conspectus. This item was formerly on the Indiana University School of Library and Information Science collection development course reading list as an illustration of use of the Conspectus by a group of libraries.

381. Stephens, Dennis, and Julia Triplehorn. "Comparison of Library Collections in Geology: A Model Based on the Pacific Northwest Conspectus." In **Collections for the Future: Archivists, Curators, Historians, Bibliographers Speak; Proceedings of the Twenty-Second Meeting of the Geoscience Information Society, October 26-29, 1987, Phoenix, Arizona**, edited by Jean T. Eaglesfield, 103-18. N.p.: Geoscience Information Society, 1988. 159p. (Proceedings of the Geoscience Information Society, vol. 18). ISBN 0-934458-15-1. ISSN 0072-1409.

This selection provides an example of how Conspectus collecting level data can be used to compare library holdings in specific subject areas. The geology collections of nearly thirty academic and special libraries in Alaska, Idaho, Montana, Oregon, and Washington are compared by means of reports supplied in September 1987 from the Pacific Northwest Conspectus Database. Nearly three-fifths of the article is devoted to tables, which present the collecting levels of sixteen libraries in the broad category "geology" and additional libraries in more specific subject headings, such as mineralogy, seismology (an earth-shaking topic), and stratigraphy.

Western Washington, Puget Sound, Idaho, Oregon State, and Montana State Universities have the strongest geologic collections. However, only three of the eight Ph.D.-granting institutions in the Pacific Northwest have reported to the database and this constitutes, in the author's words, "a major weakness of the project."

THE NORTH AMERICAN COLLECTIONS INVENTORY PROJECT

382. Buckingham, Jeanette. "NCIP, Conspectus Methodology and Canadian Health Science Collections." **Bibliotheca Medica Canadiana** 8, no. 3 (1987): 136-39.

This item begins with an account of the Conspectus methodology and Canadian participation in the NCIP. It then analyzes the problems encountered in implementing the Medical and Health Sciences Conspectus at the University of Alberta Library during the summer of 1986. Not only did the worksheets contain typographical errors and missing class ranges, but the LC and NLM class ranges indicated on the worksheets frequently did not reflect precise subject matches. The lack of standard bibliographies for checking monographic holdings posed another problem. Medicine's emphasis on serials, which are often arranged alphabetically rather than by subject, made implementation more difficult, as shelflist counts could not be used. Nevertheless, Buckingham concludes, "we feel that the conspectus methodology provides a valid collection-based assessment instrument" for the health sciences.

383. Farrell, David. "The NCIP Option for Coordinated Collection Management." **Library Resources & Technical Services** 30 (January/March 1986): 47-56.

384. Farrell, David. "The North American Collections Inventory Project (NCIP): Phase II Results in Indiana." **Resource Sharing & Information Networks** 2 (Spring/Summer 1985): 37-48. Simultaneously issued in **Coordinating Cooperative Collection Development: A National Perspective**, edited by Wilson Luquire, 37-48. New York: Haworth Press, 1986. 253p. LC 85-24847. ISBN 0-86656-543-4.

These two articles cover essentially the same subject matter, although one offers more detail. After discussing the concept of cooperative collection development and key entities in Indiana's cooperative environment, Farrell describes phase II of the NCIP, in which the Indiana, Purdue, and Notre Dame university libraries tested the Conspectus approach during 1984. Their three goals were to test the Conspectus format and training materials, gather data on the time and cost of implementation, and set a schedule to finish the Conspectus. The organizational structure and required hours for implementing seven Conspectus Divisions and applying several verification studies are then recounted, along with the benefits derived from the exercise, such as increased interaction with colleagues. The Conspectus "is leading toward closer coordination of resources," but both reports state "it is something like the Jarvik-7 artificial heart ... you will have to tolerate undesirable side effects."

385. Farrell, David, and Jutta Reed-Scott. "The North American Collections Inventory Project: Implications for the Future of Coordinated Management of Research Collections." **Library Resources & Technical Services** 33 (January 1989): 15-28.

The authors offer the best overview of the NCIP yet published. After tracing the NCIP from its origin to the complex problems facing research libraries during the late 1970s, separate sections analyze the major developments in the developmental phase (1983), the test phase (1984), the transitional years (1984-1985), the full scale implementation phase (1985-1988), the Canadian Conspectus Project, the Pacific

Northwest Project, and European use. The NCIP is then evaluated in terms of the eight rationales (e.g., to inventory the strength of North American research libraries) cited by the ARL Board of Directors when it approved the project.

Farrell and Reed-Scott next discuss three obstacles to the NCIP: 1) the Conspectus worksheets for three letters of the LC classification are not completed, 2) there are methodological concerns, especially in regard to the LC classification itself, and 3) the assessment approach evaluates collections in terms of the entire "universe of publications." It is concluded that the Conspectus "has not yet realized its potential."

386. Gardner, Jeffrey J. "National Collections Inventory Project: A Brief Description." **Encyclopedia of Library & Information Science** 41 (1987): 229-30. Supplement 6.

The purpose, objectives, and major phases of the NCIP, founded in July 1983 by ARL to employ the RLG Conspectus for the creation of a national, online database of library resources, are concisely described. A training manual was developed in phase one; pilot tests conducted at Indiana, Notre Dame, and Purdue universities in phase two; and actual implementation in phase three. Gardner's piece will be useful to anyone wishing a short introduction to the NCIP.

387. Henige, David. "Epistemological Dead End and Ergonomic Disaster?: The North American Collections Inventory Project." **Journal of Academic Librarianship** 13 (September 1987): 209-13.

As suggested in the title, this entry is highly critical of the Conspectus, and by implication, the NCIP. Henige begins by questioning whether the Conspectus offers information that is not already known, is not needed, and is "workaday true." It is argued that much Conspectus terminology, such as "research level," is inherently ambiguous and will not be interpreted consistently. The author asserts that verification studies are "nothing more than grading on the curve," because they represent comparison against other libraries rather than a fixed standard. He feels that the National Shelflist Count's "unequivocal linear measurements" are preferable to the Conspectus's "highly subjective, and abstract aggregation of selectors' opinions."

388. Marley, Carol. "The Role of NCIP (National Collections Inventory Project)." **ACML Bulletin** 60 (1986): 1-4.

This paper, presented at the Association of Canadian Map Librarians annual conference in June 1986, briefly introduces the RLG Conspectus to the uninitiated. The author explains that the Conspectus approach combines traditional quantitative and qualitative methods. Drawing on her personal experience implementing the Religion and Philosophy Conspectus as a pilot study at McGill University, in cooperation with Queens University and the National Library of Canada, Marley notes that it "is a time-consuming project" and "clearly there are special problems" for libraries not using the LC classification.

389. Miller, Robert C. "NCIP in the United States." In Association of Research Libraries, **NCIP: Means to an End; Minutes of the 109th Meeting, October 22-23, 1986, Washington, D.C.**, 11-13. Washington, D.C.: Association of Research Libraries, 1987. 127p. ISSN 0044-9652.

The Director of the Notre Dame University libraries offers some brief but perceptive observations on the NCIP and the Conspectus, often from the perspective of his experience in Indiana, where the Conspectus was implemented as a pilot project in 1982. He wryly observes, "[O]ne of the great things about it [the Conspectus] is there were lots of problems." He mentions four key elements to the NCIP: the Conspectus, the "national online tool," staff training, and the NCIP's management structure. Miller comments that Notre Dame derived more benefit from working with Indiana and Purdue than it would have completing the Conspectus alone.

390. Mosher, Paul H. "A National Scheme for Collaboration in Collection Development: The RLG-NCIP Effort." **Resource Sharing & Information Networks** 2 (Spring/Summer 1985): 21-35. Simultaneously issued in **Coordinating Cooperative Collection Development: A National Perspective**, edited by Wilson Luquire, 37-48. New York: Haworth Press, 1986. 253p. LC 85-24847. ISBN 0-86656-543-4.

Mosher analyzes the Conspectus in the context of collaboration among North American research libraries. He begins by stating that research libraries, having abandoned the myth of the "self-sufficient" library, are moving towards the new myth of "collaborative" collection development. Most of this publication is devoted to separate sections covering the RLG Conspectus and the NCIP project, although the author asserts that he has carefully avoided repeating information from the Gwinn and Mosher article (entry 327).

Particularly relevant is the author's outline of four ways the Conspectus supports collaborative collection development: 1) providing a "map" of North American research collection strengths, 2) assisting the location of significant research collections in a particular subject, 3) allowing local collecting to be related to collections at other institutions, and 4) assisting cooperative efforts in cataloging and preservation.

391. Scott, Marianne. "NCIP in Canada." In Association of Research Libraries, **NCIP: Means to an End; Minutes of the 109th Meeting, October 22-23, 1986, Washington, D.C.**, 14-18. Washington, D.C.: Association of Research Libraries, 1987. 127p. ISSN 0044-9652.

The NCIP's history in Canada is reviewed by the National Librarian of Canada. Scott notes that the University of Manitoba took part in the first Conspectus pilot study. From 1979 to 1984, the National Library was interested in resource sharing on a national scale, while in 1984 there was "a sort of coming together" of the National Library and the Association of Canadian Research Libraries concerning use of the Conspectus for a national inventory of library holdings. She emphasizes that it was necessary to "Canadianize" the Conspectus through expansion of the Canadian law, history, and literature sections and a rework of the language codes—"French is not a foreign language in Canadian libraries."

VERIFICATION STUDIES

392. Coleman, Jim. "Verification Studies: Design and Implementation." **College & Research Libraries News** 46 (July/August 1985): 338-40.

Coleman discusses the methodological issues involved in designing a verification study (an instrument for libraries to verify the accuracy of their assigned collecting levels). Because shelflist measurements are considered inappropriate for verification purposes, a sample of bibliographical citations (ranging from 300 to 600) should be developed. When checking the citations against holdings, one must decide whether to count journals, varying editions, alternate formats, and alternate languages. This short piece clarifies a number of fundamental issues regarding design of an assessment tool.

393. Larson, Jeffry. "The RLG Conspectus French Literature Collection Assessment Project." **Collection Management** 6 (Spring/Summer 1984): 97-114.

The author of the Conspectus verification instrument for French literature explains the methodology he used in compiling the 1,000-item verification checklist from the *MLA Bibliography* and 12 other sources. Particular attention was paid to sample selection and representing the appropriate periods and genres. The results of checking the list against the holdings of twenty RLG libraries are analyzed: the best result was 62 percent, compared to 86 percent for the English literature assessment. A number of inconsistencies were observed between the participating libraries' assigned collecting levels and the percentage of the checklist held. The source bibliographies for the checklist, as well as the Conspectus collecting levels and checklist results for the twenty libraries, are presented in appendixes.

394. Lucas, Thomas A. "Verifying the Conspectus: Problems and Progress." **College & Research Libraries News** 51 (March 1990): 199-220

Lucas notes that questions have been raised concerning the reliability of assigned RLG Conspectus collecting levels, with libraries often mistrusting each other's data. To remedy this situation, he recommends that the approach to verification be "redrawn and reapplied." Since 1981, RLG libraries have finished only 13 verification studies, which are time-consuming (involving checking up to 1,000 titles) and usually limited to level 4 collections. Examples of inconsistencies revealed by these studies are presented. Howard White's design of shorter verification studies (forty titles) appropriate to levels 1 through 4 is described and implicitly recommended. (See also White entry 397.)

395. Mosher, Paul. "The Nature and Uses of RLG Verification Studies." **College & Research Libraries News** 46 (July/August 1985): 336-38.

This short piece offers an excellent introduction to verification studies. Mosher explains that bibliographies, such as the *Cambridge Bibliography of English Literature*, are checked against major research collections to confirm that Conspectus collecting levels were assigned consistently among different libraries as well as to indicate relative strength and overlap. Data are reported here for verification studies in English literature and Renaissance and Baroque art history. Mosher points out that these overlap data apply to major libraries scattered across the country, whereas most overlap studies are limited to libraries in a particular area. "Supplemental Guidelines" are being developed to assist accurate collecting level assignments.

396. Signori, Donna L. "Analysis of a Verification Study of Post-1914 English Canadian Literature: Guidelines in Retrospect." **Collection Management** 11, nos. 3/4 (1989): 151-66.

The development at the National Library of Canada of the Conspectus verification instrument for post-1914 English Canadian literature is described. Preliminary steps included surveying the field as well as identifying and then selecting appropriate bibliographies. The methodological difficulties (ascertaining the exact population size and developing a sampling methodology) in deriving a 1,276-item checklist to use as the verification tool are recounted. The author notes that the bibliographic entries and statistical results were entered on diskettes, which will be distributed to other academic libraries in the United States and Canada to allow anticipated comparisons using SPSS software. Detailed results of checking the verification study instrument against the National Library of Canada's holdings are reported in two tables.

397. White, Howard D. "Evaluating Subject Collections." In **Annual Report of OCLC Research; July 1987-June 1988,** 46-48. Dublin, Ohio: OCLC Online Computer Library Center, 1988. 76p. ISSN 0894-198X.

Arguing that RLG Conspectus verification studies consisting of 1,000-item checklists are time-consuming and reflect only high collecting levels, White proposes the use of 40-item checklists, selected by subject specialists, for verification purposes. The forty titles are grouped into quartiles corresponding to Conspectus levels 1 through 4, based on the number of libraries holding them in OCLC. The ten most frequently held represent level 1, while the ten held by the fewest libraries correspond to level 4.

The method was tested in the library and information science nineteenth-century Russian literature fields at both Temple University and the University of Pennsylvania. The article concludes that "[b]oth tests discriminated well," confirming the hypothesis that fewer titles would be held at the higher levels.

THE NATIONAL SHELFLIST COUNT

398. Branin, Joseph J., David Farrell, and Mariann Tiblin. "The National Shelflist Count Project: Its History, Limitations and Usefulness." **Library Resources & Technical Services** 29 (October/December 1985): 333-42.

This excellent overview, written by a three-member task force appointed to reexamine the National Shelflist Count's role, covers its history, structure, potential uses, and limitations. The facts that only material classified according to the LC system is included in the count and that quantitative data is only one element of quality are major drawbacks. Benefits include comparative data concerning growth rates and relative size of subject collections. A figure compares the National Shelflist Count and the RLG Conspectus subject breakdowns for philosophy. The authors comment that the National Shelflist Count "can support collection assessment work required by the Conspectus."

The seven specific recommendations of the task force report, including continuing of the project and gathering data every two years, are listed. When most of these recommendations were accepted by the Chief Collection Development Officers of Large Research Libraries Discussion Group in June 1984, the project was reactivated (data had not been gathered since 1977). In February 1985, the RTSD asked the ARL libraries to participate and had received positive responses from fifty by April 1985.

399. Dannelly, Gay N. "The National Shelflist Count: A Tool for Collection Management." **Library Acquisitions: Practice & Theory** 13, no. 3 (1989): 241-50.

Dannelly explains the format and uses of National Shelflist Count data. Several statistical tables constitute an especially notable feature of this item. A table presenting data on unclassified holdings at the Boston, Brown, Columbia, Indiana, and Johns Hopkins university libraries is significant, because uncataloged material is not included in the regular count. Also of note are the statistics on total classified titles in all subjects, in literature, and in American literature from 1900 to 1960 for the forty-eight libraries participating in the 1985 count.

It is emphasized that the National Shelflist Count "cannot evaluate the quality of a collection," but with limitations "is an exceptionally useful collection management tool." Obviously, one should consult the National Shelflist Count itself (entry 403) for full data.

400. **The National Shelflist Count; Titles Classified by the Library of Congress and National Library of Medicine Classifications, 1989; prepared for the Association for Library Collections & Technical Services, a Division of the American Library Association, by the Library Research Center, the Graduate School of Library & Information Science, University of Illinois at Urbana-Champaign.** Chicago: American Library Association, 1990. 680p. ISBN 0-8389-7421-x.

The National Shelflist Count's most recent version presents holdings data for sixty libraries (the Library of Congress, "Group A" libraries that hold more than 1,100,000 titles, "Group B" libraries that contain between 800,000 and 1,100,000 titles, "Group C" libraries with fewer than 800,000 titles, the National Library of Medicine, the Smithsonian Institution, and the National Agricultural Library) according to 626 ranges of the Library of Congress and National Library of Medicine classification systems. For each classification range data are presented as follows: 1989 holdings; the range's percentage of the library's total collection; the library's holdings in the range relative to all reporting libraries, libraries in their group, and the Library of Congress; and the percentage of change in holdings between 1985 and 1989. The $125 price of the 1989 *National Shelflist Count* may be prohibitive to many, although this edition is easier to use and more complete than earlier versions.

401. Ortopan, LeRoy D. "National Shelflist Count: A Historical Introduction." **Library Resources & Technical Services** 29 (October/December 1985): 328-32.

The origin and history of the National Shelflist Count are described, often in the first person, by the individual whose name is most frequently associated with it. Ortopan relates that shelflist measurement to analyze holdings by subject classification originated at Northwestern University in the early 1960s and was further developed at Wisconsin in 1966 and Berkeley in 1971. This method evolved into the

National Shelflist Count when seventeen universities used it in 1973, twenty-six in 1975, and twenty-seven in 1977. Finally, the RTSD assumed responsibility for the project in 1985. The author concludes by asserting that the National Shelflist Count "has provided a different approach to collection analysis in research libraries" and "opened doors of communication."

402. **Titles Classified by the Library of Congress Classification: National Shelflist Count, 1981.** Chicago: Resources and Technical Services Division, American Library Association, 1987. 12 microfiche.

As the title indicates, this is the 1981 National Shelflist Count, available only in microform. It consists of holdings data tables for the Library of Congress, the National Agricultural Library, and thirty U.S. academic libraries organized into three categories: 1) more than 1 million titles, 2) one-half to 1 million titles, and 3) smaller than a half-million titles. Two pages of data are presented for each of the 490 sections of the LC classification into which the National Shelflist Count is organized. The first page includes 1981, 1979, 1975, and 1973 holdings, plus the percentage of the total collection in 1981, 1977, and 1973. The second page contains the number of volumes added between 1981 and 1979, 1977, 1975, and 1973, as well as the percent added.

This entry is less convenient to use than the later versions, because of its microfiche format and the fact that abbreviations are used for the reporting libraries. (The first fiche contains a key to the abbreviations.)

403. **Titles Classified by the Library of Congress Classification: National Shelflist Count, 1985.** Chicago: Resources and Technical Services Division, American Library Association, 1986. 610p. (looseleaf). 5 microfiche.

This item is the 1985 version of the National Shelflist Count. Counts for 1973, 1975, and 1977 were previously published, but the 1981 count was not issued until 1987 (see entry 402). Following some introductory material, the vast majority of this item is devoted to tables of holdings data for forty-six large U.S. academic research libraries, the Library of Congress, and the National Agricultural Library. The academic libraries are categorized into three groups: 1) over 1 million titles; 2) 700,000 to 1 million titles; and 3) less than 700,000 titles. Data are presented for total holdings in the LC classification, 24 broad divisions of the classification, and 490 detailed segments of the LC scheme. The Count also reports each class range as a percentage of the library's total holdings and how the library's holdings in the range compare (in percentage terms) to all other reporting libraries, all other libraries in the same size category, and the Library of Congress.

It goes without saying that the National Shelflist Count offers a wealth of basic statistics that can be used for many collection development purposes. The major drawbacks would be that these data are limited to holdings cataloged in the LC classification system.

NOTES

[1] American Library Association, Resources and Technical Services Division, Collection Development Committee, *Guidelines for Collection Development*, David L. Perkins, ed. (Chicago: American Library Association, 1979), 1-8.

[2] Paul H. Mosher, "Collaborative Collection Development in an Era of Financial Limitations," *Australian Academic & Research Libraries* 20 (March 1989): 5-15.

[3] Margaret A. Cameron, "Evaluation and Inter-Institutional Cooperation in Collection Development," *Australian Academic & Research Libraries* 20 (March 1989): 23-28.

[4] Mosher, "Collaborative Collection Development."

[5] Cameron, "Evaluation and Cooperation."

10

Evaluation of Serials

Because the escalating cost of serials — to the point of near crisis — is an issue of paramount concern to academic librarians, a significant amount has been published recently concerning serials evaluation. Serials have traditionally posed problems in many areas of librarianship, including cataloging and automation, not to mention collection development. An exasperated serials cataloger once told the author that serials do everything human beings do — they are born, they die, they join together, they split up — but even worse, they come back to life after they are dead.

This chapter annotates general discussions of serials evaluation, serials selection models, attempts to identify the core journal collection in particular disciplines, and case studies of serials evaluation, review, or cancellation projects.

The number of published case studies of serial cancellation projects has significantly increased during the last decade. Foremost among the series of issues addressed in this literature are the evaluation methodology and criteria and the organization of the project itself. Serials evaluation criteria typically include subjective quality judgments, curricular relevance, cost, use record, citation data, indexing, ILL records, extent of present holdings, and availability in nearby libraries, to name only the most obvious. Organizational issues concern the degree of faculty involvement, the project's timeframe, political and public relations aspects, the amount of preparation required, learning experiences from previous cancellation projects, and coordination with other libraries.

The chapter is divided into the following sections: general and miscellaneous discussions, serials evaluation models, identification of core journals, and serials cancellation project case studies. (Case studies of general serials evaluation projects for purposes other than cancellation were placed in the first section.) Items that analyze journal prices, patron success in using a serials catalog, or the technical services aspects of serials administration were excluded. The reader is also referred to chapter 4, which covers periodical use studies; chapter 8, which contains many entries relating to the use of citation analysis for serials evaluation; and chapter 11, which deals with journal ranking.

GENERAL AND MISCELLANEOUS DISCUSSIONS

404. Association of Research Libraries. Office of Management Studies. **Serials Control and Deselection Projects**. Washington, D.C.: Association of Research Libraries, Office of Management Studies, 1988. 117p. (SPEC Kit, 147). ISSN 0160-3582.

Written communications relating to serials review and cancellation at a dozen RLG institutions (UCLA, University of California-Riverside, Iowa, Kansas, LSU, Michigan, Minnesota, North Carolina-Chapel Hill, the RLG, SUNY-Buffalo, Texas-Austin, and Toronto) are gathered together. Documents include project justification memos, policies, criteria, and evaluation forms. The statistical data on serials costs and expenditures at various libraries is of particular interest.

405. Baldwin, Jane, and W. M. Baldwin, III. "Let the Buyer Be Aware: High Price Does Not Necessarily Mean High Quality." In **Advances in Serials Management**, vol. 3, edited by Jean G. Cook and Marcia Tuttle, 111-29. Greenwich, Conn.: JAI Press, 1989. 265p. ISBN 0-89232-965-3.

This article investigates the relationship between journal price and quality, based on price data for 1,048 of the 1,125 titles in 15 scientific subject areas ranked by impact factor in the 1987 *SCI*. Although correlational statistics were not employed, the Baldwins conclude that "there was little correlation between cost and quality as measured by impact factor." It was found that publisher type (commercial, association, university, or governmental) was more closely associated with cost than impact factor was. Fifteen tables list expensive journals in each subject area studied, along with their impact factor, cost, and cost/impact factor ratio.

Although much of this item concerns journal pricing (a timely topic, but beyond the scope of this bibliography), the authors think their analysis has application to serials evaluation, stating that "expensive titles with poor impact factors should be targeted for review."

406. Bastille, Jacqueline D., and Carole J. Mankin. "A Simple Objective Method for Determining a Dynamic Journal Collection." **Bulletin of the Medical Library Association** 68 (October 1980): 357-66.

Bastille and Mankin's rigorous study, partially funded by the National Institute of Health, seeks to identify the number of periodicals required to meet total demand as well as to develop criteria for cost-effectively reducing the periodical collection size in a hospital library. The complete usage of the Massachusetts General Hospital Library's journal collection (647 titles held in-house plus ILL requests) was analyzed, based on items reshelved and left on book carts, for the entire 1977 calendar year. A title's usage was related to subscription cost and shelf space requirements. Journals were also ranked according to "density of use," defined as total use divided by a title's linear feet of shelf space. Analysis by publication date revealed that 63 percent of usage was between 1973 and 1977. Numerous tables summarize the findings in a variety of ways.

One hundred percent satisfaction of the 79,369 uses would require 1,999 titles. However, it was concluded that the "most cost-effective decision point" would be to subscribe to the 303 titles used 36 times or more, thus meeting 90 percent of demand, but accounting for 55 percent of shelf space and 50 percent of cost. This intriguing study certainly has relevance to academic libraries. (See also Mankin and Bastille entry 145.)

407. Belanger, Sandra E., Jo Bell Whitlatch, and Robert McDermand. "Managing Business Periodicals Collections." **Collection Management** 14, no. 1/2 (1991): 99-131.

The authors focus on six methods for evaluating business periodical collections: citation analysis, use surveys, user surveys, "studies of uses" (the term the authors employ for availability studies), interlibrary loan, and indexing. Separate sections devoted to each approach explore the pros and cons of each method, cite previous studies, and present statistical results from applying the method to the business periodicals collection at the San Jose State University library at various times during the previous dozen years. The findings from a survey completed by forty-eight faculty during the spring of 1988 are analyzed in considerable detail. Particularly useful are figures that summarize the advantages and disadvantages of the six methods and the role of each method in selection, storage, and cancellation decisions. A useful four-page unannotated bibliography is appended. This article presents a valuable overview of the available serials evaluation methods in the context of data from a single university library.

408. Bensman, Stephen J. "Journal Collection Management as a Cumulative Advantage Process." **College & Research Libraries** 46 (January 1985): 13-29.

This meticulously researched paper argues that the solution to the problems posed by the "exponential growth" and "inflationary surge" of serials is for librarians to develop a "small, multidisciplinary core of heavily used titles." Synthesizing many citation studies and use studies, Bensman hypothesizes the "principle of cumulative advantage" and the "Matthew effect" (a concept introduced by the prominent sociologist Robert Merton), whereby those that have get more, result in the formation of scholarly elites and the concentration of journal usage on a relatively small number of titles. In other words, use and citation of a journal title will generate even more use and citation.

The author argues that because the Matthew effect promotes stability, frequently cited journals will retain their elite status. Thus, one can rely on *JCR* data for periodical collection evaluation. This scholarly article certainly has important practical implications for journal collection management.

409. Besson, Alain, and Ian Sheriff. "Journal Collection Evaluation at the Medical College of St. Bartholomew's Hospital." **British Journal of Academic Librarianship** 1 (Summer 1986): 132-43.

Besson and Sheriff explain a survey method to assess user satisfaction with the journal collection that was applied in the mid-1980s at one of the University of London's medical college libraries. Fifty-three faculty responded to a questionnaire in which they rated, on a 1-to-6 scale, the college library journals' importance to their work and their satisfaction with the collection. The "deficiency needs" method refined by Budd and DiCarlo (entry 55) was then applied to these results. The respondents also listed their five most important specialist journals and rated on a 1-to-6 scale how successful the college library, other libraries, personal subscriptions, and ILL were in supplying them, thus providing a comparative measure of the library's ability to satisfy patrons. Moreover, the 153 titles named by respondents were used as a checklist to evaluate holdings.

The authors assert that most journal evaluation studies (about a dozen are summarized in the preliminary section) focus on quantitative use measurement, but feel that their qualitative approach "based on users' needs and expectations" is "well worth the time and effort."

410. Blake, Monica. "Journal Cancellations in University Libraries." **Serials Librarian** 10 (Summer 1986): 73-80.

411. Blake, Monica, and A. J. Meadows. "Journals at Risk." **Journal of Librarianship** 16 (April 1984): 118-28.

These two articles report the same research project. As acknowledged by Blake, the Blake and Meadows article contains the full details of the research. A survey concerning serials cancellations, mailed to university librarians in the United Kingdom and Ireland in 1983, received thirty-three responses. It found that most had cancelled periodical subscriptions between 1974 and 1982, reaching a peak in 1981 and 1982 when 69 percent had done so. An average of 358 titles per university had been cancelled between 1980 and mid-1983. Expensive periodicals, ones that had experienced a large price increase, and foreign-language titles were most likely to be cancelled. Several tables in the Blake and Meadows article display the survey results and an appendix contains the questionnaire. This research demonstrates that the serials crisis is by no means limited to North America.

412. Bostic, Mary J. "Serials Deselection." **Serials Librarian** 9 (Spring 1985): 85-101.

The author argues that serials deacquisition promotes good long-term collection building, even though a desire for high volume counts, work pressure, and emotional attachment to the holdings often impede deselection. Most of the article is devoted to a praiseworthy recapitulation of the available serials deselection methodologies, covering major issues and important previous studies and organized into six categories: journal evaluation models, citation analysis, use studies, identification of obsolescence patterns, systematic planning based on Bradfordian distribution, and recommended standards. Bostic's essay offers a useful overview concerning serials evaluation for deselection purposes.

413. Bousfield, Wendy. "Boundary Spanners and Serials Deselection." **Serials Librarian** 10 (Spring 1986): 23-31.

This article is a reflection upon the author's experiences as a humanities subject specialist participating in a major serials cancellation project at an unnamed undergraduate university in the western United States in the early 1980s. Bousfield views a subject specialist's negotiation with faculty over serials cancellation as "boundary-spanning," a sociological concept often used in business that describes an organization's interaction and communication with its environment.

Although acknowledging that serials cancellation is an educational process, the author felt "unthanked, exhausted and battered," the collection was damaged, and rifts with the faculty developed "that were never entirely mended." Bousfield's contribution is noteworthy for both her unusually candid revelations and her introduction of a social science concept to help explain a difficult political process.

414. Bustion, Marifran, and Jane Treadwell. "Reported Relative Value of Journals versus Use: A Comparison." **College & Research Libraries** 51 (March 1990): 142-51.

The authors offer a well-done, detailed analysis of a serials cancellation project at Texas A & M University. After faculty ranked serials in their subject area on a 1 ("essential") to 5 ("not related") scale, during the spring of 1987, 540 periodicals were cancelled in the fall. During the spring of 1988, a fifteen-week follow-up use study of current issues, based on reshelving counts, was conducted for all cancelled periodicals plus a 10-percent random sample of the 3,000 titles that faculty had rated "essential." Eighty-nine percent of the cancelled periodicals received no or "low" use (defined as fifteen or fewer), while 80 percent of the titles faculty rated essential received no or low use. A bar chart displays the number of uses for cancelled and essential titles according to twenty-one major divisions of the LC classification. It is concluded that "the cancellation decisions were reaffirmed" and that faculty ratings were not a predictor of high use.

415. Diodato, Virgil P. "Original Language, Non-English Journals: Weeding Them and Holding Them." **Science & Technology Libraries** 6 (Spring 1986): 55-67.

Diodato explores, based on logical analysis, the methodological considerations involved in deciding whether to cancel foreign-language periodicals when the library also subscribes to the English-language translation, as often happens for Russian scientific and technical journals. The primary decision-making factors should be patron needs, subscription costs, time lag between both publication and indexing of the original and translation journals, whether the original or translation is cited, coverage of indexing and abstracting services, physical differences between the original and translated versions, the availability of alternate translations, and the holdings of other libraries. This narrowly focused entry is relevant to the needs of large research libraries wishing to review their foreign-language journal holdings.

416. Elder, Nancy I. "Evaluating Journals: Can Faculty Do the Job?" In **Building on the First Century; Proceedings of the Fifth National Conference of the Association of College and Research Libraries, Cincinnati, Ohio, April 5-8, 1989**, edited by Janice C. Fennell, 208-10. Chicago: Association of College and Research Libraries, 1989. 353p. ISBN 0-8389-7289-6.

This investigation explores how accurately faculty journal assessments predicted circulation at the University of Texas at Austin Life Science Library. The study was based on 653 separate evaluations (in the form of open-ended comments) of 449 journal titles by 16 faculty members. Circulation statistics from a database maintained by the library were used to assign periodicals to four use categories, ranging from "zero" to "high." Elder then reached a personal judgment concerning how well the faculty assessment matched the circulation category, concluding that 42 percent of the faculty evaluations were "good" predictors, 30 percent "fair," and 28 percent "poor." More specifically, 88 percent of the faculty predictions for high-circulation titles were "good," whereas 60 percent of the predictions for low or zero circulation periodicals were "poor." This is an intriguing study with important practical implications concerning faculty input in serials evaluation, but the methodology lacks rigor.

417.   Fabrizio, Nancy A. "Journal Evaluation in a Health Sciences Library." **Serials Review** 11 (Fall 1985): 55-57.

Fabrizio's short article is unusual in that journal evaluation for selecting new titles rather than for cancelling current ones is discussed. A four-stage process at SUNY-Buffalo is depicted: 1) priority of review is set according to origin of request, 2) a sample issue and reviews are used for evaluation by the subject specialist, 3) final decision is reached by the Serials Review Committee, and 4) for follow-up after subscription, users are asked to complete a "User Evaluation Form." The author asserts that this procedure has been used for more than 200 journal evaluations.

418.   Hastreiter, Jamie Webster, Larry Hardesty, and David Henderson, comps. **Periodicals in College Libraries**. Chicago: College Library Information Packet Committee, Association of College and Research Libraries, 1987. 116p. (CLIP Note, no. 8). ISBN 0-8389-7143-1.

This number in a series of College Library Information Packet Notes, which provide documentation on library practices to college and small university libraries, addresses periodicals management. The item begins by tabulating the results of a 55-question survey responded to by 118 college library directors from late 1986 to early 1987. The questions pertinent to evaluation revealed that 71.2 percent of the colleges "evaluate the serials collection regularly" and 20.3 percent evaluate all of the collection each year. Moreover, 35.6 percent employ use studies; 7.6 percent citation studies; 44.1 percent ILL requests; 43.2 percent recommended lists; and 64.4 percent faculty judgments.

Most of this CLIP Note is composed of documents, organized into ten sections, that are used in serials acquisition, maintenance, and deacquisition in innumerable U.S. libraries. For the purpose of this literature guide the most valuable sections present "guidelines for selection of periodicals" at seven libraries, including Bucknell and Creighton, and evaluation method forms employed in eight institutions, such as Oberlin and the University of Evansville. Like SPEC kits, CLIP Notes illustrate useful examples of library practice.

419.   Hodge, Stanley P., and Marilyn Ivins. "Current International Newspapers: Some Collection Management Implications." **College & Research Libraries** 48 (January 1987): 50-61.

This entry combines the results from a mail questionnaire of May 1985, responded to by eighteen systematically selected ARL libraries, and three user surveys, in which 313 questionnaires were completed, conducted at the Texas A & M Library during 1985. Among the useful findings is a list of ten selection criteria used by ARL libraries, headed by quality, curricular support, research, and geographic coverage. Also, a rating on a 1 (low) to 5 (high) scale of ten selection criteria by the responding ARL collection development librarians indicated that geographical representation and quality rated 4.6, while curricular support, faculty request, and perceived use rated 4.4. The user survey revealed that the most frequent reason for reading international newspapers at Texas A & M was to get "news from home" (87.9 percent). A 1984 survey at Notre Dame, reported here, indicated that 80.3 percent read these papers "to keep up with national and international news." A table lists the five most frequently read international newspapers at Texas A & M.

Other collection management data not directly relevant to evaluation or selection are also included. This item is especially significant because, as the authors note, little has been published concerning the collection management of international newspapers.

420. Holland, Maurita Peterson. "Machine-Readable Files for Serials Management: An Optimizing Program and Use Data." **College & Research Libraries** 44 (January 1983): 66-69.

A serials evaluation system, developed at the University of Michigan Engineering Library and based on machine-readable files of use and cost data, is explained in Holland's noteworthy article. A "density" figure, representing the average number of unbound periodical uses per year divided by cost, is calculated for each title. All the library's paid titles are sorted by density, in descending order, so that one can read down the list to determine the optimal subscriptions for any budget. To facilitate discussion with faculty concerning cancellation decisions, additional lists are generated by engineering discipline and subarranged by 1976-1981 use data. Low-usage titles important for nonresearch purposes, facetiously termed "sacred cows," were not considered in the evaluation process.

The technical details relating to the machine-readable data file are not covered, but this approach to serials evaluation should be brought to the attention of librarians.

421. Lancaster, F. Wilfrid, and others. "The Relationship between Literature Scatter and Journal Accessibility in an Academic Special Library." **Collection Building** 11, no. 1 (1991): 19-22.

This piece investigates the relationship between a journal's accessibility in a nearby library and frequency of retrieval through an online database. The 1,322 journals from 4,197 citations retrieved from 106 MEDLINE searches conducted at the Health Sciences Library on the University of Illinois campus during June-August 1987 were grouped into five Bradfordian zones, with journals cited less frequently from zone to zone. For example, zone 1 contained 35 extensively cited journals, while zone 5 consisted of 595 journals cited only once. The journal holdings for the five zones were then checked in four locations: the departmental library, the University of Illinois campus, availability through ILLINET, and elsewhere. It was found that lower zone journals, which are presumably less useful, were less often available in the departmental or campus libraries.

The authors correctly state that this technique could be used for journal collection evaluation, even though they conducted this investigation to satisfy "intellectual curiosity." While of considerable theoretical significance, this method could be used to develop a weighted checklist, with higher zone journals counting more.

422. Logan-Peters, Kay. "Serial Cancellation Programs in Academic Libraries in Missouri." In **Proceedings from the 1982 Spring Meeting of the Nebraska Library Association, College and University Section, Held at Concordia Teachers College, Seward, Nebraska, April 15-16, 1982**, edited by Elaine A. Franco, 36-58. Lincoln: Nebraska Library Association, 1982. 169p.

Following a brief literature review covering a number of serials cancellation projects from the 1970s, Logan-Peters reports in anecdotal manner the findings from a questionnaire survey, responded to by seventeen academic libraries in Missouri, concerning procedures and methods used in serials cancellation. It was found that: 1) 60 percent had a formal or informal deselection policy; 2) 82 percent based all or part of the cancellation decision on usage; 3) other factors considered were cost, indexing, curricular relevance, availability elsewhere, and language; 4) 41 percent indicated that faculty had input; 5) popular magazines as well as highly specialized or costly journals were most likely to be cancelled; and 6) 30 percent of the respondents thought deselection had a positive effect, while none perceived a negative consequence. The author asserts that her findings have implications for academic librarians beyond the state of Missouri.

423. Millson-Martula, Christopher. "Use Studies and Serials Rationalization: A Review." **Serials Librarian** 15, nos. 1/2 (1988): 121-36.

Following a lengthy review of numerous issues concerning periodicals collection evaluation and use studies, Millson-Martula summarizes several reports of their implementation in libraries. A nine-month use study, based on use and citation counts, conducted at St. Xavier College in Chicago during 1982-1983 is examined in detail. Two major outcomes were cancellation of 20 percent of the subscriptions and "some hostility" from the faculty, underscoring the author's emphasis on the "local politics" of periodical cancellation and evaluation. This important consideration is all too often never explicitly acknowledged in print.

424. Milne, Dorothy, and Bill Tiffany. "A Cost-Per-Use Method for Evaluating the Cost-Effectiveness of Serials: A Detailed Discussion of Methodology." **Serials Review** 17 (Summer 1991): 7-19.

The authors offer an extremely detailed description of a survey method developed at Memorial University of Newfoundland during the late 1980s for calculating the cost-effectiveness of serial titles. The survey was conducted for a full year, with a quarter of the collection surveyed each year. With each use, patrons were asked to tick paper tags affixed to current issues and the last five years of bound volumes. An adjustment factor (developed from a pilot study) was applied to the data to account for nonticked uses, while another adjustment factor, based on data from the *SCI JCR*, was used to estimate lifetime use. Titles with a cost per use exceeding $14 and less than six ticks were usually cancelled.

An especially notable section discusses three types of interference with the survey: initial blitz ticking, overticking, and removal of tags. The survey cost $30,000 to implement for three years, but resulted in $291,000 of cancellations. The authors believe that their method could be used in other libraries. (See also Milne and Tiffany entry 468.)

158 / EVALUATION OF SERIALS

425. Moore, Nicholas L. "Library Periodicals from Developing Countries: Coverage by Major Abstracting and Indexing Services." **Journal of Librarianship** 13 (January 1981): 37-45.

Moore's study, termed a "preliminary investigation," analyzes the coverage of developing countries' library and information science periodicals in five major LIS indexing and abstracting services, including *Information Science Abstract, Library & Information Science Abstracts*, and *Library Literature*. A table extending to three pages lists fifty-nine periodicals and their country of origin, as well as which indexing/abstracting services they are covered in. No overall statistical analysis is offered. The results of this study were also presented at the 46th IFLA General Conference in 1980. This entry would have some value for the evaluation of library and information science periodical collections.

426. Pao, Miranda Lee. "American Revolution: Comparison of a Bibliography with a Quality-Selected List." In **Information Interaction; Proceedings of the 45th ASIS Annual Meeting, Columbus, Ohio, October 17-21, 1982**, vol. 19, edited by Anthony E. Petrarca, Celianna I. Taylor, and Robert S. Kohn, 224-26. White Plains, N.Y.: published for the American Society for Information Science by Knowledge Industry Publications, 1982. 431p. LC 64-8303. ISBN 0-86729-038-2. ISSN 0044-7870.

427. Pao, Miranda Lee. "Characteristics of American Revolution Literature." **Collection Management** 6 (Fall/Winter 1984): 119-28.

These two items report the same research project, but this annotation focuses on the second, as it contains more detail. The article identifies the journals and monographic publishers that produce the most about the American Revolution. Analysis of *Writings in American History*, covering 1962 through 1976, found 1,095 pertinent papers in 224 journals. In a Bradfordian distribution, one journal contained 11 percent of the articles, while 25 percent of the journals accounted for 75 percent. A table lists the most productive twenty-six titles. Comparison was made with the articles listed in Shy's selected bibliography, *The American Revolution*, which listed 1,029 articles in 178 journals. A table lists the top eighteen journals in Shy, which produced 61.6 percent of the articles.

A count of the monographs listed in Shy's bibliography revealed that 227 different publishers issued the 1,014 books published between 1781 and 1971. Ten publishers produced 39 percent of the monographs. A table rank-ordering the leading twenty-two publishers, all but one still active, could be of interest (as would the journal data) to American history collection development librarians.

428. Perkins, David L. "Weed It and Reap." **Serials Librarian** 18, nos. 1/2 (1990): 131-40.

Following a discussion of escalating serials costs, three serials cancellation projects at California State University, Northridge, conducted in 1975-1976, 1976-1977, and 1988-1989 are reviewed. The first project was based on a faculty survey and usage, the second focused on titles that received no usage during a four-month survey, and the third was structured around the combined results of four previously conducted use studies.

The article concludes by offering six pieces of general advise: 1) "do usage studies"; 2) keep everyone informed; 3) involve faculty in rating journals but not directly in final deselection decisions; 4) send lists to departments for both rating and final review before cancellation; 5) for two equally rated titles, retain the unique one; and 6) do "one's homework."

429. Rice, Barbara A. "Selection and Evaluation of Chemistry Journals." **Science & Technology Libraries** 4 (Fall 1983): 43-59.

Five methods for evaluating and selecting chemistry periodicals are compared: 1) the "List of 1,000 Journals Most Frequently Cited in *Chemical Abstracts*"; 2) the 111 most frequently used titles from a 1979 SUNY-Albany study;[1] 3) the 1975 *Journal Citation Reports* citation frequency for items in category 2; 4) 42 titles from the *Chemical Abstracts* list deemed "important" by organic chemistry faculty; and 5) 832 titles identified through searching *Chemical Abstracts* in the BRS online search service. Two lengthy summary tables compare the top-ranked titles by the various methods, but no correlational statistics are used.

The pros and cons of the various ranking methods, as well as their collection development implications, are discussed. A high correspondence was found between *JCR* rankings and usage and between faculty selections and usage, but Rice concludes that no method "can identify all titles which will serve all purposes." "[C]ollection evaluation should be recognized as a subjective judgment ... different techniques produce different results."

430. Segal, Judith A. "Journal Deselection: A Literature Review and an Application." **Science & Technology Libraries** 6 (Spring 1986): 25-42.

Segal's thoroughly done article consists of several components. First, a literature review summarizes the main issues in journal deselection in academic, research, and special libraries based on examination of fifty-three articles and monographs published since 1976. Use was found to be the most frequently employed variable in the deselection process. Next, she presents a case study in which $5,000 worth of education and behavioral sciences periodicals were cancelled at Ben Gurion University of the Negev, Israel, in 1984. The author describes a mathematical deselection model she developed for this project, which incorporates such factors as completeness of holdings, cost, citation impact factor, indexing, course relevance, faculty input, and use. Finally, the paper concludes with a four-step administrative model to prepare for deselection.

431. Stankus, Tony. "Journal Weeding in Relation to Declining Faculty Member Publishing." **Science & Technology Libraries** 6 (Spring 1986): 43-53. Reprinted in **Scientific Journals: Issues in Library Selection and Management**, edited by Tony Stankus, 33-42. New York: Haworth Press, 1987. 218p. (Monographic Supplement ... to the Serials Librarian, #3) LC 87-7047. ISBN 0-86656-616-3.

After analyzing the publication records of fifty-three chemistry Ph.D.s teaching at thirty-four prestigious, small, liberal arts colleges, Stankus concludes that after four years without an article a faculty member's publishing activity has ceased. To save on subscription costs and shelf space, he advocates cancellation of serial subscriptions in the professor's research area on the assumption that they are no longer needed to support research. The author provides numerous practical tips concerning how to negotiate the cancellation (e.g., do not be judgmental or personal).

This proposal represents a creative and unusual serials cancellation methodology, but one can easily imagine enormous political problems for any librarian trying to implement it.

432. Stankus, Tony, and Barbara Rice. "Handle with Care: Use and Citation Data for Science Journal Management." **Collection Management** 4 (Spring/Summer 1982): 95-110. Reprinted in **Scientific Journals: Issues in Library Selection and Management**, edited by Tony Stankus, 173-88. New York: Haworth Press, 1987. 218p. (Monographic Supplement ... to the Serials Librarian, #3) LC 87-7047. ISBN 0-86656-616-3.

The authors explore the correspondence between journal use and citation data in the sciences, based on previously published studies and *JCR* data. They conclude that citation and use data will correlate if one compares journals of similar scope, subject, purpose, and language and there is an average of twenty-five borrowings per journal within a subject area. Comparison of journal use from a SUNY-Albany study, previously published in 1979,[2] with total citation and impact factor rankings from *JCR* in biochemistry, cell biology, and ecology (where these conditions were fulfilled) and in geosciences and mathematics (where they were not fulfilled) confirms the hypothesis. Moreover, Stankus and Rice assert that if the conditions are met, either total citation or impact factor ranking will correlate with use, but impact factor should be used for new journals or ones that publish a small number of articles. This selection provides valuable insight concerning the substitution of citation data for a local use study.

433. Swigger, Keith, and Adeline Wilkes. "The Use of Citation Data to Evaluate Serials Subscriptions in an Academic Library." **Serials Review** 17 (Summer 1991): 41-46, 52.

This scholarly study offers a sophisticated comparison of three leading serials evaluation methods (reshelving counts, subjective judgments by faculty or librarians, and citation analysis) in terms of validity, reliability, and economy, based on data from Texas Woman's University (TWU). To analyze the three approaches, the 685 different journals cited by TWU faculty between 1984 and 1989, identified through DIALOG online searches of the three ISI citation indexes, were cross-tabulated with the most frequently reshelved journals and those recommended for cancellation by faculty and by staff, using data from a late 1980s cancellation project at the TWU library.

The authors conclude that none of the three methods offers satisfactory validity, because it is uncertain what is being measured. The citation method is the most reliable. Cost, that is, economy, is difficult to assess. They also conclude that the correspondence between reshelving and citation data is "weak," while there is "no correspondence" between citation data and subjective judgments by either faculty or librarians.

434. Wallace, Danny P., and Bert R. Boyce. "Holdings as a Measure of Journal Value." **Library & Information Science Research** 11 (January 1989): 59-71.

This well-done research piece investigates whether a correlation exists between the number of libraries holding a journal, as indicated by OCLC, and other measures of journal value, such as citation data, on the premise that easily obtained OCLC holdings data would offer a valuable journal evaluation tool. Data concerning four variables—1) holdings in OCLC, 2) total citations, 3) impact factor (2 and 3 were taken from *JCR*), and 4) circulation as indicated in *Ulrich's*—were analyzed for ten samples of journals. The journal samples were compared as follows: a systematic sample of 691 science and social science journals from *SSCI* and *SCI*; eight subject samples in business, international relations, analytical chemistry, etc.; and the eight subject areas combined into a composite sample. Numerous tables and figures present correlations and scatter plots among these variables.

"Moderate to strong" correlations were found between holdings and citation measures for six of the eight subjects, although the relationship between holdings and circulation "requires further investigation." The authors conclude that "the use of holdings counts as a means of [journal] evaluation may be possible for the literature of some subjects, but not for collections as a whole."

435. Wallace, Danny P., and Susan Bonzi. "The Relationship between Journal Productivity and Quality." In **ASIS '85; Proceedings of the 48th ASIS Annual Meeting; Las Vegas, Nevada, October 20-24, 1985**, vol. 22, edited by Carol A. Parkhurst, 193-96. White Plains, N.Y.: published for the American Society for Information Science by Knowledge Industry Publications, 1985. 393p. LC 64-8303. ISBN 0-86729-176-1. ISSN 0044-7870.

The 1,931 articles distributed among 557 journals cited in Hjerrpe's 1980 bibliography on bibliometrics and citation analysis were used to test whether the "nucleus" journals in a Bradfordian distribution (i.e., the journals that contributed the greatest number of articles) were cited more frequently than non-nucleus journals. Analysis of the citations in 128 articles on bibliometrics indexed in *Library Literature* between 1981 and 1983, and a tracing of the citations to 100 articles from the Hjerrpe bibliography in the *SCI* and *SSCI* through 1983, confirmed the hypothesis that nucleus journals were more often cited than non-nucleus journals. This research piece implies that the journals contributing the most articles on a subject are also of higher quality because they receive more citations, a finding that certainly has implications for serials evaluation.

436. Weller, Ann C. "Editorial Policy and the Assessment of Quality among Medical Journals." **Bulletin of the Medical Library Association** 75 (October 1987): 310-16.

To determine whether editorial policy statements can be used as indicators of journal quality, the statements on editorial policy were analyzed in four groups of journals listed in descending order of prestige and quality: 1) 15 "perceived most prestigious medical titles," 2) 102 randomly selected titles from the *Abridged Index Medicus*, 3) 70 randomly selected titles indexed by the National Library of Medicine, and 4) 16 nonindexed titles. Many statistics are presented. It was found that more prestigious journals had longer, more elaborate statements and were more likely to cover such issues as the peer review process and ethical standards in research. Weller summarizes her findings with the statement that "the instructions section is one more decision making tool" in the journal evaluation process. (See also entry 437.)

437. Weller, Ann C. "The 'Instructions to Authors' Section as an Aid in Serials Collection Development." **Serials Librarian** 11 (December 1986/January 1987): 143-54.

162 / EVALUATION OF SERIALS

Weller offers a slightly modified and somewhat more detailed version of the research endeavor reported in entry 436. This analysis was based on the "instructions to authors" sections in five categories of medical journals: 1) 102 titles indexed in the 1986 *Abridged Index Medicus*, 2) 93 titles indexed in the 1976 *Abridged Index Medicus*, 3) 14 perceived high-quality titles, 4) 55 randomly selected titles from the *Index Medicus*, and 5) 16 nonindexed titles.

Again it was found that higher quality journals contained more information, especially regarding peer review and ethical research standards, in the instructions section. Also, the percentage of *Abridged Index Medicus* journals containing such information increased from 1976 to 1986; 23 percent referred to peer review in 1976, whereas 68 percent did so in 1986. A table presents comparative data concerning peer review statements in leading library science, education, sociology, and geology journals, but Weller states that further investigation is needed for these areas. The author notes that she was unable to locate a single citation concerning this issue.

SERIALS EVALUATION MODELS

438. Bennion, Bruce C., and Sunee Karschamroon. "Multivariate Regression Models for Estimating Journal Usefulness in Physics." **Journal of Documentation 40** (September 1984): 217-27.

This rigorous study, based on Karschamroon's doctoral dissertation, applies multiple regression models to bibliometric statistics to predict the "perceived usefulness" (PU) of physics journals. PU was calculated for 164 journals. One hundred sixty-seven physicists, selected by a systematic sample of *American Men and Women of Science*, rated the titles on a 1 (low) to 4 (high) scale of usefulness in a questionnaire. Then, four multiple regression models were developed that incorporated nine categories of data, including total citations, impact factor, immediacy index from *SCI JCR*, and circulation data from *Ulrich's*. After a statistical analysis, the authors believe their models are "excellent predictors" of perceived usefulness, and may predict the usefulness of small, specialized titles, better than survey results. They also note the data is readily obtainable and the models can easily be programmed on a microcomputer. Nevertheless, this item will probably be of more interest to researchers than to practitioners.

439. Bick, Dawn, and Reeta Sinha. "Maintaining a High-Quality, Cost-Effective Journal Collection." **College & Research Libraries News 52** (September 1991): 485-90.

Bick and Sinha propose what they term a "practical technique," developed at the Houston Academy of Medicine-Texas Medical Center Library, for reaching journal retention decisions. In-house use data were obtained by picking up unshelved journals during randomly selected one-hour periods throughout the month, for continuous fiscal years beginning in August 1989, then entering the findings along with circulation data for 3,000 titles into the Paradox database management system. An evaluation matrix, explained in detail, was used by a committee of librarians to assign weights to approximately twenty factors, including indexing, impact factor, and holdings.

The weighted evaluation criteria were then applied to each title to obtain a "journal score," which was multiplied by the number of uses to determine a "BENEFIT" factor. Next, the BENEFIT was divided by cost so the journals could be ranked by cost-benefit ratio. This fairly sophisticated model is quite fascinating.

440. Braga, Gilda Maria, and Cecilia Alves Oberhofer. "A Model for Evaluating Scientific and Technical Journals from Developing Countries." In **The Information Community: An Alliance for Progress; Proceedings of the 44th ASIS Annual Meeting, Washington, D.C., October 25-30, 1981**, vol. 18, edited by Lois F. Lunin, Madeline Henderson, and Harold Wooster, 51-54. White Plains, N.Y.: published for the American Society for Information Science by Knowledge Industry Publications, 1981. 401p. LC 64-8303. ISBN 0-914236-85-7. ISSN 0044-7870.

Braga and Oberhofer propose a model, developed at the Brazilian Institute for Information in Science and Technology, for evaluating scientific and technical journals from developing countries. A 1-to-5 scale is applied to sets of variables for seven criteria: 1) "standardization," including table of contents, abstracts, ISSN, etc.; 2) duration; 3) frequency; 4) indexing; 5) "dissemination," i.e., circulation; 6) "collaboration," i.e., wide range of contributing authors; and 7) "authority," i.e., background of editorial board members. A table illustrates application of the model for a specific title. A second table summarizes the scoring system: less than 30 points is "very bad," more than 80 is "very good."

The authors observe that this model is necessary because developing countries "are poorly represented" in the ISI citation indexes. Although it is interesting from the theoretical perspective, one wonders whether North American libraries would actually use this model.

441. Dhawan, S. M., S. K. Phull, and S. P. Jain. "Selection of Scientific Journals: A Model." **Journal of Documentation** 36 (March 1980): 24-32.

The authors propose a journal selection model based on three variables: citation, use, and coverage by abstracts. A figure with three intersecting circles illustrates the model. They advocate the following selection priority: "1) journals which are cited, abstracted, and used; 2) journals which are abstracted, used, but not cited; 3) journals which are cited, used, but not abstracted; 4) journals which are used, but neither abstracted nor cited; [and] 5) journals which are abstracted, cited, but not used."

The model was tested on 400 physics journals using *JCR, Physics Abstracts*, and use data from several Indian libraries. One hundred sixty-four of these fell into priority 1 for immediate selection. An appendix illustrates application of the model to journals at the beginning and end of the alphabet. This work is primarily of theoretical value.

442. Miller, Edward P., and Ann L. O'Neill. "Journal Deselection and Costing." **Library Acquisitions: Practice & Theory** 14, no. 2 (1990): 173-78.

Miller and O'Neill propose a model for calculating a journal's "effectiveness factor," to be used for journal deselection purposes. The model is quite flexible, as the individual library decides which elements to include as well as the weight to be assigned each element, ranging from 1 to 10. Use, curriculum, indexing, ILL availability, holdings, binding and check-in costs, publisher's reputation, format, paper quality, claiming problems, language, and microfilm are listed as suggested elements, although a library may add others. This intriguing model has never been tested in a library and one wonders whether there might be some practical problems in trying to implement it.

443. Miller, Ruth H., and Marvin C. Guilfoyle. "Computer Assisted Periodicals Selection: Structuring the Subjective." **Serials Librarian** 10 (Spring 1986): 9-22.

This article describes a numerical rating system developed and used at the University of Evansville to assist journal selection decisions. A rating of 1 to 10 is applied to seven categories: 1) indexing, 2) interlibrary loan, 3) reviews in a core list or bibliography, 4) demand by staff or patrons, 5) program support, 6) cost, and 7) miscellaneous factors. The weight for the categories ranges from 0.5 to 2. The data are maintained on an electronic spreadsheet that ranks the titles. Several figures illustrate the system's application.

Miller and Guilfoyle state that although the ranked list "provides a defensible, replicable, professional product," professional librarians must make the final decision. The approach has "proven successful" at Evansville.

444. Peters, Andrew. "Evaluating Periodicals." **College & Research Libraries** 43 (March 1982): 149-51.

A journal evaluation formula used at the Central State University library in Oklahoma is explained. Based on a model from Kraft and Polacsek,[3] except that citation frequency has been eliminated, the formula weighs: 1) relevance, subdivided into accessibility (i.e., indexing, subject importance, and format/journal reputation); 2) usage; and 3) availability, consisting of microform availability, completeness, and ownership by nearby libraries. The journals are then organized by academic department and ranked by cost/benefit ratio. Peters asserts the model promotes "knowledgeable decisions."

IDENTIFICATION OF CORE JOURNALS

445. Black, George W., Jr. "Core Journal Lists for Behaviorally Disordered Children." **Behavioral & Social Sciences Librarian** 3 (Fall 1983): 31-38.

An academic researcher and a classroom teacher listed leading journals in the field of behaviorally disordered children. Rankings calculated from the 1977-1978 JCR by discipline impact factor (the average number of times each article is cited by other journals in the discipline) for journals cited in the top four titles from the teacher and researcher were used to create two separate core lists of twenty-five journals, displayed in rank order in separate tables.

The minimal overlap between the two core lists—only two journals were common to both—"indicates a disparity between information resources found to be valuable to the teacher versus those valuable to the academic researcher." The report also contains a useful discussion concerning the use of discipline impact factor to determine core journal lists.

446. Clark, Barton M., and Sharon E. Clark. "Core Journals in Anthropology: A Review of Methodologies." **Behavioral & Social Sciences Librarian** 2 (Winter 1981/Spring 1982): 95-110.

Three different approaches to identifying the core journals in anthropology are illustrated: basic lists, user studies, and citation analysis. Over 200 journals appeared in 1 of 4 basic lists, but only the titles that were also identified through the second and third methods are named in a table. Other tables list the most frequently used journals from four previous user studies and the titles most frequently cited in seven leading anthropology journals, based on 1977-1979 *SSCI JCR* data. Finally, a composite table lists the fifty-two core journals that appeared in any of the previous tables.

The paper concludes with a brief discussion concerning the merits and demerits of each approach. While certainly not the final word, this entry is worth a look by persons interested in anthropology serials evaluation or the methodology for determining a subject's core journals.

447. Goehner, Donna M. "Core Lists of Periodicals Selected by Faculty Reviewers." **Technical Services Quarterly** 1 (Summer 1984): 17-38.

Based on the author's doctoral dissertation, this investigation used faculty selectors to identify, for academic libraries offering a master's degree, the core periodicals among the humanities, social sciences, and physical sciences. One hundred seventy-eight faculty members responded to a survey in which they indicated on lists of their subjects' periodicals from *Ulrich's* those titles they considered "basic or essential."

For each subject, titles were rank-ordered by the number of respondents who checked them. The top-ranked ones for the median number of responses were considered the core. For example, psychology respondents checked from 19 to 181 titles, with 61 the median, so the top 61 psychology journals were listed as the core. A lengthy appendix lists those, forty-one in art, ninety-one in literature, seventy-three in history, fifty in mathematics, and forty-eight in physics, along with the number and percentage of times selected, plus the price.

448. LaBorie, Tim, Michael Halperin, and Howard D. White. "Library and Information Science Abstracting and Indexing Services: Coverage, Overlap, and Context." **Library & Information Science Research** 7 (April-June 1985): 183-95.

The authors focus on the coverage and overlap of four abstracting and indexing services in library and information science (*Information Science Abstracts, Library & Information Science Abstracts, Library Literature*, and *Abstract Journal: Informatics*) plus six services from other disciplines, such as *Historical Abstracts* and *SSCI*. A total of 1,210 titles were covered. The relationships among the ten services were analyzed by a variety of methods, including multidimensional scaling and factor analysis, in this rigorous investigation. This item is significant for serials evaluation because it identifies core LIS journals based on coverage by the ten services. A table lists the one journal indexed by ten services; the three indexed in nine; the three indexed in eight; the seventeen in six; and the twenty-seven in five indexing and abstracting services.

449. Mack, Thura. "A Model Methodology for Selecting Women's Studies Core Journals." **Library & Information Science Research** 13 (April-June 1991): 131-45.

This investigation is based on an analysis of the journals cited in the women's studies periodical *Signs* during the years 1976, 1981, and 1986. A composite table reveals that 299 journals received 680 citations in 1976. Mack explains that a survey of twenty-five women's studies faculty at the University of Tennessee, Knoxville (which identified six titles recommended by three or more faculty), along with "coverage," circulation data, "scholarly focus," and recommendations in *Magazines for Libraries*, were used to select *Signs* as a source. The sixty-one unnamed journals cited at least five times in any of the three target years were considered candidates for the core. Faculty input, "subject patterns and rankings," and the frequency of citation in *Signs* were used to identify a final core of twenty journals (many outside women's studies) named in a table. A large portion of the entry, including five figures, is devoted to analysis of changes in *Signs'* subject coverage throughout the target years.

This study's usefulness lies in the core list itself rather than the selection model. In fact, the model's decision rules for selecting the final core are not explained as explicitly as would be desirable. The author notes that this piece represents the only article on the topic.

450. Rose, Robert F. "Identifying a Core Collection of Business Periodicals for Academic Libraries." **Collection Management** 5 (Spring 1983): 73-87.

A core of 283 business periodicals was identified through two methods: 1) 244 titles listed in 3 of 4 business indexes or databases (*ABI/INFORM, Business Index, Business Periodicals Index*, and *F & S Index*); or 2) 39 additional titles cited 138 times or more (the mean for business periodicals) in the 1981 *SSCI JCR*. Seventy-one titles met the second criterion, but 32 of them were listed in the indexes under the first criterion. The core titles were classified into twelve broad subject areas, such as accounting, business law, etc. A master table lists the 283 core journals, where they are indexed, their citation count, and subject classification. Rose is obviously correct in his concluding assertion, "The business specialist in academic libraries can use this list as a basis for comparison" in collection evaluation or development.

451. Sekerak, Robert J. "A Comparison of Journal Coverage in **Psychological Abstracts** and the Primary Health Sciences Indexes: Implications for Cooperative Serials Acquisitions and Retention." **Bulletin of the Medical Library Association** 74 (July 1986): 231-33.

Sekerak's short piece identifies a core list of forty-five journals (named in an appendix) in the interdisciplinary area of psychology and health care. The 315 titles indexed in both *Psychological Abstracts* and *Index Medicus* for 1983 were determined and checked against the periodicals covered by *Hospital Literature Index, Cumulative Index to Nursing and Allied Health Literature*, and *International Nursing Index*. Unfortunately, the author is unclear as to whether the forty-five core titles were covered in all five of the indexes mentioned here or merely *Psychological Abstracts* and *Index Medicus* plus one of the three hospital/nursing indexes. The potential use of these findings to a library consortium is discussed.

452. Trubkin, Loene. "Building a Core Collection of Business and Management Periodicals: How Databases Can Help." **Online** 6 (July 1982): 43-49.

Premised on the assumption that the most important journals will be covered in multiple databases, the contents of nine online databases, including *Economics Abstracts International* and the *New York Times Information Bank*, were examined to identify the core business and management journals. The 83 titles, out of 1,700 total, covered in at least 5 databases were considered the core. A table lists these journals grouped by the number of databases in which they appeared. Another table exhibits the leading journals in seven business fields, such as banking, data processing, etc. All the core titles were in English, but 46 percent were published outside the United States. Trubkin's article is of value not only for its creative methodology, but also for its listings of notable business journals.

453. Williams, Doris. "Using Core Journals to Justify Subscriptions and Services." In **IAMSLIC at a Crossroads; Proceedings of the 15th Annual Conference**, edited by Robert W. Burkhart and Joyce C. Burkhart, 123-34. N.p.: International Association of Marine Science Libraries and Information Centers, 1990. 200p. (International Association of Marine Science Libraries and Information Centers Conference Series). LC 90-81226. ISBN 0-932939-07-4.

To identify the core journals supporting the Marine Science Research Center at SUNY-Stony Brook, the author used the *Science Citation Index* to identify 271 articles published in 81 journals by MSRC faculty between 1984 and 1989. Next, every tenth journal citation in these articles was tabulated, resulting in 836 citations to 227 journals. Two tables in the appendix, which list in rank order the 81 journals published in by the faculty and the 227 they cited, could be useful to other marine science librarians. After comparing her findings with the ISI core lists in oceanography by Garfield (entry 566) and marine biology by Fuseler-McDowell (entry 571), Williams draws the noteworthy conclusion that the ISI lists "are good ones, but not a real substitute for knowing one's library users."

SERIALS CANCELLATION CASE STUDIES

454. Alligood, Elaine C., Elaine Russo-Martin, and Richard A. Peterson. "Use Study of **Excerpta Medica** Abstract Journals: To Drop or Not to Drop." **Bulletin of the Medical Library Association** 71 (July 1983): 251-59.

During a three-month period from September to November 1981, the University of Virginia Health Sciences Library reviewed separately the forty-four major sections of *Excerpta Medica*, a medical abstract comparable to *Index Medicus*. The authors describe the numerous data-gathering methods used in the project: 1) checking for duplicate holdings on the University of Virginia campus; 2) surveying reference and ILL staff concerning their perceptions of use and asking for recommendations; 3) determining patron use through shelving statistics, use records, and interviews; and 4) sending questionnaires to fifty-five health science libraries concerning their subscription policies and whether use studies had been conducted. Numerous tables report the results and compare findings from the different methods. At the end, twenty-five sections were cancelled.

Although this item will be of primary value for medical librarians, the study is noteworthy for its variety of techniques.

455. Bader, Shelley A., and Laurie L. Thompson. "Analyzing In-House Journal Utilization: An Added Dimension in Decision Making." **Bulletin of the Medical Library Association** 77 (April 1989): 216-18.

This brief communication, a follow-up to Grefsheim, Bader, and Meridith's report of an earlier serials cancellation project at the George Washington University Health Sciences Library (entry 461), describes an "easy" method for measuring in-house journal use, "data that had previously been obtainable only through laborious, time-consuming, and inaccurate methods." Journal volumes waiting to be reshelved were recorded by a portable laser bar-code reader. Every seven to ten days, the data from the bar-code reader were entered into the library's DEC PDP 11/84 minicomputer, which can produce a variety of on-demand usage reports. Data gathered by this method between January and August 1986 were used to assist journal cancellation decisions.

456. Barnard, Roy S. "A Serials Deselection Method." In **Proceedings from the 1982 Spring Meeting of the Nebraska Library Association, College and University Section, Held at Concordia Teachers College, Seward, Nebraska, April 15-16, 1982**, edited by Elaine A. Franco, 36-58. Lincoln: Nebraska Library Association, 1982. 169p.

Barnard offers a first-person narrative concerning a serials cancellation project, then still under way at the Kearney State College Library in Nebraska, begun in January 1982 in anticipation of budget cuts in the 1982-1983 budget. A Serials Review Group, composed of library staff, fairly easily agreed upon which of 169 general and library periodicals to cut by applying a three-part formula: 1) 25 percent price; 2) 25 percent index coverage; and 3) 50 percent subjective judgment by librarians. The author frankly discusses the problems that developed when faculty were asked to review their areas' periodical lists and suggest cuts of 5, 10, and 13.7 percent. For example, departments wished to cancel titles used by someone else. The author facetiously comments, "Vietnam was my only previous experience in waging an unpopular war." This piece is notable for its candid observations.

457. Carr, Barbara E. "Improving the Periodicals Collection through an Index Correlation Study." **Reference Services Review** 9 (October/December 1981): 27-32.

A systematic serials review utilizing indexes was conducted at the Kingston campus of St. Lawrence College, a community college in Ontario, beginning in the summer of 1980. First, the percentage of journals in seven core indexes received by the library, such as *Art Index* or *Readers' Guide*, was calculated. Second, *Ulrich's* was used to determine where the library's subscriptions were in fact indexed. Next, noncore indexes not including many of the library's subscriptions were cancelled. Fourth, the journals not included in the library's indexes were reviewed for cancellation, considering curricular relevance and circulation statistics. Finally, new subscriptions were placed for some periodicals indexed in the most-used indexes.

Carr stresses that "the study was time-consuming, but simple—no complicated formulae or ratios were needed." This approach is exceptional because the entire review process was built around indexing.

458. Cox, Barbara, Randy Olsen, and Richard Schockmel. "Cancelling Soviet Journals: A Demonstration Project for Utah's Coordinated Collection Development Program."* In **Preservers of the Past, Shapers of the Future; Proceedings of the Research Forum, Academic Library Section, Mountain Plains Library Association, Omaha, Nebraska, October 19-22, 1988**, edited by Douglas G. Birdsall, 84-104. Emporia, Kan.: Emporia State University Press, 1988. 113p. ISBN 0-93406-805-4.

During the late 1980s, the Brigham Young, Utah, and Utah State University libraries evaluated twelve major Soviet physics journals to reduce duplicate holdings. The methodology considered: 1) use of both bound and unbound volumes from March to May 1988; 2) citations in theses and dissertations completed between 1983 and 1987; and 3) citations in faculty publications from 1983 to 1987, at the three universities. Each journal's percentage of use, graduate citations, and faculty citations were calculated, and the journals were rank-ordered based on their average percentage for the three categories. As a result of cancellations, overlap was reduced from 80 percent to 11 percent and more than $11,000 was saved.

Cox asserts that the project "illustrated the feasibility and desirability of resource sharing." The article itself represents an interesting example of a collective serials review by three different libraries.

459. Eckman, Charles. "Journal Review in an Environmental Design Library." **Collection Management** 10, nos. 1/2 (1988): 69-84.

The journal collection at the University of California, Berkeley's Environmental Design Library was evaluated during the first half of 1986, through two methods: a three-month use study and a checklist approach. The use study revealed that 10 percent of the journals received 73 percent of the usage, 45 percent were never used, and English-language material accounted for 82.7 percent of total usage. Three tables display rank-order lists of the most frequently used architecture, planning, and landscape journals. The author notes that 38 percent of the most frequently used titles were not included in the *SSCI JCR*, leading to the conclusion that *JCR* lists should "be handled with care." The journals covered by seven major indexes were checked against the library's holdings and, using a union list of serials, against other libraries on the Berkeley campus as well as other academic libraries in California. Eckman's article offers valuable insight into the problems of journal review in a highly specialized subject area.

460. Fallon, Marcia, and Lily Liu Young. "Evaluating a Periodicals Collection." **Community & Junior College Libraries** 2 (Fall 1983): 3-8.

The authors focus on the serials evaluation methodology employed during the previous six years at the South Campus Library of the Miami-Dade Community College. A nine-point evaluation instrument was completed for each title under review for cancellation. The "determining factors" in the decision were: 1) "the annotation," i.e., a summary based on direct examination and curricular relevance; 2) circulation data; 3) availability in a local consortium; 4) requests by faculty on the Table of Contents Service; and 5) indexing. Holdings, prominence of display, price, and requestor's name serve as "background information." A table illustrates the evaluation instrument applied to four titles.

---

*Title in table of contents: "Assessing the Need for Soviet Physics Journals in Three Academic Libraries: An Example of Coordinated Serials Management."

This article differs from most other entries in this guide by describing a community college setting, but the serials review methodology is not substantially different from that used by college and university libraries.

461. Grefsheim, Suzanne, Shelley Bader, and Pamela Meredith. "User Involvement in Journal De-Selection." **Collection Management** 5 (Spring/Summer 1983): 43-52.

The authors describe an effort in the early 1980s at the George Washington University Medical Library to educate the faculty concerning the serials budget crunch and to elicit their input into journal evaluation. A "long" questionnaire asked faculty opinion concerning a list of "endangered journals," i.e., candidates for cancellation that the library staff believed to be little used. A "short" questionnaire included in unbound issues on the current periodical shelves surveyed actual usage during a two-and-one-half-month period. With "short" form usage data confirming faculty assessments on the "long" questionnaire, nine of fourteen "endangered journals" were cancelled. For a later report from the same library, see Bader and Thompson entry 455.

462. Hamaker, Charles. "Meeting the Pricing Challenge: The Serials Review Project at LSU A & M." **LLA Bulletin** 52 (Fall 1989): 61-64.

Following a short introduction to the problem of escalating serials prices (a topic on which Hamaker has published extensively), the serials review process at the Louisiana State University (LSU) Library during the late 1980s is briefly described. A list of 1,200 titles sent to faculty in April 1987 to identify cancellation candidates "did not work." Beginning in February 1988 lists of 1,200 to 2,000 titles, unsorted by subject, were sent to faculty every three to six months to be classified into one of three priority categories: "core," "research," and "peripheral." Actual cancellation focused on the "orphans" not rated by any faculty member. The article concludes by outlining seven components of the journal evaluation process used at LSU, including faculty review, circulation, and citation data.

463. Horwill, Cherry. "Periodicals Reviewing by Voting." In **Collection Development: Options for Effective Management; Proceedings of a Conference of the Library and Information Research Group, University of Sheffield, 1987**, edited by Sheila Corrall, 102-10. London: Taylor Graham, 1988. 155p. ISBN 0-947568-25-5.

An innovative voting procedure used in a serials review project at the University of Sussex in 1985 is described. A total of 1,057 teaching and research faculty plus doctoral students at the University of Sussex were sent lists of current serial subscriptions appropriate to their interest. Respondents were asked to distribute 100 votes however they pleased and add extra titles not on the list. Horwill reviews the approach's benefits, noting particularly that it resulted in a better understanding concerning "the distribution of subject interests on campus," and concludes that "the method worked." This item focuses on the voting procedure, while another piece (entry 464) offers a description of the entire review process. (See also Peasgood and Lambert entry 122.)

464. Horwill, Cherry, and Peter Lambert. "1 Man – 100 Votes: A New Approach to Reviewing Periodicals Subscriptions at the University of Sussex." **ASLIB Proceedings** 39 (January 1987): 7-16.

Although this item offers more details concerning the University of Sussex serials review project than does the article in entry 463, one wonders whether two articles were really necessary. It is explained that the voting method was intended to cover a wide range of individual interests, express varying degrees of support, and allow suggestions for new subscriptions. As a result of the project, 164 titles were cancelled and 74 new subscriptions were placed. "No money has been saved," but there was "a rebalancing of resources ... from cheaper humanities journals to more expensive science ones." Nevertheless, it is apparent that the weighted voting system approach should be brought to the attention of librarians facing cancellation projects.

465. Hunt, Richard K. "Journal Deselection in a Biomedical Research Library: A Mediated Mathematical Approach." **Bulletin of the Medical Library Association** 78 (January 1990): 45-48.

Hunt explains a formula developed specifically for a journal cancellation project in the late 1980s at the Lawrence Livermore National Laboratory's Biomedical Library. Termed the "institutional cost ratio" (ICR), the formula considers six factors: 1) annual use; 2) subscription cost; 3) size of bound collection; 4) cost of an ILL, calculated at $17.20; 5) annual cost of maintaining a subscription, calculated to be $27; and 6) shelving cost at $6 per linear foot. It computes the relative cost of obtaining requested articles through ILL versus the cost of maintaining a subscription. Use data were gathered during a six-month study. As a result of applying the formula (and review by a committee plus departmental researchers), 280 titles were cancelled, comprising 46 percent of total cost but only 8 percent of use. Two tables list the ten most used journals and the ten top-ranked journals by the ICR formula, i.e., the titles for which it would be most expensive to meet all needs by ILL. This formula apparently assumes that the backruns of cancelled titles will be weeded from the collection, thus limiting its utility to libraries not wishing to do so.

466. Marshall, K. Eric. "Evaluation of Current Periodical Subscriptions in the Freshwater Institute Library." In **IAMSLIC at a Crossroads; Proceedings of the 15th Annual Conference**, edited by Robert W. Burkhart and Joyce C. Burkhart, 117-22. N.p.: International Association of Marine Science Libraries and Information Centers, 1990. 200p. (International Association of Marine Science Libraries and Information Centers Conference Series). LC 90-81226. ISBN 0-932939-07-4.

A method, intermittently employed for ten years by the Manitoba provincial government's Freshwater Institute Library, for calculating the cost per use of current periodicals is explained. During a two-month sampling period for weeklies and a six-month period for other periodicals, patrons were requested to initial an attached slip every time they used an item. Each periodical's total yearly uses and average cost per use were then extrapolated. Data for the 400 subscriptions were maintained in the Volkswriter 3 software package, which allows sorting to identify high-cost-per-use titles as candidates for cancellation. A listing of the twenty-three marine biology core journals, based on the 1987 *SCI*, along with their U.S. prices (totaling more than $8,000), is of interest. The detailed description of the methodological procedures readily allows replication by other libraries.

172 / EVALUATION OF SERIALS

467. McReynolds, Rosalee. "Limiting a Periodicals Collection in a College Library." **Serials Librarian** 9 (Winter 1984): 75-81.

The serials librarian at Loyola University in New Orleans recounts in the first person a serials review project in the early 1980s necessitated by a severe space shortage. Responsible for writing a deselection policy for this "emotionally charged" process, the author relied entirely on published studies for citation and use pattern data in all the major branches of knowledge to identify core journals and shelf life expectancy for decision-making purposes. A number of such studies are briefly described.

The cancellation process narrated here is notable in two respects: the prime incentive was space rather than money and the methodology was based entirely on previously published research.

468. Milne, Dorothy, and Bill Tiffany. "A Survey of the Cost-Effectiveness of Serials: A Cost-Per-Use Method and Its Results." **Serials Librarian** 19, nos. 3/4 (1991): 137-49.

This piece describes a serials evaluation process, based on identifying low-usage, cost-ineffective titles, in progress at Memorial University of Newfoundland since 1986. The average cost per use ranged from $1,000 to $0.03. A major section dealing with the cost-effectiveness of serials by eight major scientific-technical publishers, such as Pergamon or Springer, indicates that 44 percent of the expenditures for their serials were cost-ineffective. Tables display a breakdown for the eight publishers but do not identify them by name.

A more detailed explanation of this project's methodology is presented in the authors' companion piece (see Milne and Tiffany entry 424). However, in light of their verbose writing style, the two contributions could probably have been combined into a single, more concisely written article.

469. Milne, Sally Jo. "Periodicals and Space Constraints." **Indiana Libraries** 9, no. 2 (1990): 55-58.

The Goshen College Library's periodicals collection was extensively reviewed during the winter of 1989 because of severe space shortages. Faculty were asked to evaluate current titles in their subject area, considering: present holdings; indexing; availability and cost of microform; the title's cost, frequency, and circulation; remarks in sources such as *Magazines for Libraries*, by Katz; and circulation of back issues during the last three years. Back issues of titles no longer subscribed to were evaluated by faculty for discard based on: shelf space used; physical condition; cost and availability of microformat; indexing; and assessment by Katz. Milne concludes that "the process worked well" and promoted "dialogue with faculty."

470. Neame, Laura. "Periodicals Cancellation: Making a Virtue out of Necessity." **Serials Librarian** 10 (Spring 1986): 33-42.

Neame believes that many libraries place too much reliance on use studies when cutting periodicals, arguing that cancellation decisions based on usage alone will not be accepted by faculty. She then recounts a major cancellation project at Okanagan College, a two-year institution in British Columbia, that employed use, cost, and perceived value by librarians and faculty as its criteria. During the project's first year, low-use titles costing over $50 were focused upon. The next year, a greater number of new titles (at lower cost, but higher usage and value potential) was added than had previously been dropped, resulting in increased strength for the collection. The project established that final responsibility for cancellation decisions belongs to the library rather than the faculty—a point stressed by the author.

471. Olsrud, Lois, and Anne Moore. "Serials Review in the Humanities: A Three-Year Project." **Collection Building** 10, nos. 3/4 (1990): 2-10.

This thoughtful piece analyzes the process whereby 2,600 of the University of Arizona's 22,000 serials were cancelled during a three-year project covering the 1986-1987, 1987-1988, and 1988-1989 academic years. The area of religion is used to illustrate the methodology. Working from INNOPACQ automated system printouts arranged by LC class, such criteria as programmatic relevance, availability elsewhere, indexing, and faculty input were used. A major section deals with the problems encountered, including timing, faculty contact, reconciliation of quality versus cost, and the unique problems of the humanities. The authors feel that not including price information during the first review was a major mistake. A useful, unannotated bibliography is attached. (See also Tallman and Leach entry 475, also describing this project.)

472. Pike, Lee E. "Conducting a Serials Review Project." **College & Research Libraries News** 52 (March 1991): 165-67.

Pike describes the process used in a comprehensive three-phase serials review during the late 1980s at the University of Alabama Business Library. The review sought to identify periodical and standing-order subscription and cancellation lists, a list of standing orders that could be converted to alternate-year purchases, and titles for which foundation funding was expiring that the library would then pay for. Separate sections recount the procedures in each of the three phases (e.g., faculty surveys in phases I and II with final decisions in phase III). This short item is useful for describing the process used to elicit faculty input.

473. Pinzelik, Barbara P. "Serials De-Acquisition." In **Projects and Procedures for Serials Administration**, compiled and edited by Diane Stine, 61-73. Ann Arbor, Mich.: Pierian Press, 1985. 325p. (Current Issues in Serials Management, no. 5). LC 85-60593. ISBN 0-87650-190-0.

The Purdue University Library's serials collection was evaluated during "a major weeding and storage project," in which 6,000 of 18,000 titles were withdrawn. The authors describe both the evaluation process and the withdrawal procedures. Titles were grouped into four broad categories: current unique, current duplicate, ceased unique, and ceased duplicate. Then a serials evaluation tree, illustrated in the article, was used to reach one of nine possible outcomes: 1) keep; 2) reevaluate; 3) cancel, then transfer and store; 4) cancel, then withdraw or transfer; 5) transfer; 6) discard; 7) withdraw; 8) store; or 9) offer to a regional depository. The half of the entry covering withdrawal procedures contains a deacquisitions flowchart and a discussion of personnel needs.

474. Sheaves, Miriam Lyness. "A Serials Review Program Based on Journal Use in a Departmental Geology Library." In **The Future of the Journal; Proceedings of the Sixteenth Meeting of the Geoscience Information Society, November 2-5, 1981,** edited by Mary Woods Scott, 59-75. N.p.: Geoscience Information Society, 1983. 97p. (Proceedings of the Geoscience Information Society, vol. 12).

174 / EVALUATION OF SERIALS

The usage of 243 bound journals at the University of North Carolina-Chapel Hill Geology Library was measured for a two-year period, beginning in October 1978, by attaching adhesive dots to the spine while reshelving titles. Subsequently, a questionnaire was sent to faculty and graduate students (forty-two responded) concerning which journals they used during the last year. There were four conclusions to the study: 1) the "collection is frequently consulted" (77 percent of the titles were used); 2) the questionnaire results were "closely parallel" to actual usage figures; 3) retrospective use was "significant," as 72 percent of usage concentrated on volumes dated 1974 or earlier; and 4) the first year's use or nonuse did not necessarily predict that of the second year. An appendix lists the forty-seven most frequently used journals. Sheaves stresses that the methodology "takes little staff time and effort."

475. Tallman, Karen Dalziel, and J. Travis Leach. "Serials Review and the Three-Year Cancellation Project at the University of Arizona Library." **Serials Review** 15 (Fall 1989): 51-60.

The same three-year serials review project described by Olsrud and Moore (entry 471) is recounted in considerable detail, except that the focus is on the entire process rather than just the humanities. The general deselection criteria used throughout the project are delineated: relevance, language, space, availability elsewhere, accessibility, format, language, requestor, cost, and holdings. The three-year schedule is outlined. Separate sections narrate the procedures, methodology, goals, staffing structure, problems, and results for years one and two. (Year three was still in progress at the time of writing.) Especially useful are sections describing the criteria and procedures for reinstatement of cancelled titles and for addition of new ones when the cancellation project was still under way.

The authors, both technical services librarians, display refreshing candor, asserting that the Central Reference staff considered the project "of second priority." The University of Arizona library is remarkable for having such a comprehensive, long-range serials review plan.

476. Vocino, Michael. "International Newspapers for U.S. Academic Libraries: A Case Study." **Collection Management** 9 (Winter 1987): 61-68.

Although a voluminous amount has been published about serials evaluation in general, very little has been written concerning the evaluation of newspaper collections. Vocino describes an assessment of the international newspaper collection at the Rhode Island University Library in the spring of 1986. Of particular interest are the six evaluative criteria used in the assessment: 1) relevance to curriculum, 2) the newspaper's reputation, 3) cost, 4) geographical/political coverage, 5) number of ethnic/national group in university community, and 6) requests from patrons. A table listing the forty-one worldwide newspapers recommended as a result of the study could be used as a checklist by other libraries.

477. Walter, Pat L. "Doing the Unthinkable: Cancelling Journals at a Research Library." **Serials Librarian** 18, nos. 1/2 (1990): 141-53.

The process whereby 923 periodicals costing $169,300 were cancelled at UCLA's Biomedical Library during 1987-1988 is depicted. Six categories of periodicals, including multiple copies, reference works, and library and information science journals, were considered for cancellation. Two lists of cancellation candidates, fifty-six and forty pages long, were then sent to the faculty for review. The cancellation decision factors were: low usage; availability elsewhere on campus, either in the University of California system or regionally; cost; indexing; subject area; ILL borrowing history; and faculty feedback.

Ending on an optimistic note, Walter concludes that a large research library "can live with itself and its users" after journal cancellations if it plans carefully, sets clear criteria, and pays attention to staff morale and faculty communication.

478. Wible, Joseph G. "Comparative Analysis of Citation Studies, Swept Use, and ISI's Impact Factors as Tools for Journal Deselection." In **IAMSLIC at a Crossroads; Proceedings of the 15th Annual Conference**, edited by Robert W. Burkhart and Joyce C. Burkhart, 109-16. N.p.: International Association of Marine Science Libraries and Information Centers, 1990. 200p. (International Association of Marine Science Libraries and Information Centers Conference Series). LC 90-81226. ISBN 0-932939-07-4.

Wible describes three data-gathering methods used to identify for cancellation ninety-three serials costing $20,000 at Stanford University's Biology Library in 1989: 1) a journal's total citations in Biology Department faculty publications during 1984-1985 and 1985-1986; 2) a count of the times a title was reshelved (the sweep method) during six sample one-week periods in 1980-1981 and 1988-1989; and 3) the *SCI JCR* 1986 impact factors. A table names the twenty-eight titles most frequently cited by faculty and displays the data mentioned here.

An instructive comparison of the three approaches is offered. The author concludes that the first two methods were extremely labor-intensive compared to easily obtained impact factor data, but warns that relying exclusively on the latter "would result in serious deselection errors." Sixteen of the one hundred most used journals had low impact factors, while three were not even ranked.

479. Williamson, Marilyn L. "Seven Years of Cancellations at Georgia Tech." **Serials Librarian** 9 (Spring 1985): 103-14.

Williamson describes three separate cancellation projects conducted at the Georgia Institute of Technology Libraries in 1976, 1979, and 1981, resulting in over 1,400 cancellations. Separate sections cover the background, procedures, methodology, and results for each project. An especially useful feature is a discussion of the evaluation guidelines used in 1976: relevance, usage, accessibility, availability, cost, format, and the criteria for foreign-language translations. By the third project, termed "massive" by the author because nearly $125,000 was cut, cost was the most important criterion.

The author concludes with some common sense advice, including the observations that serials evaluation should be a continuous process, "formal full-scale" evaluations should be conducted every three or four years, and decisions should not be based on one or two criteria.

480. Woodward, Hazel, and A. J. Evans. "Serials Cuts (and the Use of a Blunt Knife)." In **Serials '83: Proceedings of the UK Serials Group Conference; Held at University of Durham 21-24 March 1983**, edited by Rodney M. Burton, 111-22. N.p.: UK Serials Group, 1984. 144p. ISBN 0-906148-05-7. ISSN 0141-1810.

Drawing on experience at the Loughborough University of Technology as well as the published literature, the authors discuss how libraries address the problems posed by escalating journal costs. Citing Herbert White,[4] they state that libraries initially respond to budget restrictions by stopping new subscriptions, instigating a "new for old" policy, cancelling duplicate and foreign titles, sharing resources, and transferring funds from the monographic budget. Woodward and Evans then identify three stages to the cancellation process: 1) analyzing circulation and surveying use, 2) studying ILL statistics, and 3) consulting users while examining various methods for implementing these steps. They also describe an interesting use survey method employed at Loughborough: placing select titles in "closed access" so that the number of patron requests can be monitored.

NOTES

[1]Barbara Rice, "Science Periodicals Use Study," *Serials Librarian* 4 (Fall 1979): 35-47.

[2]Ibid.

[3]Donald H. Kraft and Richard A. Polacsek, "A Journal-Worth Measure for a Journal-Selection Decision Model," *Collection Management* 2 (Summer 1978): 129-39.

[4]Herbert S. White, "Strategies and Alternatives in Dealing with the Serials Management Budget," in *Serials Collection Development; Choices and Strategies*, ed. Sul H. Lee (Ann Arbor, Mich.: Pierian Press, 1981), 27-42.

11

Journal Ranking

The fairly extensive post-1980 literature concerning journal ranking is covered in this chapter. Journal ranking studies rank-order the journals within a discipline or a narrower subject focus according to some criterion of presumed value, most commonly the subjective judgment of experts in the field or some type of citation measure. Some rankings have been based on use or productivity. Typically a list of the subject's leading journals, ranked in descending order from number one, results from the study.

The earliest journal ranking has been attributed to Gross and Gross's 1927 citation analysis of chemistry journals (see entry 266), annotated in chapter 8.[1] A number of journal rankings in the scientific areas were published during the 1930s. These were usually based on crude measures such as total citation counts. Within the last two decades journal ranking has been used primarily in the social sciences. Quite frequently alternate ranking studies, based on citation measures or the perceptions of experts, have been offered for the same discipline.

Citation rankings now often use *Journal Citation Reports* data and/or impact factor. (The ISI's impact factor calculates the average number of times a journal's typical article is cited within a year, to compensate for the advantage that frequently issued journals with many articles would enjoy in a ranking by total citations received.) Perception rankings are usually compiled by surveying presumed experts in the subject who are asked to rate a list of journals, often using a predefined quality scale. The rankings themselves are based on an average qualitative rating, the number of respondents familiar with the title, or some combination of both.

The literature is replete with detailed criticisms, often quite technical, of the various ranking methods. To summarize only the major issues, criticisms of citation-based rankings include:

1. Journals with longer articles or more researchers in the field have greater opportunities to be cited

178 / JOURNAL RANKING

2. Cross-disciplinary comparisons are not valid

3. New journals have not had time to establish a citation record.

Criticisms of rankings based on subjective judgment include:

1. The respondents may be unfamiliar with the titles they are rating

2. The respondents may be biased in favor of journals in their own specialty or in which they have published

3. Important titles may have been omitted from the original list

4. The rankings may vary considerably between different categories of respondents, such as between practitioners versus academicians.

Criticisms of all ranking methods include:

1. They may be biased in favor of well-known, established journals

2. Rankings can vary over time

3. The quality of articles within a single journal can vary immensely.

Journal rankings can be used for a variety of purposes, including evaluation of promotion and tenure dossiers and assisting scholars' manuscript submission decisions. The relevance of journal ranking to collection evaluation is obvious. A table of a subject area's leading journals can be used as a checklist for evaluating journal holdings and for assisting with selection, cancellation, and weeding decisions. (It should be explained that *cancellation* means stopping the current subscription, while *weeding* refers to removing the holdings from the collection.) Ironically, if used as a checklist, journal rankings might be more useful to smaller libraries than larger ones, on the assumption that a large library would as a matter of course hold the top-ranked journals in a particular subject area.

According to Subramanyam, other collection management uses of journal ranking lists include: 1) calculating the cost of "all the journals relevant to a given subject"; 2) determining what fraction of total coverage could be obtained for a specified budget level; 3) assisting central library versus branch location decisions; and 4) assisting decisions concerning limited access storage.[2]

Moreover, the very act of ranking journals is logically connected to collection evaluation, as both involve assessments of value. Unlike most of this book's other chapters, a significant portion of the items covered were written by scholars outside the field of library and information science and published in nonlibrary journals.

Journal ranking is quite similar in concept to identifying a subject's core journals, covered in chapter 10. In fact, the two frequently overlap in the sense that core lists can be ranked and ranked lists are sometimes considered the core. Nevertheless, a number of differences can be noted:

1. Core lists are usually identified specifically for collection evaluation purposes, while ranked lists are frequently undertaken to ascertain journal value for promotion and tenure.

2. Core lists often name the titles in alphabetical order, without an explicit ranking.

3. Ranked lists are more likely to be published by scholars outside the field of library and information science and to be published in non-LIS journals.

This chapter contains both specific journal ranking studies of various subject areas and discussions of general methodological issues. Articles whose primary purpose or primary relevance to collection evaluation is to rank journals are included here. Several items in chapters 8 and 10 also incorporate journal rankings as part of broader studies. Brief critiques of specific rankings or short methodological notes, such as those frequently appearing as letters to the editor in *American Psychologist*, were generally excluded. This chapter is divided into four sections: theoretical discussions, journal rankings in business, journal rankings in the social sciences, and journal rankings in other subject areas.

THEORETICAL DISCUSSIONS

481. Archibald, Robert B., and David H. Finifter. "Biases in Citation-Based Ranking of Journals." **Scholarly Publishing** 18 (January 1987): 131-38.

This thoughtful, well-reasoned essay, based on the authors' sophisticated understanding of the topic, points out the flaws in citation-based journal ranking methods. Such rankings are biased because journals that publish more articles or longer articles, and address a larger audience or subfield, have a greater potential for citation. While the number of articles is compensated for by "impact factor," article length and field size have not been addressed by standard ranking methods. Of considerable practical value to collection development librarians are the warnings that:

1. Citation methods cannot be used for comparisons across disciplines.

2. A study focusing on a single discipline may undervalue interdisciplinary journals.

3. New journals cannot be evaluated, because they lack a citation record.

482. Boyce, Bert R., and Janet Sue Pollens. "Citation-Based Impact Measures and the Bradfordian Selection Criteria." **Collection Management** 4 (Fall 1982): 29-36.

In 1934 Bradford proposed that, in a given subject, a large proportion of significant articles appear in a few journals with a smaller number scattered in many journals.[3] To test the relationship between journal ranking by quantity (i.e., the most productive based on Bradfordian distribution) and by quality (using citation measures), a Bradfordian ranking of mathematics journals from a 1971 dissertation[4] was correlated with total citations, immediacy index, and impact factor from the 1974 *SCI JCR* and "quality weight rankings," a method similar to impact factor developed by Boyce and Funk in 1978.[5] Two tables display the correlational data. The authors assert that "none of our quality rankings correlates significantly with the quantity distribution," leading to the conclusion that one cannot rely exclusively on Bradfordian distribution for journal selection. In other words, the journals that produce the most articles on a topic may not be of the highest quality. This is an outstanding scholarly article.

483. Buffardi, Louis C., and Julia A. Nichols. "Citation Impact, Acceptance Rate, and APA Journals." **American Psychologist** 36 (November 1981): 1453-56.

The primary objective of this scholarly study is to analyze what factors predict high citation impact in psychology journals. Eight variables—number of indexes covered in, circulation, cost, publication lag, review period, early publication policy, acceptance rate, and reprint policy—were correlated with the 1977 *SSCI JCR* citation impact factor for ninety-nine psychology journals. Circulation correlated positively with impact factor, but acceptance rate correlated negatively; that is, high citation impact journals had low acceptance rates and vice versa. No other factors correlated significantly. Additional analysis revealed that American Psychological Association journals had significantly higher citation impact than non-APA journals. A table rank-orders the ninety-one psychology journals according to 1977 impact factor and also lists the percentage of submissions they accept.

The authors conclude by stating that "citation impact is probably the best single measure of journal quality we have at present." Although primarily significant for its theoretical insight, the entry is also noteworthy for the ranking of psychology journals. (See also Haynes entry 528.)

484. Christenson, James A., and Lee Sigelman. "Accrediting Knowledge: Journal Stature and Citation Impact in Social Science." **Social Science Quarterly** 66 (December 1985): 964-75.

The reputational prestige rankings of sixty-three sociology journals and sixty-three political science journals, based on surveys of academicians in those disciplines reported in 1971 by Glenn (entry 527) and 1975 by Giles and Wright (entry 526), were compared with the average 1977-1979 impact factor from the *SSCI JCR*. Separate tables present the comparative data for the two sets of journals. The authors assert that the .526 correlation for sociology and .572 for political science "are not nearly strong enough to permit us to conclude that a journal's reputation is a simple function of scholarly influence." The authors assert that reputational rankings "reflect persisting stereotypes" with very good and very bad reputations exaggerated beyond what the impact data warrant. (See also Dometrius entry 485.)

485. Dometrius, Nelson C. "Subjective and Objective Measures of Journal Stature." **Social Science Quarterly** 70 (March 1989): 197-203.

After analyzing Christenson and Sigelman's comparison of impact factor and subjective prestige rankings for political science and sociology journals (entry 484), Dometrius addresses the explanation for discrepancies between citation and subjective prestige rankings. Dometrius speculates that impact factor may be "too fair," as total citations or the number of journals that cite a title may represent better indicators of prestige. However, following statistical analysis, he concludes that impact factor offers "a robust indicator of journal stature." But, "at the same time, it is inadequate." Dometrius also stresses that the *SSCI* measures are distorted by the fact that they count citations from all periodicals in the database rather than just a discipline's central journals.

486. Gordon, Michael D. "Citation Ranking versus Subjective Evaluation in the Determination of Journal Hierarchies in the Social Sciences." **Journal of the American Society for Information Science** 33 (January 1982): 55-57.

Gordon's short, methodologically rigorous article correlates two subjective rankings ("intensity of prestige" and "extensity of prestige") of sixty-three sociology journals by academic sociologists, published by Glenn in 1971 (entry 527), with four major *SSCI Journal Citation Report* 1977 and 1978 rankings: times-cited, impact factor, immediacy index, and number of published articles. The correlational data are displayed in a table. Due to the "fairly high correlation" between the subjective measures and the citation rankings, Gordon concludes that *Journal Citation Reports* is a "useful guide" to the importance of social science journals, but states that this finding cannot be generalized to the physical sciences.

487. He, Chunpei, and Miranda Lee Pao. "A Discipline-Specific Journal Selection Algorithm." **Information Processing & Management** 22, no. 5 (1986): 405-16.

A system for journal ranking by means of a "Discipline Influence Score" is proposed. The journals in a "Candidate Set," identified through citations in key titles, are ranked according to the "sum of relative frequency of citations" to each candidate journal by titles in a "Discipline Journal Set," consisting of the discipline's most important titles. The method was tested in the area of veterinary medicine, using data from the 1983 *Journal Citation Reports*. The ranking of 146 titles did not correlate with rankings derived from a number of articles published, gross citations, impact factor, or Narin's total citation influence measure,[6] but did correlate with a ranking based on the judgment of professionals in the United States and China as well as the contents of two recommended lists. A table lists forty-six titles ranked among the top twenty by four different methods analyzed here. The authors contend that their algorithm is "easy to implement" and can be applied to all disciplines.

488. Lancaster, F. Wilfrid. "Evaluation of Periodicals." In his **If You Want to Evaluate Your Library**, 60-71. Champaign: University of Illinois, Graduate School of Library and Information Science, 1988. 193p. LC 88-91099. ISBN 0-87845-078-5.

This chapter focuses on ranking journals to assist cancellation decisions. Seven journal ranking criteria are listed: use in the library, use in other libraries, opinion, citation counts, impact factor, cost-effectiveness, and number of articles contributed to a subject area. Following an extremely valuable review of the literature comparing different periodical ranking systems, such as citation frequency versus local use, Lancaster concludes that citation data alone are not very reliable. Consequently, a hypothetical multifactor decision model incorporating use, user opinion, the subject's relevance to the institution, and cost is illustrated. He finally concludes that deselection decisions "should be made primarily on the basis of cost effectiveness." (See also Lancaster entries 15, 118, 119, and 183.)

489. Line, Maurice B. "Changes in Rank Lists of Serials Over Time: Interlending versus Citation Data." **College & Research Libraries** 46 (January 1985): 77-79.

Line, director general of the British Library Lending Division, compares changes over three- and five-year intervals in journal rankings based on requests at the BLLD and citations in both the *SCI* and the *SSCI*. A table presents the percentage of ovelap for the leading 100, 200, 300, 400, 500, and 1,000 journals for a variety of comparison points. It was found that rankings by citation data displayed much greater stability than ranking by requests at the BLDD. For example, there was only a 57 percent overlap among the top 100 journals at BLDD between 1980 and 1983, but a 95 percent overlap among the top 100 journals in the *SCI* between 1979 and 1982. Line speculates on the explanation, proposing that citations are made by authors in academic institutions while ILL requests originate from all types of libraries, but believes that more research is desirable.

490. McAllister, Paul R., Richard C. Anderson, and Francis Narin. "Comparison of Peer and Citation Assessment of the Influence of Scientific Journals." **Journal of the American Society for Information Science** 31 (May 1980): 147-52.

This rigorous article, based on contract work for the National Science Foundation, compares the subjective ranking of fifty-eight journals in ten scientific disciplines by scientists to ranking by "citation influence," a method similar to impact factor except that citations by prestigious journals receive greater weight. Two hundred ninety-seven respondents to a survey questionnaire sent to ninety-seven universities ranked the journals on a 0 (low) to 4 (high) scale according to the "scientific influence of an average article." A "strong positive" correlation (ranging around 0.9) was found between the two ranking methods in seven areas: biochemistry, botany, chemistry, geoscience, mathematics, pharmacology, and psychology. The correlation was "less striking" in the 0.4 to 0.7 range in electrical engineering, entomology, and physics. Further detailed analysis revealed that citation influence data for biochemistry correlated with peer rankings and citation data from a 1977 report.[7] This item is notable for applying a variant citation measure to ten disciplines.

491. Singleton, Alan. "Journal Rankings and Selection: A Review in Physics." **Journal of Documentation** 32 (December 1976): 258-89.

Singleton's frequently cited article offers an outstanding review of previous journal ranking studies in physics. Separate sections analyze the studies under three categories: citation analysis, use or user judgement, and productivity (i.e., number of papers, words, pages, etc.). Several tables and figures display the findings from earlier studies. An especially useful feature is a table that summarizes several options, regarding both citation source and ranking method, and then explains the theoretical implications of each option. Bradfordian distribution and Kraft's serials selection model[8] are extensively analyzed.

The author concludes that citation rankings "date fairly rapidly," while those based on use studies may not be applicable in other libraries. He predicts "continued reliance on subjective judgement of librarian and user." Although dated, this entry is still useful for illuminating some fundamental theoretical issues in journal ranking. One can observe that during the decade and a half since Singleton's article appeared, ranking studies have emphasized citations and subjective judgment rather than use or productivity measures.

492. Taylor, Roger. "Is the Impact Factor a Meaningful Index for the Ranking of Scientific Research Journals?" **Canadian Field-Naturalist** 95 (July-September 1981): 236-40.

Using the *Canadian-Field Naturalist* for illustrative purposes, Taylor argues that the *SCI JCR* distorts a journal's "worth" and is not valid for comparing journals across disciplines. This journal's 1978 impact factor was "clearly low" because it did not include self-citations (the *Canadian Field-Naturalist* is not in the ISI source database) and two 1976 issues were inexplicably excluded from the tabulation. Shorter articles have less chance to be cited. Furthermore, the fact that field research requires more time to be completed and cited than laboratory research generally contributes to a lower impact factor. A calculation method to correct the last two problems is presented.

493. Teevan, James J. "Journal Prestige and Quality of Sociological Articles." **American Sociologist** 15 (May 1980): 109-12.

Teevan adapted Glenn's methodology for ranking sociology journals (see entry 527) to the rating of specific articles within journals. Five randomly selected articles from six "general" sociological journals (ranked 1, 4, 29, 37, 41, and 45 in Glenn's study) were sent to thirty-five reviewers, full or associate professors at universities with sociology M.A. or Ph.D. programs, who were asked to assign a numerical evaluation based on a weighted standard of 10. A number of sophistical measures for ranking the six journals based on evaluation of individual articles did not correspond to Glenn's ranking. More significantly, variation in mean and median ratings was greater for articles within the same journal than between journals.

The author concludes that his "finding would be pedestrian were it not for the fact that it is often forgotten." This work is important for pointing out a major limitation of journal ranking: "highly regarded articles appear in less highly regarded journals" and vice versa. Nevertheless, librarians must still make journal selection and cancellation decisions on the basis of specific titles.

494. Todorov, Radosvet. "Evaluation of Scientific Journals: A Review of Citation-Based Measures." In **Information Research: Research Methods in Library and Information Science; Proceedings of the International Seminar on Information Research, Dubrovnik, Yugoslavia, May 19-24, 1986,** edited by Neva Tudor-Šilović and Ivan Mihel, 212-24. London: Taylor Graham, 1988. 261p. LC 89-205230. ISBN 0-94756-826-3.

In a well-done, detailed review, nearly a dozen methods for using citation data to rank scientific journals, including the ISI's familiar gross citation count, impact factor, and immediacy index, as well as refinements by several authors, are conceptualized with mathematical formulas and subjected to critical commentary. After reviewing studies that compare citation-based journal rankings with rankings based on other factors, including McAllister, Anderson, Narin (entry 490), and Gordon (entry 486), Todorov concludes that citation measures' "moderate to high correlations with subjective ratings and objective quality criteria seem to confirm their suitability for collection development decisions." This rigorous study will be of primary interest to researchers.

495. Urquhart, John A. "Has Poisson Been Kicked to Death? — A Rebuttal of the British Library Lending Division's Views on the Inconsistency of Rank Lists of Serials." **Interlending Review** 10 (November 1982): 97-99.

Urquhart argues that Clarke's comparative lists of the most frequently requested titles at the British Library Lending Division in 1975 and 1980 (entry 136) wrongly underestimate similarity of use (and thus the value of core lists) for four reasons: 1) the BLLD study did not consider changes in journal status, e.g., births, deaths, marriages, and divorces; 2) the 1975 and 1980 samples were different sizes; 3) natural variation between two samples does not reflect genuine changes in behavior; and 4) "variation may be greater because of peaking of demand over short periods." A response from the BLLD acknowledges some statistical inadequacies in the comparison, but asserts that the differences in ranking still exist as a practical matter. This entry addresses some of the theoretical difficulties involved in journal ranking.

496. Weisheit, Ralph A., and Robert M. Regoli. "Ranking Journals." **Scholarly Publishing** 15 (July 1984): 313-25.

Weisheit and Regoli, social science faculty members at Illinois State and the University of Colorado, present an illuminating discussion of several basic methodological issues involved in ranking journals. One must first define what is meant by the terms *journal* and *ranking*. Journals in a subfield may be grouped by themselves or treated as part of the broader discipline. There may be self-fulfilling prophecies whereby a journal's present ranking influences its future rankings. Finally, age and association with a professional organization may increase a journal's ranking. The authors point out that these "are theoretical concerns for which there are no unambiguously right or wrong responses."

Methodological problems in regard to ranking journals by reputation include determination of who will be surveyed, low response rates, selection of an appropriate measurement scale, and the precise meaning of the term *prestige*. The authors note that one must know the ranking's purpose before deciding which citation measure to use.

497. Wiberley, Stephen E., Jr. "Journal Rankings from Citation Studies: A Comparison of National and Local Data from Social Work." **Library Quarterly** 52 (October 1982): 348-59.

To test Line's frequently made assertion that citation rankings lack validity for journal selection decisions, Wiberley's important, well-done study compared journal rankings based on citations in a local database of 1971-1978 social work faculty publications from the University of Illinois at Chicago, with journal rankings based on three national databases: 1) the journal *Social Work*'s 1971 volume; 2) the *Encyclopedia of Social Work*; and 3) the 1971 volumes of the journals *Social Casework, Social Service Review*, and *Social Work* (repeated).

Wiberley found that fewer than half the top-ranked journals from the national databases were among the top-ranked local journals. As one proceeds down the national rankings, the journals were less likely to be cited locally. Local 1971-1974 citations were better predictors than the national databases of which journals were locally cited between 1975 and 1978. Specific titles are not mentioned. The author concludes that citation studies are "a useful, if limited and imperfect, guide" to journal selection. This item has important implications concerning the use of citations studies in journal collection evaluation.

JOURNAL RANKINGS IN BUSINESS

498. Albert, Joe, and P. R. Chandy. "Research and Publishing in Real Estate: A Survey and Analysis." **Akron Business & Economic Review** 17 (Winter 1986): 46-54.

Seventy academics and real estate professionals, randomly selected from the American Real Estate and Urban Economics Association 1983 membership list, responded to a mailed questionnaire in which they rated a "comprehensive list" of real-estate-related journals on a 0 (low) to 100 (high) scale. They also identified leading real estate articles, authors, and departments. Separate tables display the rankings of nineteen journals by academics and professionals, with each table divided into sections for journals ranked by more than half and less than half the respondents. A similarity is noted between the rankings by academics and practitioners, but no statistical analysis is undertaken. The methodology is rather primitive and not well explained, but this item is still worth mentioning.

499. Brink, David R., and Karl A. Shilliff. "Journal Preferences of Management Teaching Faculty." **Library Acquisitions: Practice & Theory** 13, no. 4 (1989): 391-99.

One hundred six managerial professors in Ohio colleges, which the authors claim are "representative of the nation," responded to a survey in which they ranked fifty-eight management and business journals by their "appropriateness as a forum for scholarly research" in management, using a 1 (low) to 4 (high) scale. A table displays, in descending order, the forty-nine journals that received a rating of 2.00 or higher. Three additional tables list the highest ranking journals by respondents classified as having a "general," "behavioral," or "quantitative" orientation, based on their subject specialties. "Significant variations" existed among the latter three rankings, but the implications are not fully elaborated upon.

Brink and Shilliff believe that their study is a better indicator of value for research and libraries than the Coe and Weinstock survey (entry 504), which was limited to deans and department chairs, or the Sharplin and Mabry study (entry 516), which omitted the quantitative area.

500. Browne, William G., and Boris W. Becker. "Perceptions of Marketing Journals: Awareness and Quality Evaluations." **AMA Educators' Proceedings** 51 (August 1985): 149-54.

Browne and Becker's investigation is based on 119 questionnaire responses from marketing department chairpersons at American Assembly of Collegiate Schools of Business [AACSB]-accredited business schools, in which respondents rated a list of fifty-two marketing journals on a 1 (high) to 4 (low) quality scale. A table displays the fifty-two journals in alphabetical order and indicates the number and percentage of responses in each of the four rating categories. Another table rank-orders the fifty-two titles by "familiarity," i.e., the number of respondents who knew the journal well enough to rate it, and also indicates the average rating and rank based on average rating. Comparison of the top ten journals with those in a similar study the authors conducted six years earlier found "little change."[9] Ratings by deans of large business schools (more than sixty faculty) showed "essentially no difference" from those of small schools. The importance of publishing for promotion and tenure is also discussed. Although their methodology is quite similar, Browne and Becker do not mention Coe and Weinstock's ranking of marketing journals (entry 501).

501. Coe, Robert K., and Irwin Weinstock. "Evaluating Journal Publications of Marketing Professors: A Second Look." **Journal of Marketing Education** 5 (Spring 1983): 37-42.

This follow-up to the authors' similar 1969 study[10] is based on 105 responses to a 1982 questionnaire mailed to marketing department chairs and coordinators at AACSB-accredited business schools. Although the article focuses on promotion-and-tenure criteria for marketing faculty, it contains significant information concerning journal rankings in that area. The chairs rated a list of fourteen journals on a 0 (low) to 9 (high) scale according to the perceived "achievement" of an author publishing in the journal. A table lists the fourteen journals in rank order and also indicates their ratings from the earlier study. Six of thirty additional journals suggested by respondents are named in the text. A .95 correlation was found between perceived journal quality and perceived acceptance rate for unsolicited manuscripts, yet the actual acceptance rate was overestimated. Besides attempting to identify top marketing journals, this entry is noteworthy for using the concept of author achievement as a ranking criterion.

502. Coe, Robert K., and Irwin Weinstock. "Evaluating the Accounting Professor's Journal Publications." **Journal of Accounting Education** 1 (Spring 1983): 127-29.

This short research item applies to accounting journals the same methodology used in the investigation described in entry 501. In a 1982 survey, 135 accounting department chairpersons from AACSB-accredited business schools rated a listing of sixteen journals on a 0 (low) to 9 (high) achievement scale. A table that rank-orders the leading fifteen titles by "mean achievement rating" also presents the results from a 1968 survey by these authors.[11] Although correlational statistics were not used, Coe and Weinstock note "the remarkable degree of stability among rankings over the fourteen year interval." An additional forty titles were named by the respondents, of which the top seven are named in the text in order of frequency. This entry is less useful than the accounting journal rankings by Howard and Nikolai (entry 510), Nobes (entry 514), and Weber (entry 518), if for no other reason than it covers fewer titles.

503. Coe, Robert K., and Irwin Weinstock. "Evaluating the Finance Journals: The Department Chairperson's Perspective." **Journal of Financial Research** 6 (Winter 1983): 345-49.

The authors' methodology described in entries 501 and 502 is used to rank finance journals. One hundred seven finance department chairpersons from AACSB-accredited business schools throughout the United States answered a mail questionnaire in which they ranked twenty finance journals from 0 (low) to 9 (high) based on the degree of "achievement" attributed to a faculty member who published in the journal. One table lists the twenty journals in rank order, while another table names the five most frequently mentioned journals not on the original list. Respondents gave the highest ranking to journals with the perceived lowest acceptance rates for submitted manuscripts, but they actually overestimated the acceptance rates by an average of 40 percent. (See also Mabry and Sharplin entry 512.)

504. Coe, Robert K., and Irwin Weinstock. "Evaluating the Management Journals: A Second Look." **Academy of Management Journal** 27 (September 1984): 660-66.

Coe and Weinstock's approach (see entries 501, 502, and 503) is applied to management journals. One hundred fourteen management department chairs from accredited business schools rated sixteen management journals on a 0 (low) to 9 (high) scale, based on "achievement by an author." A table lists the sixteen journals, in rank order, and compares their mean "achievement ratings" with the results from the authors' 1968 survey.[12] More than sixty other journals not on the list were named by respondents; the top seven of these are revealed in the text. The correlations between high ranking and low perceived acceptance rates, along with the tendency to overestimate acceptance rates, were once again confirmed. This study was criticized by Sharplin and Mabry (entry 516).

505. Davis, Gordon B. "A Systematic Evaluation of Publications for Promotion of MIS Academics." In **Proceedings of the First International Conference on Information Systems, December 8-10, 1980, Philadelphia, Pa; sponsored by ... the Society for Management Information Systems ... Association for Computing Machinery ... and the Institute of Management Sciences**, edited by Ephraim R. McLean, 206-16. N.p.: n.l., 1980. 244p.

Davis offers a framework for MIS academics to evaluate their publication records for promotion and tenure purposes. The framework is based on four criteria: the journal where the article appears, article quality, number of authors, and the number of times "essentially the same material" has been published. A scheme is proposed for placing MIS journals and proceedings into one of eight categories (each of which is briefly explained): "preferred highest," "highest," "intermediate," and "lowest" for both "scholarly" and "practitioner" journals. A figure lists thirty-five journals in implicit rank order (numbering is not used) within the framework. This item is remarkable for both its elaborate classification scheme and the fact it is based on the author's "personal observation and introspection rather than a systematic data collection."

506. Doke, E. Reed, and Robert H. Luke. "Perceived Quality of CIS/MIS Journals among Faculty: Publishing Hierarchies." **Journal of Computer Information Systems** 27 (Summer 1987): 30-33.

Doke and Luke report a ranking of computer information systems and management information systems journals, structured around eighty-two questionnaire responses from faculty at twenty-nine AACSB-accredited business schools. Respondents rank-ordered the top ten journals from a list of twenty-nine. A table displays the leading twenty-five CIS-MIS journals in rank order according to the total times ranked and "popularity/familiarity index" (a formula based on the number of respondents who ranked a journal). The "importance/prestige index" (calculated by weighted average rank) and the number of occasions ranked 1 through 10 is also revealed for each title.

The authors then speculate on whether the "popularity/familiarity index" or the "importance/prestige index" is the most meaningful indicator. They assert that intuitively the "importance/prestige index" seems "more reliable," but plan further research. (See also Luke and Doke entry 511 for an application of this methodology to marketing.)

507. Extejt, Marian M., and Jonathan E. Smith. "The Behavioral Sciences and Management: An Evaluation of Relevant Journals." **Journal of Management** 16 (September 1990): 539-51.

Extejt and Smith's excellent study rank-orders fifty-four journals concerned with the behavioral aspects of management. One hundred eighty-nine academics systematically selected from the Academy of Management and Industrial Relations Research Association membership rosters rated the journals on a 1 (high) to 4 (low) quality scale. A table names the fifty-four titles in rank order according to mean rating and also indicates the number of respondents who knew the title well enough to rate it. Another table compares Extejt and Smith's results with those from three earlier ranking systems. The authors found a .87 correlation between their findings and ranking by impact factor in the 1985 *SSCI* (for the 39 titles included in both), a -.69 correlation for the 15 journals included in Sharplin and Mabry's 1985 study (entry 516), and a .77 correlation for the 6 titles in Coe and Weinstock's 1984 investigation (entry 504).

Additional testing of specific hypotheses revealed that about 25 percent of the titles were rated higher by respondents who had published in them, but this bias "does not appear to be a consistent trend." Also, "academic journals were consistently rated higher than practitioner and mixed audience journals."

508. Fry, Elaine Hobbs, C. Glenn Walters, and Lawrence E. Scheuermann. "Perceived Quality of Fifty Selected Journals: Academicians and Practitioners." **Journal of the Academy of Marketing Science** 13 (Spring 1985): 352-61.

Three management professors at Nicholls State University analyzed 304 responses from a sample of the American Marketing Association and the Academy of Management membership, consisting of both academicians and practitioners. The perceived quality of fifty business journals was rated either Very High (4), High (3), Low (2), Very Low (1), or Unknown. The authors were surprised that 58 percent of the journals were unknown to at least 60 percent of the respondents. An unusual feature, a table displaying the distribution of responses for all titles, reveals that every journal was ranked "Very High" by at least some respondents. Another table rank-orders the fifty journals by numerical rating and classifies them into the following categories: "top of the field" (six), "prestigious" (eleven), "academically recognized" (twenty), "academically unrecognized" (ten), and "non-academic" (three). There was no statistically significant difference in the relative rankings between academicians and practitioners, although practitioners generally rated journals lower.

509. Hamilton, Scott, and Blake Ives. "Communication of MIS Research: An Analysis of Journal Stratification." In **Proceedings of the First International Conference on Information Systems, December 8-10, 1980, Philadelphia, Pa; sponsored by ... the Society for Management Information Systems ... Association**

for Computing Machinery ... and the Institute of Management Sciences, edited by Ephraim R. McLean, 203-16. N.p.: n.l., 1980. 244p.

Although the authors use the term *stratification*, their study actually ranks MIS journals according to a number of measures. There were three steps to this investigation. First, 110 MIS "experts," who held a doctorate in the field, responded to a June 1980 mailed questionnaire concerning their perceptions of 37 journals (although the rating system is not explained). Second, the articles published between 1970 and 1979 in sixteen of these journals were rated by the authors on a 0 (low) to 3 (high) scale concerning the degree to which each article belonged to the MIS field. Finally, a citation analysis was conducted on the MIS articles published in these same sixteen journals during 1979. A table rank-orders the sixteen journals according to their mean rating by MIS experts and also indicates the percentage of their articles falling within MIS and the percentage of respondents who read the journal. Another table names the sixteen most frequently cited journals. Two other tables rank the top ten journals based on the submission preferences of academics and practitioners. This study is noteworthy for its combination of ranking methods.

510. Howard, Thomas P., and Loren A. Nikolai. "Attitude Measurement and Perceptions of Accounting Faculty Publication Outlets." **Accounting Review** 58 (October 1983): 765-76.

This ranking of accounting journals is based on 311 questionnaire responses from randomly selected U.S. accounting educators holding the Ph.D. Points reflecting perceived quality were assigned to a list of journals, using an arbitrary 100 for the *Journal of Accountancy*. A table lists the fifty-one journals in rank order, while a ratio scale figure illustrates the overall ranking. Another table and ratio scale figure illustrate the top ten and bottom five journals from respondents specializing in auditing, finance, management, and taxation. Additional comparisons, using a similar format, are made between the rankings by faculty at Ph.D.-granting versus non-Ph.D.-granting institutions and between full and assistant professors. Comparison with a ranking of accounting journals conducted in 1974 by Benjamin and Brenner[13] found a .78 correlation, based on titles covered by both studies.

511. Luke, Robert H., and E. Reed Doke. "Marketing Journal Hierarchies: Faculty Perceptions, 1986-87." **Journal of the Academy of Marketing Science** 15 (Spring 1987): 74-78.

Luke and Doke apply their methodology used to rank CIS-MIS journals (see entry 506) to marketing journals. One hundred eight faculty respondents from thirty-five AACSB-accredited business schools ranked the top ten journals from a list of thirty. A table rank-orders the top twenty-five by total number of times ranked and the "popularity/familiarity index" (the two correspond). It also indicates the "importance/prestige index" and the number of times each journal was ranked at every position from 1 through 10.

The authors again discuss which of the two indexes is most valid and again assert their intuitive preference for the "importance/prestige index," but further research is planned.

512. Mabry, Robert H., and Arthur D. Sharplin. "The Relative Importance of Journals Used in Finance Research." **Journal of Financial Research** 8 (Winter 1985): 287-96.

This sophisticated, citation-based ranking of finance journals is offered as an alternative to Coe and Weinstock's 1983 perception-based ranking (entry 503). The ranking was based on the journals cited in *Journal of Finance, Journal of Financial Economics, Journal of Financial & Quantitative Analysis*, and *Journal of Money, Credit, & Banking* from 1980 through June 1985. (Use of *SSCI* data was rejected because they are based on citations from 2,500 publications rather than just the finance literature.) Tables list the top thirty journals by "simple effectiveness" (i.e., total citations), "article effectiveness" (i.e., citations adjusted by the number of articles), and "impact efficiency" (i.e., the number of citations per 10,000 words). Among the 100 titles cited in the 4 source journals, the same journals were in the leading 30 by all three methods, although their order varied. Comparison with Coe and Weinstock's ranking found a "strong difference," as eight of Mabry and Sharplin's top twenty did not even appear on Coe and Weinstock's list.

513. Nielsen, Donald A., and R. Wayne Wilson. "A Delphi Rating of Real Estate Journals." **Real Estate Appraiser & Analyst** 46 (May-June 1980): 43-48.

The authors used the Delphi technique, a social science method for achieving consensus among a group of experts, to rank real estate journals. Initially, 100 full- and part-time real estate instructors at U.S. educational institutions responded to a mailed questionnaire in which they rated an alphabetical list of journals on a 1 (low) to 20 (high) quality scale. In accordance with the Delphi methodology, the results were sent to all respondents for a second rating. The article's final ranking of seventeen titles is based on the sixty second-round responses. A table displays the rankings according to mean rating and "prestige index," defined as the mean rating multiplied by the "familiarity index" (the number of respondents who rated a journal).

Two additional tables present the mean and prestige rankings according to the degree held, primary interest (i.e., teaching or research), rank, age, tenure status, and teaching experience of the respondents. Nielsen and Wilson's entry is notable for employing the Delphi method in journal ranking. (See also Outreville and Malouin, entry 515.)

514. Nobes, Christopher W. "International Variations in Perceptions of Accounting Journals." **Accounting Review** 60 (October 1985): 702-5.

The author extends the Howard and Nikolai methodology for ranking accounting journals (entry 510) to an international set of respondents. Two hundred thirty-two full-time university faculty in the United Kingdom, Australia, and New Zealand rated a list of thirty-seven accounting journals (twenty-three from the Howard and Nikolai study plus fourteen additional ones) using 100 as a benchmark representing *Accounting Review*'s quality. A table rank-orders the thirty-seven titles by mean quality score from the three countries, while also noting the number of respondents who rated each title. The identical data are presented separately for respondents from Australia and New Zealand and for U.K. accounting and finance specialists.

For the twenty-three journals common to both, a .75 correlation was found between this international ranking and Howard and Nikolai's ranking by Americans. Because of its international perspective, this entry may be of more theoretical than practical interest.

515. Outreville, J. Francois, and Jean-Louis Malouin. "What Are the Major Journals That Members of ARIA Read?" **Journal of Risk & Insurance** 52 (December 1985): 723-33.

This investigation ranks finance and economics journals as perceived by the American Risk and Insurance Association (ARIA) membership. Employing the Delphi technique, three rounds of questionnaires were mailed out. Initially, 79 ARIA members and 161 American Economic Association members responded to a questionnaire, indicating their familiarity with each title on an alphabetical list of 255 journals. The next two rounds were limited to academic members of the ARIA. Eighty-two respondents rated a list of ninety-two titles, selected by the first round of questionnaires, on a 1 (low) to 20 (high) quality scale. Finally, these results were sent to the respondents for a final round of rating.

Two tables rank-order the forty titles that AEA and ARIA members were most familiar with. Another two-page table rank-orders the top eighty journals by mean quality rating. The top thirty or so journals according to "impact" (defined as familiarity times quality rating) are then listed for four groups of respondents, categorized by whether they teach in Ph.D.- or non-Ph.D.-granting departments and whether they teach finance as well as insurance. This entry would obviously be of interest to any academic library supporting a program in insurance.

516. Sharplin, Arthur D., and Rodney H. Mabry. "The Relative Importance of Journals Used in Management Research: An Alternative Ranking." **Human Relations** 38, no. 2 (1985): 139-49.

This outstanding study is offered as an "alternative ranking" to Coe and Weinstock's 1984 article (entry 504), of which the authors are highly critical (e.g., respondents were asked to rate an "inadequate" list of sixteen "arbitrarily chosen" titles which omitted top journals, while the "author's achievement" criterion was not defined). Sharplin and Mabry analyzed the journal citations in the 1980 to 1983 issues of *Administrative Science Quarterly* and *Academy of Management Journal*, which they consider "the two most important management journals." This process yielded over 100 that were ranked by 3 criteria: total citations, citations per article, and citations per citable 10,000 words, which the authors deem "the most appropriate measure of journal effectiveness ... for the scholar who wishes to obtain maximum research value for a minimum amount of reading." For each method, the top twenty journals, including nonmanagement titles, are listed. A final table displays the top ten management journals. This is a sophisticated journal ranking study.

517. Smith, Charles A., and George D. Greenwade. "The Ranking of Real Estate Publications and Tenure Requirements at AACSB versus Non-AACSB Schools." **Journal of Real Estate Research** 2 (Winter 1987): 105-12.

One hundred forty-five randomly selected deans of business schools (79 accredited by the American Assembly of Collegiate Schools of Business [AACSB] and 66 not accredited) responded to a mailed questionnaire in which they ranked twenty-two real estate journals on a 1 (low) to 10 (high) quality scale and also answered questions concerning tenure requirements. A table displays the average rating and number of responses (respondents only rated titles they were familiar with) for each journal. Another table lists the top twenty titles according to average rating. Both tables report the data from deans of AACSB-accredited and nonaccredited schools separately.

Deans of accredited schools consistently assigned lower quality ratings to the same journals than did deans of nonaccredited schools. The authors note "some consistency" between the two groups' relative rankings, but correlational statistics were not used. This study offers the best available rating of real estate journals.

518. Weber, Richard P., and W. C. Stevenson. "Evaluations of Accounting Journal and Department Quality." **Accounting Review** 56 (July 1981): 596-612.

This excellent study by two University of Wisconsin accounting professors is based on a mailed questionnaire (generating 782 usable responses) to all accounting faculty at AACSB-accredited business schools. A table displays, in overall rank order, thirty-two journals, rated from a list on a 1 (high) to 5 (low) quality scale by respondents, and also indicates separate rankings by accountants specializing in five areas: auditing, cost, financial, systems, and tax accounting. It is interesting that a fictitious journal received 120 responses and ranked thirtieth overall! Another table presents the top five journals for the five subareas previously noted, when respondents ranked the journals in their specialty only. A final section discusses previous studies concerning departmental rankings based on the journals in which department members publish.

Advanced statistical analysis is used to demonstrate that accountants in the five specialty areas not only evaluate journals differently, but also read and are familiar with different groups of journals, a meaningful conclusion that undoubtedly has important implications for journal ranking in other disciplines.

JOURNAL RANKINGS IN THE SOCIAL SCIENCES

519. Bayer, Alan E. "Multi-Method Strategies for Defining 'Core' Higher Education Journals." **Review of Higher Education** 6 (Winter 1983): 103-13.

This investigation ranks, according to three methods, higher education journals, which the author wishes to distinguish from general education journals. First, a computerized keyword search of the article titles published between 1977 and 1979 in 296 education journals yielded a list of 20 that had published 7 or more articles per year concerning higher education. Second, Bayer used the top fourteen journals from an unpublished 1981 study[14] based on the number of times they cited any of fifty-one Carnegie Commission on Higher Education research volumes or fifty-one selected higher education volumes published by Jossey-Bass. Third, 209 Association for the Study of Higher Education members responded to a fall 1981 survey in which they ranked the top ten journals from a list of thirty-three titles, resulting in a final ranking of fourteen titles. Three tables name, in rank order, the leading journals from each method.

Comparison of the three rankings leads to the conclusion that it is "remarkable how little correspondence there is between the results of these various strategies." Thus, "a 'core' cannot yet be readily identified." This is the only item in this guide that focuses exclusively on higher education journal ranking.

520. Blake, Virgil L. P. "In the Eyes of the Beholder: Perceptions of Professional Journals by Library/Information Science Educators and District School Library Media Center Coordinators." **Collection Management** 14, nos. 3/4 (1991): 101-48.

This detailed, well-done investigation replicates Kohl and Davis's journal ranking methodology (entry 531). Thirty-nine faculty (specializing in school media centers) at ALA-accredited LIS schools and eighty-two district level school library media coordinators throughout the United States rated a list of fifty-five journals on a 1 (low) to 5 (high) scale. They also added further titles and named the five most important journals. Nine tables exhibit the findings. They include 1) the fifty-five journals in rank order by both faculty and media coordinator rating, 2) the twelve additional journals suggested by faculty, 3) the sixty-two further titles suggested by media coordinators, 4) the twenty-six titles listed in the top five by faculty, and 5) the forty-one journals media coordinators placed in the top five. Internal consensus was also analyzed by calculating the percentage of responses that rated journals at either 4 or 5.

Perceptions by faculty and media coordinators were found to be "at variance," as were the perceptions between this faculty group and the LIS deans as reported by Kohl and Davis. Blake's objective was to evaluate journal quality for promotion and tenure purposes, but his findings have obvious relevance to LIS journal collection evaluation.

521. Colson, Harold. "Citation Rankings of Public Administration Journals." **Administration & Society** 21 (February 1990): 452-71.

This piece ranks thirty-five public administration journals by three different citation measures: 1) the average number of citations in the *SSCI JCR* between 1981 and 1986; 2) the average impact factor from *SSCI JCR* for 1981 through 1986; and 3) the most citations in five key public administration journals, such as *Public Administration Review*, from 1981 to 1986 based on *SSCI JCR* data. Colson asserts that methods 1 and 2 (which demonstrated a .88 correlation with each other) "favor works with broad academic and professional appeal," while method 3, which displayed for some journals "substantially divergent rankings" from the first two methods, "rewards periodicals that possess specific relevance to current scholarship in public administration." Comparison of the three methods with two earlier prestige rankings of public administration journals by Vocino and Elliott (entries 545 and 546) found correlations ranging from .27 to .42, termed "among the lowest ... in a social science discipline" between citation and subjective journal ranking methods.

Seven tables illustrate the various ranking methods and comparisons. Colson states that although his rankings "do not form a comprehensive citation study, they do offer many fresh and instructive assessments of journal value in public administration."

522. Fabianic, David A. "Perceived Scholarship and Readership of Criminal Justice Journals." **Journal of Police Science & Administration** 8 (March 1980): 15-20.

Thirty-eight criminal justice journals were ranked on a 1 (low) to 4 (high) scale of "scholarly quality" by 145 Academy of Criminal Justice Sciences members and 59 criminal justice educators, who also indicated if they read the journal and listed the "best" three journals in the field. A table lists the thirty-eight journals in alphabetical order and indicates their raw score and rank according to three criteria: average quality ranking score, number of nominations for the three best, and percentage of respondents who read them. Another table cross-tabulates the thirty-eight journals into high (rank 1 to 12), medium (rank 13 to 25), and low (rank 26 to 38) categories for scholarly quality and readership. Eight titles are mentioned as ranking among the top ten for scholarly quality rating and "best" nominations. This study by a Montana State University sociology professor is quite well done.

523. Feingold, Alan. "Assessment of Journals in Social Science Psychology." **American Psychologist** 44 (June 1989): 961-64.

Core journal rankings are examined in eight subject areas of social science psychology: applied, clinical/abnormal, developmental, experimental-learning and memory, experimental-perception, personality, quantitative, and social. Rankings were based on a journal's proportion of the citations to core periodicals in the official American Psychological Association publication dealing with its field as well as impact factor from *SSCI JCR*. In both ranking systems, data for 1985 and 1986 were averaged. Comparison was also made with a reputational ranking from 1975.[15] A table lists the top-ranked journals by both methods in the eight subfields, for a total of fifty-eight titles. This item is particularly notable for its focus on subareas within a discipline.

524. Garand, James C. "An Alternative Interpretation of Recent Political Science Journal Evaluations." **PS: Political Science & Politics** 23 (September 1990): 448-51.

By reworking Giles, Mizell, and Patterson's data from their ranking of seventy-eight political science journals (entry 525), this article offers an alternative ranking system. Garand created a formula that combined a journal's mean evaluative rating (used for Giles's ranking) with the proportion of respondents familiar with it, to devise what he terms an "impact" score (not to be confused with the ISI's citation impact factor). He stresses that Giles's method measures how well a journal is thought of by those familiar with it, whereas his alternative procedure considers both evaluative judgments and visibility in the profession. A table repeats the data from the earlier study by Giles and others, but also presents Garand's journal impact score and impact ranking for the seventy-eight titles. Comparison of the two systems revealed that the top journals were essentially the same, but differences were observed at lower levels. Garand quite correctly concludes that "the use of these two sets of rankings will depend upon the values that one brings to the evaluation process."

525. Giles, Michael W., Francie Mizell, and David Patterson. "Political Scientists' Journal Evaluations Revisited." **PS: Political Science & Politics** 22 (September 1989): 613-17.

This follow-up to Giles and Wright's well-known ranking of political science journals from the mid-1970s (entry 526) was based on 215 responses to a questionnaire mailed in the summer of 1988 by randomly selected political science faculty. They rated, on a 1 (low) to 10 (high) quality scale, fifty-six journals from the previous investigation that were still in print as well as twenty-two journals founded since then. A two-page table lists the seventy-eight journals in rank order by mean quality rating. It also lists the rating by specialists in the journal's subfield and the percentage familiar enough with the journal to rate it. This ranking "correlated strongly" (0.82) with the earlier study, a fact the authors attribute either to "real stability" in journal quality, "the tendency for perceptions of quality to change more slowly than reality," or both. Subfield specialists rated their areas' journals higher 80 percent of the time, while 87 percent of respondents who had published in a journal rated it higher. (See entry 524 for an alternate ranking based on this data.)

526. Giles, Michael W., and Gerald C. Wright, Jr. "Political Scientists' Evaluations of Sixty-Three Journals." **PS: Political Science & Politics** 8 (Summer 1975): 254-56.

This frequently cited piece represented the best-known ranking of political science journals for a decade and a half. Two hundred fifty-five political scientists associated with Ph.D.-granting institutions responded to a questionnaire mailed in April 1974, in which they rated on a 0 (low) to 10 (high) quality scale those titles they were familiar with from a list of sixty-three. A two-page table lists the sixty-three in rank order by mean quality score, while also indicating the number of respondents who were familiar with the title. It was found that 79 percent of subfield specialists ranked their specialty journals higher than did respondents not in the specialty, while 75 percent of respondents ranked journals they had published in higher than those who had not published in those journals. (See also entry 525 as well as Christenson and Sigelman entry 484.)

527. Glenn, Norval D. "American Sociologists' Evaluations of Sixty-Three Journals." **American Sociologist** 6 (November 1971): 298-303.

The prestige of sociology journals was assessed through a mail questionnaire, answered by 129 randomly selected professors and associate professors at sociology departments offering the Ph.D. Respondents rated the journals they were familiar with (from a list), using an arbitrary weight of 10 for *American Sociological Review* for comparison. The author distinguishes between "intensity" of prestige, the average numerical rating, and "extensity" of prestige (the number who knew the title). A table displays sixty-three sociology journals, rank-ordered by intensity, and reports the standard deviation plus how many respondents rated the journal. A correlation of .73 was found between intensity and extensity. The high standard deviations indicated a "great deal of dissensus," that is, disagreement.

Although dated, Glenn's frequently cited study, employing a rigorous and sophisticated analysis, is undoubtedly the best-known ranking of sociology journals. His work has been elaborated upon by Gordon (entry 486), Teevan (entry 493), Dometrius (entry 485), and Christenson and Sigelman (entry 484), among others.

528. Haynes, Jack P. "An Empirical Method for Determining Core Psychology Journals." **American Psychologist** 38 (August 1983): 959-61.

Discipline impact factor (based on citations from the discipline itself rather than from the entire literature covered by the ISI database) is used to identify thirty-one core psychology journals in this quantitatively sophisticated study. A complex three-iteration process, beginning with the application of a mathematical formula to citation data from the sixteen official American Psychological Association journals, was used to calculate discipline impact factor.

A comparison of the thirty-one journals, named in rank order in a table, with Buffardi and Nichols' top thirty-one (see entry 483) revealed a .69 correlation between the two lists, with nineteen titles common to both. Further analysis confirmed the findings of Buffardi and Nichols that circulation correlates positively with ranking and acceptance rate negatively. This work is of prime interest from the theoretical perspective.

529. Jones, John F., and Lois M. Jones. "Ranking Journals: A Citation Study of Social Work and Related Periodicals." **Journal of the Hong Kong Library Association,** no. 10 (1986): 9-16.

Forty journals pertinent to social work most frequently cited by the *SSCI* between 1979 and 1983 are displayed in a table in rank order. These titles were used as a checklist to evaluate the collections of Hong Kong University, the Chinese University of Hong Kong, Hong Kong Polytechnic, and City Polytechnic. The library committees of the four universities were then asked to select the ten "most useful" social work journals. Their four lists correlated with each other at a statistically significant level, but not with the *SSCI* list. A table displays, in rank order, the top twelve social work journals (all mainstream journals) based on the average rankings by the four institutions.

Most readers will not care that this study represents the first major effort to use citation analysis for journal evaluation in Hong Kong, but it is still useful for the social work journal rankings.

530. Kim, Mary T. "Ranking of Journals in Library and Information Science: A Comparison of Perceptual and Citation-Based Measures." **College & Research Libraries** 52 (January 1991): 24-37.

Kohl and Davis's (entry 531) rankings of library and information science journals based on the perceptions of LIS deans and ARL directors were correlated with rankings by nine citation-based measures, such as total citations, impact factor, etc., all of which are explained. The influence of such journal "demographic" characteristics as age, circulation, and index coverage on prestige rankings is also addressed in this rigorous, quantitative study. Three sets of hypotheses are tested. As an example of the findings, which are too numerous to be readily summarized, no statistically significant correlation was found between a journal's circulation size or age and directors' prestige ranking.

A table, listing twenty-eight titles, identifies the top twelve journals for each of fourteen different ranking methods: Kohl and Davis's two perception-based rankings, the nine citation measures addressed by Kim, and circulation, age, and index coverage. A "set" of eight "top journals" is identified. Among Kim's several conclusions, the most important is that "citation measures identified a core of journals which overlapped well with the core listings of the directors and deans." This entry is of considerable theoretical significance.

531. Kohl, David F., and Charles H. Davis. "Ratings of Journals by ARL Library Directors and Deans of Library and Information Science Schools." **College & Research Libraries** 46 (January 1985): 40-47.

A survey, conducted in the fall of 1982 and responded to by forty-three ARL directors and forty-seven North American library and information science school deans, was used to rank the field's most prestigious journals for promotion and tenure purposes. A table displays separate rankings by directors and deans of thirty-one core journals, based on the average ranking from one to five on a Likert-like scale. The directors' top eighteen and the deans' leading twenty-one journals are also rank-ordered by the "top-five" method, whereby respondents list the five most prestigious journals without regard to order. (Note, however, that the authors deem the top-five method unreliable unless strong consensus exists.) This well-done study is clearly the best known and most important ranking of LIS journals. (See Kim entry 530 and Blake entry 520 for follow-up studies.)

532. Laband, David N. "Measuring the Relative Impact of Economics Book Publishers and Economics Journals." **Journal of Economic Literature** 28 (June 1990): 655-60.

Liebowitz and Palmer's "impact-adjusted citation" methodology for journal ranking is applied to economics publishers in this important, ground-breaking article, which also compares the relative citation impact of books versus journal articles. The "impact-adjusted citations per book" were calculated, using 1981-1985 *SSCI* data, for every publisher with four or more books (excluding textbooks and directories) issued during 1980. A table rank-orders the top fifty publishers (although not noted by the author, eleven of the top twenty were university presses). The same table displays the relative citation impact of a book by that publisher compared to an article in the *Journal of Political Economy*. One could then generalize the comparison to any journal in the Liebowitz-Palmer study (entry 535), using their scaled rankings. It was found that articles in major economics journals have a "substantially greater" citation impact than do books, except for those by the top-ranked University of Chicago Press.

The article has obvious implications for economics collection development. Moreover, it is, as asserted by the author, apparently the first study of its kind.

533. Lee, David, and Arthur Evans. "American Geographers' Rankings of American Geography Journals." **Professional Geographer** 36 (August 1984): 292-300.

Two hundred eighty-nine geographers attached to American universities with graduate programs in the subject responded to a questionnaire in which they ranked thirty-four geography journals on a 1 (low) to 5 (high) scale according to "quality of scholarship." Three separate tables rank the thirty-four titles according to their mean score, the number of respondents who rated them (termed "familiarity" by the authors), and an overall ranking based on a formula that combines mean score and familiarity. A "moderately high positive correlation" (.47) was found between the mean score and familiarity rankings. Another table presents the mean score rankings for fifteen journals according to demographic characteristics of the respondents. Significant ranking differences were found for age and specialty, but not for gender or university status. A few comparisons are made with journal rankings from other social science disciplines. The authors assert that their study represents the first ranking of geography journals.

534. Lee, David, and Arthur Evans. "Geographers' Rankings of Foreign Geography and Non-Geography Journals." **Professional Geographer** 37 (November 1985): 396-402.

Lee and Evans use essentially the same methodology and format as in entry 533 to focus on foreign geography journals and non-geography journals of interest to geographers. One hundred seventy-two Ph.D. geographers at U.S. institutions offering a graduate program rated a list of sixty-five different journals (thirty-three foreign and thirty-two non-geography) on a 1 (low) to 5 (high) scale. Three separate tables rank the sixty-five titles by mean rating, the number of respondents who were familiar enough with a title to rate it, and a composite score combining the two. Another table tabulates the data in an alphabetical listing. A geographical "bias" was found, as American journals ranked highest, followed by Continental Europe, Canada, Australia and New Zealand, then Latin America and Asia. The correlation between mean score and familiarity rankings was .15, termed "considerably weaker" than the previous study. This investigation serves as a useful sequel to the authors' earlier work.

535. Liebowitz, S. J., and J. P. Palmer. "Assessing the Relative Impacts of Economics Journals." **Journal of Economic Literature** 22 (March 1984): 77-88.

Written for professional economists, this methodologically rigorous research is of interest not only for its ranking of economics journals, but also for the way it addresses several theoretical issues concerning the use of citation data for journal ranking purposes. More than 100 leading economics journals, chosen from the *Journal of Economic Literature*, are ranked according to 7 different methods based on citation data from the 1980 *Social Science Citation Index*. Two of these methods, newly created by the authors, are especially noteworthy.

In order to correct two drawbacks of *SSCI* data (weighing all citations equally, regardless of the citing journal's stature, and giving equal consideration to citations in journals outside the discipline), the authors propose a formula for ranking journals based on "impact adjusted citations," whereby citations by highly cited journals are given greater weight and citations in noneconomic journals are not counted. As a further refinement, the impact adjusted citation ranking is divided by the number of characters in the journal to compensate for the advantage enjoyed by longer journals (i.e., more opportunities to be cited). Laband (entry 532) begins his previously annotated article by stating that the Liebowitz and Palmer study "has set the standard for ranking the impact of economics journals."

536. Malouin, Jean-Louis, and J.-Francois Outreville. "The Relative Impact of Economics Journals—A Cross Country Survey and Comparison." **Journal of Economics & Business** 39 (August 1987): 267-77.

This fascinating ranking of economics journals used a two-step approach. In stage one, 384 academic economists randomly selected from the membership lists of professional organizations in the United States, United Kingdom, France, and Quebec responded to a questionnaire in which they indicated their familiarity with an alphabetical list of 284 journals. A "familiarity index" of 5 points for "known," 2 points for "aware" of, and 0 for "unknown" was applied to the results.

In step two, 194 academic economists from the 4 countries (the authors are apparently French Canadians who consider Quebec a separate country) responded to a second questionnaire. They ranked the top 130 journals from the preceding step on a 0 (lowest) to 20 (highest) prestige scale. A two-and-one-half page table rank-orders the leading 112 journals based on this prestige rating. Other tables rank-order the top 40 journals by respondents from each country, using both prestige rating and impact, defined as the prestige rating multiplied by the familiarity index. Malouin and Outreville's study is remarkable for its cross-national perspective.

537. McBride, Ruth B., and Patricia Stenstrom. "Psychology Journal Usage." **Behavioral & Social Sciences Librarian** 2 (Fall 1980/81): 1-12.

This study's objective is to compare local faculty journal use data with other data that reflects a "national perspective." Three ranked lists of core psychology journals, identified in separate tables, are compared: 1) a locally compiled list of eighteen journals read by at least 10 percent of the University of Illinois psychology faculty, based on a survey; 2) a core list of twenty-six journals used in a 1963 membership survey by the American Psychological Association, rank-ordered by total citations received in the *Annual Review of Psychology*, 1956-1960; and 3) thirty-four titles that received more than one thousand citations in the 1978 *SSCI Journal Citation Reports*.

"Considerable agreement" was found among the lists, "but there were also some differences." The authors conclude that "the usefulness of citation analysis is evident," but it cannot replace librarians' interaction with faculty.

538. Nelson, T. M., A. R. Buss, and M. Katzko. "Rating of Scholarly Journals by Chairpersons in the Social Sciences." **Research in Higher Education** 19, no. 4 (1983): 469-97.

A comprehensive study by three University of Alberta faculty members is based on survey responses from 246 departmental chairpersons in U.S. and Canadian universities who rated journals in their area on a 1-to-5 point scale. Separate tables for anthropology, economics, geography, history, philosophy, political science, and sociology, covering 20 pages, display the results for about 650 titles. Each discipline's table is organized into four sections: 1) "high visibility" journals, for which at least 75 percent of the respondents provided a rating; 2) "moderate visibility" journals, rated by 25 percent to 74 percent of respondents; 3) "low visibility" titles, rated by less than 25 percent; and 4) additional titles added by the raters. Within each section, journals are rank-ordered by average quality point rating.

This item is notable for using a uniform methodology for cross-disciplinary comparison of journals (one of the authors' goals, to assist promotion and tenure decisions) as well as for the large number of titles ranked.

539. Peery, J. Craig, and Gerald R. Adams. "Qualitative Ratings of Human Development Journals." **Human Development** 24, no. 5 (1981): 312-19.

Human development journals were ranked based on 318 mail questionnaire responses from randomly selected members of the Society for Research in Child Development. Respondents were asked to list in no particular order the ten best journals, to access visibility, then to rank-order them to evaluate quality. Table 1 displays, in rank order, the leading sixty-six journals according to the number of respondents who nominated them. Table 2 rank-orders the top thirty-one journals based on average ranking. Correlational analysis revealed that the most frequently mentioned journals received the highest prestige rankings. Although published a decade ago, this is the most recent study to focus exclusively on human development journals.

540. Poole, Eric D., and Robert M. Regoli. "Periodical Prestige in Criminology and Criminal Justice: A Comment." **Criminology** 19 (November 1981): 470-78.

The authors are quite critical of the Shichor, O'Brien, and Decker prestige ranking of criminology and criminal justice journals (entry 542). For example, they point out that the term "average importance" was not defined, the compared publications were quite different, and on average only 33 percent of the respondents rated each title. To provide an alternate ranking system, Poole and Regoli tabulated the number of citations appearing in *Criminology*, 1975-1979, to the forty-three journals rated by Shichor's study. A table rank-orders the twenty-four journals that were cited. The correlation between this citation-based ranking and Shichor's earlier prestige ranking was .75, termed a "close correspondence" by the authors. However, the fact that two journals accounted for half the citations indicated "an overwhelming dominance of a very small subset of journals ... that could not have been inferred from the subjective ratings." (See also Stack entry 543.)

541. Sellen, Mary K. "Bibliometrics in Information Science: A Citation Analysis of Two Academic Library Journals." **College & Research Libraries** 45 (May 1984): 129-32.

Sellen analyzed the citations in the 1981 volumes of *College & Research Libraries* and *Journal of Academic Librarianship*, chosen because they rank among the top five journals read by academic librarians, according to Swisher and Smith's survey (entry 544). Thus, this study's focus is obviously on material used by library practitioners.

A majority of the citations were to periodicals, although a significant number of monographs were also included. The majority of both monographic and serial citations were dated between 1975 and 1980. Separate sets of raw data were presented for each journal without summarizing percentages. The ten most cited journals in both *C&RL* and *JAL* were listed, offering yet another variation of journal ranking by a citation measure.

542. Shichor, David, Robert M. O'Brien, and David L. Decker. "Prestige of Journals in Criminology and Criminal Justice." **Criminology** 19 (November 1981): 461-69.

Forty-two criminology and criminal justice journals were rated on a 1-to-10 scale of "average importance" by 168 members of four professional organizations in criminology who answered a survey. A table rank-orders forty-three journals (respondents added a title the authors inadvertently omitted) by their average rating and indicates the number of respondents who knew the journal well enough to evaluate it. Analysis of the data respondents reported about themselves and their publications revealed "no systematic differences" in rankings based on their position (academic versus nonacademic) or academic degree. It is interesting that those who published in highly rated journals rated them lower than others, while individuals who published in low-rated titles ranked them higher than others. Although more journals are rated, this study is less sophisticated than Fabianic's (entry 522), of which the authors were unaware. Poole and Regoli's plus Stack's (entries 540 and 543) citation-based ratings critique this study.

543. Stack, Steven. "Measuring the Relative Impacts of Criminology and Criminal Justice Journals: A Research Note." **Justice Quarterly** 4 (September 1987): 475-84.

Stack begins by noting that this is the first ranking of criminology and criminal justice journals based on systematic citation data. Twenty-six journals are ranked according to three citation measures: 1) total citations received, termed "raw impact index"; 2) "age adjusted impact," defined as total citations to articles published in the preceding two years; and 3) the conventional "impact factor," as defined by Garfield. The data were taken from the 1984 and 1985 *SSCI JCR*. A table summarizes the data and indicates the ranking by the three methods. A second table compares the ranking by impact factor to Shichor, O'Brien, and Decker's reputational ranking (entry 542) as well as to Poole and Regoli's citation-count ranking (entry 540) for the twenty journals common to all three studies. Stack criticizes the latter for being based on a single source journal and not adjusting for journal age or number of articles published. Numerous correlations among the various ranking methods are calculated. Stack concludes that "further work is needed to understand fully the dynamics behind journal quality."

544. Swisher, Robert, and Peggy C. Smith. "Journals Read by ACRL Academic Librarians, 1973 and 1978." **College & Research Libraries** 43 (January 1982): 51-58.

Questions concerning the journals they read were included in questionnaires sent to a sample of ACRL librarians in 1973 and 1978. About half of this article deals with methodological issues involved in gathering the data, but this item's use for collection evaluation lies in tables that rank the seventeen most frequently read library journals in 1973 and the twenty-six most read in 1978. Even though the data are more than a decade old, academic librarians evaluating their professional reading library science collections may wish to examine these rankings. This journal ranking method differs from most other approaches, which usually employ usage, subjective judgment, or some type of citation measure.

545. Vocino, Thomas, and Robert H. Elliott. "Journal Prestige in Public Administration: A Research Note." **Administration & Society** 14 (May 1982): 5-14.

Vocino and Elliott apply to public administration Glenn's methodology for ranking sociology journals (see entry 527). Thirty-four percent of the 1,400 American Society for Public Administration members responded to a 1978 survey in which they rated forty-three journals according to their "average importance," using an arbitrary weight of 10 for the *Public Administration Review*. A table rank-orders the forty-three titles by mean weight, while also indicating the mean weights assigned by academicians and practitioners. A second table follows the same format to report the rankings of forty-one public administration journals from an identical survey conducted in 1975.[16] Two additional tables list the top ten journals, as listed by both academicians and practitioners from both the 1975 and 1978 surveys, according to "intensity" (mean weight) and "extensity" (the number of respondents who were familiar enough with a journal to rate it). It was found that academics tended to give higher ratings to more theoretically oriented journals with a political science focus.

546. Vocino, Thomas, and Robert H. Elliott. "Public Administration Journal Prestige: A Time Series Analysis." **Administrative Science Quarterly** 29 (March 1984): 43-51.

As a follow-up to the study in entry 545, 30 percent of 1,400 ASPA members responded to a 1981 survey in which the same methodology was employed to evaluate a list of forty-six journals. The authors' objective was to investigate stability in journal ranking by comparing the results with the identical 1978 and 1975 surveys. The top twenty journals in 1975, 1978, and 1981, according to both extensity and intensity by both academics and practitioners, are displayed in three tables. Two additional tables rank the overall top intensity and extensity journals by combining the three surveys' results. Although correlational statistics were not used, the authors conclude that "there is considerable stability over time" in the journal rankings by both academics and practitioners. They also observe that political science journals are becoming less important in the field of public administration.

JOURNAL RANKINGS IN OTHER DISCIPLINES

547. Chandran, D. "Evaluation of Biochemical Journals by Citation Indexing." **IASLIC Bulletin** 27 (1982): 121-26.

Chandran's ranking of biochemistry journals is based on total citations received in the 1979 volume of the *Annual Review of Biochemistry*, selected because it was the biochemistry journal with the highest 1977 impact factor. The volume contained 6,303 citations, but the author does not indicate how many were to journals. The top twenty-five journals are rank-ordered in a table that also indicates country of publication (eighteen were published in the United States) and their 1974 ranking in a study by Garfield.[17] "In general there is not much variation" in the top ten between Garfield and Chandran. Examination of citation distribution by date between 1970 and 1979, displayed for the three highest ranking journals, reveals more citations to recent dates. Although this article was published in an Indian journal, the findings are applicable elsewhere.

548. Fang, Min-Lin Emily. "Journal Rankings by Citation Analysis in Health Sciences Librarianship." **Bulletin of the Medical Library Association** 77 (April 1989): 205-11.

Online searches in the SOCIAL SCISEARCH and MEDLINE databases for articles on health science librarianship, published by health science librarians between 1982 and 1986, identified 350 articles in 70 different journals. The *Bulletin of the Medical Library Association* contained 52 percent of the articles, with 70 percent in ten journals. A table lists the twenty-one most productive journals. Fang was surprised that 61.4 percent of the journals, containing 22.6 percent of the articles, were from medicine rather than librarianship.

Next, an analysis of 1,760 citations from articles published in *BMLA* from 1982 through 1986 revealed that 63.5 percent were to journals and 26.1 percent to books. While 270 journals were cited, two-thirds of the citations were to only 20 periodicals (listed in a table). The author deems these to be the most prestigious for promotion and tenure considerations of health science librarians with faculty status. Fang considers this list the study's "most important result," although this article should be of general interest for collection evaluation in medical librarianship.

549. Garfield, Eugene. "Journal Citation Studies. 33. Botany Journals, Part 1: What They Cite and What Cites Them." **Current Contents: Social & Behavioral Sciences** 12 (August 4, 1980): 5-12.

550. Garfield, Eugene. "Journal Citation Studies. 33. Botany Journals, Part 2: Growth of Botanical Literature and Highly Cited Items." **Current Contents: Social & Behavioral Sciences** 12 (August 11, 1980): 5-15.

551. Garfield, Eugene. "Journal Citation Studies. 34. The Literature of Dental Science vs. the Literature Used by Dental Researchers." **Current Contents: Social & Behavioral Sciences** 14 (January 18, 1982): 5-11.

552. Garfield, Eugene. "Journal Citation Studies. 35. Veterinary Journals: What They Cite and Vice Versa." **Current Contents: Social & Behavioral Sciences** 14 (March 29, 1982): 5-13.

553. Garfield, Eugene. "Journal Citation Studies. 36. Pure and Applied Mathematics Journals: What They Cite and Vice Versa." **Current Contents: Social & Behavioral Sciences** 14 (April 12, 1982): 5-13.

554. Garfield, Eugene. "Journal Citation Studies. 37. Using Citation Analysis to Study Neuroscience Journals." **Current Contents: Social & Behavioral Sciences** 14 (October 11, 1982): 5-6; and "Citation Analysis of Neuroscience Journals: What They Cite and What Cites Them." **Current Contents: Social & Behavioral Sciences** 14 (October 11, 1982): 7-14.

555. Garfield, Eugene. "Journal Citation Studies. 38. Arts and Humanities Journals Differ from Natural and Social Science Journals—But Their Similarities Are Surprising." **Current Contents: Social & Behavioral Sciences** 14 (November 22, 1982): 5-14.

556. Garfield, Eugene. "Journal Citation Studies. 38.* Earth Science Journals: What They Cite and What Cites Them." **Current Contents: Social & Behavioral Sciences** 14 (December 27, 1982): 5-11.

557. Garfield, Eugene. "Journal Citation Studies. 40. Anthropology Journals—What They Cite and What Cites Them." **Current Contents: Social & Behavioral Sciences** 15 (September 12, 1983): 5-12.

558. Garfield, Eugene. "Journal Citation Studies. 41. Entomology Journals—What They Cite and What Cites Them." **Current Contents: Social & Behavioral Sciences** 16 (March 12, 1984): 3-11.

559. Garfield, Eugene. "Journal Citation Studies. 42. Analytical Chemistry Journals—What They Cite and What Cites Them." **Current Contents: Social & Behavioral Sciences** 16 (March 26, 1984): 3-12.

560. Garfield, Eugene. "Journal Citation Studies. 43. Astrosciences Journals—What They Cite and What Cites Them." **Current Contents: Social & Behavioral Sciences** 16 (May 21, 1984): 3-14.

---

*The title erroneously identifies this item as number 38. It is actually number 39.

561. Garfield, Eugene. "Journal Citation Studies. 44. Citation Patterns in Nursing Journals, and Their Most Cited Articles." **Current Contents: Social & Behavioral Sciences** 16 (October 22, 1984): 3-12.

562. Garfield, Eugene. "Journal Citation Studies. 45. Surgery Journals: Another Operation in Citation Analysis." **Current Contents: Social & Behavioral Sciences** 17 (May 27, 1985): 3-19.

563. Garfield, Eugene. "Journal Citation Studies. 46. Physical Chemistry and Chemical Physics Journals. Part 1. Historical Background and Global Maps." **Current Contents: Social & Behavioral Sciences** 18 (January 6, 1986): 3-10.

564. Garfield, Eugene. "Journal Citation Studies. 46. Physical Chemistry and Chemical Physics Journals. Part 2. Core Journals and Most-Cited Papers." **Current Contents: Social & Behavioral Sciences** 18 (January 13, 1986): 3-10.

565. Garfield, Eugene. "Journal Citation Studies. 46. Physical Chemistry and Chemical Physics Journals. Part 3. The Evolution of Physical Chemistry to Chemical Physics." **Current Contents: Social & Behavioral Sciences** 18 (January 20, 1986): 3-12.

566. Garfield, Eugene. "Journal Citation Studies. 47. Which Oceanography Journals Make the Biggest Waves?" **Current Contents: Social & Behavioral Sciences** 19 (November 30, 1987): 3-11.

567. Garfield, Eugene. "Journal Citation Studies. 48. Developmental Biology Journals: Citation Analysis Demonstrates the Multidisciplinary Nature of Modern Embryology." **Current Contents: Social & Behavioral Sciences** 20 (March 14, 1988): 3-12.

568. Garfield, Eugene. "Journal Citation Studies. 49. The Diverse Yet Essential Nutrients in the Information Diet of Nutrition Researchers." **Current Contents: Social & Behavioral Sciences** 20 (July 11, 1988): 3-15.

569. Garfield, Eugene. "Journal Citation Studies. 50. Part 1. The Core Journals of Economics." **Current Contents: Social & Behavioral Sciences** 21 (January 2, 1989): 3-11.

570. Garfield, Eugene. "Journal Citation Studies. 50. Part 2. Most-Cited Economics Papers and Current Research Fronts." **Current Contents: Social & Behavioral Sciences** 21 (January 9, 1989): 3; and Diamond, Arthur M., Jr. "Most-Cited Economics Papers and Current Research Fronts." **Current Contents: Social & Behavioral Sciences** 21 (January 9, 1989): 3-8.

571. Garfield, Eugene. "Journal Citation Studies. 51. Down to the Sea Again: Probing the Depths of Marine Biology Literature." **Current Contents: Social & Behavioral Sciences** 21 (May 8, 1989): 3-4; and Fuseler-McDowell, Elizabeth. "Documenting the Literature of Marine Biology." **Current Contents: Social & Behavioral Sciences** 21 (May 8, 1989): 4-13.

572. Garfield, Eugene. "Journal Citation Studies. 52. Acoustic Journals and Acoustic Research Activities." **Current Contents: Social & Behavioral Sciences** 21 (October 30, 1989): 3; and Cawkell, A. E. "Acoustic Journals and Acoustic Research Activities." **Current Contents: Social & Behavioral Sciences** 21 (October 30, 1989): 4-15.

573. Garfield, Eugene. "Journal Citation Studies. 52.* The Multifaceted Structure of Crystallography Research. Part 1. Core Journals, High Impact Papers, and Current Research Fronts." **Current Contents: Social & Behavioral Sciences** 22 (September 3, 1990): 5-6; and "International Crystallography Research: Where It Is Published, What It Cites, and What Cites It." **Current Contents: Social & Behavioral Sciences** 22 (September 3, 1990): 6-14.

574. Garfield, Eugene. "Journal Citation Studies. 52. The Multifaceted Structure of Crystallography Research. Part 2. A Global Perspective." **Current Contents: Social & Behavioral Sciences** 22 (September 10, 1990): 5; and "International Crystallography Research: Where It Is Published, What It Cites, and What Cites It." **Current Contents: Social & Behavioral Sciences** 22 (September 10, 1990): 5-13.

575. Garfield, Eugene. "Journal Citation Studies. 53. Agricultural Sciences: Most Fruitful Journals and High Yield Research Fields." **Current Contents: Social & Behavioral Sciences** 22 (December 17, 1990): 3-15.[18]

"Journal Citation Studies" is an ongoing series by the illustrious guru of citation studies and founder of the ISI, Eugene Garfield. (Some later items in the series have separate individual authors, although Garfield's name remains at the masthead.) Almost all the entries follow a similar format. The subject's core journals, as identified in the most recent *SCI*, are listed in rank order by impact factor. Then separate tables list, in rank order based on total citations, the fifty journals most cited by the core journals and the fifty that most frequently cite the core. Eight sets of data from the most recent *SCI* and (when a social science subject) the *SSCI* are presented in these tables: 1) citations to or from core journals; 2) citations to or from all journals; 3) self-citations; 4) percent of total citations that are core journal citations; 5) the self-citation percentage for total citations; 6) the self-citation percentage for core journal citations; 7) impact factor; and 8) the number of citable items the journal published that year. Towards the end of the series, the immediacy index was also presented. Citation patterns within each discipline, including multidisciplinarity, concentration of citations, and changing trends, are then analyzed. Additional data are often presented concerning the most frequently cited articles, research fronts in the field, and so forth. A librarian or researcher interested in a specific subject is advised to consult the appropriate article from the *Current Contents* list.

576. Garfield, Eugene. "Which Medical Journals Have the Greatest Impact?" **Annals of Internal Medicine** 105 (August 1986): 313-20.

Employing data from the *Science Citation Index Journal Citation Reports*, the top seventy-eight general and internal medicine journals were ranked according to total citations received in 1981. The leading twenty-nine titles, ranked by 1982

---

*Another numbering inconsistency: this should be 53, part 1 in the series.

impact factor, and the top thirty-one journals, ranked by the 1981 immediacy index, were then identified. Citation data from 1977 to 1982 were analyzed in detail for five leading journals, including the *New England Journal of Medicine* and the *Journal of the American Medical Association*. Although now a decade old, this entry contains a wealth of detailed citation data concerning medical journals.

577. Lal, Arjun. "Ranking of Periodicals in the Field of Soil Science." **Annals of Library Science and Documentation** 37 (June 1990): 67-73.

Lal's analysis is based on the 4,361 citations in the twenty-three soil science Ph.D. dissertations completed at Rajendra Agricultural University (India) between 1980 and 1988. The 3,161 citations (72.5 percent of the total) to 261 journals were used as the basis of the ranking. A table names in rank order the leading thirty-eight journals—half of which are published in India—according to total citations received. The leading seven journals accounted for 60.36 percent of the citations to journals. This study's value to North American libraries is significantly diminished by the fact the ranked list is skewed towards Indian journals, although librarians with large soil science collections might have some interest in this item.

578. Miranda, Michael A., and Deborah Mongeau. "An Evaluation of Journals in Physical Education, Athletics, and Sports." **Serials Librarian** 21, no. 1 (1991): 89-113.

Miranda and Mongeau's study is based on survey responses from eighty-two U.S. physical education faculty members. A list of forty-five journals were rated (the scale is not explained) according to five categories: "overall importance," "timeliness," "relevance to student needs," "relevance to faculty needs," and "reputation" (i.e., perception of its quality). Separate tables rank-order the top ten journals in each category. Another table rank-orders the top twenty according to a combined rating for the five categories. These twenty journals are annotated in an appendix. A correlation of .82 was found between ranking by relevance to student needs and relevance to faculty needs. A correlation of .89 was found between ranking by "overall importance" and "reputation." A final table presents the mean ratings in each of the five categories plus the composite rating for the forty-five journals listed in alphabetical order. Although it contains a few flaws, this is the best available ranking of physical education and sports journals.

579. Raina, Roshan. "Ranking of Journals in Phytopathology." **Herald of Library Science** 23 (July-October 1984): 187-92.

A citation analysis of twenty review articles in the 1983 *Annual Review of Phytopathology* was used to rank journals in the field of phytopathology (plant diseases). Of 1,761 citations, 62.4 percent were to journals. An appendix lists the forty-nine most frequently cited journals, which accounted for about 70 percent of the total journal citations. On the ranked list, 55.7 percent of the citations were from the United States, followed by 21.5 percent from the United Kingdom, with eight other countries represented. Analysis of the citation publication dates to the top fourteen journals (displayed in a table), revealed that slightly more than half (52 percent) date from 1979 or earlier.

580. Rao, Dittakavi Nagasankara. "Ranking of Research Journals in the Field of Physical Education." **International Library Movement** 6 (1984): 175-83.

Rao's ranking of physical education journals is based on counting every periodical citation (a total of 479) in the 1982 volume of *Research Quarterly for Exercise & Sport*. Most of the article is devoted to an extensive table, covering 7 pages, that lists all 139 cited titles in rank order. The top ten journals accounted for more than half the citations. This is clearly a crude, unsophisticated ranking system.

581. Resh, Vincent H. "Periodical Citations in Aquatic Entomology and Freshwater Benthic Biology." **Freshwater Biology** 15 (December 1985): 757-66.

Resh's investigation is primarily based on more than 10,000 periodical citations in two 1984 aquatic entomology textbooks, a 1984 freshwater benthic biology bibliography, and a 1983 limnology textbook. Extensive reference is made to two earlier limnology studies from 1968 and a 1984 study by Garfield (entry 558). The data are reported separately for each category rather than as a composite. For each citation source studied, a small percentage of cited journals (ranging from 3.3 percent to 5.3 percent) accounted for 50 percent of the citations, while a majority of the cited journals were cited only once (from 51.7 to 57.8 percent), thus confirming Bradford's law. In an unusual approach, journals that received more than 1 percent of a source's total citations, ranging from thirteen to thirty-six, were considered to be the core. Resh also calculated the cost of annual subscriptions to seven sets of core journals. The core journals are indicated in several tables that list the top-ranked journals from each source.

NOTES

[1] Harold Colson, "Citation Rankings of Public Administration Journals," *Administration & Society* 21 (February 1990): 453.

[2] Kris Subramanyam, "Citation Studies in Science and Technology," in *Collection Development in Libraries: A Treatise*, pt. B, ed. Robert D. Stueart and George B. Miller, Jr. (Greenwich, Conn.: JAI Press, 1980), 362-63. Subramanyam made these statements in regard to ranking by citation analysis, but they apply to journal rankings by any valid system.

[3] S. C. Bradford, "Sources of Information on Specific Subjects," *Engineering* 137 (January 26, 1934): 85-86.

[4] Gertrude House Lamb, "The Coincidence of Quality and Quantity in the Literature of Mathematics" (Ph.D. diss., Case-Western Reserve University, 1971).

[5] Bert R. Boyce and Mark Funk, "Bradford's Law and the Selection of High Quality Papers," *Library Resources & Technical Services* 36 (Fall 1978): 390-401.

[6] Francis Narin, Gabriel Pinski, and Helen Hofer Gee, "Structure of the Biomedical Literature," *Journal of the American Society for Information Science* 27 (January-February 1976): 25-45.

[7]National Research Council, "Report of the Committee on Biomedical Research in the Veterans Administration," Contract V101 (134) P203, 1977.

[8]Donald H. Kraft, "The Journal Selection Problem in a University Library System" (Ph.D. diss., Purdue University, 1971).

[9]William G. Browne and Boris W. Becker, "Perceived Quality of Marketing Journals," *Journal of Marketing Education* no. 2 (November 1979): 6-15.

[10]Robert K. Coe and Irwin Weinstock, "Evaluating Journal Publications: Perceptions Versus Reality," *AACSB Bulletin* 6 (October 1969): 23-27.

[11]Ibid.

[12]Ibid.

[13]James J. Benjamin and Vincent C. Brenner, "Perceptions of Journal Quality," *Accounting Review* 44 (April 1974): 360-62.

[14]C. F. Elton and J. C. Smart, "Scholarly Significance of the Carnegie Commission Sponsored Research Reports: A Citation Analysis" (Unpublished manuscript, University of Kentucky, 1981).

[15]David Koulack and H. J. Keselman, "Ratings of Psychology Journals by Members of the American Psychological Association," *American Psychologist* 30 (November 1975): 1049-53.

[16]William Hamm and Thomas Vocino, "Evaluation of Forty-One Journals by ASPA Members," *Bureaucrat* 5 (January 1977): 439-46.

[17]Eugene Garfield, *Citation Indexing: Its Theory and Application in Science, Technology, and Humanities* (New York: Wiley, 1979).

[18]Many items in this series have been reprinted in Eugene Garfield, *Essays of an Information Scientist*, 9 vols. (Philadelphia: ISI Press, 1977-1988).

12

Application of Automation to Collection Evaluation

The last decade alone has witnessed the introduction of CD-ROM, the personal computer, online public access catalogs, and integrated systems, as well as hypertext and hypermedia, to the library scene. A voluminous literature exists concerning the use of automation to perform such traditional library functions as cataloging, acquisitions, serials control, and circulation. Until fairly recently, very little has been published that deals exclusively with the application of automation to collection development or collection evaluation, although many authors had alluded to the potential offered by computers. One must conclude that the vast potential of automation is yet to be fully realized in the collection evaluation literature. This chapter annotates items that describe the use of various automated capacities to generate collection management data or to assist directly in the collection evaluation process. Included here are items pertaining to archival tapes of catalog records, the AMIGOS Collection Analysis Service, online database searching, various automated systems (integrated, online public access catalogs, and circulation), CD-ROM, and software packages.

The major advantage offered by automation is the opportunity to analyze rapidly, accurately, and inexpensively a vast amount of data. Moreover, the necessary data are often readily available as an incidental spin-off from some other use, such as an automated circulation system or online public access catalog. One could also cite the OCLC database. In this sense, many automated technologies represent what could be termed serendipitous research tools.

The use of automation in collection evaluation does not generate strong controversy, as do the RLG Conspectus, standards, or journal ranking methods. Nevertheless, a number of limitations should be mentioned:

1. Many libraries do not have their complete holdings in machine-readable form

2. Extracting the data often requires computer skills not available on all library staffs

3. Automation may generate a vast amount of data that is difficult to interpret or use

4. The original data to which computer analysis is applied may have been inaccurate or incomplete

5. The associated costs may be quite high.

Chapter 12 is organized into four sections, covering automated systems, software, online searching, and miscellaneous.

AUTOMATED SYSTEMS

582. Baker, Robert K. "Using a Turnkey Automated System to Support Collection Assessment." **College & Research Libraries** 51 (July 1990): 360-66.

The author recounts how holdings and circulation statistics by call number range, generated from the Dynix integrated automation system and entered into a microcomputer for communication to faculty using the Q & A database manager, support the ongoing collection assessment program at the Lower Columbia College Library in the Washington State community college system. The use of RECALL, a special Dynix module for data generation, is explained. An especially worthwhile feature is a table concisely summarizing the report-generation characteristics of nine leading automation systems, including Carlyle, Geac, NOTIS, and VTLS. This article is significant because it describes effective application of automation to collection evaluation in a small library.

583. Calhoun, John C., and James K. Bracken. "Automated Acquisitions and Collection Development in the Knox College Library." **Information Technology & Libraries** 1 (September 1982): 246-56.

The first half of this article describes the development during the late 1970s and early 1980s of the in-house automated acquisitions system at Knox College. The second half describes collection evaluation using special features of the system.

The publisher sort command was used to identify the fifty-eight publishers, termed "preferred publishers," that accounted for half of Knox College's 1980-1981 book orders. A table lists these along with the sixty publishers most frequently represented in *Choice*'s "Outstanding Academic Books" for 1977-1980, termed "established publishers." Next, the 2,257 outstanding books by all publishers as well as the 1,450 by established publishers were checked against the holdings. The use of the find-sort command to identify the books ordered by a particular department, as well as the proportion from established publishers, is also explained. This item offers a notable example of employing computer-generated publisher data for collection evaluation.

584. Craig, Daza Fox, and Paula Meise Strain. "Analysis of Collection Development at the National Library of Medicine." **Bulletin of the Medical Library Association** 68 (April 1980): 197-206.

The collecting patterns at the National Library of Medicine between 1965 and 1977 were studied by downloading selected fields of approximately 175,000 monographic and serial records from CATLINE (NLM's online catalog) into the ACQUIRE data management system. The records were analyzed by various combinations of subject (using both the NLM and LC classifications), form, language, and date of entry into CATLINE to create a quantitative profile of the collection. Numerous tables and figures illustrate the findings.

The authors conclude that computers allow "both quantitative analysis of an individual library's collection and qualitative comparison of that collection with the collections of other libraries." This study is particularly notable because it represents one of the earliest uses of online catalog data for collection evaluation purposes.

585. Degener, Christie T., and Marjory A. Waite. "Using an Automated Serials System to Assist with Collection Review and Cancellations." **Serials Review** 17, no. 1 (1991): 13-20.

This account of the serials review process at the University of North Carolina at Chapel Hill, Health Sciences Library, presents a serials evaluation model for which evaluative data can be stored and manipulated by an automated system. A table summarizes the options, values, and weight for the model's eleven factors: 1) indexing, 2) subject relevance to curriculum, 3) relation to information already in collection, 4) user requests, 5) language, 6) if published by a society, 7) geographic availability, 8) publisher reputation, 9) ILL borrowing history, 10) foreign or domestic geographic scope, and 11) editorial board/refereed articles. Cost and citation data are used to provide supplementary information.

It is then explained how the data for each serial title are codified and stored in the PERLINE automated serials control system. Customized lists to assist the review process can easily be generated, for instance, for non-English titles, duplicate titles, etc. The authors stress that other libraries could modify this approach to meet their own needs. This article performs a useful function by pointing out how automated serials control systems can assist collection evaluation.

586. Del Frate, Adelaide A. "Use Statistics: A Planetary View." **Library Acquisitions: Practice & Theory** 4, nos. 3/4 (1980): 248-53.

Del Frate describes an evaluation project, conducted at the NASA Goddard Space Flight Center Library, on a contract in which F. W. Lancaster was a principal. The analysis was based on circulation and book inventory data from an online circulation system developed in-house that utilized a master MARC-compatible shelflist record. For nineteen broad LC classes, circulation transactions in 1976-1977 and the first half of 1978 were compared to holdings in the class. As stated in the final contract report, quoted extensively by the author, the "goal is that the percentage of the total collection devoted to a given class should be equal or close to the percentage of the total circulation represented by books in that class." Three tables illustrate the results. This item is a relatively early example of using computer-generated data for collection analysis.

587. Gabriel, Michael R. "Online Collection Evaluation Course by Course." **Collection Building** 8, no. 2 (1986): 20-24.

An established, but often labor-intensive, collection evaluation method involves matching LC or Dewey classification numbers with courses in the curriculum, then reading the shelflist to determine the number of volumes pertinent to each course. About 40 percent of this article is devoted to an extensive analysis concerning three applications of this method: 1) at the University of Southwestern Louisiana, reported by McGrath in 1969[1]; 2) at the University of Nebraska at Omaha, reported in 1974 by Golden[2]; and 3) at SUNY-Binghamton, reported by Whaley in 1981 (see entry 66).

The author then describes an automated version tested in 1984 at Mankato State University's Urban and Regional Studies Department, whereby keyword searches in the online catalog were used to calculate the number of items supporting each course. Search strategies and results are illustrated. Gabriel asserts, undoubtedly correctly, that this is a simple and effective technique for showing the collection's comparative strengths and weaknesses, but that it cannot be expected to indicate the number of titles supporting each course with "foolproof accuracy."

588. Harer, John B., and Suzanne D. Gyeszly. "NOTIS as a Collection Evaluation and Development Tool." **Journal of Educational Media & Library Sciences** 28 (Autumn 1990): 12-25.

The ostensible purpose of this research project, first reported in a Taiwanese journal, was to analyze use patterns of business monographs at Texas A & M University. However, it presents an interesting case study illustrating both the potential and problems of using NOTIS, one of the leading integrated automation systems installed in many large university libraries, to derive data for collection evaluation.

The authors clearly explain how PROCITE software and SAS programs generated data from NOTIS files concerning the LC class numbers and patron categories for five months of circulation transactions, June through October 1989. (For technical reasons, it was easier to use return rather than checkout data.) The top twenty undergraduate and graduate majors using business books are illustrated with pie charts. It was impossible to undertake a similar analysis for faculty because the University Payroll Office tapes, which had been loaded into NOTIS, lacked departmental designations for more than 80 percent of the records and failed to distinguish faculty from staff. Harer and Gyeszly conclude that their "concept and methodology will be useful for ... all other libraries that have acquired the NOTIS system."

589. Kaiden, Phyllis. "From Periodicals Budget Cuts to Management Information Systems." **Serials Librarian** 9 (Winter 1984): 83-92.

A serials cancellation project in the early 1980s impressed upon the Union College (in Schenectady, New York) library staff the need for data to assist with serials addition, cancellation, and retention decisions. A management information system was designed in-house in conjunction with an online catalog to provide information concerning discipline, cost, format, language, call number, location, indexing, suppliers, and user access (the number of times a title was searched in the OPAC) for individual titles and the entire collection. The focus is on system functionality, though the report offers no evaluative or technical details. One presumes that the generated information would be quite relevant to serials collection evaluation, although Kaiden asserts that there had not yet been an opportunity to test the management reports' usefulness.

590. Lee, Dae Choon, and Larry A. Lockway. "Using an Online Comprehensive Library Management System in Collection Development." **Collection Management** 14, nos. 3/4 (1991): 61-73.

The authors describe use of the PALS (Project for Automated Library Systems) "online comprehensive library management system" at the St. Cloud State University Learning Resources Center to generate collection analysis statistics. Holdings, circulation, and browsing data for the 1989-1990 academic year were gathered for 164 call number ranges, impressionistically identified as high-use and low-use subject areas and subtopics by collection development librarians. Based on methods previously described by Bonn (entry 3) and Aguilar (entry 54), the proportions of holdings to circulation and holdings to browsing were calculated for these classification ranges. Seven tables exhibit the selected topics and generated reports. A major limitation is that only 240 classification ranges can be loaded into the system at once.

This report is particularly notable for its inclusion of browsing data, which were recorded with a bar-code wand when reshelving books that had not been checked out. Lee and Lockway speculate that if the capabilities of this online system were combined with a model such as the RLG Conspectus, "the result could be a highly effective collection development tool."

591. Nimmer, Ronald J. "Circulation and Collection Patterns at the Ohio State University Libraries, 1973-1977." **Library Acquisitions: Practice & Theory** 4, no. 1 (1980): 61-70.

Nimmer reports an investigation of collection growth and circulation patterns at the Ohio State University libraries between 1973 and 1977, based on data from the library's automated circulation system installed in 1972. Circulation was analyzed by 1,100 LC class ranges and 38 locations. After a brief discussion concerning how the data were generated from the master file and the circulation file, the article focuses on the statistical reports.

Major reports, illustrated here, include summary by LC class, summary by location, and location detail reports that analyze by language (English or non-English) and age of the material, divided into three broad categories. All reports contain data by user status (faculty or student) and a circulation intensity factor (a percentage calculated by dividing circulations by the number of titles in a category). The circulation intensity function is useful for comparing collections of various sizes.

592. Nutter, Susan K. "Online Systems and the Management of Collections: Use and Implications." In **Advances in Library Automation and Networking**, vol. 1, edited by Joe A. Hewitt, 125-49. Greenwich, Conn.: JAI Press, 1987. 232p. ISBN 0-89232-385-x.

Nutter's outstanding article offers a systematic overview concerning how data derived from automated library systems can be used for collection management and collection evaluation purposes. She discusses the type of data available from online catalogs, acquisitions and serials control systems, circulation systems, microcomputer applications, and external databases (such as the AMIGOS Collection Analysis Service or the Conspectus Online) and the data's potential collection management applications. For example, the database for an online catalog can produce collection assessment statistics by language, country of origin, date, subject, and format. Such statistics can serve a variety of needs, including growth projections, comparing strengths and weaknesses, etc. The data-gathering limitations of present technology, along with potential enhancements in the foreseeable future, are clearly explained.

The author concludes with warnings that automated technology's ability to produce collection management data will "outstrip" our ability to interpret the data; that collection management librarians will face responsibility for justifying the cost of management information systems; and that generated data's public availability will place librarians "under more precise and critical scrutiny."

SOFTWARE

593. Bartolo, Laura M. "Automated ILL Analysis and Collection Development: A Hi-Tech Marriage of Convenience." **Library Acquisitions: Practice & Theory** 13, no. 4 (1989): 361-69.

After reviewing previous reports concerning the use of ILL data for collection analysis purposes, Bartolo concludes that the time and effort required to gather the data placed "constraints" on these studies. However, present technology now allows data analysis to be readily incorporated into ILL workflow. Five ILL software packages (ACQUILLA, ILLRKS, ILL Log, ILL Office Program, and SAVEIT) are evaluated, based on telephone calls to the vendors, in terms of: 1) data elements included (publisher, date, etc.), 2) statistical reports, 3) incorporation into ILL workflow, 4) ability to capture holdings data from other libraries, and 5) availability of software. A table summarizes the findings in a checklist format.

594. Daugherty, Robert Allen. "System Statistics from the Library Computer System (LCS) at the University of Illinois." **Library Acquisitions: Practice & Theory** 4, no. 1 (1980): 71-74.

This report describes how the statistical package developed for the University of Illinois Library Computer System can generate data to assist collection evaluation. The master bibliographic file provides holdings data by location and by subject, using up to 255 defined ranges of the Dewey or LC classification. It can also report circulation for up to 255 ranges, as well as the ratio of circulation to holdings. Each location can define a different set of ranges, which may overlap and be changed as needed. The patron file provides data by user category, including academic department. Moreover, the system will combine data by subject category and user status. Reports can be generated monthly, quarterly, by semester, and annually.

595. Palmer, Judith, and Lois Sill. "Keeping Track: The Development of an Ongoing Journal Usage Survey." **Serials** 1 (July 1988): 30-33.

After reviewing the standard journal-use survey methods and finding them deficient, Palmer and Sill describe an approach developed in the late 1980s at the Rothamsted Experimental Station Library in the United Kingdom. VAX Datatrieve software, available from the Rothamsted Computing Unit, was used to create a database recording serials usage. Data were entered into seven fields covering the title, the user, and the user's department, as well as the type and number of uses. They stress that the system offers the advantage of continuous monitoring while requiring minimal staff time (forty-five minutes per day). The authors do not explain how one gathers the data prior to entry into the system.

596. Pinnell-Stephens, June. "Local Conspectus Applications." **PNLA Quarterly** 53 (Spring 1989): 22-23.

The collection development librarian from the Fairbanks, Alaska North Borough Public Library illustrates how the library uses the Excel software on a Macintosh computer to create a database recording the number of missing books each month, according to the categories of the Pacific Northwest Conspectus. A figure illustrates the application in forty-nine Conspectus subject groups. The entry's focus is on the final product rather than the technical details of the application. This approach could be employed by academic libraries that use the Conspectus.

597. Schmidt, Sherrie, Jane Treadwell, and Gloriana St. Clair. "Using dBaseIII+ to Create a Serials Review List." **Microcomputers for Information Management** 5 (September 1988): 169-82.

This item describes how the dBaseIII+ database management software was used to create a serials database to assist the review of 15,603 active serials subscriptions at the Texas A & M University Library during the late 1980s. The authors explain which fields were entered into the database: title, country, price, etc. A major section covers the "political process" used to involve faculty in the review. Each department was sent a list of titles to rank on a scale of 1 (high) to 5 (low) according to their importance to teaching and research at the university. The faculty rankings were entered into the database, sorted by department. Collection development librarians reviewed these lists to compile a cancellation list for final faculty review. The article contains several illustrative figures and tables, including a flowchart of the review project. The authors conclude that a dBaseIII+ created-database provided a "decision-making tool."

598. Slater, Jack. "Online Collection Statistics: A Comparison of BASIC and SAS." **Drexel Library Quarterly** 17 (Winter 1981): 61-74.

The author briefly outlines the major features, benefits, and drawbacks of using BASIC, a general programming language, and SAS (Statistical Analysis System), a commercially available software package, for generating online collection statistics. Nine figures in an appendix illustrate and compare reports, especially by subject and format, produced by each software product. Slater's conclusion that "packaged software should be considered as an alternative to general languages such as BASIC" (for writing small programs intended for in-house use) is even more applicable a decade later.

599. Swartz, B. J. "Biology Serials: A Useful and Continuing, Though Statistically Inaccurate Study at the Rutgers–Camden Library." **New Jersey Libraries** 20 (Spring 1987): 14-17.

Swartz describes use of the PC-File software, a database management program, to maintain biology serials data at the Rutgers–Camden Library. Each record contains fields for: 1) title; 2) frequency; 3) fund code; 4) cost; 5) LC number; 6) use from 1984 onward, broken down by the publication decade of the used item from the 1920s through the 1980s; and 7) ILL requests from 1985 on, again analyzed by decade from the 1920s through 1980s. The file can be sorted by use or ILL requests, in ascending or descending order, to identify titles to be considered for purchase or cancellation. The author observes that this data should not serve as the only decision criterion, because several of the database sources "are highly suspect in their accuracy."

600. Townley, Charles T. "Using SPSS to Analyze Book Collection Data." **Drexel Library Quarterly** 17 (Winter 1981): 87-119.

Townley illustrates, based on a sample of 1,063 titles from the Pennsylvania State University, Capitol Campus library, how the Statistical Package for the Social Sciences can be used for univariate, bivariate, and multivariate statistical analysis concerning book use, book loss, and duplication. The paper is aimed at practicing librarians, but an understanding of statistics and programming or access to technical assistance is assumed. Although dated, this item is worth noting because few similar articles have been published.

601. White, Howard D. "Computer Techniques for Studying Coverage, Overlaps, and Gaps in Collections." **Journal of Academic Librarianship** 12 (January 1987): 365-71.

This item explains how the Statistical Package for the Social Sciences (SPSS) can be used to analyze coverage, overlap, and gaps in the holdings of a library consortium, assuming that a master file of bibliographic records already exists. The article focuses on the SPSS commands to be used, the reports that can be generated (displayed here), and the interpretation of the reports. A 300-book sample of holdings data for 72 major academic libraries is used for illustrative purposes, although White stresses that he is not evaluating these libraries. He gives examples of the commands used to generate various lists, such as the books not held by any library, the books held in common by two libraries, etc.

The author claims to give enough information on SPSS commands to allow a library manager to delegate the actual work "to anyone who understands the rudiments of SPSS." This is the best available article concerning the use of SPSS for collection analysis.

ONLINE SEARCHING

602. Bronars, Lori, and Katherine Branch. "Cost-Cutting Uses of New SCISEARCH Feature." **Database** 13 (December 1990): 53-58.

Bronars and Branch demonstrate a journal evaluation method, developed at Yale University, in which SCISEARCH is used to ascertain which journals faculty publish in or cite, on the implicit assumption that such journals are more valuable to the library. This technique became feasible in September 1988 when DIALOG enhanced SCISEARCH by allowing display of the CW (Cited Work) field, which lists the references cited by an author. The authors also explain how the Crosstalk communications software and WordPerfect can be used to reduce online charges to one-third the level they would otherwise be. The precise search strategies are illustrated in numerous figures. The authors conclude that this approach can be employed for journal cancellation, transfer, or subscription decisions, but caution that other factors, such as usage and professional judgment, should also be considered.

603. Clark, Katharine E., and William R. Kinyon. "The Interdisciplinary Use of Physics Journals." **College & Research Libraries News** 50 (February 1989): 145-50.

This article depicts the use of online searching at Texas A & M University to establish the importance and interdisciplinary nature of thirty-six physics journals when the library had to decide quickly whether to transfer the journals to a branch location. After abandoning a cumbersome attempt to search specific articles, the journal titles were searched online in eight non-physics databases, including *Chemical Abstracts, Engineering Index,* and *Mathematical Reviews,* to identify the number of entries for 1983 through 1985. This number was then compared to the total number of articles published by each journal between 1983 and 1985, determined from the *SCI JCR,* so that the percentage coverage for each title in the eight databases could be calculated. The findings are displayed in a two-page table. Because coverage in non-physics databases demonstrated the journals' interdisciplinarity, they were retained in the central library.

The authors conclude that the online searching provided "a fast and efficient solution." The evaluation was completed within a week at a cost of approximately 100 staff hours and $1,000 in online charges.

604. Delman, Bruce S. "Tailoring Periodical Collections to Meet Institutional Needs." **Bulletin of the Medical Library Association** 72 (April 1984): 162-67.

This entry illustrates the application of Delman's PAJS method (problem-oriented approach to journal selection)[3] to three hypothetical medical libraries at: 1) a large academic medical center; 2) a large teaching, nonresearch hospital; and 3) a small community hospital. To identify for a large medical center the core journals supporting the topic "Prostatic Diseases," that term was searched in the MEDLARS online database. The yield was 205 journals containing 970 articles. The 37 journals that accounted for 75 percent of the citations are listed in a table. For the other two types of libraries, narrower searches were conducted, using various subheadings such as "Prostatic Diseases—Diagnosis." Journals containing at least six articles were considered the core. A table presents the twenty-seven core journals for a medical center, seventeen for a teaching hospital, and fourteen for a community hospital.

Although not stated by the author, this method could be adapted as an evaluation tool for nonmedical subjects by providing a checklist of core journals.

605. Fenichel, Carol H. "Combining Reference with Collection Development: Using Pro-Cite to Produce a Faculty Bibliography and as an Aid in Journal Selection." **Medical Reference Services Quarterly** 9 (Spring 1990): 69-75.

Fenichel explains how a bibliography of faculty publications can be quickly compiled using Pro-Cite, PC software for formatting citations, and Biblio-Link, software for converting downloaded records to Pro-Cite format. This method was used to create a list of faculty publications from the Mental Health Sciences Department at Hahnemann University, in Philadelphia, using records downloaded from the SCISEARCH and SOCIAL SCISEARCH online databases. The list was then sorted by journal frequency and compared to the current subscription list to identify journals in which faculty often publish that were not held by the library. Two new subscriptions were placed based on this project. Although libraries in these times are obviously more likely to be cancelling journals than selecting them, this article nevertheless offers a new selection methodology.

606. Kaniki, Andrew M. "The International Agricultural Collection of The Pennsylvania State University Libraries: A Collection Evaluation." **Quarterly Bulletin of the International Association of Agricultural Librarians & Documentalists** 32, no. 4 (1987): 217-24.

The use of online databases to generate a checklist for collection evaluation is described in this interesting article. Three agricultural databases initially yielded 2,484 citations covering international agriculture. Because the cost of printing them would have exceeded $1,000, the project was scaled down by printing only citations from the subdivision "Education, Extension, and Advisory Work" in the AGRIS-INTERNATIONAL and AGRICOLA databases, at a cost of $85. The final list of 58 serials and 254 monographic titles was checked against the Pennsylvania State University collection by means of the online catalog. This approach's benefits are discussed: it is quick, it is up-to-date, online databases are easily manipulated to generate the desired list, and the list can be used for selection. It is apparent that this method would be useful for libraries that can afford the expense and are interested in evaluating a small segment of the collection.

MISCELLANEOUS

607. Armbrister, Ann. "Library MARC Tapes as a Resource for Collection Analysis: The AMIGOS Service." In **Advances in Library Automation and Networking**, vol. 2, edited by Joe A. Hewitt, 119-35. Greenwich, Conn.: JAI Press, 1988. 257p. ISBN 0-89232-673-5.

An AMIGOS Bibliographical Council staff member provides the most detailed description available concerning the AMIGOS Collection Analysis Service, in which the catalog tapes of a library or group of libraries are used to extract data to analyze collecting patterns or overlap. Following brief discussions of the RLG Conspectus and the significance of the MARC format for gathering collection analysis data, the author describes the service's history, file processing procedures, statistical reports, and data interpretation problems, as well as the potential uses for the results. An appendix illustrates three types of statistical reports generated by the service.

The description of the processing procedures, written in easy-to-comprehend layman's language, is particularly illuminating. Receiving reports in two stages is suggested for coping with their "sheer volume." Detecting gaps, revealing strengths, setting preservation priorities, aiding cooperative collection development, and formulating funding requests are among the many mentioned applications for the resulting data.

608. Dillon, Martin, and others. "Design Issues for a Microcomputer-Based Collection Analysis System." **Microcomputers for Information Management** 5 (December 1988): 263-73.

The authors describe a prototype automated collection analysis system developed at OCLC. Based on a microcomputer and CD-ROM disc drive, the system contains OCLC holdings data and allows a library to compare its holdings in at least 500 subject areas with predefined or selected library peer groups. Eight specific uses of the system are outlined, including various evaluation, budgeting, and acquisitions functions. After describing the RLG Conspectus, the authors predict that "automated approaches will be merged with the Conspectus effort to the benefit of both."

The authors then illustrate and explain the reports that the system generates. A subject area can be evaluated by comparing the evaluating library's holdings data with that of peer groups. Specific titles not owned by the evaluating library can be identified in descending order by the number of peer group libraries that hold them. Although not mentioned by name, this is obviously the prototype of the AMIGOS Collection Analysis Service.

609. Hodson, James. "The Use of Microcomputers for Collection Evaluation." **Library Software Review** 9 (July-August 1990): 231-32.

This "executive summary" of a presentation at the March 1990 "Computers in Libraries Conference," at Crystal City near Washington, D.C., begins by noting that the area of collection development has been "relatively untouched" by microcomputers. Hodson emphasizes that one can generate useful collection evaluation information through searching online or CD-ROM databases, downloading records, and manipulating the data through microcomputer software. For instance, by searching the author affiliation field, one can create a list of publications by local faculty as a means of analyzing collection need.

610. Johnson, Susan W. "Collection Analysis from OCLC/AMIGOS." **Information Retrieval & Library Automation** 25 (December 1989): 1-3.

The OCLC/AMIGOS Collection Analysis compact disc is briefly described by Johnson. This CD-ROM package allows a library to analyze subject overlap and uniqueness in its holdings compared to 14 other library categories, such as ARL institutions, academic libraries with more than 700,000 volumes, etc. The database used for comparison contains 1.6 million abbreviated bibliographic records from OCLC, published between 1977 and 1987, excluding serials, dissertations, and government documents. It is noted that the product first became available in July 1989 and had been sold to eleven libraries by December 1989. Technical requirements for operating this CD-ROM system are listed. This item serves as evidence that CD-ROMs can be used for applications more sophisticated than supporting traditional library functions.

611. Kim, David U. "OCLC-MARC Tapes and Collection Management." **Information Technology & Libraries** 1 (March 1982): 22-27.

Based on his experiences at the University of Lowell Libraries, the author discusses how OCLC-MARC tapes of a library's cataloging records can generate data to analyze collecting patterns by LC class range, curriculum area, language, location, intellectual level, physical format, place of publication, and publication date (as well as combining these categories through Boolean operators). Kim briefly explains how the needed portions of the bibliographical records can be extracted from the tapes into an excerpt file for more efficient manipulation.

The approach can be applied to either current acquisitions or the entire holding, if retrospective conversion has been completed. Numerous figures illustrate the type of data that can be gathered. The article's last sentence reads, "OCLC-MARC tapes contain a wealth of information that has yet to be exploited." (See also Payson and Moore entry 614.)

612. Kountz, John. "What's in a Library? Comparing Library Holdings to the Constituencies Served." **Library Hi Tech** 9, no. 2 (1991): 31-48, 61.

This stimulating, but somewhat verbose article, explains how library holdings can be correlated with enrollment by using data from OCLC archival tapes. Title data for 8,256,143 monographic records (as of October 1989) were extracted from the OCLC tapes of nineteen university libraries in the California State system and entered on floppy disks to be manipulated with IBM-compatible desktop computers using Lotus' Symphony software. Titles held and student credit units were compared in a variety of ways. For example, absolute numbers and percentage growth from 1986-1987 through 1988-1989, were analyzed in twenty-two broad subject categories condensed from the HEGIS taxonomy. Nine bar charts display the results.

Composite findings for the nineteen campuses are presented and a sidebar indicates individual results made available to the participating libraries. Because this method requires that the LC classification numbers extracted from the archival tapes be converted into the appropriate HEGIS subject category, a four-page appendix illustrates the corresponding numbers in the two systems. This item depicts not only a creative use of both OCLC archival tape data and the HEGIS subject classification but also an approach that "provide[s] meaningful insights" into collection analysis by correlating holdings with enrollment rather than with the curriculum per se.

613. Kreyche, Michael. "BCL3 and NOTIS: An Automated Collection Analysis Project." **Library Acquisitions: Practice & Theory** 13, no. 4 (1989): 323-28.

Kreyche reports the preliminary results of a collection analysis project at the Kent State University Library using *Books for College Libraries* (3d ed., 1988) in machine-readable form (*BCL3-MR*) with complete MARC records. *BCL3-MR*'s two benefits are automated searching to determine the proportion of entries in *BCL* held by the library (assuming the library's catalog is in machine-readable form) and a sophisticated statistical analysis of what is held, by subject, language, place and date of publication, etc. A SAS profile of *BCL3*'s contents, presented in a table, reveals that 61.4 percent of the entries have been added since *BCL2* and that 97.7 percent are in English. A large portion of the article discusses the technical aspects of matching items in Kent State's NOTIS database with *BCL3-MR*, i.e., determining that the library definitely owns a *BCL3* entry.

Many libraries are using *BCL3-MR* to reduce the drudgery of manually searching *Books for College Libraries*, a long-used evaluation tool. Kreyche performs an important service by publicizing this approach.

614. Payson, Evelyn, and Barbara Moore. "Statistical Collection Management Analysis of OCLC-MARC Tape Records." **Information Technology & Libraries** 43 (September 1985): 220-32.

Citing the University of Wisconsin-Whitewater Library, Payson and Moore illustrate the use of OCLC archival tapes, supplemented by COBOL and SAS programs, to generate collection management data. The analysis was based on certain fields extracted from the archival tapes. Reports were then produced by type of material, location, and subject, according to 423 categories of the LC classification, for 1) a three-month period, 2) the fiscal year, and 3) totals to date. Several tables and figures illustrate the generated reports and the SAS program codes. The potential for using SAS programs on extracted OCLC data for more sophisticated analysis, such as departmental ordering by subject and publication date, is also explored. The authors conclude that SAS is preferable to a standard programming language such as COBOL. (See also Kim entry 611.)

615. Piccininni, James C. "Using the Higher Education General Information System (HEGIS) to Enhance Collection Development Decisions in Academic Libraries." **Collection Management** 10, no. 1/2 (1988): 15-24.

The use of the HEGIS collection analysis approach at the SUNY, New Paltz library is explained. The 550 HEGIS subject divisions have been correlated with the LC classification system. When the SUNY Course and Section Analysis tapes were run against the OCLC archival tapes, data were generated concerning the number of books held in each HEGIS category. This figure was then compared to five other data elements for each HEGIS category: number of enrolled students, total credit hours, total contact hours, faculty workload data, and faculty contact hour data. The reports, which are illustrated, also provide percentages and divide the student statistics into lower division, upper division, beginning graduate, and advanced graduate categories. This method allows comparison of the total books held in a subject with the "potential demand" that could be placed on the area. Piccininni correctly notes a major shortcoming in the fact that the data are strictly quantitative and tell nothing about the quality of the books.

The HEGIS approach has been explored by the SUNY system for at least a decade and a half. This study offers the best available explanation of the method except for Glen Evans's work,[4] which, as a library in-house publication, is beyond this bibliography's scope.

616. Potter, William Gray. "Modeling Collection Overlap on a Microcomputer." **Information Technology & Libraries** 2 (December 1983): 400-407.

An established expert on overlap studies describes in layman's terms how an IBM personal computer can be used to analyze collection overlap. A pilot project was conducted using the databases of the Southern Illinois, Northern Illinois, Illinois State, and Southern Illinois-Edwardsville libraries, all members of the twenty-three-library Library Computer System network.

Potter explains which fields are extracted from the bibliographical record; for example, title key (the first four characters from the first significant word plus the initial five characters from the second word), subject code, or format code. A software program then uses this data to determine which records match each other, in order to calculate uniqueness and overlap. In the pilot study, the matching scheme approached 95 percent accuracy. The author concludes that a personal computer connected to a large bibliographical database has many potential uses.

617. Sanders, Nancy P., Edward T. O'Neill, and Stuart L. Weibel. "Automated Collection Analysis Using the OCLC and RLG Bibliographic Databases." **College & Research Libraries** 49 (July 1988): 305-14.

This study's objective is "to test the feasibility of using the databases of the bibliographic networks for computerized collection analysis to reduce the labor required." Random samples of 500 monographic titles dated between 1978 and 1983, in mathematical analysis and botany, were taken from the OCLC database. These samples were used to analyze the holdings (taken from OCLC and RLN), including uniqueness and overlap, of the Committee on Institutional Cooperation libraries (i.e., the Big Ten universities plus Chicago). Holdings had to be verified locally because "holdings indicated by the bibliographic networks may not accurately reflect [what is held in] a library's collection." Several tables and figures exhibit the holdings and overlap patterns of the eleven universities.

The authors concluded that data revealing the percentage of available books held in a subject compared to other libraries represents a "viable approach to collection evaluation." However, the authors feel the expense of this process would restrict its use to selected subjects.

NOTES

[1] William E. McGrath and Norma Durand, "Classifying Courses in the University Catalog," *College & Research Libraries* 30 (November 1969): 533-39.

[2] Barbara Golden, "A Method for Quantitatively Evaluating a University Library Collection," *Library Resources & Technical Services* 18 (Summer 1974): 268-74.

[3] Bruce S. Delman, "A Problem-Oriented Approach to Journal Selection for Hospital Libraries," *Bulletin of the Medical Library Association* 70 (October 1982): 397-410.

[4] Glen T. Evans, and others, *Collection Development Analysis Using OCLC Archival Tapes, Final Report* (Albany, N.Y.: State University Libraries, 1977).

Glossary

Archival tape. A computer tape containing the machine-readable records for the items a library has cataloged through a bibliographical utility, such as OCLC, RLIN, or WLN. Analysis of a library's archival tape or tapes can reveal considerable information about its collecting patterns, especially in terms of subject, date, format, and language.

Associated Colleges of the Midwest (ACM). A consortium of private, liberal arts colleges with headquarters in Chicago.

Bibliometrics. A term, coined by the British librarian Alan Pritchard in 1969, meaning the application of statistical analysis to books, journal articles, citations, and patterns of scholarly communications. Citation analysis is a major, but not the only, form of bibliometrics.

Bradfordian distribution. Named after the prominent British librarian and information scientist, S. C. Bradford. As stated by Boyce and Pollens, in 1934 "Bradford found that if he collected papers on a particular topic, created a list of journals publishing these papers and then ranked the journals by the number of papers each contributed, there would be a few with many papers, a large number with a moderate number, and many others with only a few."[1] This pattern has subsequently been found to apply in journal use and citation studies.

Checklist method. One of the oldest, most traditional collection evaluation techniques, in which a list of bibliographical items is checked against the holdings of a library.

Clapp-Jordan Formula. A quantitative method, originally published in 1965 by Verner W. Clapp and Robert T. Jordan, for calculating the total number of volumes required for minimum-level collection adequacy in an academic library. Weights are assigned for various factors, such as FTE faculty, FTE students, etc. For details, see entry 245.

Client-centered. A collection evaluation method or technique that focuses on how the collection is being used and how well it is meeting patron needs. Examples would be circulation studies, in-house use studies, or availability studies. Often called patron-centered or use-centered.

Collection-centered. In contrast to client-centered techniques, an evaluation method that focuses on the collection itself or compares the collection to some external standard. Checklists, the RLG Conspectus, formulas, direct examination, or comparative statistics are examples of collection-centered methods.

Conspector. In terminology used in the United Kingdom, an individual who implements the Conspectus.

Core collection. The important materials that form the center of the collection that most libraries collecting in the area would wish to hold. The concept can apply to the books or journals for a particular subject area, such as the core journals in political science, or to the entire collection, such as the core books for a college library.

Document delivery tests. A method developed by Richard H. Orr and colleagues during the 1960s to test how rapidly a library can provide documents requested by a patron. See the introduction to chapter 5 for a more thorough explanation.

Formula. In the collection evaluation context, a quantitative method for calculating whether a library's collection contains enough volumes for minimal adequacy. Weights are assigned to factors such as number of degrees, faculty, students, etc. Examples include the Clapp-Jordan Formula and the ACRL Standards for College Libraries.

Higher Education General Information Surveys (HEGIS). Statistical data concerning institutions of higher education in the United States, compiled by the National Center for Educational Statistics and organized into a few dozen broad academic divisions. These divisions are subdivided into several hundred subject areas. HEGIS statistics and the HEGIS subject classification or taxonomy have been used for a number of collection analysis purposes. In this book the original acronym HEGIS is used, although the current term is IPEDS (Integrated Postsecondary Education Data System).[2]

Impact factor. The generally accepted definition is the one used by the ISI: a citation measure that calculates how frequently a journal's "average article" is cited within a year. As stated in the *SSCI JCR*, the impact factor represents "a ratio between citations and citable items published."[3] Journal ranking by impact factor rather than total citations received compensates for the advantage that journals publishing more items (because they are older, larger, or issued more frequently) would otherwise enjoy. Other definitions have been offered.

Immediacy index. A citation measure used by the ISI to determine how quickly a journal's "average article" is cited. A journal's 1990 immediacy index is calculated by dividing the number of times its 1990 articles were cited in 1990 by the total number of source articles the journal published in 1990. This measure has been used in a number of journal-ranking studies.

Institute of Scientific Information (ISI). Founded by Eugene Garfield, and located in Philadelphia, the ISI publishes *Current Contents,* the *Science Citation Index*, the *Social Science Citation Index*, and the *Arts & Humanities Citation Index*. Much citation data used in serials evaluation originates from the ISI.

Journal Citation Reports (JCR). Contains a wide variety of journal citation data, including rankings by total citations, impact factor, and immediacy index. Data from this source has been used in innumerable collection evaluation, citation, and journal-ranking studies. Through 1988, both the *Science Citation Index* and the *Social Science Citation Index* annual subscriptions automatically included a bound volume of the *JCR* as part of the set. (It now must be purchased separately and is available only in a microfiche format.)

Library and Information Resources for the Northwest (LIRN). A program, funded in 1983 by a private foundation, through which over 200 libraries of all types in Alaska, Oregon, Washington, Idaho, and Montana implemented the Pacific Northwest Conspectus.

MARC (machine-readable cataloging). A standardized format developed in the 1960s for storing library catalog records in machine-readable form. Data concerning a variety of factors, such as subject, publication date, or language, can be extracted from MARC records and used for collection analysis purposes.

Metropolitan Reference and Research Library Agency (METRO). A library consortium in New York State.

National Shelflist Count. A project organized in the early 1970s by the ALA's RTSD to compile data concerning the holdings of major North American research libraries according to 490 divisions of the Library of Congress classification system.

North American Collections Inventory Project (NCIP). (Formerly the National Collections Inventory Project.) A project begun in 1983 through which the Association of Research Libraries members began implementing the RLG Conspectus in their libraries.

Northwestern Online Total Integrated System (NOTIS). An integrated automation system, developed at Northwestern University, used in many academic libraries.

Pittsburgh Study. A major study of the usage of library materials conducted at the University of Pittsburgh during the 1970s. It reported that approximately 40 percent of the roughly 35,000 books purchased in 1969 never circulated during the seven years after they were purchased.

Reliability. A method or approach is considered *reliable* if it offers consistent results.

RLG Conspectus. A collection analysis instrument developed by the Research Libraries Group (RLG). Collection assessments ranging from 0 to 5 are assigned to approximately 7,000 subjects, usually corresponding to small segments of the LC classification. See the introduction to chapter 9 for a detailed explanation.

SCISEARCH. The *Science Citation Index* online, accessible through DIALOG.

Shelf Availability Test. A measure of how frequently patrons can immediately find the material they are seeking on the shelf. During the 1970s, Paul B. Kantor developed a branching technique for analyzing non-availability of materials. For a detailed explanation, see the introduction to chapter 5.

Shelflist. An inventory, in call number order, of the titles owned by a library. Traditionally, shelflists contained a card or cards for each title, but contemporary versions often assume an electronic format.

Shelflist measure. A traditional collection evaluation technique that uses or measures the shelflist to count the number of items held in a particular subject area. The segment of the DDC or Library of Congress classification corresponding to the subject is determined; the shelflist is then consulted to ascertain the number of titles or volumes within the range.

SPEC Kit. A collection of in-house library documents, issued on a regular basis by the Systems and Procedures Exchange Center (SPEC) of the ARL's Office of Management Studies, illustrating how a particular problem or issue is being addressed by large research libraries. Each kit is devoted to a specific theme, such as retrospective conversion or information desks. A number of SPEC kits have addressed issues pertinent to collection evaluation.

Statistical Analysis System (SAS). A software package of statistical programs applicable to a variety of library applications, including collection evaluation.

Statistical Package for the Social Sciences (SPSS). A software package for statistical analysis of data, frequently used in library and information science research.

Trueswell's 80/20 Rule. A bibliometric pattern, first observed by Richard W. Trueswell in 1969, in which approximately 20 percent of a library's holdings account for 80 percent of the circulation. See entry 129.

Qualitative approaches. Collection evaluation techniques that ask "how good" the material in a collection is. Examples would be the checklist method, direct examination, or hiring a subject specialist.

Quantitative approaches. A collection evaluation method, often contrasted with qualitative approaches, that counts or asks "how many." Examples include data concerning collection size and growth, comparative statistics, and formulas.

Validity. A technique is considered *valid* if it actually measures what it is supposed to measure.

Virginia Tech Library System (VTLS). An integrated automated system developed at Virginia Tech University.

NOTES

[1] Bert R. Boyce and Janet Sue Pollens, "Citation-Based Impact Measures and the Bradfordian Selection Criteria," *Collection Management* 4 (Fall 1982): 29.

[2] John Kountz, "What's in a Library? Comparing Library Holdings to the Constituencies Served," *Library Hi Tech* 9, no. 2 (1991): 34.

[3] *Social Science Citation Index Journal Citation Reports; 1987 Annual* (Philadelphia: Institute for Scientific Information, 1988), 10A.

Author/Title Index

Index is to both entry numbers and page numbers. Entry numbers are listed first, and page numbers follow after **p.** or **pp.**

Abell, Millicent D., 320
ABI/INFORM, 450
"The ABN Database," 215
Abridged Index Medicus, 436-37
Abstract Journal: Informatics, 448
Academic Libraries: Research Perspectives, 273
Academy of Management Journal, 504, 516
Accounting Review, 224, 510, 514, 518
"Accrediting Knowledge: Journal Stature and Citation Impact in Social Science," 484
ACML Bulletin, 388
"Acoustic Journals and Acoustic Research Activities," 572
"The Acquired Immune Deficiency Syndrome," 304
"Acquisition Rates in University Libraries," 251
Acquisitions '90; Conference on Acquisitions, Budgets, and Collections, 64, 349, 372
Acquisitions Librarian, 339
Acquisitions Management and Collection Development in Libraries, 18-19
ACRL. *See* Association of College and Research Libraries
"ACRL Guidelines for Branch Libraries in Colleges and Universities," 226
Adams, Gerald R., 539
Adewole, Segun, 254
Administration & Society, 521, 545
Administrative Science Quarterly, 516, 546
Advances in Librarianship, 21
Advances in Library Administration and Organization, 37

Advances in Library Automation and Networking, 374, 592, 607
Advances in Serials Management, 174, 405
Advani, N., 130
AECT (Association for Educational Communications and Technology), p.83
African Journal of Academic Librarianship, 247
Agnew, Grace, 103
Agricultural Administration, 255
Aina, L. O., 154, 255
Akron Business & Economic Review, 498
ALA. *See* American Library Association
ALA Resources and Technical Services Division, 1, 321
ALA Resources Section Executive Committee, 4
ALA Yearbook; A Review of Library Events 1980, 126
Alabi, G. A., 154
Alafiatayo, Benjamin O., 294
Albert, Joe, 498
Alexandria, 354
Alldredge, Noreen S., 131
Allen, G. G., 361
Allen, William R., 64, 242
Alligood, Elaine C., 454
Alt, Martha S., 84, 97
"An Alternative Interpretation of Recent Political Science Journal Evaluations," 524
"Alternatives to the Shelflist Measure for Determining the Size of a Subject Collection," 71
AMA Educators' Proceedings, 500
Ambia, Golam, 132

230 / AUTHOR/TITLE INDEX

American Association of Junior Colleges, p.83
American Book Publishing Record, 35, 209
American Council on Education, p.83
"American Geographers' Rankings of American Geography Journals," 533
American Journal of Agricultural Economics, 311, 315
American Libraries, 23
American Library Association (ALA), 1, 4, 7, 65, 85, 99, pp.x, xiv, 37, 61, 83-84, 120
  Reference and Adult Services Division, 38
  Resources and Technical Services Division, 1, 321
  Resources Section Executive Committee, 4
American Men and Women of Science, 438
American Political Science Review, 272, 291
American Psychologist, 268, 483, 523, 528, p.179
"American Revolution: Comparison of a Bibliography with a Quality-Selected List," 425
American Sociologist, 493, 527
"American Sociologists' Evaluations of Sixty-Three Journals," 527
American Sociological Review, 527
"Analysis of a Verification Study of Post-1914 English Canadian Literature," 396
"Analysis of an Inductive Method of Evaluating the Book Collection of a Public Library," 59
"Analysis of Collection Development at the National Library of Medicine," 584
"Analysis of the Differences Between Density-of-Use Ranking and Raw-Use Ranking of Library Journal Use," 145
"Analyzing In-House Journal Utilization," 455
Anderson, Richard C., 490
"An Annotated Bibliography of Items Relating to Collection Evaluation in Academic Libraries, 1969-1981," 40, p.xiv

Annals of Library Science and Documentation, 577
"Annual Report of OCLC Research; July 1987-June 1988," 397
Annual Review of Biochemistry, 547
Annual Review of Information Science and Technology, 203
Annual Review of Psychology, 537
Annual Review of Sociology, 53
"Application of a Methodology Analyzing User Frustration," 192
"The Application of Relative Use and Interlibrary Demand in Collection Development," 54
"An Approach to Collection Analysis," 66
Aquilar, William, 54
Archibald, Robert B., 481
"Are We There Yet? Evaluating Library Collections, Reference Services, Programs, and Personnel," 23
Armbrister, Ann, 607
Arrigona, Daniel R., 104
Art Documentation, 144, 326
Art Index, 144, 457
Arts & Humanities Citation Index, 133, 318, p.98
ASIS '85; Proceedings of the 48th ASIS Annual Meeting, 435
ASIS '86; Proceedings of the 49th ASIS Annual Meeting, 313
ASLIB Proceedings, 464
"Assessing Assessment," 375
"Assessing Collection Use by Surveying Users at Randomly Selected Times," 72
"Assessing Current Periodical Use at a Science and Engineering Library," 148
"Assessing the Relative Impacts of Economics Journals," 535
"Assessment of Journals in Social Science Psychology," 523
Association for Educational Communications and Technology (AECT), p.83
Association of College and Research Libraries (ACRL), 226, pp.83-85
  and Association for Educational Communications and Technology, 237-40
  Audiovisual Committee, 228

Community and Junior College
  Libraries Section, 229
Library Standards Committee, 230-31
Standards and Accreditation
  Committee, 232-33
Undergraduate Librarians Discussion
  Group, 234
Undergraduate Librarians Discussion
  Group and University
  Libraries Section, 235
University Libraries Section, 227
University Library Standards Review
  Committee, 236
Association of Research Libraries
  (ARL), 85
  Office of Management Studies, 322,
    404
"Attitude Measurement and Perceptions
  of Accounting Faculty
  Publication Outlets," 510
*Australian Academic & Research
  Libraries*, 93, 102, 176, 218-19,
  362-63, 364-66, 368-70
Australian Library Journal, 361
"Automated Acquisitions and Collection
  Development in the Knox College
  Library," 583
"Automated Collection Analysis Using
  the OCLC and RLG Biblio-
  graphic Databases," 617
"Automated Collection Assessment:
  CASSI as a Tool," 207
"Automated ILL Analysis and Collec-
  tion Development," 593
"Availability Analysis," 180
"Availability Analysis Report," 187
" 'Availability' as a Performance
  Measure for Academic
  Libraries," 190
"Availability Studies in Libraries," 184
"Availability Survey in Co-operation
  with a School of Librarianship
  and Information Studies," 191

Bachmann-Derthick, Jan, 174, 181
Bader, Shelley A., 455, 461
Baker, Robert K., 582
Baker, Sharon L., 2, 16, 105-6, 175, p.x
"Balancing Library Objectives with
  Book Circulation," 172
Baldwin, Jane, 405
Baldwin, W. M., III, 405

Barling, Cathryn H., 35
Barnard, Roy S., 456
Bartlett, J. A., p.30
Bartolo, Laura M., 593
Basak, Nanda Dulal, 278
A Basic Music Library, 99
Bastille, Jacqueline D., 145, 406
Baughman, James C., 295
Bayer, Alan E., 519
"BCL3 and NOTIS," 613
Becker, Boris W., 500
*Behavioral & Social Sciences
  Librarian*, 48, 53, 342, 445-46,
  537
"The Behavioral Sciences and
  Management," 507
Belanger, Sandra E., 407
Belgum, Kathie, 67
Benenfeld, Alan R., 179
Bennion, Bruce C., 438
Bensman, Stephen J., 408
Bentley, Stella, 204, 227
Besson, Alain, 409
"Biases in Citation-Based Ranking of
  Journals," 481
"A Bibliography on Standards for
  Evaluating Libraries," 41,
  pp.xiv, 83
"Bibliometrics: Library Use and
  Citation Studies," 273
"Bibliometrics in Information Science,"
  541
Bibliotheca Medica Canadiana, 382
Biblische Zeitschrift, 283
Bick, Dawn, 439
"Biochemistry and Environmental
  Biology," 309
Biological Abstracts, 309
"Biology Serials," 599
Biometrika, 278
Birdsall, Douglas G., 458
Black, George W., Jr., 68-69, 445
Blake, Monica, 410-11
Blake, Virgil L. P., 65, 520
Bland, Robert N., 279, 293
Bobick, James E., 256, 271
Bonn, George S., 3, 16
Bonzi, Susan, 435
"Book Availability as a Performance
  Measure of a Library," 189
"Book Availability at the University
  of California, Santa Cruz,"
  178

"Book Availability in the University of Minnesota Bio-Medical Library," 200
"Book Availability Study as an Objective Measure in a Health Sciences Library," 182
Books for College Libraries 2 (BCL2), 125
Books for College Libraries 3 (BCL), 48, 77, 210, 279, 613, p.xvii
Books in Print Plus, 77
Borkowski, Casimir, 159-60
Bostic, Mary J., 412
"Boundary Spanners and Serials Deselection," 413
Bousfield, Wendy, 413
Bowman, Michael, 257, 263
Boyce, Bert R., 434
Bracken, James K., 583
Bradley, Kate, 371
Braga, Gilda Maria, 440
Branch, Katherine, 602
Branin, Joseph J., 398
Bremer, Thomas A., 72
Brill, Margaret S., 296
Brink, David R., 499
British Journal of Academic Librarianship, 122, 357, 409
Britten, William A., 107
Brittonia, 302
Broadbent, Marianne, 176
Broadus, Robert N., 73, 108-11, 133, 161, 258-59, 269, p.97
Broderick, Dorothy, 5
Bronars, Lori, 602
Brown, Helen M., p.84
Browne, William G., 500
Brug, Sandra, 39
Bryant, Bonita, 321
Buckingham, Jeanette, 382
Buckland, Michael K., 205
Budd, John, 55, 77, 260, 297
Buffardi, Louis C., 483
"Building a Core Collection of Business and Management Periodicals," 452
"Building Collections Together," 373
Building Library Collections, 5
Building on the First Century; Proceedings of the Fifth National Conference of ACRL, 204, 208, 416

Bulletin of the Medical Library Association, 56, 82, 88, 147, 149, 182, 200-202, 217, 275, 282, 292, 406, 436, 451, 454-55, 465, 548, 584, 604
Burkhart, Joyce C., 32, 264, 453, 466, 478
Burkhart, Robert W., 32, 264, 453, 466, 478
Burrell, Quentin L., 112
Burton, Rodney M., 480
Bushing, Margaret, 367
Business Index, 450
Business Periodicals Index, 450
Buss, A. R., 538
Bustion, Marifran, 414
Buzzard, Marion L., 280
"By the Numbers: The Fallacy of Formula," 44
Byrd, Gary D., 56
Byrne, Elizabeth Douthitt, 86

Cairns, Paul M., 206
Calhoun, John C., 583
California Librarian, 24
Cambridge Bibliography of English Literature, 395
Cameron, Margaret A., 364
Campbell, Judith, 362
Canadian Field-Naturalist, 309, 492
Canadian Historical Review, 316
Canadian Library Journal, 332
"Canceling Soviet Journals," 458
Cann, Sharon Lee, 38
Carpenter, Raymond L., 243-44
Carr, Barbara E., 457
"A Case against Conspectus," 361
"*CASSI* and Collection Assessment," 208
CASSI (Chemical Abstracts Service Source Index), 207
Catalogue & Index, 212
"Catching Up on Collection Evaluation," 102
Catholic Biblical Quarterly, 283
Catholic Library World, 375
Cauchi, Simon, 298
"Causes and Dynamics of User Frustration in an Academic Library," 193
Cave, Roderick, 298
Cawkell, A. E., 572

Cenzer, Pamela S., 339
Chandran, D., 547
Chandy, P. R., 498
"Changes in Rank Lists of Serials Over Time," 489
Chapman, Michael, 308
"Characteristics of American Revolution Literature," 427
"Characteristics of Journal Citations in the Social Sciences," 314
"Characteristics of References in Selected Scholarly English Literary Journals," 305
"Characteristics of the Literature of Literary Scholarship," 318
"The Characteristics of the Literature Used by Historians," 308
"Characteristics of the Monographic Literature of British and American Literary Studies," 299
"Characteristics of Written Scholarship in American Literature," 297
Chemical Abstracts, 72, 429
Chemical Abstracts Service Source Index (CASSI), 208
The Chicago Manual of Style, p.xiii
Choice, 225
Christenson, James A., 484
Christiansen, Dorothy E., 4
Chrzastowski, Tina E., 134-35
Chweh, Steven Seokho, 55, 57
Ciliberti, Anne C., 177, p.61
Cipolla, Wilma Reid, 234
"Circulation and Collection Patterns at the Ohio State University Libraries, 1973-1977," 591
"Circulation and In-Library Use of Government Publications," 155
"Circulation Studies and Collection Development," 45
"Circulation Studies Cannot Reflect Research Use," 173
"Citation Analysis in the Social Sciences," 303
"Citation Analysis of the Literature of Systematic Botany," 302
"Citation-Based Impact Measures and Bradfordian Selection Criteria," 482
"Citation Characteristics in Library Science," 317
"Citation Characteristics of French and German Literary Monographs," 300
"Citation Characteristics of Italian and Spanish Literary Monographs," 301
"Citation Data for Selected Journals in Reproductive Biology," 256
"Citation Impact, Acceptance Rate, and APA Journals," 483
"Citation Patterns in the History of Technology," 312
"Citation Ranking versus Subjective Evaluation in the Determination of Journal Hierarchies in the Social Sciences," 486
"Citation Rankings of Public Administration Journals," 521, 545
"Citation Studies in Science and Technology," 277
"A Citation Study of American Literature," 260
"Citations in Bibliography," 298
Clapp, Verner W., 245
Clark, Barton M., 446
Clark, Katherine E., 603
Clark, Sharon E., 446
Clarke, Ann, 136
Clayton, Peter, 363
"Co-operative Approaches in Scotland," 355
Coale, Robert Peerling, 87
Coe, Robert K., 501-4
Cole, F. J., p.97
Coleman, Jim, 392
"Collaborative Collection Development," 333
"The Collection: Evaluation," 39
"Collection Adequacy: Meaningless Concept or Measurable Goal?" 46
"Collection Analysis and the Humanities," 336
"Collection Analysis from OCLC/AMIGOS," 610
"Collection Analysis in Modern Librarianship," 337
"Collection Assessment in a Regional Consortium," 372
"Collection Assessment in Science Libraries," 32

234 / AUTHOR/TITLE INDEX

"Collection Assessment in the Pacific Northwest," 374
"Collection Assessment in the 1980s," 14
Collection Assessment Manual, 85
Collection Assessment Manual for College and University Libraries, 79
"Collection Assessment of Biotechnology Literature," 91
"Collection Assessment Using the RLG Conspectus," 345
Collection Building, 8, 14, 25, 29, 44, 47, 52, 185, 257, 284, 307, 333, 335, 421, 471, 587
Collection Description and Assessment in ARL Libraries, 85
Collection Development: Options for Effective Management, 355, 463
Collection Development and Acquisitions, 1970-1980, 39, p.xiv
Collection Development for Australian Libraries, 13
Collection Development for Libraries, 11-13
Collection Development in Libraries: A Treatise, pt. B, 20, 45, 277, 303
"Collection Development in the British Library," 350
"Collection Development Using Interlibrary Loan Borrowing and Acquisitions Statistics," 56
"Collection Evaluation," 5, 25
"Collection Evaluation: A Practical Guide to the Literature," 26
"Collection Evaluation: Materials-Center Approaches," 2
"Collection Evaluation: Nine Techniques Discussed in the Literature," 22
"Collection Evaluation: Practices and Methods in Libraries of ALA Accredited Graduate Library Education Programs," 37
"Collection Evaluation: Theory and the Search for Structure," 81
"Collection Evaluation: Use-Centered Approaches," 105
"Collection Evaluation and Development Using Citation Analysis Techniques," 264
"Collection Evaluation and Standards," 9

"Collection Evaluation and the Conspectus," 368
"Collection Evaluation in a Developing Country," 95
"Collection Evaluation in Fine Arts Libraries," 36
"Collection Evaluation in the Research Library," 29
"Collection Evaluation or Analysis," 20
Collection Evaluation Techniques: A Short, Selective, Practical, Current Annotated Bibliography 1980-1990, 38, p.xiv
"Collection Evaluation Techniques in the Academic Art Library," 31
"Collection Evaluation Workshops Project," 367
"Collection Growth and Evaluation at Texas A & M University, 1978 and 1988," 89
Collection Management, 49-50, 54, 58, 65, 72, 78, 80, 83, 89, 92, 94, 97, 98, 101, 103, 109, 117, 124-25, 134, 153, 161, 166, 220, 260, 270, 272, 276, 282-83, 306, 337, 345, 393, 396, 407, 427, 450, 459, 461, 476, 482, 520, 590, 615
Collection Management; Background and Principles, 27
Collection Management: Current Issues, 29
Collection Management in Academic Libraries, 46
"Collection Mapping," 60
"Collection Overlap in Hospital Health Sciences Libraries," 217
"Collection Overlap in the LCS Network in Illinois," 213
"The Collection Use Survey," 116
Collections for the Future, 381
College & Research Libraries, 40-41, 61, 70, 76, 96, 121, 123, 177-78, 192-93, 198, 209, 211, 223, 243-45, 250-51, 258-59, 263, 269, 280, 299, 318, 325, 327, 329, 377, 408, 414, 419-20, 444, 489, 530-31, 541, 544, 582, 617, p.xiv
College & Research Libraries News, 116, 137, 226-40, 253, 276, 371, 392, 394-95, 439, 472, 603, p.85

"College Libraries: A Comparative Analysis in Terms of the ACRL Standards," 243
"College Libraries and Chemical Education," 266
"College Library Formulas Applied," 253
"College Textbook as a Tool for Collection Evaluation, Analysis and Retrospective Collection Development," 279
Colson, Harold, 521
"Combining Reference with Collection Development," 605
Comer, Cynthia, 47
"Commentary on 'Report on the Study of Library Use at Pitt by Professor Allen et al.'," 168
Communicating Information; Proceedings for the 43rd ASIS Annual Meeting, 179
"Communication of MIS Research," 509
Community & Junior College Libraries, 281, 460
"Comparative Analysis of Citation Studies, Swept Use, and ISI's Impact Factors as Tools for Journal Deselection," 478
"A Comparative Periodical Use Study," 162
"Comparing Quarterly Use Study Results for Marginal Serials at Oregon State University," 139
"A Comparison between Library Holdings and Citations," 288
"Comparison of Journal Coverage in *Psychological Abstracts* and the Primary Health Sciences Indexes," 451
"Comparison of Library Collections in Geology," 381
"Comparison of Peer and Citation Assessment of the Influence of Scientific Journals," 490
"Computer Assisted Periodicals Selection," 443
"Computer Techniques for Studying Coverage, Overlaps, and Gaps in Collections," 601
"Conducting a Serials Review Project," 472

"Conferences: The RLG Conspectus and Collection Evaluation," 362
Conservation Administration News, 340
"The Conspectus: Issues and Questions," 320
"Conspectus and the National Library of Australia," 370
"The Conspectus as a Collection Development Tool for College Libraries and Consortia," 349
"Conspectus as a Tool for Art Libraries in Australia," 369
"Conspectus at the Coal-Face," 357
"The Conspectus Experience," 353
"The Conspectus in Alaska and How We're Using It," 379
"The Conspectus in North America and Western Europe," 359
"Conspectus in Scotland: Report to SCONUL," 358
Conspectus in Scotland Newsletter, p.122
Conspectus in the British Library, 352
"Conspectus in the United Kingdom," 354
"Conspectus Reconsidered," 363
Contemporary Sociology, 48, 53
Cook, Jean G., 174, 405
Cook, Kevin L., 155-56
"Cooperative Collection Development – National Trends and New Tools," 326
"Coordinating Collection Development: The RLG Conspectus," 327
Coordinating Cooperative Collection Development: A National Perspective, 376, 380, 384, 390
Corbin, John, p.ix
"Core Analysis in Collection Management," 125
"Core Journal Lists for Behaviorally Disordered Children," 445
"Core Journals in Anthropology: A Review of Methodologies," 446
"Core Lists of Periodicals Selected by Faculty Reviewers," 447
"Core Literature of the Two Social Psychologies," 267
Corrall, Sheila, 355, 463
"Cost-Cutting Uses of New SCISEARCH Feature," 602

236 / AUTHOR/TITLE INDEX

"Cost-Per-Use Method for Evaluating the Cost-Effectiveness of Serials," 424
"Counteracting the Divergence Between Professional Accreditation and the Evaluation of Library Science Collections," 65
Cox, Barbara, 458
Craig, Daza Fox, 584
"Crerar/Chicago Library Merger," 206
Criminology, 540, 542
Crissinger, John D., 261
"A Critical Analysis and Evaluation of Russian Language Monographic Collections at the University of Alaska-Fairbanks," 101
"Cross-Disciplinary Citation Patterns in the History of Technology," 313
Crowe, Cathryn, 46
Cullars, John, 299-300
Cumulative Index to Nursing and Allied Health Literature, 451
Curley, Arthur, 5
Current Contents: Social & Behavioral Sciences, 549-75
"Current International Newspapers," 419
Current Issues in Fine Arts Collection Development, 36
"Current Legal Periodicals," 140
"Current Social Theory," 53
Currie, William W., 281

Dannelly, Gay N., 399
Das, Binod Bihari, 278
Das Deutsche Buch, 219
Database, 602
Daugherty, Robert Allen, 594
Davis, C. Roger, 4
Davis, Charles H., 531
Davis, Gordon B., 505
De Klerk, Ann, 162
De Prospo, Ernest R., 184
Decker, David L., 542
Deffenbaugh, James T., 283
Degener, Christie T., 585
Del Frate, Adelaide A., 586
Delendick, Thomas J., 302
Delman, Bruce S., 604

"A Delphi Rating of Real Estate Journals," 513
"Departmental Evaluation and Maintenance of the Library Sociology Collection," 35
"Design Issues for a Microcomputer-Based Collection Analysis System," 608
"Determining the Mutual Dependence between Two Disciplines by Means of Citation Analysis," 319
"Developing a Quantitative Formula for the Book Collection in Small Academic Technical Libraries," 242
"Developing a Scale of Comprehensiveness to Serve as a Collection Evaluation Criteria," 43
Developing Library and Information Center Collections, 6
"Development and Use of the RLG Conspectus," 334
"Development of Methodologic Tools for Planning and Managing Library Services," 201
Devin, Robin B., 48, 262-63
Dhawan, S. M., 441
DiCarlo, Mike, 55
Dillon, Martin, 608
Diodato, Virgil P., 415
"A Discipline-Specific Journal Selection Algorithm," 487
"Distribution of Middle Eastern Periodicals in the UK Libraries," 221
"The Distribution of Use of Library Materials," 115
"Document Delivery Capabilities of Major Biomedical Libraries in 1968," 202
"Documenting the Literature of Marine Biology," 571
"Doing the Unthinkable," 477
Doke, E. Reed, 506, 511
Dombrowski, Theresa, 282
Dometrius, Nelson C., 485
Dorn, Knut, 218
Drexel Library Quarterly, 31, 60, 598, 600
"Duplication in Library Collections," 185

Author/Title Index / 237

"Dutch Cooperative Collection Development and the Conspectus Method," 360

Eaglesfield, Jean T., 381
Eales, Nellie B., p.97
Eckman, Charles, 459
Economics Abstract International, 452
"Editing the RLG Conspectus to Analyze the OCLC Archival Tapes of Seventeen Texas Libraries," 330
"Editorial Policy and the Assessment of Quality among Medical Journals," 436
"EGOS: A Study of Stock Overlap in the Libraries of the Universities of Glasgow and Edinburgh," 212
"The 80/20 Rule," 112
Elder, Nancy I., 416
Elenchus Bibliographicus Biblicus, 319
Eliot, Charles W., p.37
Elliott, Robert H., 545-46
Elzy, Cheryl Asper, 58
"An Empirical Method for Determining Core Psychology Journals," 528
Encyclopedia of Library & Information Science, 386
Encyclopedia of Social Work, 497
English Historical Review, 308
English Studies, 305
"Epistemological Dead End and Ergonomic Disaster?" 387
ERIC, p.xiv
"Establishment of Standards for Bookstock in West African University Libraries," 247
"Estimating Collection Size Using the Shelf List in a Science Library," 68
"Evaluating a Periodicals Collection," 460
Evaluating Acquisitions and Collection Management, 339
"Evaluating Collections by Their Use," 117
"Evaluating Journal Publications of Marketing Professors," 501
"Evaluating Journals: Can Faculty Do the Job?" 416
"Evaluating Periodicals," 444

"Evaluating Research Library Collections in Psychology," 342
"Evaluating Subject Collections," 397
"Evaluating the Accounting Professor's Journal Publications," 502
"Evaluating the Collection of a Two-Year Branch Campus by Using Textbook Citations," 281
"Evaluating the Conspectus Approach for Smaller Library Collections," 377
"Evaluating the Finance Journals," 503
"Evaluating the Geoscience Collection," 346
"Evaluating the Management Journals," 504
"Evaluating the Sociology Collection," 48
"Evaluation," 6, 18
"Evaluation: Problems of Criteria and Methodology," 24
"Evaluation and Analysis," 27
"Evaluation by Type of Library," 17
"Evaluation of a Geoscience Library Collection," 348
"Evaluation of a Scholarly Collection in a Specific Subject Area by Bibliographic Checking," 51
"Evaluation of Biochemical Journals by Citation Indexing," 547
"Evaluation of Current Periodical Subscriptions in the Freshwater Institute Library," 466
"An Evaluation of East Asian Collections in Selected Academic Art Libraries in the United States," 220
"Evaluation of In-House Use," 106
"An Evaluation of Journals in Physical Education, Athletics, and Sports," 578
"Evaluation of Library Collection Support for an Off-Campus Degree Program," 289
"Evaluation of Materials Availability," 175
"Evaluation of Periodicals," 488
"Evaluation of Scientific Journals," 494
"Evaluation of the Collection," 3, 16, 19
"Evaluation of the Collection: Analysis of Use," 118

238 / AUTHOR/TITLE INDEX

"Evaluation of the Collection: Formulae, Expert Judgment and Use of Bibliographies," 15
"Evaluation of the Extent to Which the Holdings of Four United States Research Libraries Would Have ...," 222
"Evaluation of the Government Documents Collection," 33
"An Evaluation of the Music Collection at Louisiana State University," 99
"An Evaluation of the Vertebrate Zoology Collection at the R. M. Cooper Library," 92
"Evaluations of Accounting Journal and Department Quality," 518
"An Evaluative Checklist for Reviewing a College Library Program," 248
Evans, A. J., 480
Evans, Arthur, 533-34
Evans, G. Edward, 6
Evans, Josephine King, 137
Excerpta Medica, 454
" 'Existing Collection Strength' and Shelflist Count Correlations in RLG's Conspectus for Music," 329
Extejt, Marian M., 507
Eyman, David H., 113

F & S Index, 450
Fabianic, David A., 522
Fabrizio, Nancy A., 417
Fachan, Karen W., 39, p.xiv
"Faculty Audiovisual Materials Use and Collection Planning at Georgia State University," 103
"A Faculty Response from the University of Pittsburgh," 159
Faigel, Martin, 7
"Failure in the Library," 188
Fallon, Marcia, 460
Fang, Min-Lin Emily, 548
Farrell, David, 383-85, 398
Faulkner, Ronnie W., 246
Fedunok, Suzanne, 372
Feingold, Alan, 523
Fenichel, Carol H., 605
Fennell, Janice C., 113, 135, 204, 208, 416
Ferguson, Anthony W., 323-25
Ferguson, Douglas K., 376

Ferl, Terry Ellen, 178
Fertility & Sterility, 256
Finifter, David H., 481
Fitzgibbons, Shirley A., 303
Fjallbrant, N., 138
Flesch, Juliet, 219
Flynn, Roger R., 162-63
Forcier, Peggy J., 373-74
"Format Citation Patterns and Their Implications for Collection Development in Research Libraries," 257
"Forms of Literature Studies in Agricultural Economics," 315
Forney, Christopher D., 304
Franco, Elaine A., 422, 456
Franklin, Hugh, 139
Freshwater Biology, 581
Frohmberg, Katherine A., 179
"From Periodicals Budget Cuts to Management Information Systems," 589
Fuseler-McDowell, Elizabeth, 264, 571
Fussler, Herman H., 114
Futas, Elizabeth, 8, 28, 30, 42
Future of the Journal; Proceedings of the Sixteenth Meeting of the Geoscience Information Society, 474

Gabriel, Michael R., 587
Gallagher, Kathy E., 88
Galvin, Thomas J., 164
Garand, James C., 524
Gardner, Jeffrey J., 386
Gardner, Richard K., 9
Garfield, Eugene, 549-76, p.98
Garland, Kathleen, 43
Gasset, Ortega y, p.x
"Gathering Useful Circulation Data in the Documents Department," 156
Geahigan, Priscilla, 71
Genaway, David C., 64, 349, 372
"Geographers' Rankings of Foreign Geography and Non-Geography Journals," 534
"German Collecting in the Social Sciences in Australian Libraries," 219
Giles, Michael W., 525-26
Gilman, Lelde B., 342
Gjerdet, Nils Roar, 149

Gleason, Maureen L., 10, 283
Glenn, Norval D., 527
Godden, Irene P., 39, p.xiv
Goehner, Donna M., 447
Goldblatt, Margaret A., 140
Goldhor, Herbert, 15, 22, 47, 58-59
Gordon, Martin, 141
Gordon, Michael D., 486
Gorman, G. E., 11-13
"Government Documents Usage in an Academic Library," 154
"Government Documents Use by Superintendent of Documents Number Areas," 157
Government Information Quarterly, 296
"Government Publications as Bibliographic References in the Periodical Literature of International Relations," 296
Government Publications Review, 33-34, 154, 157-58, 255
Gozzi, Cynthia I., 339
Granade, Warner, 195
Grant, Joan, 324-25
"Graphing: A Tool for Collection Development," 82
"Greater Midwest Regional Medical Library Network and Coordinated Cooperative Collection Development," 344
Greenwade, George D., 517
Grefsheim, Suzanne, 461
Griffith, Belver C., 292
Grimes, David, 375
Griscom, Richard, 265
"Groping toward National Standards for Collection Evaluation," 341
Gross, E. M., 177, 266, p.97
Gross, P. L. K., 177, 266, p.97
Grover, Mark L., 14
Guide for Written Collection Policy Statements, 321, p.120
"Guide to Collection Evaluation through Use and User Studies," 4
Guide to the Evaluation of Library Collections, 1, 4, 37, pp.x, xiv
"Guidelines for Audiovisual Services in Academic Libraries," 228
"Guidelines for Branch Libraries in Colleges and Universities," 227
"Guidelines for Extended Campus Library Services," 232
"Guidelines for Library Services to Extension/Noncampus Students," 233
Guidelines for the Formation of Collection Development Policies, 321, 328
"Guidelines for Two-Year College Learning Resources Programs (Revised), Part I," 237, 240, 252
"Guidelines for Two-Year College Learning Resources Programs (Revised), Part II," 238, 240, 252
Guilfoyle, Marvin C., 443
Gupta, M. G., 130
Guy, Wendell A., 142
Gwinn, Nancy E., 326-27
Gyeszly, Suzanne D., 89, 588

Hacken, Richard D., 78
Haley, Anne, 376
Hall, Blaine H., 79-80
Halperin, Michael, 448
Hamaker, Charles, 462
Hamilton, Scott, 509
Handbook of Latin American Studies, 87
"Handle with Care," 432
Hanger, Stephen, 350, 352
Hansen, Inge Berg, 143
Hanson, David J., 267
Hardesty, Larry, 165-66, 268, 418
Harer, John B., 588
Harrell, Jeanne, 89
"Has Poisson Been Kicked to Death?" 495
Hass, Stephanie C., 284
Hastreiter, Jamie Webster, 418
Hatfield, V. Sue, 196
Hayes, Robert M., 115
Haynes, Jack P., 528
He, Chunpei, 487
Heaney, Henry, 351
Heim, Kathleen M., 158
Heinzkill, Richard, 49, 305
Henderson, David, 418
Henderson, Madeline, 162, 440
Hendrickson, Kent, 236
Henige, David, 387
Henri, James, 364
Henty, Margaret, 364, 365
Herald of Library Science, 315, 579

AUTHOR/TITLE INDEX

Herubel, Jean-Pierre V. M., 90, 285-86, 306
Hewitt, Joe A., 374, 592, 607
Hickey, Doralyn J., 18
Historical Journal, 308
History of Commerce, p.30
History of International Law, p.30
Hitchcock, Eloise R., 307
Hodge, Stanley P., 419
Hodson, James, 609
"Holdings as a Measure of Journal Value," 434
Holicky, Bernard H., 116
Holland, Maurita Peterson, 420
Holt, Brian G. F., 352
Horacek, John, 366
Horne, Esther E., 37
Horwill, Cherry, 463-64
Hospital Literature Index, 451
"How Are Collections Evaluated?" 13
"How Are We Doing? Using a Materials Availability Survey in an Academic Library," 196
"How Many Psychology Journals Are Enough?" 268
Howard, Thomas P., 510
Howes, B. R., 11-13
Hughes, Katherine E., 56
Hulme, E. W., p.97
Human Development, 539
Human Relations, 516
Hunt, Richard K., 465
Hurd, Julie M., 313
Hyman, Ferne, 29

IAMSLIC at a Crossroads; Proceedings of the 15th Annual Conference, 32, 264, 453, 466, 478
IASLIC Bulletin, 547
"Identifying a Core Collection of Business Periodicals for Academic Libraries," 450
IEEE Transactions on Computers, 277
If You Want to Evaluate Your Library, 2, 15, 118-19, 183, 488
Ifidon, Sam E., 247, p.xiv
IFLA Journal, 241, 333
Illinois Libraries, 344
"Improving the Periodicals Collection through an Index Correlation Study," 457

"An In-Depth Collection Evaluation at the University of Manitoba Library," 62
"In-House Use," 119
"In the Eyes of the Beholder," 520
"Increases in Book Availability in a Large College Library," 179
Index Medicus, 437, 451, 454
Indian Journal of Agricultural Economics, 311, 315
Indian Library Association Bulletin, 278
Indiana Libraries, 10, 210, 286, 469
The Information Community: An Alliance for Progress; Proceedings of the 44th Annual Meeting, 440
Information Interaction; Proceedings of the 45th ASIS Annual Meeting, 43, 426
"Information Needs of Humanities Scholars," 108
Information Processing & Management, 205, 254, 487
Information Research: Research Methods in Library and Information Science, 494
Information Retrieval & Library Automation, 610
Information Science Abstracts, 425, 448, p.xiv
Information Technology & Libraries, 215, 583, 611, 614, 616
INSPEL, 221
" 'Instructions to Authors' Section as an Aid in Serials Collection Development," 437
"The Interdisciplinary Use of Physics Journals," 603
Interlending & Document Supply, 146
Interlending Review, 136, 495
"Internal Uses of the RLG Conspectus," 323, 324
"The International Agricultural Collection of the Pennsylvania State University Libraries," 606
"International Crystallography Research," 573, 574
International Federation of Library Associations and Institutions (IFLA), 241
International Journal of Information & Library Research, 222

Author/Title Index / 241

International Library Movement, 580
International Library Review, 294, p.xiv
"International Newspapers for U.S. Academic Libraries," 476
International Nursing Index, 451
"International Variations in Perceptions of Accounting Journals," 514
Intner, Sheila S., 30
"An Investigation of Collection Support for Doctoral Research," 280
Irricab, 51
Irvine, Betty Jo, 144
"Is the Impact Factor a Meaningful Index for the Ranking of Scientific Research Journals?" 492
"Issues in Collection Development: Collection Evaluation," 8
Ives, Blake, 509
Ivins, Marilyn, 419

Jain, S. P., 441
JCR (*Journal Citation Reports*), 177, 429, 432, 441, 487
Jewett, Charles Coffin, 21, pp.30, 97
Johnson, Margaret Ann, 228
Johnson, Susan W., 610
Johnston, Christine, 207-8
Joncich, M. J., 16
Jones, Clyve, 308
Jones, John F., 529
Jones, Lois M., 529
Jones, William G., 194
Jordan, Robert T., 245
Joshi, Y., 287
"Journal Availability at the University of New Mexico," 174
"Journal Cancellations in University Libraries," 410
"Journal Citation Reports as a Deselection Tool," 275
Journal Citation Reports (*JCR*), 177, 429, 432, 441, 487
"Journal Citation Studies. 52. Acoustic Journals and Acoustic Research Activities," 572
"Journal Citation Studies. 53. Agricultural Sciences," 575
"Journal Citation Studies. 42. Analytical Chemistry Journals," 559

"Journal Citation Studies. 40. Anthropology Journals," 557
"Journal Citation Studies. 38. Arts and Humanities Journals Differ from Natural and Social Science Journals," 555
"Journal Citation Studies. 43. Astrosciences Journals," 560
"Journal Citation Studies. 33. Botany Journals, Part 1," 549
"Journal Citation Studies. 33. Botany Journals, Part 2," 550
"Journal Citation Studies. 44. Citation Patterns in Nursing Journals, and Their Most Cited Articles," 561
"Journal Citation Studies. 48. Developmental Biology Journals," 567
"Journal Citation Studies. 51. Down to the Sea Again," 571
"Journal Citation Studies. 38*. Earth Science Journals," 556
"Journal Citation Studies. 41. Entomology Journals," 558
"Journal Citation Studies. 50. Part 1. The Core Journals of Economics," 569
"Journal Citation Studies. 50. Part 2. Most-Cited Economics Papers and Current Research Fronts," 570
"Journal Citation Studies. 46. Physical Chemistry and Chemical Physics Journals. Part 1," 563
"Journal Citation Studies. 46. Physical Chemistry and Chemical Physics Journals. Part 2," 564
"Journal Citation Studies. 46. Physical Chemistry and Chemical Physics Journals. Part 3," 565
"Journal Citation Studies. 36. Pure and Applied Mathematics Journals," 553
"Journal Citation Studies. 45. Surgery Journals," 562
"Journal Citation Studies. 49. The Diverse Yet Essential Nutrients in the Information Diet of Nutrition Researchers," 568
"Journal Citation Studies. 34. The Literature of Dental Science vs. the Literature Used by Dental Researchers," 551

242 / AUTHOR/TITLE INDEX

"Journal Citation Studies. 52*. The Multifaceted Structure of Crystallography Research. Part 1," 573
"Journal Citation Studies. 52. The Multifaceted Structure of Crystallography Research. Part 2," 574
"Journal Citation Studies. 37. Using Citation Analysis to Study Neuroscience Journals," 554
"Journal Citation Studies. 35. Veterinary Journals," 552
"Journal Citation Studies. 47. Which Oceanography Journals Make the Biggest Waves," 566
"Journal Collection Cost-Effectiveness in an Academic Chemistry Library," 134
"Journal Collection Evaluation at the Medical College of St. Bartholomew's Hospital," 409
"Journal Collection Management as a Cumulative Advantage Process," 408
"Journal Deselection," 430
"Journal Deselection and Costing," 442
"Journal Deselection in a Biomedical Research Library," 465
"Journal Evaluation in a Health Sciences Library," 417
"Journal Evaluation Using Journal Citation Reports as a Collection Development Tool," 282
Journal of Academic Librarianship, 68, 77, 138, 155, 159, 167, 170-73, 186, 199, 290, 387, 541, 601
Journal of Accountancy, 510
Journal of Accounting Education, 502
Journal of Biblical Literature, 283
Journal of Computer Information Systems, 506
Journal of Documentation, 112, 438, 441, 491
Journal of Economic Literature, 532, 535
Journal of Economics & Business, 536
Journal of Education for Librarianship, 203
Journal of Education for Library & Information Science, 336
Journal of Educational Media & Library Sciences, 588

Journal of Finance, 512
Journal of Financial Research, 503, 512
Journal of Garden History, 306
Journal of Interdisciplinary History, 286
Journal of International Affairs, 296
Journal of Librarianship, 190, 298, 308, 350, 353, 356, 411, 425
Journal of Library Administration, 57, 324
Journal of Management, 507
Journal of Marketing Education, 501
Journal of Money, Credit & Banking, 512
Journal of Police Science & Administration, 522
Journal of Political Economy, 532
Journal of Politics, 272
Journal of Real Estate Research, 517
Journal of Risk & Insurance, 515
Journal of Rural Economics & Development, 255
Journal of Social History, 286
Journal of the Academy of Marketing Science, 508, 511
Journal of the American Chemical Society, 266
Journal of the American Society for Information Science, 145, 180, 189, 271, 274, 302, 486, 490
Journal of the American Statistical Association, 278
Journal of the American Veterinary Medical Association, 152
Journal of the History of Ideas, 286
Journal of the Hong Kong Library Association, 529
"Journal Preferences of Management Teaching Faculty," 499
"Journal Prestige and Quality of Sociological Articles," 493
"Journal Prestige in Public Administration," 545
"Journal Rankings and Selection," 491
"Journal Rankings by Citation Analysis in Health Sciences Librarianship," 548
"Journal Rankings from Citation Studies," 497
"Journal Review in an Environmental Design Library," 459
"Journal Use in a Clinical Librarian Program," 147

"Journal Weeding in Relation to Declining Faculty Member Publishing," 431
"Journals at Risk," 411
"Journals Read by ACRL Academic Librarians, 1973 and 1978," 544
Justice Quarterly, 543

Kaag, Cynthia Stewart, 38
Kaiden, Phyllis, 589
Kaniki, Andrew M., 606
Kantor, Paul B., 174-75, 177-82, 184, 186, 190, 192-94, 199-200, p.61
Karschamroon, Sunee, 438
Kaser, David, 248, p.84
Kaske, Neal K., 194
Katz, Bill, 44, 50
Katzko, M., 538
Kazlauskas, Edward John, 179
Keeping Current with Geoscience Information: Proceeding of the Fifteenth Meeting of the Geoscience Information Society, 261
"Keeping Track," 595
Kehoe, Kathleen, 91
Kelland, John Laurence, 92, 309
Kellogg, Martha, 263
Kent, Allen, 164, 167-69
Kent, Philip, 46
Kidd, Claen M., 346
Kieffer, Karen, 199
Kim, David U., 611
Kim, Mary T., 530
Kinyon, William R., 603
Kniesner, Daniel L., 64, 242
Knightly, John J., 209
Kohl, David F., 531
Kohn, Robert S., 43, 426
Kolner, Stuart J., 182
Konopasek, Katherine, 74
Korenic, Lyn, 144
Kountz, John, 612
Kreissman, Bernard, 37
Kreyche, Michael, 613
Kusnerz, Peggy Ann, 31

Laband, David N., 532
LaBorie, Tim, 448
Lal, Arjun, 577
Lambert, Peter J., 122, 464

Lancaster, F. Wilfrid, 2, 15-16, 51, 58, 83, 105-6, 117-19, 175, 183, 293, 421, 488, p.x
The Landscape of Literatures: Use of Subject Collections in a University Library, 120
Larson, Jeffry, 393
Lauer, Joseph J., 70
Law Library Journal, 67, 140
Leach, J. Travis, 475
Lee, Ching-Tat, 93
Lee, Dae Choon, 590
Lee, David, 533-34
Lee, Kate, 284
Lein, Edward, 328
"Let the Buyer Be Aware," 405
Lewis, D. E., 288
LIBER Bulletin, 360
LIBER News Sheet, 358-59
"Liberal Arts College Library Acquisitions," 113
Libraries and the Literacy Challenge, 196
Libraries Unlimited, p.xiii
Library & Information Research News, 288
Library & Information Science, 314
Library & Information Science Abstracts, 425, pp.x, xiv, xv
Library & Information Science Research, 108, 184, 216, 260, 297, 309, 312, 434, 448-49
Library Acquisitions: Practice & Theory, 7, 26, 107, 160, 168, 262, 279, 293, 343, 364, 399, 442, 499, 586, 591, 593-94, 613
"Library Acquisitions Policy by Consultation Out of Conspectus," 365
"Library and Information Science Abstracting and Indexing Services," 448
Library Collections: Their Origin, Selection and Development, 9
"Library Collections and Academic Curricula," 209
Library Effectiveness: A State of the Art, 194
Library Herald, 130
Library Hi Tech, 612
Library Journal, 42, 164, 373, p.37
Library Literature, 435, pp.x, xiv

244 / AUTHOR/TITLE INDEX

Library Literature—The Best of ..., 39
"Library MARC Tapes as a Resource for Collection Analysis," 607
"Library Materials on the History of Christianity at Ohio State University," 97
Library of Congress Shelflist, 66
Library of Congress Subject Catalogs, 66
"Library Periodicals from Developing Countries," 425
Library Quarterly, 188, 213, 295, 300-301, 305, 497
Library Research, 55, 71, 115, 165, 214, 317
Library Resources & Technical Services, 4, 39, 42, 62-63, 66, 100, 111, 206, 291, 330, 383, 385, 398, 401
Library Review, 191
"Library Services to the Academically Disadvantaged in the Public Community College," 229
Library Software Review, 609
"Library Support of Faculty Research at the Branch Campuses of a Multi-Campus University," 290
Library Trends, 3, 17, 28, 30, 81, 248-49, 252
Libri, 51, 59, 95, 132, 247, 311, 319, 351
Liebowitz, S. J., 535
"Limiting a Periodicals Collection in a College Library," 467
Lincoln, Tamara, 94, 101
Line, Maurice B., 258, 269, 310, 489
"List-Checking as a Method for Evaluating Library Collections," 47
"List-Checking in Collection Development," 50
Litchfield, Charles A., 121
Literary History of the United States, 100
LLA Bulletin, 99, 462
"Local Conspectus Applications," 596
Lockett, Barbara, 1
Lockway, Larry A., 590
Loertscher, David V., 2, 60
Logan-Peters, Kay, 422
"Longitudinal Studies of Book Availability," 194
"Looking at a Collection in Different Ways," 58

Lopez, Manuel D., 15, 22, 61
"The Lopez or Citation Technique of In-Depth Collection Evaluation Explicated," 61
Lucas, Thomas A., 394
Luke, Robert H., 506, 511
Lundin, Anne H., 50
Lunin, Lois F., 162, 440
Luquire, Wilson, 376, 380, 384, 390
Lynch, Beverly P., 241, 249
Lynch, Mary Jo, 273

Mabry, Robert H., 512, 516
MacEwan, Bonnie, 343
"Machine-Readable Files for Serials Management," 420
Mack, Thura, 449
Macleod, Murdo J., 159-60
Magazines for Libraries, 449, 469
Magrill, Rose Mary, 17-19, 270, 276, p.ix
Mahapatra, M., 311
"Maintaining a High-Quality, Cost-Effective Journal Collection," 439
Makino, Yasuko, 220
Makooi, Aref, 221
Malouin, Jean-Louis, 515, 536
"The Management and Social Science Literatures," 274
"Managing Business Periodicals Collections," 407
Manitoba Library Association Bulletin, 22, 316
Mankin, Carole J., 145, 406
Mansbridge, John, 184, p.61
Manual for the North American Inventory of Research Library Collections, 331
Maps in the Geoscience Community; Proceedings of the Nineteenth Meeting of the Geoscience Information Society, 346
"Marketing Journal Hierarchies," 511
Marley, Carol, 388
Marsh, Spencer S., 222
Marshall, K. Eric, 466
"Material Availability: A Study of Academic Library Performance," 177
"Materials Availability and Use," 197

Author/Title Index / 245

"Materials Provision Survey at the University of Ife Library, Nigeria," 96
"Materials Used in Historical Scholarship," 306
"Materials Used in the Research of State History," 307
Matheson, Ann, 353-56
Mathews, Eleanor, 104
McAllister, Paul R., 490
McBride, Ruth B., 537
McCabe, Gerald B., 37
McCain, Katherine W., 271, 312-13
McCandless, Patricia, 192
McClure, Charles R., 197
McDermand, Robert, 407
McGinty, Stephen, 272
McGrath, William E., 45, 81, 329
McLean, Ephraim R., 505, 509
McReynolds, Rosalee, 467
Meadows, A. J., 411
The Measurement and Evaluation of Library Services, 2, 16, 105-6, 175
"Measurement of Availability Using Patron Requests and Branching Analysis," 181
"The Measurement of Periodicals Use," 73
"Measures of User Evaluation at Two Academic Libraries," 55
"Measuring a Library's Capability," 203
Measuring Academic Library Performance: A Practical Approach, 197
"Measuring Academic Library Use," 126
"Measuring Collections Use at Virginia Tech.," 121
Measuring the Book Circulation Use of a Small Academic Library Collection, 128
Measuring the Circulation Use of a Small Academic Library Collection, 127
"Measuring the Relative Impact of Economics Books Publishers and Economics Journal," 532
"Measuring the Relative Impacts of Criminology and Criminal Justice Journals," 543
Medical Reference Services Quarterly, 605
"Meeting the Pricing Challenge," 462

Meneely, William E., 103
Meredith, Pamela, 461
Merry, Karen, 146
Merton, Robert, 408
"Methodological Problems in Assessing the Overlap Between Bibliographical Files and Library Holdings," 205
"A Methodology for Estimating the Size of Subject Collections, Using African Studies as an Example," 70
"Methods and Issues in Collection Evaluation Today," 7
"Methods of Collection Evaluation," 11
Metz, Paul, 120-21, 184, 273
Microcomputers for Information Management, 597, 608
Micros, Minis, and Geoscience Information; Proceedings of the Twentieth Meeting of Geoscience Information Society, 348
Mihel, Evan, 494
Milam, Carl, p.84
Miller, Arthur Jr., 128
Miller, Edward P., 442
Miller, George B., Jr., 20, 45, 277, 303
Miller, Naomi, 147
Miller, Robert C., 389
Miller, Ruth H., 210, 443
Miller, Tamara J., 211
Millson-Martula, Christopher A., 344, 423
Milne, Dorothy, 424, 468
Milne, Ronald, 357
Milne, Sally Jo, 469
Miranda, Michael A., 578
"Missing the Brass Ring in the Iron City," 171
"The Mission of a University Undergraduate Library," 234, 235
Mission of the Librarian, p.x
Miwa, Makiko, 314
Mizell, Francie, 525
MLA International Bibliography, 297, 300-301, 393
"A Model for Evaluating Scientific and Technical Journals from Developing Countries," 440
"A Model Methodology for Selecting Women's Studies Core Journals," 449

"Modeling Collection Overlap on a Microcomputer," 616
Modern Language Review, 305
Moffett, William A., 179
Mongeau, Deborah, 578
"Monograph Support Provided by the National Library of Medicine ...," 292
Moody, Marilyn K., 157
Moore, Anne, 471
Moore, Barbara, 211, 614
Moore, Nicholas L., 425
Morris, Jacquelin M., 230-31
Mosher, Paul H., 20-21, 87, 327, 364, 379, 390, 395, p.ix
Mosley, Madison, 229
Moulden, Carol M., 289
Mowat, Ian R. M., 212
"Multi-Method Strategies for Defining 'Core' Higher Education Journals," 519
"Multi-User Subjects, Multi-Subject Users," 122
"Multivariate Regression Models for Estimating Journal Usefulness in Physics," 438
Murfin, Marjorie E., 186
Musib, S. K., 311, 315
"The Myth of Accessibility," 186

Nakayama, Kazuhiko, 314
Narin, Francis, 490
"National Collections Inventory Project," 386
"The National Plan for Collections Inventories," 332
"A National Scheme for Collaboration in Collection Development," 390
"National Shelflist Count: A Historical Introduction," 401
"The National Shelflist Count: A Tool for Collection Management," 399
The National Shelflist Count, 98, 400
"The National Shelflist Count Project," 398
"The Nature and Uses of RLG Verification Studies," 395
Naylor, Maiken, 148
"NCIP, Conspectus Methodology and Canadian Health Science Collections," 382

NCIP: Means to an End; Minutes of the 109th Meeting, 320, 323, 334, 389, 391
"NCIP in Canada," 391
"NCIP in the United States," 389
NCIP News, p.122
"The NCIP Option for Coordinated Collection Management," 383
Neal, James G., 290
Neame, Laura, 470
Neeley, James D., Jr., 274
Nelson, Harriet, 71
Nelson, T. M., 538
New, Doris E., 280
New Jersey Libraries, 599
New York Times Information Bank, 452
New Zealand Libraries, 367
Newby, Jill, 345
Nichols, Julia A., 483
Nielsen, Donald A., 513
Niemeier, Martha W., 210
Nigerian Agricultural Journal, 255
Nikolai, Loren A., 510
Nimmer, Ronald J., 591
Nisonger, Thomas E., 22, 40, 61, 62, 291, 316, 330, p.xiv
Nobes, Christopher W., 514
"The Non-Use of Periodicals," 131
"The North American Collections Inventory Project (NCIP): Phase II Results in Indiana," 384
"The North American Collections Inventory Project," 385
"North American Inventory Project," 343
"NOTIS as a Collection Evaluation and Development Tool," 588
Nutter, Susan K., 592
Nuzzo, Nancy B., 329

Oberg, Larry R., 377
Oberhofer, Cecilia Alves, 440
Objective Performance Measures for Academic and Research Libraries, 178, 181
O'Brien, Nancy Patricia, 74
O'Brien, Robert M., 542
"Observations of Browsing Behavior in an Academic Library," 123

"OCLC/MARC Tapes and Collection Management," 611
O'Connell, Jon Brian, 95
The Off-Campus Library Services Conference Proceedings, 289
O'Herron, Virginia, 64, 242
Olaosun, Adebayo, 96
Olden, Anthony, 222
Olsen, Randy, 458
Olsrud, Lois, 471
Oltmanns, Gail, 268
"On Citations, Uses, and Informed Guesswork," 258
"1 Man—100 Votes," 464
"A One-Year Journal Use Study in a Veterinary Medical Library," 152
O'Neil, Ann L., 442
O'Neill, Edward T., 617
Online, 452
"Online Collection Evaluation Course by Course," 587
"Online Collection Statistics," 598
"Online Systems and the Management of Collections," 592
Orbis, 296
"Organization of Periodicals Collection Based on Citation Analysis," 278
"Original Language, Non-English Journals," 415
Orr, Richard H., 5, 184, 201-3, p.62
Ortopan, LeRoy D., 401
Osburn, Charles B., p.37
Ottersen, Signe, 41, pp.xiv, 83
Output Measures for Public Libraries, 197
Outreville, J. Francois, 515, 536
"Overlap and Description of Psychology Collections in Research Libraries," 204
"Overlap of Monographs in Public and Academic Libraries in Indiana," 216

Pacific Northwest Collection Assessment Manual, 378
"The Pacific Northwest Collection Assessment Project," 376
Pacific NW Collection Assessment & Development Newsletter, p.122
Palais, Elliot, 187
Palmer, J. P., 535
Palmer, Judith, 595
Palmer, Trevor, 146
Pao, Miranda Lee, 426-27, 487
Parkhurst, Carol A., 435
Paskoff, Beth M., 63
Paton, Barbara, 46
Patterns in the Use of Books in Large Research Libraries, 114
"Patterns of Access and Circulation in a Depository Document Collection Under Full Bibliographic Control," 158
"Patterns of Journal Use in a Departmental Library," 271
Patterson, David, 525
Payson, Evelyn, 614
Peasgood, Adrian N., 122
Peat, W. Leslie, 170
Pedersen, Wayne A., 82
Peery, J. Craig, 539
Penner, Rudolf Jacob, 203
"Perceived Quality of CIS/MIS Journals among Faculty," 506
"Perceived Quality of Fifty Selected Journals," 508
"Perceived Scholarship and Readership of Criminal Justice Journals," 522
"Perceptions of Marketing Journals," 500
"Periodical Citations in Aquatic Entology and Freshwater Benthic Biology," 581
Periodical List, 69
Periodical List Supplement, 69
"Periodical Prestige in Criminology and Criminal Justice," 540
"Periodical Use at a Small College Library," 141
"Periodical Use in a University Music Library," 265
"A Periodicals Access Survey in a University Library," 198
"Periodicals and Space Constraints," 469
"Periodicals Cancellation," 470
Periodicals in College Libraries, 418
"Periodicals Reviewing by Voting," 463
Peritz, Bluma C., 317
Perkins, David L., 428
Perrault, Anna H., 63, 99
Peters, Andrew, 444
Peterson, Richard A., 454
Petrarca, Anthony E., 43, 426

"Pharmacy Faculty Members' Exposure to Current Periodicals," 142
"The Philosophy Collection," 90
"Philosophy Dissertation Bibliographies and Citations in Serials Evaluation," 285
Phull, S. K., 441
Physics Abstracts, 441
Piccininni, James C., 615
Pierce, Sydney J., 338
Pike, Lee E., 472
Pinnell-Stephens, June, 596
Pinselik, Barbara P., 473
"The Planning and Implementation of Conspectus in Scotland," 356
PNLA Quarterly, 379, 596
"Political Science Publishers," 272
"Political Scientists' Evaluations of Sixty-Three Journals," 526
"Political Scientists' Journal Evaluations Revisited," 525
Poole, Eric D., 540
Porta, Maria A., 51
Potter, William Gray, 213-14, 616, p.74
Powell, Nancy, 367, 374, 378
"A Practical Journal Usage Technique," 76
"The Practice of Collection Development," 10
"Preservation Planning and the Conspectus at Yale University," 340
Preservers of the Past, Shapers of the Future; Proceedings of the Research Forum, 458
"Prestige of Journals in Criminology and Criminal Justice," 542
Pringle, R. V., 358
Pritchard, Alan, p.97
"Procedures for Collection Evaluation," 12
Proceedings from the 1982 Spring Meeting of the Nebraska Library Association, 422, 456
Proceedings of the First International Conference on Information Systems, 505, 509
Professional Geographer, 533-34
"Project CoEd," 100
Projects and Procedures for Serials Administration, 473
Promis, Patricia, 345

"A Proposed Method for Eliminating Titles from Periodical Subscription Lists," 259
Pruett, Nancy Jones, 261
PS: Political Science & Politics, 524-26
Psychological Abstracts, 451
Psychological Reports, 267
"Psychology Journal Usage," 537
"Public Administration Journal Prestige," 546

Qualitative Collection Analysis: The Conspectus Methodology, 322
"Qualitative/Quantitative Evaluation of Academic Library Collections," p.xiv
"Qualitative Ratings of Human Development Journals," 539
"Quality and Library Collections," 21
"Quantitative Approaches to Qualitative Collection Assessment," 52
"Quantitative Criteria for Adequacy of Academic Library Collections," 245
"Quantitative Standards for Two-Year Learning Resources Programs," 240
Quarterly Bulletin of the International Association of Agricultural Librarians & Documentalists, 143, 287, 347, 606

Radford, Neil A., 188
Raina, Roshan, 579
Randall, William M., p.84
"The Range of Subject Literatures Used by Humanities Scholars," 109
"Ranking and Evaluating the ARL Library Map Collections," 223
"Ranking Journals," 496, 529
"Ranking of Journals in Library and Information Science," 530
"Ranking of Journals in Phytopathology," 579
"Ranking of Periodicals in the Field of Soil Science," 577
"The Ranking of Real Estate Publications and Tenure Requirements at AACSB versus Non-AACSB Schools," 517
"Ranking of Research Journals in the Field of Physical Education," 580

Rao, Dittakavi, Nagasankara, 580
Rashid, Haseeb F., 189
"Rating of Scholarly Journals by Chairpersons in the Social Sciences," 538
"Ratings of Journals by ARL Library Directors and Deals of Library and Information Science Schools," 531
"Rationalization of Periodical Holdings," 138
"Rationalizing Library Acquisitions Policy," 287
Readers' Guide, 186, 457
"Readers Utilization of Journals in Maulana Azad Medical College Library," 130
"The Readership of the Current Periodical and Newspaper Collection in the Slavic and Baltic Division of the New York Public Library," 151
Real Estate Appraiser & Analyst, 513
"A Rebuttal," 167
Reed-Scott, Jutta, 4, 331, 359, 385
"Reference Collection Development Using the RLG Conspectus," 338
Reference Librarian, 338
Regoli, Robert M., 496, 540
"The Relationship between Journal Productivity and Quality," 435
"The Relationship between Literature Scatter and Journal Accessibility in an Academic Special Library," 421
"Relative Impact of Economics Journals," 536
"The Relative Importance of Journals Used in Finance Research," 512
"The Relative Importance of Journals Used in Management Research," 516
"Report on the Kent Study of Library Use," 160
"Reported Relative Value of Journals versus Use," 414
"The Representation of German Social Science Titles in Australian Libraries," 218
"Research and Publishing in Real Estate," 498
Research in Higher Education, 538

"Research Journal Usage by the Forestry Faculty at the University of Florida Gainesville," 284
"The Research Literature of Agricultural Economics," 294
Research Quarterly for Exercise & Sport, 580
"The Research Value of Siberia Content Monographs in Polar Collections of the University of Alaska-Fairbanks," 94
Resh, Vincent H., 581
Resource Sharing & Information Network, 376, 380, 384, 390
"Responsibilities of Technical Service Librarians to the Process of Collection Evaluation," 30
"Retrospective Collection Development in English Literature," 49
Review of Higher Education, 519
"A Review of Local Journal Use Studies," 153
Revill, D. H., 190-91
Rice, Barbara A., 429, 432
Richards, Daniel T., 32
Rindel, Gene E., 192
Riordan, Paul J., 149
RLG Collection Development Manual, 85
RLG Conspectus, 27
"The RLG Conspectus: Its Uses and Benefits," 325
"The RLG Conspectus Down Under," 364
"The RLG Conspectus French Literature Collections Assessment Project," 393
Robbins-Carter, Jane, 23
Robinson, Margaret G., 178
Robinson, William C., 33-34
Rochester, Maxine K., 215
Roeder, Christine S., 64
"Role of NCIP (National Collections Inventory Project)," 388
"The Role of Public Services in Collection Evaluation," 28
Roles and Responsibilities in Geoscience Information; Proceedings of the Eighteenth Meeting of the Geoscience Information Society, 225
Rooke, Su, 75
Rose, Robert F., 450

250 / AUTHOR/TITLE INDEX

Rosenberg, Betty, 24
Ross, Johanna, 123
Rowell, Unni Havem, 225
RQ, 104, 156
Russo-Martin, Elaine, 454
Rutstein, Joel, 324-25

Sanders, Nancy P., 617
Sandler, Mark, 35, 52
Saracevic, T., 186, 193
Sauer, Jean S., 150
Saunders, Stewart, 71
Saye, Jerry D., 292
Schad, Jasper G., 167, 171
Schless, Arthur P., 202
Schmidt, Jannie, 364, 368
Schmidt, Sherrie, 597
Schockmel, Richard, 458
Scholarly Publishing, 110, 481, 496
SCI JCR, 275, 482
Science, 266
Science & Technology Libraries, 91, 142, 242, 304, 415, 429-31
Science Citation Index, 148, 259, 453, p.98
Science Citation Index JCR, 148
"Science Collections in Community College Libraries," 371
Science Progress, p.97
Scientific Journals: Issues in Library Selection and Management, 431-32
Scott, Marianne, 332, 391
Scott, Mary Woods, 474
"Searching the Scriptures," 283
Sears, Jean L., 157
Seavey, Charles A., 223
Segal, Judith A., 430
Sekerak, Robert J., 451
"Selecting Livestock Periodicals through Citation Analysis Technique," 254
"Selection and Evaluation of Chemistry Journals," 429
"Selection of Scientific Journals," 441
Sellen, Mary K., 541
"Serial Cancellation Programs in Academic Libraries in Missouri," 422
"The Serial/Monograph Ratio in Research Libraries," 263
Serials, 595

Serials '83: Proceedings of the UK Serials Group Conference, 480
Serials Control and Deselection Projects, 404
"Serials Cut (and the Use of a Blunt Knife)," 480
"Serials De-Acquisition," 473
"Serials Deselection," 412
"Serials Deselection Method," 456
Serials Librarian, 69, 74, 75, 131, 133, 139, 141, 150-51, 163, 265, 268, 285, 412-13, 423, 428, 437, 443, 467-68, 470, 477, 479, 578, 589
Serials Review, 73, 148, 417, 424, 433, 475, 585
"Serials Review and the Three-Year Cancellation Project at the University of Arizona Library," 475
"Serials Review in the Humanities," 471
"A Serials Review Program Based on Journal Use in a Departmental Geology Library," 474
"Service at San Jose State University," 199
"Seven Years of Cancellations at Georgia Tech," 479
Sharplin, Arthur D., 512, 516
Shaw, Debora, 216
Shaw, J. Margaret, 369
Shaw, W. M., Jr., 76, 186, 193-94
Sheaves, Miriam Lyness, 474
"Shelf Availability," 183
Sheriff, Ian, 409
Shichor, David, 542
Shiels, Richard D., 84, 97
Shilliff, Karl A., 499
Shoemaker, Sarah, 29
Show-Me Libraries, 341
Siemaszkiewicz, Wojciech, 151
Sigelman, Lee, 484
Signori, Donna L., 396
Signs, 449
Sill, Lois, 595
Simon, Julian L., 114
"Simple Citation Analysis and the Purdue History Periodical Collection," 286
"A Simple Objective Method for Determining a Dynamic Journal Collection," 406
Singer, Loren, 36
Singleton, Alan, 491

Sinha, Reeta, 439
Slater, Jack, 598
Slote, Stanley J., p.37
Smith, Barbara J., 290
Smith, Charles A., 517
Smith, Charles R., 89
Smith, Jonathan E., 507
Smith, Patricia A., 39, p.xiv
Smith, Peggy C., 544
Smith, Rita, 195
Smith, Thomas E., 275, 282
Snow, Marina, 98
Social Casework, 497
Social Science Citation Index, 535, pp.xv, 98
Social Science Citation Index Journal Citation Reports, 48, 258-59, 269, p.xiv
Social Science Information Studies, 310
Social Science Quarterly, 484-85
Social Sciences & Humanities Index, 295
Social Service Review, 497
Social Work, 497
Sociological Abstracts, 48
"Some Behavioral Patterns of Library Users: The 80/20 Rule," 129
"The Sources of Canadian History," 316
Southeastern Librarian, 90
Spornick, Charles, 339
Spurlock, Sandra, 174, 181
Sridhar, M. S., 124
SSCI, 274
SSCI JCR, 282, 459, 483, 486, 521
St. Clair, Gloriana, 270, 276, 597
Stack, Steven, 543
Stam, David H., 333-35
"Standards for College Libraries" (1975), 243, 248
"Standards for College Libraries" (1982), 248
"Standards for College Libraries, 1985," 230
"Standards for College Libraries, 1986," 231, 246, 253
"Standards for Community, Junior and Technical College Learning Resources Programs," 239
"Standards for Two-Year College Learning Resources Programs," 240
Standards for University Libraries, 241
"Standards for University Libraries," 236

"Standards for University Libraries" (1979), 236, 249
Stankus, Tony, 431-32
Stark, Marilyn M., 346
"Statistical Assumption-Making in Library Collection Assessment," 78
"Statistical Collection Management Analysis of OCLC-MARC Tape Records," 614
"Statistical Determination of Bound Volume Journal Holdings in a Science Library," 69
Statistical Theory & Methods Abstract, 278
Stein, Elida B., 91
Stelk, Roger Edward, 83, 293
Stenstrom, Patricia, 537
Stephens, Dennis, 348, 379-81
Stern, Madeleine, 318
Stevenson, W. C., 518
Stielow, Frederick J., 336-37
Stiffler, Stuart A., 125
Stine, Diane, 473
"A Stitch in Time: The Alaska Cooperative Collection Development Project," 380
Strain, Paula Meise, 584
Stroyan, Sue, 217
"A Structural Analysis of the Literature of Sociology," 295
"The Structure of Social Science Literature as Shown by Large-Scale Citation Analysis," 310
Stubban, Vanessa L., 347
Stubbs, Kendon, 250
"Studies of Collection Overlap," 214
"A Study of Collection Overlap in the Southwest Indiana Cluster of SULAN," 210
Stueart, Robert D., 20, 45, 277, 303
"Subject and Longitudinal Use of Books by Indian Space Technologists," 124
"Subject Collection Evaluation, Quantitative and Qualitative," 93
"Subject Dispersion Studies in Agricultural Economics," 311
"Subject and Objective Measures of Journal Stature," 485
Subramanyam, Kris, 277, p.178

"Suggestions for Formulating Collection Development Policy Statements for Music Score Collections in Academic Libraries," 328
"Survey of Major Library Collections in the Geosciences in the State of Victoria, Australia," 225
"Survey of Periodical Use in an Academic Art Library," 144
"Survey of the Cost-Effectiveness of Serials," 468
"Surveying Non-Usage of Serials," 75
Swartz, B. J., 599
Swigger, Keith, 433
Swisher, Robert, 544
"System Statistics from the Library Computer System (LCS) at the University of Illinois," 594
Systematic Botany, 302
"A Systematic Evaluation of Publications for Promotion of MIS Academics," 505

"Tailoring Periodical Collections to Meet Institutional Needs," 604
Tallman, Karen Dalziel, 475
Taranto, Cheryl, 99
Taylor, Celianna I., 43, 426
Taylor, Roger, 492
Teaching Sociology, 12, 35
Technical Services Quarterly, 207, 447
Technology & Culture, 313
Teevan, James J., 493
Tennessee Historical Quarterly, 307
"A Test of Two Citation Checking Techniques for Evaluating Political Science Collections ...," 291
Tezla, Kathy E., 338
Thaxton, Lyn, 103
"Theatre Arts Collection Assessment," 98
"Think Globally — Act Locally," 335
Thomas, D. A., 56
Thompson, Laurie L., 455
Thompson, Ronelle K. H., 196
Tibbo, Helen R., 336-37
Tiblin, Mariann, 398
Tiffany, Bill, 424, 468
"Title Overlap," 211

Titles Classified by the Library of Congress Classification: National Shelflist Count, 1981, 402
Titles Classified by the Library of Congress Classification: National Shelflist Count, 1985, 403
Tjoumas, Renee, 37, 65
Todorov, Radosvet, 494
Tolliver, Don L., 211
"A Tool for Comparative Collection Analysis," 63
Townley, Charles T., 600
"Tracking Periodical Usage in a Research Library," 137
"Translating the Conspectus," 339
Treadwell, Jane, 339, 414, 597
Triplehorn, Julia, 348, 381
Trochim, Mary Kane, 126-28
Trubkin, Loene, 452
Trueswell, Richard W., 129, 145, 152, 172
Try, Eleane Hobbs, 508
Tudor-Silovic, Neva, 494
Tuttle, Marcia, 174, 405
"Two-Year College Learning Resources Standards," 252
"Two-Year College Libraries," 244
"Tying the Curriculum to Book Collection Development," 64

Ueda, Shuichi, 314
Ulrich's, 434, 438, 447, 457
"Undergraduate Library Availability Study 1975-1977," 195
"Undergraduate Term Paper Citation Patterns by Disciplines and Levels of Course," 270
"Undergraduate Term Paper Citations," 276
"University Libraries: Standards and Statistics," 250
"University Library Collections of Accounting Periodicals," 224
"University Library Standards," 249
University of Chicago Library, 114
"The University of Pittsburgh Study of Journal Usage," 163
"Unused Current Issues," 150
Urbancic, Frank R., 224
Urquhart, John A., 495
"Use by Humanists of University Press Publications," 110

Author/Title Index / 253

"Use Involvement in Journal De-Selection," 461
"Use of a University Library Collection," 164
"Use of Citation Data for Periodicals Control in Libraries," 269
"Use of Citation Data to Evaluate Serials Subscriptions in an Academic Library," 433
"The Use of Government Documents by Researchers in Agricultural Economics ... Nigeria," 255
"Use of Journal Citations in Theses as a Collection Development Methodology," 261
Use of Library Materials; The University of Pittsburgh Study, 169
"Use of Library Materials at a Small Liberal Arts College," 165
"Use of Library Materials at a Small Liberal Arts College: A Replication," 166
"The Use of Microcomputers for Collection Evaluation," 609
"The Use of Periodical Literature in a Norwegian Dental Library," 149
"Use of Periodicals by Humanities Scholars," 133
"Use of Periodicals in Physics in Delhi University Science Library," 132
"The Use of Reach Libraries," 170
"The Use of Serial Titles in Libraries with Special Reference to the Pittsburgh Study," 161
"Use of Serials at the British Library Lending Division in 1983," 146
"The Use of Serials at the British Library Lending Division in 1980," 136
"The Use of Shelflist Samples in Studies of Book Availability," 83
"Use of Textbooks in Evaluating the Collection of an Undergraduate Library," 293
"Use of the Danish Veterinary and Agricultural Library ...," 143
"Use of the RLG Conspectus as a Tool for Analyzing and Evaluating Agricultural Collections," 347
"A Use Statistic for Collection Management: The 80/20 Rule Revisited," 107
"Use Statistics: A Planetary View," 586
"Use Studies and Serials Rationalization," 423
"Use Studies of Library Collections," 111
"A Use Study of an Academic Library Reference Collection," 104
"Use Study of *Excerpta Medica* Abstract Journals," 454
"User Criteria for Evaluation of Library Service," 57
User Surveys and Evaluation of Library Services, 187, 195
"Using a Turnkey Automated System to Support Collection Assessment," 582
"Using an Automated Serials System to Assist with Collection Review and Cancellations," 585
"Using an Online Comprehensive Library Management System in Collection Development," 590
"Using Core Journals to Justify Subscriptions and Services," 453
"Using dBaseIII+ to Create a Serials Review List," 597
"Using SPSS to Analyze Book Collection Data," 600
"Using the Higher Education General Information System (HEGIS) to Enhance Collection Development Decisions in Academic Libraries," 615
"The Utility of a Recommended Core List," 77

Van Heijst, Jacob, 360
Van House, Nancy A., 197
Veenstra, Robert J., 152-53
"Verification Studies," 392
"Verifying the Conspectus," 394
"The Victorian Chemistry Conspectus Pilot Project," 366
Vidor, David L., 42
Vocino, Michael, 476
Vocino, Thomas, 545-46
Voigt, Melvin J., 22, 173, 251
"Volume Equivalents of Microforms— A Question," 67
Voos, Henry, 25

Wainwright, Eric, 46, 364, 370
Waite, Marjory A., 585

AUTHOR/TITLE INDEX

Walcott, Rosalind, 225
Walker, Gay, 340
Wallace, Danny P., 434-35
Wallace, James O., 252, p.83
Walter, Pat L., 477
Watson, Paula D., 158
Watson, William, 198
Webb, William, 100
Weber, Richard P., 518
Wedgeworth, Robert, 126
"Weed It and Reap," 428
Weeding and Maintenance of Reference Collections, 338
Weibel, Stuart L., 617
Weil, Beth T., 197
Weinstock, Irwin, 501-4
Weisheit, Ralph A., 496
Welch, Eric C., 182
Weller, Ann C., 436-37
West, C. Eugene, 94, 101
West Virginia Libraries, 246
"West Virginia Public Colleges and the Latest ACRL Standards," 246
"Western European Interest in Conspectus," 351
Whaley, John H., Jr., 66, 341
"What Are the Major Journals That Members of ARIA Read?" 515
"What Constitutes a 'Good' Collection?" 42
"What Is Collection Evaluation?" 13
"What's in a Library?" 612
"Where Does the Money Go?" 135
"Which Medical Journals Have the Greatest Impact?" 576

White, Howard D., 397, 448, 601
White, Phillip M., 246, 253
Whitehead, Derek, 102, 364
Whitlatch, Jo Bell, 199, 407
"Who Wins? Who Loses? User Success and Failure in the State Library of Victoria," 176
"Who's Using What?" 262
Wiberley, Stephen E., Jr., 497
Wible, Joseph G., 478
Wiemers, Eugene, Jr., 26
Wilkes, Adeline, 433
Williams, Doris, 453
Williamson, Marilyn L., 479
Wilson, Wayne R., 513
Wilson Library Bulletin, 129
Winter, Michael F., 53
Wood, Richard, 349
Woods, Pamela Carr, 308
Woodward, Hazel, 480
Wooster, Harold, 162, 440
World Politics, 296
Wortman, William A., 27
Wright, Gerald C., Jr., 526
Wright, James C., 153
"Writing the Collection Assessment Manual," 80
Writings in American History, 427
Wulff, Yvonne, 200

Yitzhaki, Moshe, 319
Young, Arthur P., 273
Young, Lily Liu, 460

Zweizig, Douglas L., 23

Subject Index

AACSB (American Assembly of Collegiate Schools of Business), p.xvii
  journal ranking, 517
AALL (American Association of Law Libraries), p.xvii
AALS (American Association of Law Schools), p.xvii
ABA (American Bar Association), p.xvii
ABN (Australian Bibliographic Network), p.xvii
Academic libraries
  collection evaluation, p.xi
  standards, p.84
Academically disadvantaged library service, p.84
  standards, 229
Accounting periodicals
  journal ranking, 502, 510, 514
  overlap studies, 224
ACM. *See* Associated Colleges of the Midwest
ACML (Association of Canadian Map Librarians), p.xvii
Acoustics, journal ranking, 572
Acquisitions statistics, 56
ACRL (Association of College and Research Libraries), p.xvii
AEA (American Economic Association), p.xvii
AECT (Association for Educational Communications and Technology), p.xvii
African books, overlap study, 222
African studies, 70
Agricultural economics, citation studies, 294, 311, 315
Agriculture
  citation study, 255
  journal ranking, 575
  online searching, 606
AIDS, citation study, 304

ALA. *See* American Library Association
Alaska, Pacific Northwest Conspectus, 379-80
Albion College library, Pacific Northwest Conspectus, 377
ALCTS (Association for Library Collections and Technical Services), p.xix
American Assembly of Collegiate Schools of Business (AACSB), p.xvii
  journal ranking, 517
American Association of Law Libraries (AALL), p.xvii
American Association of Law Schools (AALS), p.xvii
American Bar Association (ABA), p.xvii
American Economic Association (AEA), p.xvii
American Library Association (ALA), pp.xvii, 61-62
  Ralph R. Shaw Award for Outstanding Contribution to Library Literature, 16
American literature, citation studies, 260, 297
American Psychological Association (APA), p.xvii
American Revolution, serials evaluation, 426-27
American Risk and Insurance Association (ARIA), p.xvii
  journal ranking, 515
American Society for Information Science (ASIS), p.xvii
American Society for Public Administration (ASPA), p.xvii
AMIGOS Collection Analysis Service, 607, p.209
Analytical chemistry, journal ranking, 559

255

256 / SUBJECT INDEX

Ancient Near-East studies, citation study, 319
Annotations, p.xiii
Anthropology
  core journal identification, 446
  journal ranking, 557
APA (American Psychological Association), p.xvii
Aquatic entomology, journal ranking, 581
Archival tape, defined, p.223
ARIA (American Risk and Insurance Association), p.xvii
  journal ranking, 515
Arizona State University Libraries, availability study, 187
Arkansas State University, government documents use, 155-56
ARL. *See* Association of Research Libraries
ARL Collection Analysis project, 80
ARL libraries, overlap study, 223
Arnold and Marie Schwartz College of Pharmacy, periodical use study, 142
Art libraries
  overlap study, 220
  periodical use study, 144
  survey works, 31, 36
Arts and humanities, journal ranking, 555
ASIS (American Society for Information Science), p.xvii
ASLIB (Association of Special Libraries and Information Bureaux), p.xvii
ASPA (American Society for Public Administration), p.xvii
Associated Colleges of the Midwest (ACM), p.xvii
  defined, p.223
  model, use studies, 126
Association for Educational Communications and Technology (AECT), p.xvii
Association for Library Collections and Technical Services (ALCTS), p.xix
Association of Canadian Map Librarians (ACML), p.xvii
Association of College and Research Libraries (ACRL), p.xvii
Association of Research Libraries (ARL), pp.xvii, 120-21

Association of Special Libraries and Information Bureaux (ASLIB), p.xvii
Astrosciences, journal ranking, 560
Auburn University Veterinary Medical Library, periodical use study, 152
Audiovisual materials and services, 103, p.84
  standards, 228
  use studies, 103
Augustana College library, availability study, 196
Australia, RLG Conspectus, 361-66, 368-70
Australian Bibliographic Network (ABN), p.xvii
  overlap studies, 215
Australian libraries, overlap study, 218-19
Australian National University Library, RLG Conspectus, 365
Automated systems, 582-92
  acquisitions, 583
  ILL, 593
  Knox College Library, 583
  National Library of Medicine, 584
  NOTIS, 588
  Ohio State University Libraries, 591
  serials, 585
  St. Cloud State University, 590
  University of North Carolina at Chapel Hill, 585
Automation in collection evaluation, pp.209-10
Availability studies, 174-200, pp.61-62
  Arizona State University Libraries, 187
  Augustana College library, 196
  branching techniques, pp.61-62
  Case Western Reserve University, 180, 189, 193-94
  Liverpool Polytechnic Library Service, 190-91
  Oberlin College library, 179
  San Jose State University library, 199
  State Library of Victoria, 176
  University of British Columbia, 198
  University of California, Santa Cruz Library, 178
  University of Illinois at Urbana-Champaign library, 192

University of Illinois Health Sciences Center, 182
University of Minnesota Bio-Medical Library, 200
University of New Mexico Library, 174
University of Sydney Library, 188
University of Tennessee Undergraduate Library, 195
William Patterson College Library, 177

BASIC, 598
BCL (Books for College Libraries), p.xvii
Behaviorally disordered children, core journal identification, 445
Bellevue Community College, Pacific Northwest Conspectus, 371
Biblical studies, citation studies, 283, 319
Bibliographies
  citation studies, 298
  survey works, 38-41
Bibliometrics, p.97
  citation studies, 273
  defined, p.223
Biochemistry
  citation study, 309
  journal ranking, 547
Biology, journal ranking, 571
Biomedical, serials cancellation case study, 465
Biotechnology, 91
BLLD. *See* British Library Lending Division
BMLA (Bulletin of the Medical Library Association), p.xvii
Books for College Libraries (BCL), p.xvii
Botany, journal ranking, 549-50
Bradfordian distribution, defined, p.223
Branch campuses, citation study, 290
Branch libraries, standards, 226-27
Branching techniques, pp.61-62
Brigham Young University library, 80, 85
Brillouin information measure, 43
British Library Lending Division (BLLD), p.xvii
  journal ranking, 495
  periodical use studies, 136, 146

British Library, RLG Conspectus, 350, 352
Browsing behavior, use study, 123
Bulletin of the Medical Library Association (BMLA), p.xvii
Business periodicals
  core journal identification, 450, 452
  serials evaluation, 407
Business, journal rankings, 498-518

CALC (Charleston Academic Libraries Consortium), p.xvii
California State University at Sacramento, 98
California State University, Northridge, serials evaluation, 428
Canada, NCIP, 382, 391
Canadian history, citation studies, 316
Cancellation, p.178
Carnegie-Mellon University, Pittsburgh Study, 162
Case studies, p.30
  in single libraries, 84-102, p.30
Case Western Reserve Health Sciences Library, availability study, 189
Case Western Reserve University Libraries, 43, 76
  availability study, 180
Case Western Reserve University Sears Library, availability studies, 193-94
CASSI (Chemical Abstracts Service Source Index), p.xvii
  overlap studies, 207-8
CD-ROM (Compact-disc read-only memory), 608, 610, p.xvii
Central Plantation Crop Research Institute, citation study, 287
Central State University library, serials evaluation model, 444
Chalmers University of Technology, Sweden, periodical use study, 138
Charleston Academic Libraries Consortium (CALC), p.xvii
  RLG Conspectus, 349
Checklist method, 58, p.30
  defined, p.223
  English literature, 49
  irrigation collection, 51
  methods and methodology, 47-53
  social theory, 53
  sociology, 48

258 / SUBJECT INDEX

Chemical Abstracts Service Source Index (CASSI), p.xvii
  overlap studies, 207-8
Chemical physics, journal ranking, 563-65
Chemistry Division of Pacific Northwest Conspectus, RLG Conspectus, 366
Chemistry journals, serials evaluation, 429
Christianity, 84, 97
Ciliberti, Anne C., p.61
CIS (Computer information systems), p.xvii
Citation analysis, p.98
Citation rankings, pp.177-78
Citation studies, pp.37, 97-99
  agricultural economics, 294, 311, 315
  agriculture, 255
  AIDS, 304
  American literature, 260, 297
  Ancient Near-East studies, 319
  Biblical studies, 283, 319
  bibliography, 298
  bibliometrics, 273
  biochemistry, 309
  branch campuses, 290
  Canadian history, 316
  Central Plantation Crop Research Institute, 287
  citation analysis, 278-93
  DePauw University, 268
  deselection, 275
  doctoral research, 280
  ecology, 309
  English history, 308
  English literary journals, 305
  Firelands College, 281
  forestry, 284
  French and German literary monographs, 300
  garden history, 306
  general and miscellaneous, 254-77
  government documents, 255
  history, 286
  Indian Statistical Institute Library, 278
  Indiana University, 265, 268
  international relations, 296
  Italian and Spanish literary monographs, 301
  library science, 317
  limitations, p.98
  literary scholarship, 318
  livestock periodicals, 254
  Loughborough University, 288
  management literature, 274
  medical behavioral sciences, 292
  monographs, 299
  music, 265
  National Animal Production Research Institute, Nigeria, 254
  off-campus degree program, 289
  Pennsylvania State University libraries, 290
  philosophy, 285
  political science, 272, 291
  Pomona College, 266
  Purdue University, 285-86
  reproductive biology, 256
  science and technology, 277
  serial/monograph ratio, 263
  social psychology, 267
  social sciences, 274, 303, 310, 314
  sociology, 295
  state history, 307
  systemic botany, 302
  technology history, 312-13
  Temple University, 271
  textbooks, 279, 281, 293
  undergraduate term papers, 270, 276
  University of California, Irvine, 280
  University of Florida, Gainesville, 284
Citation-based, journal ranking, 481-84, 494, 497
Clapp-Jordan Formula, 22
  defined, p.223
  standards, 245
Classic articles, p.xi
Clemson University Library, 92
Client-centered, defined, p.223
Clinical medicine, periodical use study, 147
CLIP Notes, 418
Collection adequacy, 46
Collection assessment, 79-80
Collection evaluation
  academic libraries, p.xi
  annotations, p.xiii
  benefits, pp.ix-x
  boundaries of, p.x
  classic articles, p.xi
  defined, p.ix
  evaluation of serials, pp.xii-xiii
  macroevaluation, p.x

methodology, pp.xiv-xv
microevaluation, p.x
North American audience, p.xi
organization, pp.xii-xiv
other bibliographic works, p.xiv
scope, pp.xi-xii
selection and weeding, p.xii
special libraries, p.xi
Collection evaluation case studies
  biotechnology, 91
  California State University at Sacramento, 98
  Christianity history, 97
  Clemson University Library, 92
  Columbia University Library, 91
  engineering, 95
  French program, 96
  Louisiana State University, 99
  music, 99
  Newberry Library, 87
  Ohio State University Library, 84, 97
  ophthalmology, 88
  philosophy, 90
  Russian language monographs, 101
  Siberiana, 94
  social work, 93
  SPEC (Systems and Procedures Exchange Centers) kits, 85, p.226
  State Library of Victoria, 102
  Texas A & M University, 89
  theatre arts, 98
  University of Alaska-Fairbanks, 94, 101
  University of Cincinnati, 86
  University of Colorado, 100
  University of Guanajuato, 95
  University of Ife Library, Nigeria, 96
  University of Mississippi, 90
  vertebrate zoology, 92
  Washington University Medical Library, 88
  Western Australian Institute of Technology, 93
Collection mapping, 60
Collection profiling method, 63
Collection-centered
  defined, p.224
  versus client-center methods, p.1
Collective evaluations of two or more library collections, 218-25, p.75
College learning resources programs, standards, 237-40

College libraries
  serials evaluation, 418
  standards, 230-31, 243-44, 246, 248, 252-53, p.84
Colorado School of Mines, RLG Conspectus, 346
Columbia University Library, 91
Compact-disc read-only memory (CD-ROM), 608, 610, p.xvii
Computer information systems (CIS), p.xvii
Conspector, defined, p.224
Conspectus Online database, p.121
Conspectus, software, 596
Core analysis, use study, 125
Core collection, defined, p.224
Core journal identification, pp.178-79
  anthropology, 446
  behaviorally disordered children, 445
  business periodicals, 450, 452
  faculty reviewers, 447
  health care, 451
  library and information science, 448
  management, 452
  Marine Science Research Center SUNY-Stony Brook, 453
  psychology, 451
  women's studies, 449
Core lists, 77
Cornell College, use study, 125
Criminology and criminal justice, journal ranking, 522, 540, 542-43
Criteria, serials evaluation, p.150
Crystallography, journal ranking, 574
Curricular needs, 66
Curriculum-centered collection development, 64

Danish Veterinary and Agricultural Library, periodical use study, 143
dBaseIII+, 148, 597
DDC (Dewey Decimal Classification), pp.xvii, 121
Delhi University Libraries, periodical use study, 132
Dental science, journal ranking, 551
DePauw University
  citation studies, 268
  Pittsburgh Study, 165
Deselection, citation studies, 275

260 / SUBJECT INDEX

Design, architecture, and art collection, 86
Developing countries
   serials evaluation, 425
      models, 440
Developmental biology, journal ranking, 567
DeVry Institute of Technology, 64
Dewey Decimal Classification (DDC), pp.xvii, 121
Doctoral research, citation study, 280
Document delivery tests, 201-3, p.62
   defined, p.224

Earth science, journal ranking, 556
East Asian collections, overlap study, 220
Eckerd College, Pittsburgh Study, 166
Economics, journal ranking, 532, 535-36, 569-70
Editorial policy, serials evaluation, 436
Education, journal ranking, 519
Engineering, 95
English Canadian literature verification study, 396
English history, citation study, 308
English literary journals, citation study, 305
Entomology, journal ranking, 558
Environmental biology, citation study, 309
Environmental design, serials cancellation case study, 459
Evaluation of serials, pp.xii-xiii
Extended campus library services, 232-33

Faculty assessments
   core journal identification, 447
   serials evaluation, 416
Finance, journal ranking, 503, 512
Firelands College, citation study, 281
Footnotes, p.98
Forestry, citation study, 284
Formulas, 44
   defined, p.224
Franklin & Marshall College Library, periodical use study, 141
French literature, verification study, 393
French monographs, citation study, 300
French program, 96

Freshwater Institute Library, serials cancellation case study, 466
FTE (Full-time equivalent), p.xvii
Full-time equivalent (FTE), p.xvii

Gaps, p.74
Garden history, citation study, 306
General and miscellaneous use studies, 103-29
General survey works, 1-27
Geography, journal ranking, 533-34
Geology
   Pacific Northwest Conspectus, 381
   serials cancellation case study, 474
Georgia State University, use study, 103
Georgia Tech, serials cancellation case study, 479
Geosciences
   overlap studies, 225
   RLG Conspectus, 346, 348
German monographs, citation studies, 300
Glasgow University Library, RLG Conspectus, 357
GMRMLN (Greater Midwest Regional Medical Library Network), p.xviii
GMRMLN Conspectus Project, RLG Conspectus, 344
Goldhor's inductive method, 15, 22, 58-59
Goshen College Library, serials cancellation case study, 469
Government documents
   citation study, 255
   survey works, 33-34
Government documents use studies
   Arkansas State University, 155-56
   Ibadan University, Nigeria, 154
   Miami University, 157
   SuDocs number areas, 157
   University of Illinois at Urbana-Champaign, 158
GPO (Government Printing Office), p.xviii
Graphing, 82
Greater Midwest Regional Medical Library Network (GMRMLN), p.xviii

Harrassowitz (book dealer), 218
Health sciences
  core journal identification, 451
  journal ranking, 548
  overlap study, 217
  serials evaluation, 417
HEGIS (Higher Education General Information Surveys), 224, 615, p.xviii
Higher Education General Information Surveys (HEGIS), 224, 615, p.xviii
History, citation study, 286
Holdings, serials evaluation, 434
Houston Academy of Medicine-Texas Medical Center Library, serials evaluation models, 439
Human development, journal ranking, 539
Humanities
  periodical use study, 133
  RLG Conspectus, 336
  serials cancellation case study, 471
  use studies, 108-10

IAMSLIC (International Association of Marine Science Libraries and Information Centers), p.xviii
IASLIC (Indian Association of Special Libraries and Information Centres), p.xviii
Ibadan University, Nigeria, government documents use, 154
IFLA (International Federation of Library Associations and Institutions), p.xviii
ILL (Interlibrary loan), p.xviii
Illinois State University, 58
Immediacy index, defined, p.225
Impact factor, p.177
  defined, p.224
In-house journal use
  serials cancellation case study, 455
  use studies, 106, 119
Index correlation study, serials cancellation case study, 457
Indian Association of Special Libraries and Information Centres (IASLIC), p.xviii
Indian Space Research Centre Library, use studies, 124

Indian Statistical Institute Library, citation study, 278
Indiana
  NCIP, 384, 389
  overlap study, 216
Indiana University Fine Arts Library, periodical use study, 144
Indiana University, citation studies, 265, 268
Input methods, 25
Institute of Scientific Information (ISI), p.xviii
Instructions to authors, serials evaluation, 437
Interlibrary loan (ILL), p.xviii
  borrowing statistics, 56
International Association of Marine Science Libraries and Information Centers, (IAMSLIC), p.xviii
International Federation of Library Associations and Institutions (IFLA), p.xviii
International newspapers
  serials cancellation case studies, 476
  serials evaluation, 419
International relations, citation study, 296
Iowa State University, use study, 104
Irrigation collection, checklist method, 51
ISI (Institute of Scientific Information), p.xviii
  defined, p.225
Italian monographs, citation study, 301

JCR (*Journal Citation Reports*), p.xviii
  defined, p.225
Jewett, Charles Coffin, 21, p.30
John Crerar Library, overlap study, 206
Journals. See Periodicals; Serials
Journal Citation Reports (JCR), p.xviii
  defined, p.225
Journal deselection
  cancellation case study, 461
  evaluation, 430
  model, 442
Journal ranking, pp.177-79
  AACSB schools, 517
  accounting, 502, 510, 514, 518
  acoustics, 572
  agricultural sciences, 575
  analytical chemistry, 559

262 / SUBJECT INDEX

Journal ranking—*Continued*
  anthropology, 557
  aquatic entomology, 581
  ARIA, 515
  arts and humanities, 555
  astrosciences, 560
  biochemical, 547
  biology, 571
  botany, 549-50
  British Library Lending Division, 495
  business, 498-518
  chemical physics, 563-65
  citation-based, 481-84, 494, 497
  criminal justice, 522
  criminology, 540, 542-43
  criticisms, pp.177-78
  crystallography, 574
  dental science, 551
  developmental biology, 567
  earth science, 556
  economics, 532, 535-36, 569-70
  education, 519
  entomology, 558
  finance, 503, 512
  geography, 533-34
  health science librarianship, 548
  human development, 539
  library and information science, 520, 530-31, 541
  management, 499, 504, 507-8, 516
  management information systems (MIS), 505-6, 509
  marketing, 500-501, 511
  mathematics, 553
  medical, 576
  neuroscience, 554
  nursing, 561
  nutrition, 568
  oceanography, 566
  physical chemistry, 563-65
  physical education, 578, 580
  physics, 491
  phytopathology, 579
  political science, 524-26
  psychology, 528, 537
  public administration, 521, 545-46
  real estate, 498, 513, 517
  science, 490, 494, 547-77, 579, 581
  social science psychology, 523
  social sciences, 486, 519-46
  social work, 497, 529
  sociology, 493, 527
  soil science, 577
  surgery, 562
  theoretical discussions, 481-97
  uses, p.178
  veterinary science, 552

Kansas State University, RLG Conspectus, 347
Kantor's branching method, p.xi
Kantor, Paul B., p.61
Kearney State College Library, serials cancellation case study, 456
Kent State University, 613
Knox College Library, automated systems, 583

Latent need, 183
Latin-American history, 87
Lawrence Livermore National Laboratory Library, serials cancellation case study, 465
LC (Library of Congress), pp.xviii, 121
LCS (Library Computer System), 213, 594
LIBER (Ligue des Bibliotheques Europeenes de Recherche), p.xviii
Library and Information Resources for the Northwest (LIRN), pp.xviii, 121
  defined, p.225
Library and information science (LIS), p.xviii
  citation studies, 317
  collections methods, 65
  core journal identification, 448
  journal ranking, 520, 530-31, 541
  schools, 37
Library Computer System (LCS), 213, 594
Library of Congress (LC), pp.xviii, 121
Ligue des Bibliotheques Europeenes de Recherche (LIBER), p.xviii
Limitations of automation in collection evaluation, pp.209-10
LIRN (Library and Information Resources for the Northwest), p.xviii
  defined, p.225
  Pacific Northwest Conspectus, 373, 376
List checking, 47

Literary scholarship, citation study, 318
Literary studies, citation study, 299
Literature scatter, serials evaluation, 421
Liverpool Polytechnic Library Service, availability studies, 190-91
Livestock periodicals, citation study, 254
LLA (Louisiana Library Association), p.xviii
Lopez method, 15, 22, 61-62
Loughborough University
  citation study, 288
  serials cancellation case study, 480
Louisiana Library Association (LLA), p.xviii
Louisiana State University, 63, 99
  serials cancellation case study, 462
Loyola University, serials cancellation case study, 467

Machine-readable cataloging (MARC), p.xviii
  defined, p.225
Machine-readable files, serials evaluation, 420
Macroevaluation, p.x
Management
  citation study, 274
  core journal identification, 452
  journal ranking, 499, 504, 507-8, 516
Management information systems (MIS), p.xviii
Mansbridge, John, p.61
Map collections, overlap study, 223
MARC (machine-readable cataloging), p.xviii
MARC tapes, 607, 611-15
Marine Science Research Center SUNY-Stony Brook, core journal identification, 453
Marketing, journal ranking, 500-501, 511
Materials availability, 197
Mathematics, journal ranking, 553
Measurement of holdings
  methods and methodology, 67-71
  microforms, 67
  shelflist measurement, 68
Measurement of use, methods and methodology, 72-76
Medical behavioral sciences, citation study, 292

Medical College of Pennsylvania, periodical use study, 147
Medical library network, RLG Conspectus, 344
Medical science
  journal ranking, 576
  online searching, 604
  serials cancellation case study, 454
  serials evaluation, 409
Memorial University of Newfoundland, serials cancellation case study, 468
Methodological discussions, 42-46
Methods and methodology, pp.xiv-xv, 15
  acquisitions statistics, 56
  checklist method, 47-53
  collection mapping, 60
  collection profiling, 63
  curricular needs, 66
  interlibrary loan borrowing statistics, 56
  library and information science collections, 65
  measurement of holdings, 67-71
  measurement of use, 72-76
  methodological discussions, 42-46
  miscellaneous, 77-83
  other methods, 54-66
  public libraries, 55, 59
  relative use and interlibrary demand, 54
Pacific Northwest Conspectus, 372, 375
METRO (Metropolitan Reference and Research Library Agency), p.xviii
  defined, p.225
  Pacific Northwest Conspectus, 372, 375
Metropolitan Reference and Research Library Agency (METRO), p.xviii
  defined, p.225
  Pacific Northwest Conspectus, 372, 375
Miami University, government documents use, 157
Miami-Dade Community College, serials cancellation case study, 460
Microcomputer-based collection evaluation, 608-9
Microevaluation, p.x

264 / SUBJECT INDEX

Microforms, measurement of holdings, 67
Middle eastern periodicals, overlap study, 221
MIS (Management information systems), p.xviii
  journal ranking, 505-6, 509
Models of serials evaluation, 438-44
Montana State University Library, 72
Mountain Plains Library Association (MPLA), p.xviii
MPLA (Mountain Plains Library Association), p.xviii
Multiple regression, serials evaluation model, 438
Music, 99
  citation studies, 265
  RLG Conspectus, 328-29

National Agricultural Library, RLG Conspectus, 347
National Animal Production Research Institute, Nigeria, citation study, 254
National Humanities Center (NHC), p.xviii
  periodical use study, 133
  use studies, 108-10
National Library of Australia (NLA), p.xviii
  overlap study, 219
  RLG Conspectus, 370
National Library of Medicine (NLM), p.xviii
  automated systems, 584
National Shelflist Count, 398-403, p.122
  defined, p.225
NCIP (North American Collections Inventory Project), 382-92, pp.xviii, 225
  defined, p.225
  Canada, 382, 391
  Indiana, 384, 389
  RLG Conspectus, 343, 390
  University of Alberta Library, 382
NDLA (North Dakota Library Association), p.xviii
Netherlands, RLG Conspectus, 360
Neuroscience, journal ranking, 554
New York City Libraries, Pacific Northwest Conspectus, 372

New York Public Library, periodical use study, 151
New Zealand, RLG Conspectus, 367
NHC (National Humanities Center), p.xviii
NLA (National Library of Australia), p.xviii
NLM (National Library of Medicine), p.xviii
Non-English journals, serials evaluation, 415
Non-use of periodicals, 131
North America, RLG Conspectus, 359
North American Collections Inventory Project. *See* NCIP
North Dakota Library Association (NDLA), p.xviii
Northeast Louisiana University, 55
Northwestern Online Total Integrated System (NOTIS), 588, p.xviii
  defined, p.226
NOTIS (Northwestern Online Total Integrated System), 588, p.xviii
  defined, p.226
Nursing, journal ranking, 561
Nutrition, journal ranking, 568

Oberlin College library, availability study, 179
Oceanography, journal ranking, 566
OCLC (OCLC Online Computer Library Center), p.xviii
  database, 617
  RLG Conspectus, 330
OCLC Online Computer Library Center (OCLC), p.xviii
OCLC/AMIGOS Collection Analysis compact disc, 610
Off-campus degree program, citation study, 289
Off-campus library services, p.84
Ohio State University libraries, 84, 97
  automated system, 591
  collection evaluation case studies, 84
Okanagan College, British Columbia, serials cancellation case study, 470
Online Public Access Catalog (OPAC), p.xviii
Online searching, 602-6
  agriculture, 606
  medical, 604

Subject Index / 265

physics journals, 603
Pro-Cite, 605
SCISEARCH, 602, 605
SOCIAL SCISEARCH, 605
OPAC (Online Public Access Catalog), p.xviii
Ophthalmology, 88
Oregon State Library Foundation, p.121
Oregon State University Library, periodical use study, 139
Organizational issues, serials evaluation, p.150
Orr, Richard H., p.62
Output methods, 25
Overlap studies, 204-17, pp.74-75
   accounting periodicals, 224
   African books, 222
   ARL libraries, 223
   art libraries, 220
   Australian Bibliographic Network (ABN), 215
   Australian libraries, 218-19
   CASSI, 207-8
   computer modeling, 616
   East Asian collections, 220
   geosciences collections, 225
   health science libraries, 217
   Indiana libraries, 216
   John Crerar Library, 206
   Library Computer System, 213, 594
   map collections, 223
   Middle Eastern periodicals, 221
   National Library of Australia, 219
   SULAN, 210
   United Kingdom libraries, 221
   University of Chicago, 206
   University of Edinburgh, 212
   University of Glasgow, 212
   University of Wisconsin, 211
   vendor records, 218
   Victoria, Australia libraries, 225

Pacific Northwest Conspectus, pp.121, 371-81
   Alaska, 379-80
   Albion College library, 377
   Bellevue Community College, 371
   geology, 381
   LIRN, 373, 376
   METRO, 372, 375
   New York City Libraries, 372
   science, 371

Pacific Northwest Library Association (PNLA), p.xviii
PC-File, 599
Pennsylvania State University (PSU), p.xviii
Pennsylvania State University libraries, citation studies, 290
Perception rankings, p.177
Performance measurement, p.61
Periodical use studies, 73. *See also* Journals; Serials
   Arnold and Marie Schwartz College of Pharmacy, 142
   art library, 144
   Auburn University Veterinary Medical Library, 152
   British Library Lending Division, 136, 146
   Chalmers University of Technology, Sweden, 138
   clinical medicine, 147
   Danish Veterinary and Agricultural Library, 143
   Delhi University Libraries, 132
   Franklin & Marshall College Library, 141
   humanities, 133
   Indiana University Fine Arts Library, 144
   legal periodicals, 140
   Medical College of Pennsylvania, 147
   National Humanities Center, 133
   New York Public Library, 151
   Oregon State University Library, 139
   ranking, 145
   Slavic holdings, 151
   SUNY-Buffalo Science and Engineering Library, 148
   SUNY-New Paltz Library, 150
   Texas A & M University, 131
   University of Bergen School of Dentistry Library, 149
   University of Delhi Medical College Library, 130
   University of Illinois at Urbana-Champaign Chemistry Library, 134-35
   University of South Florida, 137
   Washington University Law Library, 140
Periodicals use, Pittsburgh Study, 161-63

266 / SUBJECT INDEX

Philosophy, 90
  citation studies, 285
Physical chemistry, journal ranking, 563-65
Physical education, journal ranking, 578, 580
Physics
  journal ranking, 491
  serials evaluation models, 438
Physics journals, online searching, 603
Phytopathology, journal ranking, 579
Pittsburgh Study, pp.xi, 38, 159-73
  Carnegie-Mellon University, 162
  defined, p.226
  DePauw University, 165
  Eckerd College, 166
  periodicals use, 161-63
Plymouth Polytechnic Library, United Kingdom, 75
PNLA (Pacific Northwest Library Association), p.xviii
Political science
  citation studies, 272, 291
  journal ranking, 524-26
Pomona College, citation studies, 266
Preservation, RLG Conspectus, 340
Pro-Cite, 605
PSU (Pennsylvania State University), p.xviii
Psychology
  core journal identification, 451
  journal ranking, 528, 537
  RLG Conspectus, 342
Public administration, journal ranking, 521, 545-46
Public libraries
  methods, 55, 59
Public services, 28
Purdue University Calumet, use studies, 116
Purdue University Library, serials cancellation case studies, 473
Purdue University, citation studies, 285-86

Qualitative approaches, defined, p.227
Qualitative standards, p.84
Quantitative standards, 242, 245, 247, p.84
Quantitative versus qualitative methods, p.1

Ralph R. Shaw Award for Outstanding Contribution to Library Literature, ALA, 16
Ranking, serials evaluation model, 443
Real estate, journal ranking, 498, 513, 517
Reference collections, RLG Conspectus, 338
Reference study, p.98
Relative use and interlibrary demand, 54
Reliability, defined, p.226
Religion, use studies, 125
Reproductive biology, citation study, 256
Research Libraries Group (RLG), 617, pp.xviii, 120
Research Libraries Information Network (RLIN), p.xviii
Research library, survey works, 29
Resources and Technical Services Division (RTSD), p.xix
RLG (Research Libraries Group), 617, pp.xviii, 120
RLG Conspectus, pp.120-23
  assessment, p.121
  Australia, 361-66, 368-70
  British Library, 350, 352
  Charleston Academic Libraries Consortium, 349
  Chemistry Division of Pacific Northwest Conspectus, 366
  Colorado School of Mines, 346
  criticisms, p.122
  defined, p.226
  Divisions, p.120
  Europe, 350-60
  general, 320-41
  geosciences, 346, 348
  Glasgow University Library, 357
  GMRMLN Conspectus Project, 344
  humanities, 336
  Kansas State University, 347
  medical library network, 344
  music, 328-29
  National Agricultural Library, 347
  National Library of Australia, 370
  national standard, 341
  NCIP, 343, 390
  Netherlands, 360
  New Zealand, 367
  North America, 342-49, 359
  OCLC tapes, 330
  organization, p.120

Subject Index / 267

preservation, 340
psychology, 342
reference, 338
Scotland, 353, 355-56, 358
Subject Categories, p.120
Subject Groups, p.120
United Kingdom, 354
University of Alaska-Fairbanks, 348
University of Missouri-Columbia Libraries, 343
verification studies, p.74
western Europe, 351, 359
Yale University Preservation Planning Task Force, 340
RLIN (Research Libraries Information Network), pp.xviii, 121
RTSD (Resources and Technical Services Division), p.xix
Russian language monographs, 101

San Jose State University library, availability studies, 199
SAS (Statistical Analysis System), pp.xix, 598
  defined, p.226
School of Library and Information Science (SLIS), p.xix
SCI (*Science Citation Index*), p.xix
Science
  journal rankings, 490, 494, 547-77, 579, 581
  Pacific Northwest Conspectus, 371
  serials evaluation, 432
    models, 441
  shelflist measurement, 68
  survey works, 32
Science and technology, citation study, 277
Science Citation Index (*SCI*), p.xix
SCISEARCH
  defined, p.226
  online searching, 602, 605
SCONUL (Standing Conference on National and University Libraries), p.xix
Scotland, RLG Conspectus, 353, 355-56, 358
SDLA (South Dakota Library Association), p.xix
Selection and weeding, p.xii
Serial/monograph ratio, citation study, 263

Serials. *See* Journals; Periodicals
Serials cancellation case studies, 454-80
  biomedical, 465
  environmental design, 459
  Freshwater Institute Library, 466
  geology, 474
  Georgia Tech, 479
  Goshen College Library, 469
  humanities, 471
  in-house journal use, 455
  index correlation study, 457
  international newspapers, 476
  journal deselection, 461
  Kearney State College Library, 456
  Lawrence Livermore National Laboratory Library, 465
  Loughborough University of Technology, 480
  Louisiana State University Library, 462
  Loyola University, 467
  medical, 454
  Memorial University of Newfoundland, 468
  Miami-Dade Community College, 460
  Okanagan College, British Columbia, 470
  Purdue University Library, 473
  serials deselection, 456
  Soviet journals, 458
  Stanford University Biology Library, 478
  UCLA Biomedical Library, 477
  University of Alabama Business Library, 472
  University of Arizona, 471, 475
  University of California, Berkeley, 459
  University of North Carolina-Chapel Hill, 474
  University of Sussex, 463-64
  University of Virginia Health Sciences library, 454
Serials cancellation, 410-11, 414, 422, 436
Serials deselection
  serials cancellation case studies, 456
  serials evaluation, 412-13
Serials evaluation, pp.150-51
  American Revolution, 426-27
  business periodicals, 407
  California State University, Northridge, 428

268 / SUBJECT INDEX

Serials evaluation—*Continued*
  cancellations, 410-11, 414, 422
    case studies, 454-80
  chemistry journals, 429
  college libraries, 418
  criteria, p.150
  developing countries, 425
  editorial policy, 436
  faculty assessments, 416
  general and miscellaneous, 404-37
  health sciences library, 417
  holdings, 434
  identification of core journals, 445-53
  instructions to authors, 437
  international newspapers, 419
  literature scatter, 421
  machine-readable files, 420
  medical, 409
  models, 438-44
  non-English journals, 415
  organizational issues, p.150
  science, 432
  serials deselection, 412-13
  SUNY-Buffalo, 417
  Texas A & M Library, 419
  Texas Woman's University, 433
  University of Michigan Engineering Library, 420
  University of Texas at Austin, 416
Serials evaluation models
  Central State University library, 444
  developing countries, 440
  Houston Academy of Medicine-Texas Medical Center Library, 439
  journal deselection, 442
  multiple regression, 438
  physics, 438
  ranking, 443
  science, 441
Serials identification of core journals, 445-53
Serials, nonuse, 75
Shelf Availability Test, defined, p.226
Shelflist measure, defined, 71, p.226
Shelflist
  defined, p.226
  samples, 83
Siberiana collection, 94
Skidmore College, use study, 113
Slavic holdings, periodical use study, 151
SLIS (School of Library and Information Science), p.xix

Small academic libraries, use studies, 127-28
Smithsonian Library, 21, p.30
Social psychology, citation study, 267
Social Science Citation Index (*SSCI*), p.xix
Social science psychology, journal ranking, 523
Social sciences
  citation studies, 303, 310, 314
  journal rankings, 486, 519-46
SOCIAL SCISEARCH, 605
Social theory, checklist method, 53
Social work, 93
  journal ranking, 497, 529
Sociology
  checklist method, 48
  citation study, 295
  journal ranking, 493, 527
  survey works, 35
Software, 593-601
  automated ILL, 593
  BASIC, 598
  conspectus, 596
  dBaseIII+, 597
  LCS, 594
  PC-File, 599
  SAS, 598
  SPSS, 600-601
  University of Illinois, 594
Soil science, journal ranking, 577
South Dakota Library Association (SDLA), p.xix
Southeastern Louisiana University, 55
Southern Illinois University at Carbondale, 68-69
Soviet journals, serials cancellation case study, 458
Spanish monographs, citation study, 301
SPEC (System and Procedures Exchange Centers) kits, 85
  defined, p.226
Special libraries, p.xi
SPSS (Statistical Package for the Social Sciences), 600-601, p.xix
  defined, p.227
SSCI (*Social Science Citation Index*), p.xix
St. Cloud State University, automated systems, 590

Standards, pp.83-85
  academically disadvantaged students, 229
  audiovisual services, 228
  branch libraries, 226-27
  Clapp-Jordan Formula, 245
  college learning resources programs, 237-40, 252
  college libraries, 230-31, 243-44, 246, 248, 253
  extended campus library services, 232-33
  official statements, 226-41
  technical libraries, 242
  university libraries, 236, 241, 249-51
  undergraduate libraries, 234-35
  West African university libraries, 247
Standing Conference on National and University Libraries (SCONUL), p.xix
Stanford University Biology Library, serials cancellation case study, 478
Stanford University library, 85
State history, citation study, 307
State Library of Victoria, 102
  availability study, 176
State University Library Automation Network (Indiana) (SULAN), p.xix
  overlap study, 210
State University of New York (SUNY), p.xix
Statistical Analysis System (SAS), p.xix
  defined, p.226
Statistical Package for the Social Sciences (SPSS), 69, p.xix
  defined, p.227
Statistics in collection assessment, 78
Subject collections, verification study, 397
SuDoc (Superintendent of Documents), p.xix
  number areas, government documents use, 157
SULAN (State University Library Automation Network) (Indiana), p.xix
  overlap study, 210
SUNY (State University of New York), p.xix
SUNY-Buffalo, 61
  serials evaluation, 417

SUNY-Buffalo Science and Engineering Library, periodical use studies, 148
SUNY-New Paltz Library, periodical use study, 150
Superintendent of Documents (SuDoc), p.xix
Surgery, journal ranking, 562
Survey works, p.1
  art libraries, 31, 36
  bibliographies, 38-41
  general, 1-27
  government documents, 33-34
  library and information science schools, 37
  public services, 28
  research library, 29
  science libraries, 32
  sociology collections, 35
  technical services, 30
Surveying library users, 72
Systemic botany, citation studies, 302
Systems and Procedures Exchange Centers (SPEC) kits, 85, p.226

Technical libraries, standards, 242
Technical services, survey works, 30
Technology history, citation studies, 312-13
Temple University, citation study, 271
Texas A & M University, 89
  periodical use studies, 131
  serials evaluation, 419
Texas Woman's University, serials evaluation, 433
Textbooks, citation studies, 279, 281, 293
Theatre arts, 98
Theory of collection evaluation, 81
Title file rate, 196
Trueswell's 80/20 Rule, 107
  defined, p.227
  use studies, 112, 129

U.S. Government Printing Office (GPO), p.xviii
UCLA Biomedical Library, serials cancellation case study, 477
Undergraduate term papers, citation studies, 270, 276
Unique title, p.74

United Kingdom libraries
  overlap studies, 221
  RLG Conspectus, 354
University library standards, 236, 241, 249-51, p.84
University of Alabama Business Library, serials cancellation case study, 472
University of Alaska-Fairbanks, 94, 101
  RLG Conspectus, 348
University of Alberta Library, NCIP, 382
University of Arizona, serials cancellation case studies, 471, 475
University of Bergen School of Dentistry Library, periodical use study, 149
University of British Columbia, availability study, 198
University of California at Davis, use study, 123
University of California, Berkeley, serials cancellation case study, 459
University of California, Irvine, citation study, 280
University of California, Santa Cruz Library, availability study, 178
University of Chicago Library, use study, 114
University of Chicago, overlap study, 206
University of Cincinnati, collection evaluation case study, 86
University of Colorado, 100
University of Delhi Medical College Library, periodical use study, 130
University of Edinburgh, overlap study, 212
University of Florida, Gainesville, citation study, 284
University of Glasgow, overlap study, 212
University of Guanajuato, 95
University of Ife Library, Nigeria, 96
University of Illinois, 51
  software, 594
University of Illinois at Urbana-Champaign Chemistry Library, periodical use studies, 134-35
University of Illinois at Urbana-Champaign library, availability study, 192
University of Illinois at Urbana-Champaign Undergraduate Library, 83
University of Illinois at Urbana-Champaign, government documents use, 158
University of Illinois Health Sciences Center, availability study, 182
University of Illinois Undergraduate Library, 74
University of Iowa Law Library, 67
University of Manitoba, 62
University of Massachusetts, use study, 129
University of Michigan Engineering Library, serials evaluation, 420
University of Minnesota Bio-Medical Library, availability study, 200
University of Mississippi, 90
University of Missouri-Columbia Libraries, RLG Conspectus, 343
University of New Mexico Library, availability study, 174
University of North Carolina at Chapel Hill
  automated systems, 585
  serials cancellation case study, 474
University of Pittsburgh, p.38
  use studies, 115
University of South Florida, periodical use study, 137
University of Sussex
  serials cancellation case studies, 463-64
  use study, 122
University of Sydney Library, availability study, 188
University of Tennessee at Knoxville, use study, 107
University of Tennessee Undergraduate Library, availability study, 195
University of Texas at Austin, serials evaluation, 416
University of Texas Health Science Center Library, 82
University of Virginia Health Sciences library, serials cancellation case study, 454
University of Wisconsin, overlap study, 211

Subject Index / 271

University presses, use study, 110
University undergraduate libraries, standards, 234-35
Use studies, 105, pp.37-38
  ACM model, 126
  audiovisual materials, 103
  browsing behavior, 123
  criticisms, p.38
  core analysis, 125
  Cornell College, 125
  general and miscellaneous, 103-29
  Georgia State University, 103
  government documents, 154-58
  humanities, 108-10
  in-house use, 106, 119
  Indian Space Research Centre Library, 124
  Iowa State University, 104
  National Humanities Center, 108-10
  periodical use, 130-53
  Pittsburgh Study, pp.38, 115, 159-73
  Purdue University Calumet, 116
  reference, 104
  religion, 125
  serials use, 122
  Skidmore College, 113
  small academic libraries, 127-28
  Trueswell's 80/20 Rule, 112, 129
  University of California at Davis, 123
  University of Chicago Library, 114
  University of Massachusetts, 129
  University of Sussex, 122
  University of Tennessee at Knoxville, 107
  university presses, 110
  Virginia Tech Library, 120, 121

Validity, defined, p.227
Vendor records, overlap study, 218
Verification studies, 392-97, p.121
  English Canadian literature, 396
  French literature, 393
  subject collections, 397

Vertebrate zoology, 92
Veterinary science, journal ranking, 552
Victoria, Australia libraries, overlap study, 225
Virginia Tech Library System (VTLS), p.xix
  defined, p.227
  use studies, 120, 121
Voigt current acquisitions model, 22
VTLS (Virginia Tech Library System), p.xix
  defined, p.227
  use studies, 120, 121

Washington University Law Library, periodical use study, 140
Washington University Medical Library, 88
Weeding, pp.37, 178
West African university library standards, 247
Western Australian Institute of Technology, 93
Western Europe, RLG Conspectus, 351, 359
Western European Studies Section of the ACRL (WESS), p.xix
Western Library Network (WLN), pp.xix, 121
William Patterson College Library, availability study, 177
WLN (Western Library Network), pp.xix, 121
Women's studies, core journal identification, 449

Yale University Preservation Planning Task Force, RLG Conspectus, 340

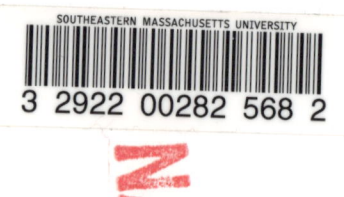